William Allen

A history of Kentucky

Embracing gleanings, reminiscences, antiquities, natural curiosities, statistics and biographical sketches of pioneers

William Allen

A history of Kentucky
Embracing gleanings, reminiscences, antiquities, natural curiosities, statistics and biographical sketches of pioneers

ISBN/EAN: 9783337135416

Printed in Europe, USA, Canada, Australia, Japan

Cover: Foto ©ninafisch / pixelio.de

More available books at **www.hansebooks.com**

A HISTORY OF KENTUCKY,

EMBRACING

GLEANINGS, REMINISCENCES,

ANTIQUITIES, NATURAL CURIOSITIES, STATISTICS,

AND

BIOGRAPHICAL SKETCHES

OF

Pioneers, Soldiers, Jurists, Lawyers, Statesmen, Divines, Mechanics, Farmers, Merchants, and other leading men, of all occupations and pursuits.

BY

WILLIAM B. ALLEN

AUTHOR OF THE KENTUCKY OFFICERS' GUIDE.

LOUISVILLE, KY.
BRADLEY & GILBERT, PUBLISHERS.
1872.

TO
DR. CHRISTOPHER GRAHAM, M. D.,
WHO WAS BORN IN THE WILDWOODS OF KENTUCKY FIVE YEARS BEFORE IT BECAME A STATE; WHO IS HIMSELF

A LIVING HISTORY OF KENTUCKY,

AND ONE OF THE FEW LINKS NOW LEFT IN THE LONG CHAIN THAT BINDS THE PRESENT GENERATION TO THE FIRST SETTLERS OF THE "DARK AND BLOODY GROUND;"

WHO IS THE BEST RIFLE SHOT IN AMERICA, AND UNEQUALED AS A TARGET-SHOOTER;

AND WHILE ALREADY NUMBERED AMONG THE MOST MUNIFICENT BENEFACTORS OF THE STATE HAS ONCE MORE EVINCED HIS LIBERALITY BY THE CONTRIBUTION OF HIS EXTENSIVE CABINET OF NATURAL HISTORY TO THE PUBLIC LIBRARY OF KENTUCKY, ESTIMATED TO BE WORTH $25,000—TO THIS MAN SO WORTHY OF OUR HIGHEST ESTEEM IS THIS BOOK DEDICATED BY

THE AUTHOR.

PREFACE.

The aged actors in the scenes connected with the early settlement of Kentucky have passed away, and all are now slumbering with the dead. To preserve in a durable form such of those events as have not been recorded in history, we have to rely on oral tradition, or to the recollection of the sons of those ancient worthies who participated in the scenes of those stirring times, and who in infancy were witnesses of some of the scenes, or else received them traditionally from their fathers.

Much of the primitive history of Kentucky, which would be exceedingly interesting even to the youth of this day, is now forever lost, and lies buried with those venerable witnesses who have long since passed from earth to that bourn from which there is no return. Many mementoes of the past, however, both useful and interesting to the rising generation, have been collected and preserved by the author, and will, in future, occupy a conspicuous place in history. Many things recorded in this volume were delivered me in my youth from the lips of my venerated father, and from my uncle, and others who participated in the scenes of those times, and which would, probably, have ever been lost had it not been for my predilection for such knowledge.

I have derived great advantage and assistance from the History of Kentucky, by Lewis Collins, written nearly thirty years ago, as well as from Marshall's and Butler's, written some time previously. Many of the biographical sketches given in this work are an abridgment from those works, especially those of the earliest settlers. Many, also, from a Dictionary of Congress, by Charles Lanman, and from any and every other source from which I could derive certain and reliable information. A great number of them are written from my own recollection and knowledge of the persons described, with such information as I could collect from their descendants or intimate friends and relatives. I have indulged much throughout the work in biography, looking upon biographies as landmarks, to which the larger portion of the world refers, and which is of itself, for the most part, a history of the times in which the persons lived who are described. Instance the lives of Plutarch of the most distinguished men of Greece and Rome; the lives of the signers of the Declaration of Independence of the United States; the life of Napoleon Bonaparte, &c., &c. I have endeavored all along to possess the reader with useful, interesting, correct, and entertaining matter; and with narrations so plain as to be easily understood, even by those of the humblest pretensions to learning. My object has been to state facts, stripped of all unnecessary ornament. I have given also a historical sketch, without partiality or sectarian predilection, of each of the leading denominations of Christians in Kentucky, including Roman Catholics, Episcopalians, Baptists, Methodists, Presbyterians, Cumberland Presbyterians, and Christian Church, and have added also an account of the Shakers and of the Mormon Religion; and have given biographical sketches of the most distinguished ministers in each of these churches. The interest and usefulness of this work would have been considerably augmented had all the persons to whom we wrote for information on particular subjects have communicated the information desired, but many failed or neglected to do so. To many, however, we acknowledge our indebtedness and tender our thanks; particularly the Rt. Rev. B. B. Smith, D. D., of Frankfort, Bishop of the Diocese of Kentucky of the Episcopal Church; Rt. Rev. Wm. McClosky, D. D., of Louisville, Bishop of the Diocese of Louisville of the Roman Catholic Church; Drs. Humphrey and Wilson, of Louisville, ministers of the Presbyterian Church; Rev. Thomas Marshall, of Green County, minister of the Cumberland Presbyterian Church; Rev. John James, of Columbia, Adair County, minister of the Baptist Church; Dr. McDaniel, of Greensburg, circuit minister of the Methodist Episcopal Church South; Mrs. Elizabeth H. Scott, for a sketch of her father's life; the Rev. Isaac Hodgen, of the Baptist Church; Mrs. Judy Wakefield, daughter of Creed Haskins, deceased; Rev. W. K. Asbill, of Columbia, of the Christian Church; Hon. John B. Huston and Rev. James H. Mulligan, of Lexington; General Walter C. Whitaker, of Louisville; Christopher Graham, M. D., of Louisville.

I have ever thought that the way to spend most profitably our leisure moments was by the perusal of good books, and especially historical works; and of these, the first to be preferred, aside from the Bible, is the history of our own State and country. I have endeavored so to arrange the work as to make it not only a pleasing and interesting study, but instructive also; and if I have succeeded in ever so small a degree in redeeming from oblivion any mementoes of the past which deserve a place in history, my highest expectations will have been accomplished. *Multum in parvo* have been my watch-words; and I have consequently contracted the statements of facts and events as much as possible, so as to render the book of such size and price as to be accessible to all, even those of small pecuniary means.

WM. B. ALLEN.

INDEX.

CHAPTER I.
PAGE.

Boundaries and Situation—Face of the Country—Surroundings of Fayette County—Southeastern Portion of the State Mountainous, &c.—Timber of the State—Springs—Ohio River, and other Principal Rivers of Kentucky—Their Situation, &c.—Iron Ore—Lead Ore—Salt Water—Sandstone—Nitrate of Lime—Saltpetre—Mineral Springs—Organic Remains—Fossil Remains—Blue Limestone—Bones of Quadrupeds—Big Bone Lick—Mastodon—Peale's Museum—Soil, Character of Manners and Customs in Early Settlement—Amusements and Feelings—Their Fare—Christian Observances—Clothing—Table Furniture—Food—Dress—Forts and Cabins.................................. 17

CHAPTER II.

Earliest condition of Kentucky—Tribes of Indians which disputed first Settlement—Monuments of a Superior Race—First Visits to Kentucky—Col. George Croughan—Daniel Boone's first Visit—Col. James Knox's Visit—Gen. George Washington's Visit—Thomas Bullitt's Visit—James Harrod erects Log Cabins at Harrodsburg—Boonesborough, foundation of laid—Boone's Family arrive in Kentucky—Simon Kenton erects a Cabin and raises Corn—Arrival of three more Ladies—Calloway and Logan arrive with their Families—Misses Calloway's Capture by the Indians—Colonel George Rodgers Clark's First Visit—Kentucky formed a County of Virginia—First Court held at Harrodsburg—Forts Assailed—Kentucky invaded by Indians and Canadians—Boone Captured while making Salt—His Escape—Captain Duquesne attacks Boonesborough—Clark's Expedition against British Posts—Louisville, foundation laid—Robert Patterson erects Block Houses at Lexington—Occupying Claimant Law passed—Kentucky divided into three Counties—Indian Hostilities renewed—Estill Killed—Hostilities ceased for a time in 1783—Settlements advanced rapidly—Kentucky erected into a District—Dry Goods Store at Louisville—Gen. James Wilkinson visits Kentucky—Life of Daniel Boone, sketch of—Simon Kenton, sketch of—Col. George Rodgers Clark, sketch of—Benjamin Logan, sketch of—Also James Harrod, Anthony

(viii)

Wayne, James Sandusky, John Lancaster, Col. William Whitley, Robert McAfee, James Estill, Col. William Russell, Col. Richard Henderson, Stephen Trigg, Col. John Todd, John Howard, John Bradford, Capt. William Hardin, John Breckinridge—List of other names distinguished in Kentucky History.................................... 21

CHAPTER III.

Independent Government of Kentucky Favored by Spain as well as by Leading Men of Kentucky—Nine Conventions within eight years, with a view of Admission into the Union—Account of their Meetings and Action—Efforts to separate Kentucky from the Union—Don Gardoqui, Connelly—Spanish and British Intrigues in Kentucky—Indians Troublesome—Expedition of Clark—General Wilkinson Obtains Permit to Import Tobacco for Spanish King's Stores at New Orleans—Kentucky an Independent State, June 1st, 1792—First Constitution \Formed—Isaac Shelby First Governor—Commissioners to fix the Capital—Frankfort Selected—Legislature—First Session—New Counties Formed—Governor Shelby—Sketch of Treaty with Spain to Navigate Mississippi to Ocean, and Deposit at New Orleans—Spain Intriguing up to 1806—Thomas Power—Benjamin Sebastian—Colonel Gayoso—Carondelet in 1797—His Scheme Unfolded—Disposition by Spain to Violate Treaty—Powers Escapes—Aaron Burr's First Visit to Kentucky—Visits again in Spring of 1806—Plan of his Southern Enterprise—The Cause—Duel with Alexander Hamilton—Blennerhasset—General Adair—Newspaper "Western World"—Burr Denounced as a Traitor—Joseph H. Davis—Burr's Prosecution and Trial—Popular Current—Burr Acquitted—His Death—Sebastian Resigned—Inquiry as to Judge Innis—James Garrard Second Governor—His Administration—Dissatisfaction with the Constitution—New Constitution of 1799—Garrard Re-elected Governor—Treaty with Spain Violated—Mr. Monroe Minister to France—Purchase of Louisiana from Bonaparte—Sketch of Governor Garrard—Christopher Greenup Elected Governor—Sketch of his Life—Scott Elected Governor—Sketch of his Life—John Allen.. 61

CHAPTER IV.

Isaac Shelby Elected Governor a Second Time—He Enters the Field in Person in the War of 1812—Defeat of Raisin—The Fall of John Allen at Raisin—General Dudley; his Defeat—Battle of Tippecanoe—Fall of Joseph H. Davies—Battle of Mississinaway—Fort Stephenson—Battle of Thames—Victory of New Orleans—Battle of Erie—Tecumseh—Moravian Towns on the River Thames—Colonel Richard M. Johnson wounded—Tecumseh Killed—Proctor Fled—General Jackson at New Orleans—George Madison Elected Governor—His Death—Gabriel Slaughter Acted as Governor—New Election Question—Governor Madison, Sketch of—John Pope—Sketch of Governor Slaughter—Independent Banks, Forty Odd Chartered—Twelve Months' Replevy Law—Commonwealth Bank Chartered—Party Names in Kentucky—Judge Clark's Decision—Summoned before the Legislature—Denunciation of Court of Appeals—Their Firmness—Judges of the Court of Appeals Summoned before Legislature—Victory for the Judges—Reorganizing Act Passed—Great Excitement—Robert Wickliffe Denounces Relief Party—New Court Organized—Both Courts Continued to Hold Sessions—Names of Parties at that Time—Array of Parties at that Time—Old Court Triumphant—General John Adair Elected Governor—His Opponents—General Adair, Sketch of—General Joseph Desha Elected Governor—A Sketch of his Life—New Party Names Assumed—Election Excitement in 1828—Metcalfe and Barry Opponents for Governor—Metcalfe Elected—His Administration—Breathitt Elected Governor over Buckner—Sketch of Breathitt—His First Public Speech—Removal of his Father to Kentucky..................................... 78

CHAPTER V.

James Clark elected Governor—Sketch of his Life—Robert P. Letcher elected Governor—Sketch of his Life—William Owsley elected Governor—Sketch of his Life—John J. Crittenden elected Governor—Sketch of his Life—Sketch of James T. Morehead—Sketch of Charles A. Wickliffe—Beriah Magoffin elected Governor—Sketch of his Life—Acting Governor Robinson—Thomas E. Bramlette elected Governor—Sketch of his Life—John L. Helm elected Governor—Sketch of his Life—Mrs. Governor Helm—Ben. Hardin Helm—Hon. H. W. Bruce—Thomas Hays—John W. Stevenson acting Governor—Elected at Regular Election—Sketch of his Life—Successor of Thomas L. McCreery in U. S. Senate—Hon. P. H. Leslie, acting Governor until August Election, 1871, when Election takes place regularly.............. 96

CHAPTER VI.

The Antiquities, Curiosities, Minerals, &c., of Adair County—Of Barren County—Of Boone County—Of Bourbon County—Of Bracken County—Of Bullitt County—Of Carroll County—Of Clinton County—Of Cumberland County—Of Edmonson County—Of Grayson County

Of Green County—Of Greenup County—Of Garrard County—Of Hancock County—Of Hart County—Of Henry County—Of Kenton County—Of Larue County—Of Laurel County—Of Lewis County—Of Lincoln County—Of Meade County—Of Mercer County—Of McCracken County—Of Montgomery County—Of Nicholas County—Of Nelson County—Of Owen County—Of Pendleton County—Of Rockcastle County—Of Union County—Of Woodford County—Of Warren County—Of Whitley County.. 111

CHAPTER VII.

Centennial Celebration at Camp Knox; Great Crowd in Attendance; Bountiful Repast; Speaking on the Occasion—Long Hunters, Visit of—Colonel James Knox—Doctor Walker—Christopher Gist—George Croughan—Colonel James Smith—John Findley—General George Washington visits Kentucky; Account of same—Boone and Knox—James Stewart—Green River—Friendship of an Indian—Mt. Gilead—Skin-house Branch—Return of Long Hunters—Immense Immigration—Surveyors in the Country—Earliest Settlers in Green, Names of—Cane Creek Fort—Indian Annoyances—Colonel William Whitley—Nickajack Towns; their Capture—Troubles ended in Southern Kentucky — Long Hunters revisit Kentucky — Encampment near Bowlinggreen—Names Cut upon Beech Trees—William Skaggs, Incidents of; his Death... 143

CHAPTER VIII.

Counties of Kentucky; When Formed; County-seats—Population and Increase—First Constitution of Kentucky—Where Convention was Held—Names of the Members and Counties Represented—Frankfort the Seat of Government—Convention met in 1799 to form New, or Second Constitution—Members Composing that Body and Counties Represented—Third Constitution Ratified 11th of June, 1850—Counties Represented—The Congress of 1776, which Declared Independence—Its Author—Declaration—States Represented and Names of Members—Confederation of the Thirteen Original States; Ratification of—States Represented and Names of Members—Names of Presidents and Vice Presidents of United States—Date of Adoption of United States Constitution—When Ratified by the Several States—Electors of Presidents, &c., of United States in Kentucky from her Admission—Their Names and who they Voted for—Population of Kentucky, with Increased Per Cent. from 1820 to 1870—Speakers of the House of Representatives of United States from Kentucky—

Presidents of the Senate—Chaplains of United States Senate and House of Representatives.. 150

CHAPTER IX.

Historical Sketches of the Leading Denominations of Christians in the State of Kentucky, including the Catholic, Baptist, Presbyterian, Episcopalian, Methodist, Cumberland Presbyterian, Christian, &c., with Brief Biographical Notices of the most Distinguished among the Pioneers... 170

CHAPTER X.

Henry Clay, Sketch of his Life—John Breckinridge, Sketch of—Mrs. Breckinridge—George Nicholas, Sketch of—Chilton Allan—Samuel Hanson—Joseph H. Daviess—Richard C. Anderson, Jr.—Wm. T. Barry—Solomon P. Sharp—George M. Bibb—Humphrey Marshall—Jesse Bledsoe—Harry Innis—George Robertson—John Speed Smith—John B. Thurston—David Trimble—John. White—Henry Grider—James Harlan—Judge William McClung—Alexander D. Orr—John Coburn—John T. Johnson—Robert P. Henry—Thomas Chilton—James B. Clay—Thomas Corwin—Martin D. Hardin—James S. Jackson—Wm. P. Duval—Joshua H. Jewett—Francis Johnson—Sherrod Williams—Elijah Hise—James Guthrie—John Boyle—Daniel Breck—F. M. Bristow—Presley Ewing—Henry C. Burnett—Thomas J. Helm—Joshua F. Bell—John Calhoon—Beverly L. Clark—Albert G. Haws—James Love—Richard H. Menifee—Stephen Ormsby—Wm. Wright Southgate—General Leslie Combs—William J. Graves—Archibald Dixon—Thomas P. Moore—Richard French—Benjamin Tobin—General Samuel Hopkins—Captain William Hubbell—General Jefferson Davis—President Abraham Lincoln—William Mitchell—Colonel Acquilla Whitaker—James S. Whitaker—Richard T. Whitaker—Christopher Graham, M. D.. 236

CHAPTER XI.

History of Kentucky more particularly relating to Green County—When Established—Its present Area—First Representative, Richard Thurman—Sketch of General James Allen, first Lawyer of Greensburg—Sketch of his Life and Family—Incidents in the Life of himself and Brothers, John, Robert, and David—David Kills an Indian—Early Military Services—Clerk of both the Courts in the County—Military Service in the War of 1812—In the Legislature of Kentucky

INDEX. xiii

PAGE.

—Governor Shelby's Confidence in him—General Adair's Opinion of him—His Death, &c.—John Emerson, Sketch of—Alexander McGinty—Isham Talbot—James Nourse—Ninian Edwards—John Rowan—Felix Grundy—Judge Allen M. Wakefield—Robert Coleman—Samuel Work—George Semple—Samuel Brents—Ezekiel Allen—Robert Wickliffe, Sketch of—Judge John Bridges—Judge Henry P. Broadnax—Francis Emerson—Benjamin Hutcheson—W. W. Irvine—General John E. King—Richard A. Buckner—Nathan Haggard—David Walker—Wm. Owens—John A. Coke—Thomas M. Emerson—Wm. J. Adair—Wm. T. Willis—Wm. B. Booker—Benjamin G. Burks—Thomas Waller Lisle—Christopher Tompkins—Jesse Craddock—George Washington Towles—James T. Goalder—John Pope—Benjamin Hardin—General Samuel A. Spencer.................................. 338

CHAPTER XII.

First Settlers of Green, where from—Of High Character and Good Property—Names given of Early Settlers—Names of Early Ministers of the Gospel—Rev. Manoah Lasley, Sketch of—Rev. Thomas Lasley, Sketch of—Rev. John White, Baptist Minister—John Chandler and James Larimore, Baptist Ministers—Isaac Hodgen, Baptist Minister, Sketch of his Life—First Judges of Green Quarter Session Court, Sketch of them—General Barbee, the Founder of Deaf and Dumb Asylum—An Account of it—Colonel Wm. Casey, Sketch of his Life—John Tucker, Sketch of—A Number of Names of Emigrants to Green in 1795 and 1796—Nathaniel Owens, Sketch of—Joseph Logston, Sketch of—William Skaggs—His Trial for Murder—The Last Judges of Quarter Session Court, Jonathan Cowherd, John Chandler, and John C. Allen, Sketch of them—John Y. Taylor and David Willock, first Assistant Judges of Green Circuit Court, Sketch of—First Circuit Court, its Officers—First Order of Record—First Constable—First Licensed Tavern-keeper—First Overseer of Road—First Pauper—First Mill—First Reviewers of a Road—First Administrator of an Estate—First Deputy Sheriffs—First Coroner, and first Commissionors to take Depositions—First Lawyer Sworn to Practice—First Keeper of Standard Measures—First Ferry on Green River—First Jailer—First Inspectors of Tobacco—First Keeper of Stray Pen—First Merchant, Daniel Brown, Sketch of—John Barret, Sketch of—Names of his Deputies who acquired Distinction—Robert Barret, Sketch of—First Silversmith—First Hatter—First Tanner—First Saddler—Captain William Hobson, Sketch of—Alexander Irvin, first Physician, Sketch of—Most noted Tavern, an account of it—Incidents there Occurring—David Allen, Incidents related of him—Silas

Burks, Sketch of—Jenkens Asten—Fight with Burks—First Tailor Shop—First Dancing School—First Classical School—First Tobacco Warehouse Established—Wm. H. King, Sketch of—First Tobacco Manufactory — Distinguished Arbitrators — First Singing School Taught—First Resident Carpenters—Robert Ball—Thos. Parsons, Sketch of—Revolutionary Pensioners—Wm. Finn, Centenarian—List of Earliest Justices of the Peace, Constables, and Assessors—Creed Haskins, Sketch of—First Baptist Church Organized—List of Early Coroners—First Undertakers of Public Buildings—First Man Tried for Vagrancy—First Will Admitted to Record—Gabriel and Benjamin Chisham—Jonathan Hobson, Sketch of—Bank at Greensburg, its Officers—Uncommon Names who were Early Settlers of Green—Life and Villainies of Carrington Simpson, the Murderer, in Detail—The Harpes... 375

APPENDIX.

The Alien and Sedition Laws.. 419
The Late Great Rebellion... 423
Government of Kentucky... 428
States and Territories of the Union.. 440

HISTORY OF KENTUCKY.

CHAPTER I.

Boundaries and Situation—Face of the Country—Surroundings of Fayette County—Southeastern Portion of the State Mountainous, &c.—Timber of the State—Springs—Ohio River, and other Principal Rivers of Kentucky —their Situation, &c.—Iron Ore—Lead Ore—Salt Water—Sandstone— Nitrate of Lime—Saltpetre—Mineral Springs—Organic Remains—Fossil Remains—Blue Limestone—Bones of Quadrupeds—Big Bone Lick—Mastodon—Peale's Museum—Soil, Character of—Manners and Customs in Early Settlement—Amusements and Feelings—Their Fare—Christian Observances—Clothing—Table Furniture—Food—Dress—Forts and Cabins.

The State of Kentucky is situated between 36 degrees 30 minutes and 39 degrees 10 minutes, north latitude; and between 81 degrees 50 minutes and 89 degrees 26 minutes, west longitude; and includes all that portion of territory which lies south and westward of a line, beginning on the Ohio River, at the mouth of Big Sandy River, and running up the same, and the main, and northeasterly branch thereof, to the great Laurel Ridge, or Cumberland Mountains; thence southwest along said mountains to a line of North Carolina. It is bounded north by Illinois, Indiana, and Ohio; east by Virginia; south by Tennessee; and west by the Mississippi River, which separates it from the State of Missouri. It is 300 miles in length from east to west, and 150 miles in mean breadth; and contains 42,600 square miles, or about twenty-seven million of acres.

The face of the country is diversified, having every variety of surface, and every quality of soil. Fayette County, and the surrounding counties in that portion of the State, extending to the Ohio River, has been appropriately called the Garden of Kentucky, though there are remarkably productive lands in almost every county in the State, but not in such large bodies as is found in that portion which I have mentioned. The eastern and southeastern portion of the State may be said to be mountainous, the balance of the State for the most part agreeably undulating, the soil generally deep, loose, and without sand, and exceedingly luxuriant in its productions. It is one of the finest timbered countries in the Union, producing trees of as great variety as perhaps any other State, and certainly as large in size as can be found anywhere else. There is scarcely any portion of the State that does not abound with springs of the purest water. The entire northern boundary of the State is washed by the beautiful Ohio, and large creeks, or navigable streams, flow through every portion of the State. The principal rivers of Kentucky are the Ohio, which flows along the northern boundary a distance of over six hundred miles, following its meanderings; the Mississippi, which washes the western boundary a hundred miles; Tennessee, Cumberland, Kentucky—from which last mentioned the State takes its name—Green, Licking, Big and Little Sandy, Salt, and the Rolling Fork of Salt River. Big and Little Sandy rivers lie in the eastern extremity of the State. Cumberland and Tennessee rivers intersect the western extremity; the Cumberland rises in the eastern part of the State, and flows into the State of Tennessee, then returns to Kentucky, and flows into the Ohio. The Kentucky, Licking, Salt, Rolling Fork, and Green rivers flow through the interior of the State. I have elsewhere spoken of the metals and other useful minerals of the State, which renders a particular account unnecessary in this place. Several varieties of iron ore are found in great abundance in many portions of the State. Veins of lead ore have also been found in many localities, but nowhere as yet in sufficient quantities to justify mining operations.

Salt water is obtained of good quality and in great abundance in many portions of the State, especially in eastern and middle Kentucky. The sandstone, which overlies the slate, seems to furnish the salt springs of this State. The salt stream, or basin, in some localities is not reached under a depth of 1,000 feet; in other localities it is reached by boring from three hundred to five hundred feet. Nitrate of lime is found in great abundance in most of the caves so numerous in Kentucky, which is converted into saltpetre by leaching through wood ashes. Gypsum (plaster of Paris) and hydraulic limestone are also found in many places in Kentucky.

Mineral springs abound in Kentucky. Sulphur, chalybeate, or epsom, are found in every part of the State, and in the watering seasons many of them are places of great resort, not only for invalids, but for the votaries of pleasure also. I have elsewhere given a detailed account of the most popular watering places in Kentucky—the Blue Licks, Drennon's Lick, Big Bone Lick, Harrodsburg, Crab Orchard, and the springs in Rockcastle, Estill, Bath, Lewis, and Grayson counties. I have also spoken elsewhere of the organic remains, which abound more or less in all the strata of the State. Fossil remains, too, are exceedingly abundant. In many places the blue limestone is composed almost entirely of marine animals. Slate and sandstone are destitute of any organic remains. In some of the rocks are sometimes found the bones of quadrupeds long since extinct. I have, in another place, described the bones of extraordinary animals, now extinct, which have been dug up about Big Bone Lick and other places in Kentucky. The hugely large animal called the mastodon must at some period have roamed through this State, perhaps through the whole country, for nearly a complete skeleton of one was found in the State of New York, eleven feet high, and measuring fifteen feet in length, which was put up by Mr. Peale in the museum of Philadelphia. How long since this large class of animals became extinct, or why they perished, are facts totally unkown to us at this remote day.

Geologists have ascertained, beyond doubt, that the character of the soil of Kentucky depends upon the underlying rock, and is formed by its decomposition, and varies with it; the blue limestone forms the richest soil; slate and sandstone form poor soils generally; the soil over coal measures varies in its qualities, but as a general thing is poor.

In the early settlement of Kentucky the manners and customs of the people at that day were necessarily, or unavoidably, rude; yet, with all their rudeness, they were honest and hospitable, and lived together in their settlements and forts, working, fighting, feasting, or suffering in cordial harmony. They were warm in their friendships, but bitter in their resentments. They divided their rough fare freely with a neighbor or stranger, without asking or even expecting pay in return. There was very little of Christian observances among them; Sunday was merely regarded as a rest day for the old, and a play day for the young. Most of the articles in common use among them were of domestic manufacture. Table furniture usually consisted of wooden vessels, either turned or coopered; spoons or forks, of metal, or even tin cups, were seen but seldom. Their food was plain, but of the most wholesome and nutrative kind. The dress was simple; the hunting shirt was universally worn by the men, made of linsey, linen, or dressed deer skins, fastened by a belt; the bosom served as a sort of wallet, in which they could carry their provisions and other things deemed necessary on their hunting excursions. To the belt on the right side was suspended the tomahawk, and on the left side the butcher or scalping knife. Their hats were usually of the native fur; moccasins for the feet, made of dressed deer skin, were more generally worn than shoes; shirts and jackets were of the common fashion. The forts in which the early settlers lived consisted of cabins, block houses, and stockades. The cabins usually occupied one side of the fort; the cabins were separated from each other by partitions of logs. The whole of the work about a fort was made without the use of a nail, or even a spike of iron, as such articles could not be obtained in the country.

CHAPTER II.

Earliest condition of Kentucky—Tribes of Indians which disputed first Settlement—Monuments of a Superior Race—First Visits to Kentucky—Col. George Croughan—Daniel Boone's first Visit—Col. James Knox's Visit—Gen. George Washington's Visit—Thomas Bullitt's Visit—James Harrod erects Log Cabins at Harrodsburg—Boonesborough, foundation of laid—Boone's Family arrive in Kentucky—Simon Kenton erects a Cabin and raises Corn—Arrival of three more Ladies—Calloway and Logan arrive with their Families—Misses Calloway's Capture by the Indians—Colonel George Rodgers Clark's First Visit—Kentucky formed a County of Virginia—First Court held at Harrodsburg—Forts Assailed—Kentucky invaded by Indians and Canadians—Boone Captured while making Salt—His Escape—Captain Duquesne attacks Boonesborough—Clark's Expedition against British Posts—Louisville, foundation laid—Robert Patterson erects Block Houses at Lexington—Occupying Claimant Law passed—Kentucky divided into three Counties—Indian Hostilities renewed—Estill Killed—Hostilities ceased for a time in 1783—Settlements advanced rapidly—Kentucky erected into a District—Dry Goods Store at Louisville—Gen. James Wilkinson visits Kentucky—Life of Daniel Boone, sketch of—Simon Kenton, sketch of—Col. George Rodgers Clark, sketch of—Benjamin Logan, sketch of—Also James Harrod, Anthony Wayne, James Sandusky, John Lancaster, Col. William Whitley, Robert McAfee, James Estill, Col. William Russell, Col. Richard Henderson, Stephen Trigg, Col. John Todd, John Howard, John Bradford, Capt. William Hardin, John Breckinridge—List of other names distinguished in Kentucky History.

Of all the States of this great confederacy of ours, there is none whose history is richer in variety and interest than the State of Kentucky. Before it was ever visited by any of the Anglo-Saxon race, it was a dark forest and cane thicket, and formed the vast hunting ground of several tribes of Indians both north and south of the territory which separated them. The tribes north, which disputed the first settlement of this wilderness country with the whites, were the Shawanoes, the Delawares, and the Wyandottes; and the tribes south were the Cherokees, Creeks, and Catawbas. The fierce contests which occurred between these tribes and the first white settlers of Kentucky were frequent, of long continuance, and disastrous to the whites in the extreme before their final expulsion.

It is believed by many experienced and knowing ones (and not without good reason) that this vast wilderness lying between the Allegheny Mountains and the Mississippi River was occupied hundreds of years ago, by a race of people greatly superior in arts and knowledge to the rude tribes we have mentioned. As monuments of their superiority, there are evidences of their having worked the copper mines of the West, and they had copper tools for working in wood and stone. Their pipes and utensils of various kinds, fashioned from clay, show their superiority in mechanism; whilst they prove their progress in the military art over the tribes I have named by their extensive fortifications, contrived to resist in the best manner a formidable foe, with which no doubt they had often to contend. Many of their fortifications were well constructed, and of solid masonry. That such a race of men occupied portions of Kentucky at some period cannot be doubted; but no investigation has been able to fix upon the time with any accuracy. The best informed fix the period at not less than eight hundred years ago. The examination which has been made of some of the fortifications and cemeteries show conclusively even a greater period than that mentioned. Who they were, or how they became extinct, can only be conjectured.

The first account we have of a visit of any of the Anglo-American race to Kentucky was by Dr. Walker, of Virginia, in the year 1750, to the northeastern portion. Another account, however, says that he visited the eastern and southeastern parts in 1747. In 1751 Christopher Gist was sent out by what was called the Ohio Company, on an exploring expedition, and descended the Ohio River to the Falls, where Louisville is now situated. The next account we have of a visit to Kentucky was June 8, 1765, when Col. George Croughan, a British officer, descended the Ohio from Fort Pitt to a point below the Wabash, where he was encountered and taken prisoner by the Indians. In 1766 Kentucky was visited by Col.

James Smith. In 1767, by John Findley, on a trading expedition. In 1769 Daniel Boone first visited Kentucky, and was accompanied by John Findley and others. The party built a rude hut to protect themselves from the storms, and remained two years, traversing in the meantime the northern and middle regions with great attention. The visits by whites to the country previous to this time were obscure, and of but little importance. In 1770 Col. James Knox visited the country. The party led by him was called the Long Hunters; they were from Holston, on Clinch River, and explored thoroughly the middle and southern regions of Kentucky. Boone was a native of Pennsylvania, but had emigrated to North Carolina; both these parties were in the country at the same time, but never met. It was in this year that General Washington descended the Ohio as far as the northeastern part of Kentucky. Boone's party was greatly annoyed by the Indians, and James Stewart, one of the party, was killed by them, and Boone himself was taken prisoner, but afterwards escaped. They returned in 1771, and gave such glowing accounts of the country, its fertile soil, its climate, great abundance of game, &c., that considerable emigration soon set in from the western part of Virginia and North Carolina.

The Virginia troops who had served in the French War were given bounty lands in Kentucky, and in 1773 surveyors were sent out to survey those lands upon the Ohio River. Thomas Bullitt conducted a party of surveyors down the Ohio to the Falls (now Louisville), where they erected a fortification for their protection from the Indians. A great number of surveys were made in Kentucky during this expedition, and much of the country explored with a view to future settlement. James, George, and Robert McAfee accompanied Bullitt in this expedition, but separated from him at the mouth of the Kentucky River, explored extensively, and made surveys in various places.

In 1774 James Harrod erected a log cabin where Harrodsburg now stands, which soon grew to be a station, and which was probably the oldest in Kentucky.

Daniel Boone, having been employed by Richard Henderson

to survey the country, to which he had set up claim by purchase from the Indians, and to select favorable situations, in the spring of 1775 laid the foundation of Boonesborough; by the middle of April the fort was completed; and by the middle of June of that year, Boone's wife and daughters arrived, and resided in the fort; the first white woman as far as known who ever stood on Kentucky soil. This same year Simon Kenton, the renowned pioneer, erected a log cabin, and raised a crop of corn where the town of Washington, Mason County, now stands. In the fall of that year he removed to Boonesborough. The renowned Kenton was the maternal uncle of Col. Wm. Owen, late of Adair County, personally well known to the writer, and of whom I shall give a more extended account hereafter. In September, 1775, three more ladies arrived in Kentucky, and, with their husbands and children, settled at Harrodsburg, to-wit: Mrs. Denton, Mrs. McGary, and Mrs. Hogan. In 1776 Col. Richard Calloway brought his wife and two daughters to Boonesborough, and Col. Benjamin Logan his wife and family to Logan's Fort, near where Stanford now stands, in Lincoln County. In the summer of this year Boone's daughter and two of the Misses Calloway, out at play near the fort, were taken prisoners by the Indians, but were rapidly pursued by Boone and Floyd, and eight others, and, about forty miles distance from the fort, were overtaken, the Indians dispersed, and the girls recovered. During the summer of this year Col. George Rodgers Clark visited Kentucky for the first time. He employed the greater part of his time in hunting alone, visited the different stations, but made no locations.

In the winter of 1775 Kentucky was formed into a county of Virginia. The first Court of Quarter Sessions was held at Harrodsburg, composed of John Todd, John Floyd, Benjamin Logan, John Bowman, and Richard Calloway. Levi Todd was clerk. About this time Harrodsburg, Boonesborough, and Logan's Fort were successively assailed by the Indians, They withstood the furious attacks made upon them; not, however, without great loss. During the succeeding summer they were considerably reinforced by a number of men from

North Carolina, and about one hundred under Col. Bowman from Virginia.

In 1778 Kentucky was invaded by an army of Indians and Canadians under the command of Captain Duquesne; and the expedition of Col. George Rodgers Clark against the English Post of Vincennes and Kaskaskia took place this year. In February of this year Boone, with about thirty men, was engaged in making salt at the Lower Blue Licks, when he was surprised by about two hundred Indians. The whole party surrendered upon terms of capitulation. The Indians carried them to Detroit, and delivered them all up to the commandant, except Boone, whom they carried to Chilicothe. Boone soon effected his escape and returned to Boonesborough in time to give them information of an intended attack of a large body of Indians on that place. In consequence of the escape of Boone, the progress of the Indians who were collected at Chilicothe was greatly disconcerted and delayed. After a delay of some weeks, however, Captain Duquesne, with about five hundred Indians and Canadians, made his appearance before Boonesborough, and besieged the fort for the space of nine days, but finally decamped with the loss of thirty men killed, and a much greater number wounded. The loss of the garrison was two killed and four wounded; beside this, much of their stock was taken off, and great destruction of their improvements. In 1776 Col. George Rodgers Clark started upon an expedition against the British Posts in the northwest, and, having descended the Ohio in boats to the Falls, he there landed thirteen families who had accompanied him from Pittsburgh; and by these emigrants the now flourishing city of Louisville was laid. About the first of April, 1779, Robert Patterson erected a block house, with some adjacent defenses, where the city of Lexington now stands. This year, the celebrated land law of Kentucky was passed by the Legislature of Virginia, usually called the Occupying Claimant Law. The great defect of this law was, that Virginia, by this act, did not provide for the survey of the country at the expense of the State, and its subdivisions into sections, half sections, &c., as it is now done by the United States Government. Such a course would have prevented unnumbered lawsuits and vexatious litigation. Each one holding a warrant could locate it where he pleased, and survey it at his own cost. The law required that entries should be made with great precision, in order to avoid difficulties; this, however, was not often observed by the unskillful hands of pioneers and hunters, and surveys were lapped and piled upon each other all over the country in endless perplexity; the consequence of this law was, however, a flood of emigration during the years 1780 and 1781. During this period the emigrants were greatly annoyed by the frequent incursions of the Indians, and their entire destruction sometimes seemed almost inevitable. This law was a great feast for the lawyers of that day, many of whom amassed great wealth, especially in lands. Some of the brightest intellects of any State in the confederacy adorned the bar of Kentucky shortly after that period.

In November, 1780, Kentucky was divided into three counties, bearing the names of Fayette, Lincoln, and Jefferson. We had now three County Courts, holding monthly sessions, and three Quarter-Session Courts, whose highest jurisdiction was of misdemeanors only; no court nearer than Richmond, Virginia, that could try capital offenses.

In 1782, Indian hostility was earlier, more active and shocking than it had ever been in the country before; a great battle was fought upon Hinkston's Fork of the Licking, near where Mt. Sterling now stands, in which the Indians were victorious. In this battle, Estill, who commanded the whites, and nearly all of his officers, were killed.

Near the Blue Licks another battle was soon afterwards fought with Captain Holder, in which the whites were again defeated; in both these last mentioned battles the contending foe were Wyandottes. In this year also, an attack by five hundred Indians was unexpectedly made on Bryant's Station. In this attack the Indians were finally repulsed on the second night of the siege. The garrison at Bryant's Station being reinforced, and numbering one hundred and sixty men, on the 18th of August started in pursuit of the retreating Indians, and on the 19th overtook them beyond Licking River, where a desperate battle ensued, commanded on the part of the whites by Major McGary, who was totally routed on that occasion, losing in the flight about sixty officers and men killed, seven taken prisoners, and the number of the wounded was never ascertained. McGary was too impatient for the pursuit of the Indians to wait for the forces Logan was raising in Lincoln, and when he returned from the battle to the fort the next night, he there met Logan with a force of four hundred and fifty men. Among those who were killed in this battle, on the field, were Todd, Trigg, Harland, McBride, Bulger, and Gordon. McGary, though in the midst of the fight, escaped unhurt. Logan, with his force, immediately proceeded to the battle-ground, where he collected and buried the dead; and finding that the foe had crossed the Ohio, and were beyond his reach, returned to Bryant's Station and disbanded his troops. Soon afterwards, Colonel George Rodgers Clark determined on retaliation, and with the State troops stationed at Louisville, and the militia of the country who joined him, in all, one thousand men, penetrated to the heart of the Indian country, and, unresisted, reduced their towns to ashes, cut up their corn, and laid waste their whole country; and, having destroyed everything within reach, returned to Kentucky. Peace was made with Great Britain in 1783, and hostilities ceased; hostilities with the Indians also for a time seemed suspended, but were soon renewed with greater violence than ever. During the cessation of hostilities with the Indians, settlements in Kentucky advanced rapidly.

In 1784, Simon Kenton, who had been absent from his family some twelve or thirteen years, returned to Virginia and brought his family to Kentucky, and reclaiming his settlement at Washington, erected a block-house where Maysville now stands. The general course of emigration from that time was down the Ohio River to Maysville, and thence to the interior.

In the spring of 1783, by an act of the Virginia Legislature, Kentucky was erected into a district, with criminal as well as civil jurisdiction co-extensive with the district. In the spring of this year the first court under the law was held at Harrodsburg; John Floyd and Samuel McDowell, Judges; John May, Clerk; and Walker Daniel, Prosecuting Attorney. During the summer a log court-house and jail were erected where Danville now stands. In the same year a dry goods store was opened in Louisville by Daniel Broadhead, being the first establishment of the kind in the district. This year Gen. James Wilkinson came to Kentucky and settled in Lexington. Wilkinson was aid-de-camp to Gates at Saratoga, and for his distinguished services in that campaign he was promoted by Congress to the rank of Brigadier General. He was said to be in embarrassed circumstances at the time pecuniarily, and one great object of his visit was to improve his fortune. He had distinguished himself in the war of Independence, and very soon after his arrival in Kentucky distinguished himself as a politician and a party leader. His fine address, amiable manners, acknowledged hospitality, and perseverance made him very popular with the mass of the people, and he occupied high position in the early civil conflicts of Kentucky.

Daniel Boone has always been regarded as most distinguished among the pioneers to Kentucky, from the fact, perhaps, that he was the first white man who made a permanent settlement in the country, and underwent more fatigue, trials, and hardships than any other man, perhaps, who ever visited the country at that early period; I therefore deem it proper in this place to give a more detailed account of his life and character.

I remember, when I was a boy, with what delight and satisfaction I listened to the tales rehearsed by my father of the daring deeds, miraculous escapes, bloody fights, and heart-rending sufferings of the early adventurers to Kentucky. They made an impression on my mind then that I shall never forget; and such rehearsals inspired me with such love for the reading of history as was ever an advantage to me.

Daniel Boone was born in Bucks County, Pennsylvania, on Delaware River, on the 11th of February, 1731, and was just about one year older than General George Washington, who was born on the 22d of February, 1732. Boone was near forty years old when he first visited Kentucky, and of his life but little is known previous to that time. It is said that his ancestors were among the original Catholic settlers of Maryland; of this, however, but little is known with certainty. In his boyhood, his father moved first to Reading, on the headwaters of the Schuylkill, and subsequently to a valley of South Yadkin, North Carolina. Here Boone continued to reside until his first visit to Kentucky. All we can learn of him previous to this time is, that he was fond of the exciting pleasures of the chase, and the thrilling solitude of forests and wild wood, where the foot of man but seldom trod.

As we have stated in a previous chapter, he left his family upon the Yadkin, and in company with Findley and four others, in 1769, started on an exploring expedition to a country of which he had heard so favorable an account. Having reached Red River, on the borders of what is now the State of Kentucky, they built a cabin, as has been before stated, and devoted themselves to hunting, and killed immense quantities of game. On the 22d of December of that year he was captured by the Indians, the incidents of which have before been stated. Boone was followed by his brother, Squire Boone, from North Carolina, who fortunately soon met with him. Boone's companions had all been killed except one, and that one becoming disheartened by the perils to which they were continually exposed, returned home, leaving Boone and brother alone in the wilderness, with nothing but rifles. Their ammunition running short, Squire Boone returned to North Carolina for a fresh supply, leaving Daniel in charge of the camp, and to roam the forests in solitude until his return. On the 27th of July, 1770, the younger brother returned with the ammunition, and the brothers continued to range through the country without injury until March, 1771, when they returned to North Carolina. Boone had been absent from his family three years, and during that time had never tasted bread or salt, nor beheld the face of a single white man, excepting his brother, and the friends who had been killed.

On the 25th of September, 1771, Boone, having sold his farm and all his property except what he brought with him, took leave of his friends and started again to Kentucky with his family. In Powell's Valley he was joined by five more families and forty men, well-armed. Near Cumberland Mountains they were attacked by a large party of Indians; Boone, with his force, compelled them to retreat, with the loss, however, of six men killed and wounded, and among the killed, Boone's eldest son. They were so discouraged by this disaster that they retreated to the settlement on Clinch River, forty miles from the scene of action, where they remained until 1774. During this interval Boone was employed by Gov. Dunmore, of Virginia, to conduct a party of surveyors through the wilderness to the Falls of the Ohio, eight hundred miles distant. After his return he was placed by Gov. Dunmore in command of three frontier stations, and engaged with several affairs with the Indians. It was about that time he attended the treaty of Wataga, with the Cherokees, for the purchase of the lands south of the Kentucky River. On the 22d of March, 1775, Boone arrived within fifteen miles of where Boonesborough was afterwards built. Here he had a severe contest with the Indians, and repulsed them, with a loss on his part of four men killed and wounded. The attack was again renewed the next day, with a loss of five more of his men. On the 1st of April they reached the southern bank of the Kentucky River, and began to build the fort afterwards known as Boonesborough. The fort was soon completed, and Boone returned to Clinch River for his family. The little garrison at Boonesborough, for a considerable time, was exposed to the incessant assaults of the Indians, which were withstood with indomitable firmness and courage. I have before spoken of the capture by the Indians of Boone's daughter and the two Misses Calloway, and of their recapture by Boone and eight men in July, 1776, in which Boone sustained no loss whatever. The loss of the Indians was two men killed and a complete rout. The garrison was considerably annoyed during the spring, but the most they suffered was the destruction of their property.

On the 15th of April the fort was attacked by a large body of Indians, and again on the 4th of July by two hundred warriors, but were repulsed on both occasions with some loss. Whilst

Boone was a prisoner with the Indians in March, 1778, he accompanied them on a visit to Detroit, where Gov. Hamilton offered a hundred pounds for his ransom, but the Indians had formed such affection for him that the offer was refused. Boone was in captivity about six months with the Indians before he was enabled to effect his escape, and when he returned to Boonesborough, his wife and family, supposing him dead, had returned to North Carolina. In the fall of this year Boone went to North Carolina for his family, and in the summer of 1780 brought them back, and again settled at Boonesborough. In August, 1782, was fought the memorable and disastrous battle of the Blue Licks, in which Boone bore himself with distinguished gallantry, and where fell a son and many of his dearest friends. Boone afterwards accompanied Colonel George Rodgers Clark in his expedition against the Indian towns, undertaken to avenge the disaster of the Blue Licks. After this it does not appear that Boone was ever engaged in any other expedition or adventure. Upon the establishment of the Commissioner's Court in Kentucky, in 1779, Boone laid out the main part of his property to procure landwarrants, and had raised about $20,000 in paper money (Continental money, I suppose,) with which he intended to purchase them. On his way to the city of Richmond he was robbed of the whole, and left destitute of the means of procuring more. The few lands he was afterwards enabled to procure were all lost by better claims. Becoming greatly dissatisfied with the ill-fortune which had attended him, he went to Missouri in 1795, which country then belonged to Spain, and devoted the remainder of his life principally to the employments of the chase; even after his energies became enfeebled from age he would wander to the remotest wilderness he could reach. As late as 1816 he made such an excursion to Fort Osage, a hundred miles from his residence. Three years after this, in 1819, as says Governor Morehead in his Boonesborough speech, a patriotic solicitude to preserve his portrait prompted a distinguished American artist to visit him at his dwelling on the banks of the Missouri, and from him the following particulars were received: He found him in a rude log-cabin, indisposed, and reclining on his bed. A slice from the loin of a buck, twisted round the rammer of his rifle, was roasting before the fire. Several other cabins there, in parallelogram form, marked the spot of a dilapidated station. They were occupied by his descendants; here he lived in the midst of them. His withered energies and locks of snow indicated that the sources of his existence were nearly exhausted. The year after (1820) he died of fever at the house of his son-in-law, in Flanders, Calloway County, at the advanced age of eighty-nine years. Upon the announcement of his death, the Legislature of Missouri, being in session, passed a resolution in respect to his memory, that the members should wear the usual badge of mourning for the space of twenty days. In person he was of robust and powerful proportions; five feet ten inches in height; his countenance mild and contemplative. His ordinary habiliments were those of a hunter, shirt and moccasins always comprising a part of them.

At a session of the Legislature of Kentucky of 1844-5, measures were adopted to have the remains of Boone and his wife removed from the banks of the Missouri to the cemetery at Frankfort. The consent of the surviving relations having been obtained, the removal was effected, and the 13th of September, 1845, was fixed upon as the time when the ashes of the venerable dead would be committed with fitting ceremonies to their place of final repose.

An immense concourse of citizens from all parts of the State were present on the occasion, and the ceremonies were deeply impressive. The procession extended more than a mile. The hearse, decorated with evergreens and flowers, and drawn by four white horses, occupied the position assigned in the line. The pall-bearers were the distinguished Col. Richard M. Johnson, Gen. James Taylor, Capt. James Ward, General Robert B. McAfee, Peter Jordan, Waller Bullock, Thomas Joice, Landon Sneed, Col. John Johnston, of the State of Ohio, Major Z. Williams, and Col. William Boone.

The procession was accompanied by several military companies, and the Masonic and Odd-Fellow fraternities in rich regalia. At the grave the funeral services were performed. The hymn was given out by the Rev. Mr. Godell, of the Baptist Church, oration by the Hon. John J. Crittenden, closing prayer by Rev. J. J. Bullock, of the Presbyterian Church, and benediction by Rev. P. S. Fall, of the Christian Church.

Next to Boone, as one of the principal actors in the first settlement of Kentucky, the name of the justly renowned Simon Kenton deserves to be ranked. He was born of obscure parentage in Fauquier County, Virginia, on the 15th day of May, 1755. His father was an Irishman, and his mother of Scotch descent. His education was quite limited, though he was a man of strong natural intellect. A calamity which befell him at sixteen years of age gave direction to his whole future life. He lost his sweetheart; not by death, but she was won from him by a more favored rival, whose name was Wm. Veach. Kenton went to the wedding uninvited, and unceremoniously thrust himself between the newly-married couple, who were seated upon a bed, when he was immediately pounced upon by Veach and his brothers, who gave him a tremendous beating. Kenton, soon afterwards meeting with Veach, informed him that he was not satisfied, and a severe fight ensued, in which Veach, this time, got a sound whipping. Veach, attempting to rise from his entanglement in a bush, fell back insensible. Kenton became alarmed, believing him to be dead, and fled precipitately to the woods. Having lost his sweetheart, and killed (as he supposed) his rival and former friend and companion, to remain at home he regarded as threatening too much danger, and he started at once to the wilderness of the unexplored West. Traveling by night and lying concealed by day, after many sufferings he arrived on Cheat River, in April, 1771, and changed his name to Simon Butler. After some months' stay at this place, having earned by his labor a good rifle, he joined a party who were going to Fort Pitt. At this place he met with and formed the acquaintance of the notorious Simon Girty. In company with George Yeager and John Strader, Kenton from this point proceeded down the Ohio River as far as the mouth of the Kentucky River. Yeager, who had represented to Kenton that the country was covered with cane, was to some extent mistaken, for really cane grew nowhere on the banks of the Ohio above the mouth of the Kentucky River, although the interior was covered with it. The party not finding the description of country they were hunting for, returned up the Ohio to the mouth of Big Kanawha, and, in the winter of 1771-2, they built a camp on a branch of the Great Kanawha, and hunted and trapped successfully; here they remained until the spring of 1773. In March, 1773, while the three hunters were quietly reposing in their camp, they were fired upon by the Indians. Yeager was killed, and Kenton and Strader fled, and effected their escape, barefooted and naked, without food, having on nothing but their shirts. They wandered six days in this condition, suffering from hunger and exhaustion, and several times laid themselves down to die. On the sixth day they met a party of hunters on the Ohio, who gave them food and clothed them. During the winter of 1773-4, Kenton spent his time with a hunting party on the Big Sandy, and, when the war broke out with the Indians, he retreated into Fort Pitt, with other settlers. When Lord Dunmore raised an army to punish the Indians, Kenton volunteered, and was employed as a spy, and he also acted in the same capacity with Colonel Lewis. In the fall of this year he returned with Thomas Williams to the old hunting-ground on Big Sandy.

In the spring of 1775, having disposed of his peltries to a French trader, he descended the Ohio River once more, in search of the "cane land." They put in at the mouth of Cabin Creek, in the present county of Mason, about sixteen miles above Maysville. Having examined the country about that place on the next day, he became enraptured with the richness of the soil, and returning to his canoe, sunk it, with the view of remaining a while at least. In May, 1775, he and Williams built their camp in about a mile of where the town of Washington now stands. They made a small clearing, and planted about an acre of corn, and here ate the first roasting ears, planted by the whites, that ever grew on the north side of Kentucky River. In the fall of 1775, Kenton, in his rambles, met at the Lower Blue Licks with one Michael

Stoner, who had come to Kentucky the year before with Daniel Boone. He now discovered that he and Williams were not the only white men inhabiting the cane lands, so gathering up his property, he and Williams accompanied Stoner to the settlement in the interior.

Kenton passed the winter of 1775-6 at Hinkston Station, about forty miles from his corn-patch, in what is now Bourbon County. In 1776 the Indians became so troublesome that the weaker stations were abandoned. The settlers at Hinkston went to McClelland's Fort (where Georgetown now stands), Kenton accompanying them. About the beginning of the year 1777, McClelland's Fort becoming too weak to withstand the frequent and desolating attacks of the Indians, was abandoned, and the settlers all went to the fort at Harrodsburg, where Kenton also took up his abode. Major Clark, who now had command of the settlements, sent Kenton and five others to Hinkston, to break flax and hemp. Upon their approach the fort was surrounded by the Indians, and the party led by Kenton were compelled to retreat.

So annoying had the Indians become, that six spies were appointed by Clark to watch the Indians and give timely notice of their approach, and for their payment pledged the faith of Virginia. Two were appointed for Boonsborough, of whom Kenton was one; two for Harrodsburg, and two for Logan's Fort, all of whom performed good service. Two men in the fields being fired upon by the Indians, immediately fled, and the Indians pursued them, and a warrior overtook and tomahawked one of them within seventy yards of the fort, and was proceeding to scalp him, when Kenton, standing in the gateway, observed and shot the daring savage dead, and with his companions gave chase to the others. Boone, hearing the noise, hastened to his assistance with ten men. At this time Kenton observed an Indian taking aim at Boone's party, and he instantaneously leveled his rifle at him, pulled trigger, and the Indian fell dead on the spot. Boone having advanced some distance, found that a large body of Indians had gotten between him and the fort. By the command of Boone a desperate charge was made, and seven of the fourteen whites were wounded, Boone among the number, whose leg was broken. An Indian sprang upon him with uplifted tomahawk, but before the blow was given Kenton killed the Indian, shooting him in the breast, and bore his gallant leader into the fort. When all in the fort was secure, Boone, addressing Kenton, said, "Well, Simon, you have behaved yourself like a man to-day; indeed, you are a fine fellow." Kenton deserved the praise, for he had saved the life of Boone, and killed three Indians.

Boonesborough sustained three sieges this year, in every one of which Kenton bore an active and gallant part. Kenton continued as a spy until June, 1778, when he joined Clark's expedition against Kaskaskia. The result of this expedition was entirely successful, and Kenton returned to Harrodsburg by way of Vincennes, and communicated such information to Clark as enabled him afterwards easily to take that post also. After this, Kenton joined a party of Boone's, consisting of nineteen men, to go against a small Indian town on Paint Creek. On arriving near the village, Kenton, as usual, was in advance, and heard loud laughter in a cane-brake just before him, and he suddenly saw two Indians mounted on a pony, seemingly unconscious of danger, one facing the animal's tail, the other his head. He aimed, pulled trigger, and both fell, one killed, and the other mortally wounded. He hastened to scalp them, but was immediately surrounded by about forty Indians, when he commenced dodging from tree to tree to avoid being shot, until Boone with his party, coming up, furiously attacked and signally defeated the Indians.

Boone returned to the fort, learning that a war-party had gone against it, but Kenton and Montgomery proceeded to the village, in hopes to get another shot at them, and also get some of their horses. Lying in wait, the second night they succeeded in getting two of their best horses, and put off to Kentucky, and the day after the Indians raised the siege of Boonesborough they cantered into the fort on their stolen horses. In September of the same year he, in company with George Clark, went to Chilicothe on a similar expedition, and succeeded in haltering seven horses, and the succeeding day arrived with them on the Ohio, a few miles below Maysville, but the river was so rough that they could not cross with any safety. To relieve their burthen they turned four of the horses loose, but afterwards relenting they endeavored to recover them, and with this view they separated to search for them. Kenton had not gone far before he heard the whoop of Indians behind him, and, instead of trying to make his escape, he dismounted from his horse, tied him, and then crept back in the direction of the noise. Two Indians and a white man made their appearance; he raised his rifle, pulled trigger, and the gun flashed; he then took to his heels, but it was too late, and he was taken prisoner. The party was furious towards him, and beat him without mercy, then secured him for the night by tying him on his back fast to stakes, both hand and foot. His captivity was more than eight months, during which time his sufferings were extreme, and, as stout as he was, almost insupportable. He was compelled to run the gauntlet eight times; three times tied to a stake, and providentially relieved; once nearly killed by a blow with an axe, and subjected to many hardships and privations most of the time. He was finally, through the influence of Logan, the Mingo chief, purchased by a Canadian trader named Druyer, who delivered him over to the British commandant at Detroit. Here he remained until the summer of 1779, when he effected his escape by the assistance of a Mrs. Harvey, the wife of an Indian trader. Kenton at this time was but twenty-four years of age, and is described as "fine looking, of dignified and manly deportment, a soft and pleasing voice, and, wherever he went, a favorite among the ladies." Mrs. Harvey had provided Kenton with a rifle, ammunition, food, and clothing, preparatory to his escape. Returning many thanks to the kind lady, he took his departure. He never saw her afterwards, but remembered her with gratitude and admiration as long as he lived. Kenton, with his two companions, Bullitt and Coffee, arrived safely at Louisville in July, 1789. Soon after this he visited his old companion in arms, Major Clark, at Vincennes. This post he found entirely quiet, so he returned by way of the Falls to Harrod's Station, where he was joyfully received by his old companions. We can not, in these gleanings, go into the minutiæ of Kenton's life and great services in the first settlement of this country. It would require a volume to write them down, for he was a principal actor in almost every important event that occurred in Kentucky until Indian aggressions were entirely extirpated, which was about the year 1793. About that time Clark raised an army of eleven hundred men for retaliation, after the fall of Martin's and Ruddle's forts. Kenton commanded a company of volunteers from Harrod's Station, and shared in all the dangers and successes of this army. Chilicothe, Pickaway, and many other towns were burnt, and their crops destroyed. For two years after this period the stations enjoyed comparative peace, and Kenton passed his time in hunting, or as a spy, or with surveying parties. In the fall of 1782 he heard for the first time since he had been in this country that his father yet lived, and that he had not killed his old friend and companion, Wm. Veach, as he had supposed. The information pleased him much. For eleven years he had wandered in the wilderness, with remorse for the rash deed which he supposed he had committed.

In the fall of 1782, Clark, to avenge the disaster of the Blue Licks, led another army, fifteen hundred strong, against the Indian towns. Kenton again commanded a company on this occasion, and was again the pilot of the army. After this campaign he settled on his land on Salt River, built some rude block-houses, planted corn, and, in the fall, having gathered his corn, determined to visit his father and bring him to Kentucky. The reunion was joyful to all, especially to those who thought him dead. He saw Veach and his wife, and the old feud was forgotten. He gathered up his father's family and started for Kentucky, and had proceeded as far as Red-Stone Fort, on the Monongahela River, when his father died. He, with the rest of the family, proceeded on their journey, and arrived at his settlement in safety in the winter of 1784. In July, 1784, he went to his old camp, in Mason County, but soon returned again to Salt River on account of his trouble with the Indians. In the fall, however, he built some block-houses at his old camp, and was joined by several families. In the spring of 1785 many new settlements were made around Kenton's Station.

In 1786 Kenton sold (or gave, as one says) one thousand acres of land to Fox and Wood, on which they laid out the town of Washington. Old Ned Waller had settled at Limestone (now Maysville) the year before.

In 1786, to put a check to the predatory incursions of the Indians, a force, seven hundred strong, was gotten up, under the command of Colonel Logan. Kenton commanded a company, and, as usual, piloted the army into the enemy's country. They defeated the Indians in several engagements, and burnt four of their towns. An expedition, the next year, was gotten up by Kenton, commanded by Colonel Todd, of which the former commanded a company of gallant young men, trained by himself, and, as usual, piloted the expedition. A detachment, led by Hinkston and Kenton, fell upon and defeated a large body of Indians before Todd came up. Chilicothe was burnt, and the expedition returned without the loss of a man.

From 1788 to 1793 the Indians ceased their incursions into Kentucky. In 1793, when Wayne came down the Ohio for his expedition against the Indians, Kenton, then a Major, joined him with his battalion, and proceeded to Greenville, where he was conspicuous with the army on account of his superior skill and activity. The Indians, being defeated by Wayne, sued for peace, and the war ended.

The value of lands increased greatly after the peace of Greenville, owing to the immense immigration, and Kenton was regarded as immensely wealthy; but, like Boone, he lost all by older claims and expensive lawsuits, and, finally, his body was taken for debt upon the covenant in deeds to lands, and for twelve months he lay in prison upon the very spot where he first built his cabin, and where he planted the first corn. Poor and penniless, in 1802 he moved to Ohio and settled in Urbana. In 1805 he was elected a Brigadier General of the Ohio millitia, and in 1810 joined the Methodist Episcopal Church. In 1813 he joined the Kentucky troops under Governor Shelby, and was admitted a privileged member of his military family, and was in the battle of the Thames. He remained in Urbana until 1820, when he removed to Logan County, Ohio. He had owned some mountain lands in this State, which had been sold for the taxes, and in 1824 he undertook a trip to Frankfort to try and prevail with the Legislature to release the claim of the State upon his lands. The Legislature, without hesitation, released her claim, and Congress shortly afterwards granted him a pension of $240 a year, in order to secure his old age from absolute want. In April, 1836, he died, in sight of the place where, fifty-eight years before, the Indians proposed to torture him to death, at peace with his God and all mankind.

Intimately connected with the history of the early settlements of Kentucky, and scarcely less distinguished than any other, is the name of Colonel George Rodgers Clark, a detailed account of whose life and services it would be impossible to give in the plan designed. I shall, therefore, confine myself to the principal events of his eventful career.

He was born in Albemarle County, Virginia, on the 19th of November, 1752. But little is known of his early years, except that in his youth he engaged in the business of surveying, an occupation very common with many of the enterprising young men of his day. He commanded a company in Dunmore's war against the Indians; at the close of this war he was offered a commission in the British service, but declined it. In the spring of 1775, as I have elsewhere stated, he came to Kentucky, and remained here until fall, when he returned to Virginia. During this visit he was placed in the temporary command of the settlements. In the spring of 1776 he again came to Kentucky, with the intention of making it his permanent home. Soon after his arrival, upon the suggestion of Clark, a meeting was held at Harrodsburg for the purpose of appointing agents to the Legislature of Virginia, to negotiate with them for the recognition of the colonists, as being within her jurisdiction and under her protection; and, in the event of Virginia's refusal to afford them means of protection, to establish an independent State. Clark and Gabriel Jones were selected; but when they arrived at Williamsburg, the then seat of government, the Legislature had adjourned, and Jones left for the Holston, leaving Clark to attend to the mission alone. By the indefatigable and persevering exertions of Clark, he finally succeeded with the Council in obtaining five hundred pounds of gunpowder, for the use of the people of Kentucky, and the transportation of the powder to Pittsburgh, to be delivered to Clark or his order. This order was made the 23d of August, 1776. At the fall session of the Legislature, this year, through the influence of Clark and Jones, aided by others, in opposition to Henderson and Campbell, Kentucky was formed into a county of Virginia. Clark and Jones returned home by the way of Pittsburgh, and, with the assistance of seven men, were enabled to reach the landing at Maysville in safety with the powder, whereby the colonists were abundantly supplied with an indispensable means of defense against the constant inroads of the Indians.

Clark was universally looked up to by the settlers as the master spirit of the times, and was always among the foremost in the conflicts which ensued in that quarter. After this, his expedition against Kaskaskia and Vincennes was undertaken, which resulted so gloriously, and of which I have heretofore spoken. Clark's plans for the reduction of these posts were submitted to the Legislature of Virginia in December, 1777; his scheme was fully approbated, and £1,200 ($4,000) were advanced to defray the expenses, and the commandant at Fort Pitt ordered to supply Clark with ammunition, boats, and all other necessary equipments. Proceeding down the river, on the evening of the 4th of July, 1778, they arrived in the neighborhood of Kaskaskia, having left their boats where Fort Massae was afterwards built.

That night the town and fort were captured without the effusion of a drop of blood; the British Governor was taken in his chamber. Clark then directed his attention to the French village of Cahokia, sixty miles higher up the Mississippi. The expedition reached the town without being discovered, and took possession of it. The people took the oath of allegiance, and in a few days the utmost harmony prevailed. After this, by the assistance of a Catholic priest, named M. Gibault, who influenced the people of his pastoral charge to join Clark, Vincennes was taken without difficulty. The inhabitants threw off their allegiance to the British, and the American flag was displayed from the ramparts of the fort. Clark, with a view to conciliate the various tribes of Indians who inhabited this portion of the country, and were continually disturbing the peace and quietude of Kentucky, entered into negotiations with many of the tribes, and succeeded in pacifying, in a great degree, their hostility.

In January, 1769, Clark received intelligence that Governor Hamilton, of Detroit, had marched against Vincennes, and had re-established the British power in that fort. He immediately made preparations for another expedition against that fort. He commenced his march with a force of one hundred and seventy-five men, on the 7th of February, having previously dispatched Captain Rogers with a force of forty-six men and two four-pounders in a boat to ascend the Wabash and station themselves a few miles below White River until further orders. In eleven days Clark, through much difficulty and great privations, arrived near enough to hear the morning and evening guns of the fort, and encamped within nine miles of the town, below the mouth of Embaras River.

On the 20th of February, having crossed the river, they were in sight of Vincennes. Having captured a man who was shooting ducks in the neighborhood of the town, Clark sent a letter to the inhabitants by him, letting them know that he should take possession of the town that night. The inhabitants were taken entirely by surprise. On the 23d he took possession of the heights back of the town, and commenced firing with great spirit. On the evening of the next day the British commandant, apprehensive of a disastrous result on his part, sent a flag asking a truce for three days. This was refused, and on the 24th of February, 1779, the fort was surrendered, and the garrison made prisoners of war. On the 25th possession was taken, the stars and stripes again hoisted, and thirteen guns fired in celebration of the victory.

Soon after this Louisville was settled, and Clark made his headquarters there. In 1780 he built Fort Jefferson, on the Mississippi River. In the course of this year he led an expedition of about one thousand men with some artillery from the Falls against the Indians of Ohio. The Indian town was reached before the enemy had any intimation of their approach. A conflict ensued, which resulted in a loss of about seventeen men on each side. The Indians fled, the town was reduced to ashes, and their gardens and fields laid waste; and the whites received no further trouble that season.

Clark had conceived a plan for the reduction of the British fort at Detroit, and had gone to Richmond to obtain an appropriation of means for that purpose, but before the arrangements could be completed a British force from New York, under the traitor Benedict Arnold, carried hostilities into the heart of the State, and Clark took a temporary command under Baron Steuben, and participated in the active operations of that campaign.

Two thousand men were raised in 1781, and on the 15th of March rendezvoused at the Falls, and Clark was raised to the rank of Brigadier General, but instead of moving on Detroit was confined to defensive operations. In September of this year he led one thousand men against the Indian towns on the Miami and Scioto. The Indians fled before them. Twelve of their men were killed and taken.

In 1786 an army was raised to march against the Indians on the Wabash, and Clark, at the head of one thousand men, again entered the Indian territory; but this expedition proving unfortunate was abandoned.

General Clark was never married. He suffered a long time from rheumatic affection, which terminated in paralysis and deprived him of the use of one of his limbs. He died in February, 1818, and was buried at Locust Grove, near Louisville.

Another name, whose history is intimately connected with the early settlements in Kentucky, is that of Benjamin Logan. He was of Irish parentage, who lived first in Pennsylvania, and afterwards moved to Augusta County, Virginia, where Benjamin was born. The father having died, left Benjamin, at fourteen years of age, the head of the family. By the right of primogeniture, under the law as it then stood, he was entitled to all the lands of which his father died possessed, to the exclusion of the other children. He did not, however, avail himself of the advantage which the law gave him. He therefore sold the land not subject to division, and divided the proceeds with the other children. Adding his portion with that of a brother, he purchased a tract of land on James River for the use of his mother during her life, with the remainder to his brother in fee. Having settled his mother, he removed to Holston himself, purchased lands, married, and commenced farming. At an early age he accompanied Colonel Beauquette in an expedition against the Indians of the North. In 1774 he was with Governor Dunmore in his expedition to the northwest of Ohio In 1775 he came to Kentucky, accompanied only by two or three slaves, to see the lands, and make a settlement. In Powell's Valley he met with Boone and others, also on their way to Kentucky, with whom he traveled; but afterwards he separated from them, and in a few days more pitched his tent in Lincoln County, about a mile from where Stanford now stands, and there built a fort called Logan's Fort.

On the 20th of May, 1777, this fort was invested with one hundred Indians, and one man was killed outside of the fortifications and two wounded; the rest, who were out, escaping into the fort and closing the gate. Harrison, one of the wounded men, ran a few paces and fell, and his cries exciting the sympathies of Logan, he rushed to him, threw him on his shoulders, and carried him in the fort amidst a shower of bullets which whistled about him from the Indians in a canebrake near by. The fort was now vigorously assailed for many days, and there were only twelve or fifteen men to defend it, and they destitute of ammunition. In this trying emergency Logan left the fort under cover of the night, and crept through the Indian lines, accompanied by two others. who made their way to Holston, where he procured ammunition, and, intrusting it to his companions, arrived at the fort himself within ten days from the time he left it. In a few days the appearance of Colonel Bowman's party compelled the Indians to retire. The first year of his arrival at Asaph's or Logan's Fort, he, with William Glasby, raised a small crop of corn. In the fall of this year he removed his cattle and the rest of his slaves from Holston to his camp. In 1776 he removed his family to Kentucky, and for their greater security placed them at Harrod's Station, whilst he with his slaves cultivated his farm.

In the spring of 1777 Mrs. Logan returned to her husband. This same year he discovered a camp of Indians at Big Flat Lick, two miles from his station. He immediately returned, raised a party of men, and attacked them with great resolution. The Indians immediately fled, sustaining but little loss. He was afterwards at the same lick in search of game, when he was fired on by concealed Indians, which broke his right arm, and wounded him slightly in the breast. He came very near falling into their hands, they being once so near as to catch hold of his horse's tail.

Logan was second in command, Colonel Bowman being commander-in-chief, in the expedition to Chilicothe, in 1779, of which we have spoken elsewhere. Logan was in full march, but was unable to participate in the battle of the Blue Licks with his well-appointed force. He proceeded to the battle-ground the next day, and buried the dead of that disastrous affair; after which he disbanded his men and returned home. In the summer of 1788 he conducted an expedition against the northwestern tribes of Indians, doing but little other damage than burning their towns and destroying their corn.

General Logan was a member of the convention which formed the Constitution of 1792. He was also a member of the convention which formed the Second Constitution of Kentucky, in 1799. He was repeatedly a member of the Legislature, and was highly esteemed as such. He died at an advanced age, beloved by all who knew him. He was the father of Wm. Logan, for many years Judge of the Court of Appeals of Kentucky.

Another important character connected with the history of the first settlers of Kentucky was James Harrod. His name is particularly distinguished as being the builder of the first log cabin in Kentucky. He immigrated to the country in the year 1774. It is said of him, that in person he was tall, erect, commanding, bold, resolute, active, and energetic; of a generous nature, familiar with danger, capable of enduring hardships, expert with the rifle, a successful hunter, and though an unlettered man by no means an ignorant one, and ranked high as a leader of the pioneers. He delighted in the chase, and was ever ready, when necessary, to attach himself to any party for exploration or expedition against the Indians. On the 10th of October, 1774, he was with Lewis in his victorious enterprize against the northwestern savages. His station was the most prominent of any for refuge and resort in times of greatest danger. Whilst he lived he never relinquished his fondness for the solitudes of the wilderness. Though blessed with an interesting family, he often left home on protracted hunting excursions, and it was on one of these occasions, in a distant part of the country, that he never returned to his home.

Though General Anthony Wayne was not a Kentuckian, and had never lived here, yet his history is in some degree connected with it. After St. Clair's inglorious and disastrous defeat by the Indians on the northwestern frontier, Wayne, a citizen of Pennsylvania, was appointed by General Washington, then President of the United States, as his successor, and brought the Indian war in that quarter to a peaceful termination. On the 20th of August, 1794, near the river of the Miami, he fought and gained one of the greatest victories of the times, and in 1795 he concluded a treaty of peace with the Indians. This may be regarded as an end of all the difficulties with the Indians in the West, and terminated hostilities entirely with the Indians of the Northwest. Many of Kentucky's noble sons shared the honors of that glorious victory, under his command.

General Wayne was born in Chester County, Pennsylvania, January 1, 1745. He received a good education, and early commenced the business of surveying. He was chosen, in 1774, Provincial Deputy to consider the affairs of Great Britain. In 1775 he was elected to the Legislature, and was a member of the Convention of Safety. In January, 1776, he was appointed by Congress a Colonel of one of the Pennsylvania regiments, and joined the army of General Lee, at New York.

In 1777 he was promoted to the rank of Brigadier-General. At the battle of Brandywine he commanded the division stationed at Chad's Ford. He was in the battles of Germantown and Monmouth. In July, 1779, he stormed the strong fortress of Stony Point, by a night attack. He witnessed the surrender of Lord Cornwallis at Yorktown. He was then sent to the South, and remained until peace was made. He died in December, 1796.

In the year 1776 James Sandusky removed from Virginia to Washington County, and built Sandusky's Station, on Pleasant Run. His brother Jacob is believed to be the first white man that descended the Ohio and Mississippi rivers, except French and Spanish. In 1774 he traveled to the Cumberland River, and descended it and the Ohio and Mississippi to New Orleans, where he took shipping and went round to Virginia by Baltimore. Shortly afterwards he returned to Kentucky and settled with James at Sandusky's Station.

In 1788 John Lancaster came to Washington County, and was afterwards a prominent citizen. In descending the Ohio River, on his way to Kentucky, he was taken prisoner by the Indians, and was treated very cruelly by them, but eight days afterwards effected his escape. Previous to his escape, however, he was adopted as a brother of one of the Indians, with great ceremony, in place of one who had been slain the previous year, and they called him Kioba, or the Running Buck, from his remarkable fleetness of foot. In two or three weeks after his departure he landed at the Falls, and soon joined his friends at Sandusky's Station. He lived many years to recount his adventures, and died in Washington County, at a good old age, surrounded by a numerous offspring.

One of the most distinguished of the early pioneers to Kentucky was Colonel William Whitley. He was born on the 14th of August, 1749, in that part of Virginia then called Augusta, and which afterwards furnished the territory of Rockbridge County. He had but poor opportunities for mental acquirements in early life, and followed the occupation of a tiller of his native soil until he was about twenty-six years old. Soon after he attained manhood he married Esther Fullin, in whom he found a wife in every way worthy of him. Becoming inspired with the spirit of enterprize, in 1775, with his axe and plow, gun and kettle, he set out for Kentucky in company with his brother-in-law, George Clark. In the wilderness they were joined by seven others. We have no detailed account of Whitley's adventures in Kentucky from 1775 to 1785, though we know they were numerous, great, and daring. In 1785 McClure's camp in Lincoln was assaulted at night by the Indians, and six whites killed and scalped. Mrs. McClure escaped from the camp with her four children, the youngest in her arms an infant, which kept up so continued a crying as to give the Indians notice of their place of concealment; by forsaking the infant she might save herself and the three larger children; but this, as a mother, she could not do, and preferred to die rather than forsake it. The Indians, attracted by the crying of the child, soon came upon them, and brutally murdered the three older children and took the mother and infant captive. She was taken by the Indians back to the camp, and compelled to cook for her captors. In the morning she was mounted on an unbroken horse and started off with them. Whitley, getting intelligence of the affair, started with twenty-one men in pursuit of them. They had stopped on their path to divide the plunder they had stolen, and Whitley in the meantime had gained the path in advance of them and prepared for their arrival, his men being concealed in a favorable position. As the Indians approached they were met by a deadly fire from Whitley's men, killing two of them, wounding two more, dispersing the rest. They rescued Mrs. McClure, her child, and a negro woman, and retook the six scalps taken by the Indians at the camp.

Ten days after this a Mr. Moore and his party, emigrating to the country, were attacked by Indians on the same road, nine of whom were killed, and the rest dispersed. Upon hearing this news Whitley, with thirty men, started in pursuit of them, and in six days met with them in a cane-brake. The Indians, twenty in number, were mounted on good horses, but as soon as they discovered the whites, they dismounted and took to their heels. Whitley pursued them, killed three, retook eight scalps, and captured twenty-eight horses, fifty pounds in cash, and a quantity of clothing and household furniture, which the Indians had stolen.

Whitley was with Bowman and Clark in their respective expeditions against the Indians. In the years 1792-93-94, the southern Indians gave great annoyance to the southern and southwestern portions of Kentucky, and made frequent inroads upon what was called the outside settlements, especially in the neighborhood of Crab Orchard, Logan's and McKinney's stations. To put an end to this, Whitley conceived the project of conducting an expedition against their towns, on the south side of the Tennessee River.

In 1794 he informed Major Orr, of Tennessee, of his contemplated design, and asked his assistance, which was readily acceded to, and the two corps, six or seven hundred in number, rendezvoused at Nashville. Their expedition was known by the name of Nickajack, being the name of the principal town against which they directed their operations. The Indians were taken greatly by surprise, and in the battle which ensued were defeated with great loss of life, their towns burnt, and their crops destroyed. This was Whitley's last hostile expedition against the Indians during the war. Soon after the general peace he went to some of the southern Indian towns to reclaim some negroes that had been taken in the contest. They told Whitley at first that he could not get the negroes, and put him several times in great fear for his life. He finally succeeded in getting the negroes, however, and returned home. He visited the Cherokees some time after this, and was everywhere received in the most friendly manner.

In 1813, then in the sixty-fifth year of his age, he volunteered with the Kentucky militia, under Governor Shelby, and was killed in the battle of the Thames, the 5th day of October of that year. Whitley is described as a man above the ordinary size, capable of enduring great fatigue and privation, with courage unquestionable, having been foremost in seventeen battles with the Indians, and one with a more civilized foe, in which he fell at the first fire. His memory is cherished by all Kentuckians as a patriot and hero.

In March, 1777, Harrodsburg was attacked by a party of forty-seven Indians, under the command of a celebrated chief named Blackfist. General James Ray, two of his brothers, and others were chopping wood outside of the fort. The Indians suddenly rushed upon them, killed one of his brothers, and took the other prisoner. James being uninjured, fled to the fort. Several of the swiftest Indians took after him, but he distanced them all, and reached the fort in safety, which very much attracted the admiration of the Indians, and Blackfist himself remarked to Boone, after his capture at the Blue Licks the next year, that some boy at Harrodsburg had outrun all his warriors. It was fortunate for the garrison that Ray got in in time for preparation for the attack, which was soon made by the Indians. The attack was commenced by firing an out-cabin on the east side of the town. This manœuver of the Indians had the effect which they desired, which was to decoy the whites out, and then intercept their return to the fort. The whites, however, retreated, keeping up a random fire until they got to the woods, just where the courthouse now stands, and each taking a tree soon made the Indians give back, and the garrison regained the fort. In the conflict only one Indian was killed, while four of the whites were wounded, one of whom afterwards died. The same year Ray and a man named McConnell were shooting at a mark near the fort, when McConnell was shot by the Indians. A large body of them suddenly appearing, Ray took to his heels, amidst a shower of bullets. When he arrived at the fort the gate had been shut, and he could not get in. He threw himself behind a stump at the fort wall, during four hours delay, the Indians keeping up a fire all the time. He was finally taken in by the garrison digging a hole under the wall just where he lay, and he was soon in the embraces of a fond mother and his friends. This year (1777) the fort was surrounded and beset by Indians nearly the whole time. General Clark on one occasion sallied out from the fort, and came upon the rear of some Indians, four of whom were killed, one by Clark, and another by Ray. Clark complimented Ray with the gun of the Indian he had shot, the first one he had ever killed.

Robert McAfee, (father of Robert B. McAfee), with his brothers, Samuel and James, settled a station and built a cabin in the neighborhood of Harrod's Station, in 1779, at the same place where the son Robert lived many years and died. The garrison at this station had many conflicts with the Indians, generally with success. The McAfees were sensible men, good Indian-fighters, and worthy citizens, often filling important stations.

Captain James Estill was a native of Augusta County, Virginia, and moved to Kentucky at an early period. He built a station at Muddy Creek, in Madison County. In 1781 one of his arms was broken by a rifle-shot from an Indian. In 1782, with twenty-five men, he pursued about the same number of Wyandotte Indians across Kentucky River, into Montgomery County, where was fought one of the most bloody battles on record, considering the number of men engaged. Captain Estill and South, his lieutenant, were both killed in their retreat. Estill came up with the Indians at the Hinkston Fork of Licking. When he first opened fire on the Indians they manifested a disposition to retreat, but their chief, who was badly wounded, ordered them to stand and fight. They immediately each took a tree, from which they returned the fire of the whites. Estill's men also protected themselves in the same way. The fight on both sides was maintained with great deliberation and coolness. The combatants being equal, each singled out his man, and only fired when the mark was presented, both sides standing firmly for nearly two hours. The loss on each side was nearly equal. In the charge which compelled Estill to retreat, he and eight of his men were killed and four others badly wounded, but they made their escape. In the affair the Indians lost more than half their number; the loss of the whites was greater.

Another important character in the first settlement of Kentucky was Colonel William Russell, who was born in Culpepper County, Virginia, in 1758. In the year 1774, at the age of fifteen, he accompanied Boone's expedition against the southern Indians; from that period to 1779 he was engaged in frequent excursions against the savages, who waged a continual warfare against the whites. In the spring of 1780 he visited Kentucky again, and went thence to Nashville, where a settlement had just been effected. Here he spent the summer, aiding the settlers in their defense against the assaults of the savages, when he returned to Virginia and joined the army fighting for independence, and bore himself valiantly in the battle of King's Mountain, and was the leader of a company in that action. After this he was in an expedition against the Cherokee Indians, which resulted in a treaty of peace. In the capacity of lieutenant he marched under Col. Campbell to the assistance of the Southern army, and fought in the battle of Whitsett's Mills, and also in the memorable battle of Guilford. After the conclusion of the Revolutionary War he returned to Kentucky and settled in Fayette County. After his migration to Kentucky he was in each of the expeditions conducted by Governor Scott and General Winchester against the Indian towns in the northwestern territory. In the expedition under Wayne he commanded a regiment of Kentucky volunteers. In 1789 he was elected a delegate to the Virginia Legislature, which passed the act separating Kentucky from Virginia as a separate State. Immediately after the organization of the State government he was annually returned a member of the Legislature of Kentucky from Fayette, except for one or two years, until 1808. In 1808 President Madison appointed him to the command of a regiment in the regular army. In 1811, after the battle of Tippecanoe, General Harrison assigned him to the frontier command for the protection of Indiana, Illinois, and Missouri.

He, with Governor Edwards, of Illinois, planned an expedition against the Peoria Indians. In 1823 he was again elected to the Legislature, and afterwards urgently solicited to offer as a candidate for Governor by some of the most distinguished men in the State. Few men were more useful in society than he. He died in the spring of 1825 at the age of sixty-seven years.

Colonel Richard Henderson came to Kentucky at a very early period. No history that we have examined, however, shows that he was ever engaged in any of the wars with the Indians, or experienced any of the troubles which their numerous and repeated incursions produced, but the incidents connected with his history in Kentucky are worthy of notice.

He was born in the State of North Carolina, and was emphatically a self-made man. His parents were poor, and he had grown to maturity before he could either read or write. This knowledge he acquired by his own unaided exertions. When a young man he filled the office of constable, and afterwards that of under-sheriff. After learning to read he devoted his leisure time to the reading of such law books as he could procure, and obtained license to practice law in the inferior courts of the county, and in due time was admitted to the bar of the superior courts. He soon became distinguished as an advocate, and for the uniform success of his efforts, and his general accurate knowledge of the details of his profession. In short, he established a high reputation as a lawyer, was promoted to the bench, and received the appointment of Associate Chief Judge of the Province of North Carolina. He is described as being ambitious and ostentatious. He became involved in speculations which embarassed his pecuniary relations, but being bold and adventurous he engaged in one of the most stupendous speculations ever recorded in the history of this country. He formed a company for that purpose, and succeeded in negotiating with the head chiefs of the Cherokee Indians, (known as the treaty of Watega), by which he and his associates became the proprietors of all that country which comprises now more than one-half of the State of Kentucky. All that country lying between the Cumberland and Kentucky rivers, and south of the Ohio River, was transferred to the company for a reasonable consideration. This was done in the year 1775. The company immediately proceeded to establish a proprietary government, of which Henderson was president, and which had its seat at Boonesborough, and bore the name of Transylvania. The first Legislature held its sittings at Boonesborough, under the shade of a large elm tree near the fort. The members were Squire Boone, Daniel Boone, William Coke, Samuel Henderson, Richard Moore, Richard Calloway, Thomas Slaughter, John Sythe, Valentine Harmon, James Douglass, James Harrod, Nathan Hammond, Isaac Hite, Azariah Davis, John Todd, Alexander Dandridge, John Floyd, and Samuel Wood. Thomas Slaughter was elected chairman, and Matthew Jewit, clerk. This is the earliest popular body that ever assembled in Kentucky.

A compact was entered into by the proprietors and the colonists establishing a free, manly, and liberal government over the territory. It was provided that the election should be annual; that there should be perfect freedom of opinion in matters of religion; that the judges should be appointed by the proprietors, but answerable for malconduct to the people; the convention to have the sole power of appropriating all moneys and electing their treasurer. The compact was signed by the proprietors, acting for the company, and by Thomas Slaughter, acting for the colonists.

The Virginia Legislature afterwards annulled the purchase made by Henderson & Co., as being contrary to the rights of that State. But, as a compensation to the proprietors for their services in opening the wilderness and preparing for civilization, they were granted a tract of land twelve miles square, on the Ohio below Green River.

Henderson was regarded as a man of a high order of talents, and entitled to a distinguished place among the early pioneers.

Another distinguished pioneer to Kentucky was George M. Bedinger. In 1779 he acted as Adjutant in the unfortunate expedition of Col. Bowman against the Indian town of Chilicothe. In 1782 he was a Major at the fatal battle of the Blue Licks, and bore himself gallantly as a brave and efficient officer. In 1792 he was elected a Representative to the first Legislature of Kentucky, from Bourbon County, of which Nicholas County then constituted a part. In 1802 he was elected a member of Congress, and served two terms in that body. He lived to an advanced age, and died on his farm near the Lower Blue Licks.

Another conspicuous character in the annals of Kentucky history was that of Stephen Trigg. He came to Kentucky in the fall of 1779, as a member of the Land Commissioners' Court; and in the spring of 1780, after the dissolution of that body, he determined to make Kentucky his permanent home. The same year he settled a station at the mouth of Dix River, and soon became noted for his activity against the Indians. He fell two years afterward at the fatal battle of the Blue Licks, while bravely leading his men to the charge. He was endeared to the hearts of the people of Kentucky by his amiable qualities, and his memory will ever be cherished as one of the noblest of Kentucky's early pioneers.

A thousand instances might be given of the intrepid bravery, hair-breadth escapes, and intolerable sufferings of individuals, men, women, and children, in the early settlement of Kentucky; but such relations, in detail, would occupy volumes, and is without the pale of our design in this work. My object is to present in a more tangible form than has been heretofore given the most important facts or events connected with the early settlement of Kentucky, and biographical sketches of those who participated most in the events of those times. I have, therefore, taken the pains to examine the best histories on the subject, often detailing the facts related in the very language of the author. Many of them, however, are traditional, and have never before been published, but handed down by my father and other old settlers in the middle part of the State, who participated in the transactions of those times, and from whom I received them in my youth, and treasured them in my recollection.

Among the most distinguished of the early emigrants to Kentucky the name of Colonel John Todd stands conspicuous. He was born in Pennsylvania, and educated in Virginia, at his uncle's, the Rev. John Todd. When he completed his education he studied law, obtained license to practice, and settled himself in the town of Fincastle, Virginia, where he was engaged in the practice of his profession for several years. But

Todd, lured with the description of the country, as given by those who had visited Kentucky, soon prepared for his journey, and arrived at Boonesborough about the year 1775, where he found Henderson and others. He joined Henderson's party, obtained a pre-emption right, and located sundry tracts of land in Madison County in the land-office of Colonel Henderson. He afterwards returned to Virginia, where he remained until 1786, when he came to Kentucky again, and improved two places in the vicinity of where Lexington now stands, one for himself and the other for John May; for both of which he obtained certificates of settlement and pre-emption of fourteen hundred acres adjoining to, and in the immediate vicinity of Lexington. He accompanied Colonel Clark in his expedition against Kaskaskia and Vincennes, and was at the capture of both those places. Colonel Todd was appointed to succeed Clark in the command at Kaskaskia. In 1777 the Legislature of Virginia passed an act by which all that part of the Northwestern territory conquered by Clark, and all other of her territory northwest of the Ohio River, was erected into the county of Illinois, and Colonel Todd was appointed Colonel Commandant and County Lieutenant, with all the civil powers of Governor. He was seldom absent from his government up to the time of his death. He was authorized to raise a regiment by enlistment of volunteers for the defense of the frontier, which he did; and though raised only for one year, they continued in service until 1779, when Virginia added four other regiments for the same object, two of which were placed under the command of Colonel Joseph Crockett, and the other two under Colonel Todd. In 1780 Colonel Todd was sent a delegate to the Legislature of Virginia from Kentucky County. While attending the Legislature he married, and, returning to Kentucky, settled his wife in the fort at Lexington, but again visited the county of Illinois. He was assiduous in attention to his affairs, both civil and military, and was but seldom with his family, until the summer of 1782, when Bryant's Station was besieged by the Indians in great force.

Colonel Todd fell in the battle of the Blue Licks, in the prime of life, and in the midst of his usefulness, leaving a wife and one child (a daughter twelve months old.) This daughter afterwards became the wife of R. Wickliffe, Esq. Colonel Todd was an accomplished gentleman, of high talents and fine personal appearance—was universally beloved, and died without an enemy or a stain upon his character.

John Howard was also an early adventurer to this country, and settled at Boonesborough in 1775. He served in the Revolutionary War, was a volunteer at the battle of Guilford, and was in that battle attacked by Tarleton's light-horse while he was in the act of taking a wounded man from the field, and himself received five wounds, three of which at the time were pronounced mortal by the surgeon who attended him. He was a native of Virginia, of fine education, and was afterwards president of Princeton College. He was a devoted Christian, and lived an exemplary member of the Presbyterian Church eighty years of his life. His only son was Benjamin Howard, Governor of Missouri, who died at St. Louis in 1814. Mr. John Howard died at the residence of Major Woolley, in Lexington, Kentucky, who married his granddaughter. Having survived all his family but one (his second daughter), he died at the advanced age of one hundred and three years.

Another distinguished name in the early history of Kentucky is that of John Bradford, who was born in 1749 in Fauquier County, Virginia. He was married in 1761, and served a short time in the army of the Revolution, and came to Kentucky in the fall of 1779. He was in the battle with the Indians at Chilicothe. In 1785 he removed his family to Kentucky, and settled four miles north of Lexington, on Cane Run. In 1787 he, in conjunction with his brother Fielding, established the first paper ever published in Kentucky, called the "Kentucky Gazette," at Lexington, the first number of which was issued on the 11th of August of that year. The next year Fielding Bradford withdrew from the concern, and it was conducted by John, alone, until the 1st of April, 1802, when he conveyed the establishment to his son, Daniel Bradford, who conducted it for many years more before it changed hands, and it is, perhaps, yet in existence under the name of the Lexington Gazette.

Captain William Harding next claims our attention. At a very early period he erected a station in what is now Breckinridge County. He was a noted hunter and Indian-fighter, of dauntless courage and resolution, cool, calm, and self-possessed in the midst of danger, and perfectly skilled in all the arts of border warfare. Soon after the erection of his station he received information that the Indians were building a town on Saline Creek, in the now State of Illinois, not very far from his station, though on the opposite side of the Ohio River. He soon collected around him a force of eighty-six men determined to dislodge them, all accustomed to the most perilous adventures. They started off and approached the town cautiously, and found in its possession three warriors who had been left to guard the camp. The warriors were immediately fired upon, and two of them killed. The third was shot down as he ran. He gained his feet, however, and leaped up a bank six feet high, and fell dead. Harding, supposing that the main body of the Indians were out on a hunting expedition, placed his men in a favorable situation, and awaited their return, ordering his men to post themselves behind trees, and not to fire until the Indians should approach within twenty-five yards. They soon discovered the Indians rapidly approaching, eighty or a hundred in number, and when they had arrived in about one hundred yards, the impatience of one man made him forget his captain's order, and he fired. The Indians charged immediately. At the first fire Captain Harding was shot through the thighs. Without resigning his command, or yielding to the pain occasioned by the shot, he sat himself upon a log, giving his orders, and encouraging his men during the action, until success finally crowned his efforts. It was frequently a hand-to-hand contest. Some thirty of the Indians fell, and the loss of the whites was very considerable. It was regarded, generally, as one of the most fiercely contested battles ever fought in the West.

John Breckinridge, better known as a statesman than as a military man or Indian-fighter, did not remove to Kentucky until 1793, about the time that Indian hostilities ceased. He was born in Augusta County, Virginia, on the 2d of December, 1769. His parents were of Scotch-Irish descent; that is, Presbyterians from the north of Ireland, but originally from Scotland. Mr. Breckinridge practiced law in Albemarle County, Virginia, from 1785 until his removal to Kentucky. He died at his residence (Cabbell's Dale), near Lexington, December 14, 1805, when he had just completed his forty-sixth year. As a lawyer, no man of his day excelled him, and but few could compare with him. He amassed a large fortune. He was of spotless reputation, of great popularity, and took a leading part in all the great questions that agitated Kentucky whilst he lived. The Constitution of 1799 was more the work of his hands than any other one man of the Convention. He was the undoubted leader of the old Democratic party, which came in power with Jefferson. He was appointed by Jefferson Attorney General of his administration. He was a Senator in Congress, a member of the Kentucky Legislature, and made the first great movement in that body against the alien and sedition laws, by offering the resolutions in the Kentucky Legislature of 1798, of which he was the sole and true author. He was in stature tall, muscular, and slender, about the middle size, of great power, and noble appearance. He had clear grey eyes and brown hair, inclining to a slight shade of red; grave and silent in ordinary intercourse, courteous and gentle, and loved by all who knew him. He was the grandfather of the distinguished John C. Breckinridge.

Time would fail me to recount in detail the exploits and public services of all those who most distinguished themselves in the early settlement of Kentucky, many of whom were equally meritorious with those I have named particularly; but, as I have said before, it would require volumes to do so. I have given, for the most part, the history of those whose lives, characters, and actions afford most light upon the subject of the early history of Kentucky. There are other names, however, occasionally mentioned in these pages, whose memories will be cherished ever with fond recollection by their descendants, and by all who love Kentucky chivalry and prowess. We can never forget such names as McGary, Bowman, Harlan, McBride, Chapline, Holden, Bulger, Hinkston, Knox, Bullitt, Thompson, Hart, Allen, Todd, Jones, Rogers, Benham, Proctor, Bryant, Miller, Stewart, McClelland, Hubble, Stucker, Templeton, Mitchell, Perry, Herndon, Squire Boone, Floyd, Wells, Rowan, Simpson, Kincheloe, and a host of others, too numerous to mention, each and all of whom rendered themselves memorable by their valor and services in the first settlement of the country, and converting the wilderness into one of the noblest and proudest States of this Confederacy.

CHAPTER III.

Independent Government of Kentucky Favored by Spain as well as by Leading Men of Kentucky—Nine Conventions within eight years, with a view of Admission into the Union—Account of their Meetings and Action—Efforts to separate Kentucky from the Union—Don Gardoqui, Connelly—Spanish and British Intrigues in Kentucky—Indians Troublesome—Expedition of Clark—General Wilkinson Obtains Permit to Import Tobacco for Spanish King's Stores at New Orleans—Kentucky an Independent State, June 1st, 1792—First Constitution Formed—Isaac Shelby First Governor—Commissioners to fix the Capital—Frankfort Selected—Legislature—First Session—New Counties Formed—Governor Shelby—Sketch of Treaty with Spain to Navigate Mississippi to Ocean, and Deposit at New Orleans—Spain Intriguing up to 1806—Thomas Power—Benjamin Sebastian—Colonel Gayoso—Carondolet in 1797—His Scheme Unfolded—Disposition by Spain to Violate Treaty—Powers Escapes—Aaron Burr's First Visit to Kentucky—Visits again in Spring of 1806—Plan of his Southern Enterprise—The Cause—Duel with Alexander Hamilton—Blennerhasset—General Adair—Newspaper "Western World"—Burr Denounced as a Traitor—Joseph H. Davis—Burr's Prosecution and Trial—Popular Current—Burr Acquitted—His Death—Sebastian Resigned—Inquiry as to Judge Innis—James Garrard Second Governor—His Administration—Dissatisfaction with the Constitution—New Constitution of 1799—Garrard Re-elected Governor—Treaty with Spain Violated—Mr. Monroe Minister to France—Purchase of Louisiana from Bonaparte—Sketch of Governor Garrard—Christopher Greenup Elected Governor—Sketch of his Life—Scott Elected Governor—Sketch of his Life—John Allen.

As early as 1784 the people of Kentucky became strongly impressed with the necessity of the organization of a regular government, and gaining admission into the Union as a separate and independent State; but their efforts were continually perplexed and baffled for the space of eight years before their desire was fully accomplished. And though they were often tempted by Spain with the richest gifts of fortune if she would declare herself an independent State; and although the Congress of the Confederated States continually turned a deaf ear to her reiterated complaints and grievances, and repulsed her in every effort to obtain constitutional independence, she maintained to the last the highest respect for law and order, and the most unswerving affection for the Government. Some of the most talented and leading men of the country favored a separate and independent government for Kentucky. Among the great number were such men as General Wilkinson, Brown, Innis, and Sebastian. But other distinguished men opposed any other separation than that of constitutional independence, desiring to become a co-equal sovereign State of the Union. Among these were Marshall, Muter, Allen, Crockett, Christian, and others.

With the view to admission into the Union as an independent State, there were elected and held nine Conventions in Kentucky within the space of eight years. The first Convention met at Danville the 27th of December, 1784, at which the subject of a separation from Virginia was discussed with great gravity and decorum. Samuel McDowell was the president of the Convention, and Thomas Todd clerk. There was a division of opinion on the subject of separation, yet a resolution was adopted declaratory of their views by an overwhelming majority, and it was agreed to hold a second Convention in Danville, in May, 1785, to determine whether separation was expedient. In this interval the subject of separation was warmly discussed in the primary assemblies held by the people in different parts of the country, and the almost unanimous expression of opinion seemed to be in favor of constitutional separation only.

On the 23d day of May, 1785, the second Convention met, and adopted resolutions in favor of a constitutional separation, and decided that an address to the Legislature of Virginia be prepared, and that an address to the people of Kentucky should be published; also that another election of delegates should take place in July, to meet at Danville again the following August, to whom these matters should be referred for final action, this Convention being the third. New petitions and addresses were ordered to be drawn up in a more exaggerated and impassioned form, copies of which were multiplied with the pen, there being at that time no printing press in Kentucky. The Chief Justice of the District, George Muter, and the Attorney General, Harry Innis, were deputied to present the petition to the Legislature of Virginia (which was done), and in January, 1786, the Legislature passed an act according with the wishes of Kentucky, but requiring a fourth Convention to assemble in 1786, to determine whether it was the will of the District to become an independent State of the Confederacy, on the conditions in the act enumerated; and they were to fix upon a day upon which the authority of Virginia was to cease, provided that Congress should assent to said act, and receive Kentucky into the Union previous to the first of June, 1787.

Kentucky, in the meanwhile, was smarting under the scourge of Indian warfare, without any settled government at home, and, being separated from the capital of Virginia by a wilderness of five or six hundred miles, was totally unprotected by that State. No press in the country, and no mail facilities. In this condition, the intelligence reached Kentucky that several States in Congress had voted to barter away the right to navigate the Mississippi River, in consideration of commercial advantages to be yielded by Spain to the Eastern States, and in which Kentucky, more interested than any other, would enjoy no benefit.

This was the time for foreign schemers and intriguers to show their hands for a severance of Kentucky from the Union by other than constitutional means. This sort of means was resorted to, the principal actor on the part of Spain being the minister, Don Gardoqui. Dr. Connelly was also in Kentucky in 1788, as a British agent. In 1789 a correspondence took place between General Washington and Colonel Thomas Marshall, of Kentucky, respecting the British and Spanish intrigues in Kentucky.

The elections to the fourth Convention took place in the spring of 1786. General Wilkinson was a candidate, and favored separation without the slow formalities of the law, which he thought the exigencies of the country could not await. His notion produced a great sensation in Fayette, and there was violent opposition to his views; yet, on account of his tact, talent, adroitness, and address, he was elected, whilst four others elected from the same county were utterly opposed to his views. In the other counties there was but little excitement, and the prescribed number was elected, who were all willing to await the formalities of the law for the admission of Kentucky into the Union.

About this time the Indians became very troublesome, and the expedition of Clark against the Wabash Indians so interfered that a quorum could not be had in September. They continued their meeting by adjournment until January, 1787, when they again expressed their feelings in favor of separation, and called another Convention, to be held in the fall.

A second act of the Virginia Legislature had been passed the previous year, for the postponement of the separation until January 1, 1789.

On the 17th of September, 1787, the fifth Convention met, and unanimously decided in favor of separation on the terms offered by Virginia. It was in June of this year that General Wilkinson descended the Ohio and Mississippi rivers to New Orleans with the first cargo from Kentucky, and obtained a permit to import tobacco for the Spanish King's stores.

On the 28th of June, 1788, the Virginia Convention met for the purpose of adopting or rejecting the Federal Constitution. A very large majority of the people of Kentucky were opposed to the adoption of the Constitution, yet three out of fourteen delegates to that Convention from Kentucky voted in favor of its adoption. The Federal Constitution was, however, adopted by Virginia by a vote of 88 to 78.

On the 3d of July, 1788, Congress referred the subject of the admission of Kentucky into the Union to the new Government.

On the 28th of July the sixth Convention met, and adjourned without any action of importance, other than calling another Convention invested with full discretionary powers.

On the 4th of November the seventh Convention met. A temperate and respectful address to the Legislature of Virginia was adopted, praying the assistance of Virginia in procuring the admission of Kentucky into the Union.

On the 27th of December Virginia passed her third act in favor of separation, and on the 20th of July, 1789, the eighth Convention assembled, and remonstrated strongly against the conditions of separation contained in the third act of the Virginia Legislature. The 18th of December, afterwards, Virginia passed her fourth act, complying fully with the wishes of Kentucky.

On the 26th of July, 1790, the ninth Convention assembled, accepted the terms of Virginia, and fixed June 1, 1792, for the independence of the State of Kentucky. On the 4th of February, 1791, Congress agreed to admit her into the Union on the 1st of June, 1792.

In December, 1791, the tenth and last Convention was elected, and in April following met at Danville and formed the first Constitution, which, being adopted, the officers under it were elected in May, 1792.

The first Governor of Kentucky elected under the new Constitution was Isaac Shelby. Alexander Bullitt was chosen Speaker of the Senate, and Robert Breckinridge, Speaker of the House of Representatives. James Brown was the first Secretary of State, and George Nicholas the first Attorney General. John Brown and John Edwards, when the Legislature met, were elected, by joint ballot, Senators to Congress.

Frankfort and Danville each contended for the seat of Government. Commissioners were chosen by joint ballot, empowered to fix upon the capital, and Frankfort was selected. Several ineffectual attempts to remove it since that time have been made. Louisville has been most prominent in her efforts, and has offered greater inducements than any other place heretofore proposed. I think it probable, however, that when the Ohio and Cumberland Railroad shall be completed, that Lebanon, being centrally situated and accessible from every quarter of the State, and besides growing to be a city of no inconsiderable importance, may calculate, with better reason than any other place, on being designated as the future capital of Kentucky, if it is removed at all.

The Legislature at its first session was principally engaged in the organization of the new government, regulating the revenue and the judiciary department. A supreme court was established; county courts, and courts of quarter session, the latter having common law and chancery jurisdiction over five pounds; also a court of oyer and terminer. A number of new counties were formed at this session, and many other matters of interest to the State attended to.

Shelby was forty-two years of age when he was inaugurated Governor of Kentucky. His administration was regarded as wise, prudent, and discreet. He was born near Hagerstown, in Maryland, where his father and grandfather settled after their arrival from Wales. Having acquired a knowledge of surveying, he took up his residence in Western Virginia. He was a lieutenant in the company of his father in the memorable battle fought at the mouth of the Kanawha, the 10th of October, 1774. The Indians in this battle were commanded by the celebrated chief, Cornstalk. Shelby continued with the troops until they were disbanded in July, 1775. After this he proceeded to Kentucky, and was employed as a surveyor under Henderson & Co., who styled themselves proprietors of the country under their purchase from the Cherokees, and had established a regular land office.

After a residence here of twelve months he returned home. In 1776 he was appointed Captain of a minute company by the Committee of Safety of Virginia. In 1777 he was appointed by Governor Henry Commissary of Supplies for an extensive body of militia. In 1778 he was engaged in the Commissary Department. In the spring of 1779 he was elected a member of the Virginia Legislature from Washington County, and in the fall of that year was commissioned a Major by Gov. Jefferson in the escort of guards to the Commissioners for extending the boundary line between that State and North Carolina. By the extension of that line his residence was found to be in the limits of North Carolina, and he was shortly afterwards appointed by Governor Caswell as Colonel of the county of Sullivan. In 1780 he returned to Kentucky and engaged in locating and securing lands he had previously marked out for himself. In the interim he was in many battles and skirmishes of the Revolution, acting as Colonel commandant at the most critical period of the war.

Colonel Shelby distinguished himself in the great victory achieved at the battle of King's Mountain, and the Legislature of North Carolina passed a vote of thanks to him and other officers, and each was presented with a sword for their patriotic conduct on that occasion, the 7th of October, 1780. The resolution for the sword presentation passed during the summer of 1813. Colonel Shelby was the originator of this expedition, which terminated so gloriously to our arms. Generals Gates and Green approved the suggestions of Shelby in regard to the expedition, and acted accordingly, and the result of his advice was the victory at the battle of the Cowpens.

In 1781 Colonel Shelby served under General Marion. In September he was called by General Green to the Lower Country, with five hundred riflemen, to aid him in the interception of Cornwallis, who he supposed would endeavor to retreat through North Carolina, being at that time blockaded by the French fleet in the Chesapeake. But upon Cornwallis' surrender in Virginia, Shelby was attached to Marion's command on the Santee. After the surrender of the British fort at Fairlawn, and their retreat to Charleston, no further active service being contemplated, Colonel Shelby obtained leave of Marion to attend the Assembly of North Carolina, of which he was a member. In 1782 Colonel Shelby was elected a member of the North Carolina Assembly, and was appointed one of the Commissioners to settle the pre-emption claims, and lay off the lands allotted the officers and soldiers of North Carolina, on Cumberland River, south of where Nashville now stands. Having performed this service, he returned to Boonesborough in April, 1783, where he married Susannah, the second daughter of Captain Nathaniel Hart.

He settled himself on the first settlement and pre-emption granted in Kentucky, where he resided at his death, which occurred forty-three years afterwards. He was a member of the early Conventions which met at Danville, with a view to separation from Virginia, and was a member of the Convention in 1792 to form the first Constitution of Kentucky; and in

May of that year was elected the first Chief Magistrate of Kentucky, as before stated.

At the close of his term as Governor, he returned to his farm in Lincoln County. He was a distinguished agriculturist, as well as statesman and military officer. He was several times an elector of President, and voted for Jefferson and Madison.

At the commencement of the War of 1812 he was again elected to the Chief Magistracy of Kentucky. The Legislature of 1812–13 passed a resolution requesting the Governor to assume personal command of the State troops, whenever, in his judgment, such a step would be necessary. In organizing his forces, Generals Henry and Desha were assigned to the command of the two divisions, and Generals Calmes, Caldwell, King, Chiles, and Galloway to the brigades. Adair, Crittenden, and Barry, with others, constituted his staff. General Harrison recognized Shelby as the senior Major General of the Kentucky troops. Both the Legislature of Kentucky and Congress expressed their sense of his gallant conduct in appropriate resolutions. By a vote of Congress, after the victory of Thames, a gold medal was assigned to both Shelby and Harrison.

Governor Shelby extended great aid to the General Government during the progress of the war, by sending men to defend the country around Detroit, and for the defense of New Orleans. His second term as Governor expired in the fall of 1815, and he once more retired to his farm in Lincoln. In March, 1817, President Monroe selected him to fill the Department of War, but, preferring private life at his advanced age, he declined the proffered honor.

In 1818 he was commissioned by the President to act in conjunction with General Jackson in holding a treaty with the Cherokee Indians, for the purchase of their lands west of the Tennessee River, within the limits of Kentucky and Tennessee, and they obtained a cession of lands to the United States. This was his last public act.

In February, 1820, he was attacked with paralysis, which disabled his right arm, and occasioned him also to walk lame on his right leg. He died of apoplexy, on the 18th of July, 1826, in the seventieth year of his age.

Governor Shelby had been for many years a consistent member of the Presbyterian Church, and was the chief instrument in erecting a house of worship on his own farm in Lincoln County.

In October, 1795, a treaty of peace was concluded with Spain, in which the right to navigate the Mississippi to the Ocean was conceded, together with a right to deposit at New Orleans, which had been all along the great desire of Kentucky. We had now made peace with the Indians, all the posts in the country had been surrendered, and the navigation of the Mississippi had been obtained; but still a negotiation or intrigue on the part of Spain was going on with some of the most important citizens of Kentucky, even up to the year 1806, the full extent of which was never known.

In July, 1795, the Spanish Governor, Carondolet, sent Thomas Power with a letter to Benjamin Sebastian, then a Judge of the Court of Appeals in Kentucky. In this he alludes to the former correspondence which had passed between them, and also to the confidence which his predecessor, General Miro, had reposed in him.

In this communication he said the King of Spain was willing to open the navigation of the Mississippi to the Western Country, and desired Sebastian to have agents appointed by Kentucky to meet Colonel Gayoso at New Madrid, where all matters could be adjusted.

Sebastian, with the advice of Judge Innis, George Nicholas, and William Murray, met Gayoso at New Madrid, to hear what he had to propose. He met him, and a treaty was agreed to, but before the matter was fully concluded intelligence was received that the United States Government had concluded a treaty with Spain, by which the navigation of the Mississippi was effectually secured.

All correspondence then ceased until 1797, when the agent of Carondolet again appeared in Louisville with a letter to Sebastian. The scheme unfolded in this letter was, that they should withdraw from the Federal Government, and that

$100,000 should be appropriated to Sebastian, Nicholas, Innis, and Murray, in consideration of their time and services in the enterprise. In withdrawing from the Federal Union, they were to form an independent western government. To effect this end it was proposed by Power that twenty field-pieces of artillery, with a large supply of small arms and munitions of war, and $100,000, should be immediately furnished Kentucky in aid of the enterprise. Fort Massae was to be seized instantly, and the Federal troops to be dispossessed of all posts on the western waters. For the addition of this territory to the dominion of his Catholic Majesty, the King of Spain, it seems he was willing, by treachery and intrigue, to violate his treaty but lately solemnly made. Power, however, had finally to make his escape from the country, under a guard provided by General Wilkinson, for fear of arrest by the General Government. In 1806 it became public that Sebastian had received a pension from the Spanish Government, from about 1795 to 1806, of $2,000 a year.

In 1805 Aaron Burr made his first appearance in Kentucky, visiting Lexington and Louisville, then passing on to Nashville, St. Louis, Natchez, and New Orleans, and again returned to Lexington, where he remained some time.

In the spring of 1806 there was a prospect of an outbreak between the United States and Spain. The Spanish forces had advanced to the Sabine in somewhat hostile array, and General Wilkinson, who had command of the United States forces in that quarter, had received orders to be on the alert, and repel them if they attempted to cross that barrier.

At this juncture Burr again came to the West, spending a large portion of his time at Blennerhasset's Island, but was seen at Lexington, Nashville, and Louisville. Burr in 1801 had been elected Vice President of the United States, but had quarreled with the President, and had become somewhat odious to the Republican party; but hoping, as is supposed, to retrieve his political fortunes, he became a candidate in New York for Governor, in opposition to the regular Republican or Democratic ticket. But he was beaten, chiefly by the influence of Alexander Hamilton, who had represented him publicly as unworthy of political trust. Deeply stung by his defeat, he challenged Hamilton to mortal combat, and killed him in a duel.

After this Burr found himself abandoned pretty much by all parties. In this state of his political condition he came to the West, and engaged in some great scheme of daring, the object of which, I think, was never fully known. The essential features of the plan, as far as understood, was to organize a military force on the western waters, descend the Mississippi, and wrest from Spain a portion of her territory adjoining the Gulf of Mexico; and that the southern portion of the United States, which at that time embraced New Orleans and the territory adjacent, was to become a part of this new empire, of which New Orleans was to be the capital, and Burr the chief ruler, governor, emperor, or whatever title he might choose to assume; and if circumstances were favorable, the whole country west of the Alleghenies was to be wrested from the United States and made part of his empire.

For the accomplishment of his object, whatever it might have been, by his talents and superior address he ingratiated his scheme into the favor of many of the distinguished men of the West. His eye was particularly fixed on Blennerhasset, who owned and occupied the beautiful island by that name in the Ohio River opposite Marietta, which lay exactly in his path. Blennerhasset was an Irishman of great wealth. Burr visited him, won his favor, and gained complete power, not only over his will, but his wealth also. General Adair concurred in his scheme, under the belief that it was merely an expedition against the Spanish provinces. Burr held frequent intercourse with General Wilkinson, and relied with certainty on his co-operation, and many other distinguished generals in the West, who were never informed fully of Burr's real object.

During the summer of 1806 rumors became rife in Kentucky that some secret and mysterious schemes were going on. What it was, however, no one pretended to know, and doubt and mystery hung over all, until a paper published at Frankfort, called the "Western World," came out with bold and defiant charges against Sebastian as being an intriguer with and pensioner on Spain. Judge Innis, John Brown, and General Wilkinson were all implicated. At the same time Burr was denounced as a traitor, and his scheme unfolded.

Great excitement prevailed, and the Legislature, which had been elected that year, were called upon to inquire into the conduct of Judge Sebastian.

On the 3d of November, of that year, Joseph H. Davis, Attorney General of the United States, made application in open court, before Judge Innis, for process against Burr, to answer a charge of high misdemeanor, in organizing a military expedition against a friendly power within the territory and jurisdiction of the United States. This motion created tremendous sensation at the time, from the fact that Burr was very popular in Kentucky, and caressed by her most eminent, patriotic, and distinguished citizens.

Public feeling at the time showed itself warmly in favor of Burr, and against the Attorney General, who, though an avowed Federalist, acted boldly and manfully in the discharge of his duties. Judge Innis took time to consider the application, and, after two days, overruled the motion. Burr was then at Lexington, but hearing of the application came immediately to Frankfort, and, addressing the Judge, spoke of his great surprise of such a motion being made; said the Judge had treated it as it deserved, but as the Attorney might renew the motion in his absence he preferred that the Judge would entertain it now, and he had voluntarily appeared to give the Attorney an opportunity of proving his charge. All this was said in a lofty and imposing manner, which only tended to increase the general prepossession in his favor. Davis promptly accepted the challenge, and said he would proceed as soon as he could procure the attendance of his witnesses. Henry Clay and John Allen were the counsel of Burr, both men of eloquence and superior powers of intellect, young as they then were. The case was continued from time to time to procure witnesses. First General Adair, then General Floyd, were wanted as witnesses. Several incidental questions arose during the delay, which were warmly and ably debated by Davis on one side and Clay on the other. Finally, the day of trial arrived, and the witnesses sent before the Grand Jury, who, having finished their investigation, on the 5th of December, 1806, returned the indictment "*not a true bill,*" accompanied with a written declaration, signed by all the jury, in which they say: "From all the evidence before us, we completely exonerate Burr from any design inimical to the peace or well-being of the country." The popular current was greatly in his favor, and the United States Attorney, for the time, was overwhelmed with obloquy. The acquittal of Burr was celebrated in Frankfort by a brilliant ball; then another ball was given to Mr. Davis by those who believed the charge against Burr to be just. At one of those parties the editor of the "Western World," who had sounded the alarm, was attacked with the view of driving him from the ball-room, and was rescued with difficulty. A month had not elapsed from Burr's exultant acquittal before his impudent and daring intrigues came sufficiently to light to render him, in the estimation of all good and true men, extremely odious; and he soon sunk so low in public estimation as never, through his long life which remained, to be able to rise above the degradation which enveloped him. He lived in poverty and obscurity for thirty years afterwards, and died in the city of New York, in September, 1836, at the advanced age of eighty-five years.

The Legislature, when it assembled, instituted an inquiry into the conduct of Judge Sebastian. He, hoping to stifle the inquiry, resigned his office; but being a judge of the Federal Court, the Legislature of Kentucky had no authority to investigate his conduct. At the succeeding session, however, they passed a resolution recommending an inquiry into the conduct of Judge Innis, who was also strongly implicated. This inquiry was had, and resulted in his acquittal.

Under the first Constitution of Kentucky, formed in 1792, the Governor and Senate were elected by electors, as the President of the United States is now elected, and at the general election in May, 1796, an election was held for electors for Governor and Senate, as well as for members of the House of

Representatives, and James Garrard was chosen as the successor of Shelby. The Legislature convened in November of this year, and passed many acts of deep interest and great importance to the State.

About this time, or soon after, great dissatisfaction began to be manifested in regard to the Constitution, although it had been in operation but a few years, and in 1797 the sense of the people on the question of calling a convention to revise the Constitution was taken, but not being satisfactory, a similar vote was taken in May, 1798, and of the 11,853 votes returned, 8,804 were in favor of a convention. The Constitution required the concurrence of a majority of all the votes at two successive elections to authorize the calling of a convention, or else a majority of two-thirds of the Legislature. The convention having failed with the people, owing to a good many of the counties not making a due return of their votes, the Legislature ordered a convention by a constitutional majority. In the spring of 1799 the members of the convention were elected, and in July of that year the convention assembled and adopted the second Constitution of Kentucky, which went into operation the 1st of June, 1800.

Under the new Constitution James Garrard was re-elected Governor of Kentucky, and continued in office another term of four years. Alexander Bullitt was elected Lieutenant Governor.

In the winter session of 1801 the Legislature repealed the act establishing district courts, and established circuit courts, as they now exist. At this same session an insurance company was chartered at Lexington, with banking powers, and this may be called the first bank that was ever chartered in Kentucky.

In the treaty with Spain, in 1795, the navigation of the Mississippi was secured to the United States, but in 1802 the right of deposit at New Orleans was suspended, in violation of the treaty, which was a vital blow to the commerce of the West, and threw Kentucky into a great commotion. This was done by Morales, the Spanish Intendant. About this time it was understood that Louisiana was ceded to France, and that Napoleon Bonaparte, the First Consul of that republic, was then in possession of and holding that important point. Mr. Monroe, afterwards President of the United States, was sent by our Government to France to arrange the matter in some way. On his arrival he found Napoleon on the eve of a rupture with England, and not expecting to be able to retain possession of that point, he determined to place it out of the power of the English, by selling that country to the United States for the very low price of $15,000,000, and this was the first great accession to the territory of the United States. A number of others have been made since, and it is still expected that others at no distant day will be added; perhaps Nova Scotia and the Island of St. Domingo.

James Garrard's second term of office expired in 1804, having served eight consecutive years as Governor, with wisdom and general satisfaction to the State. Governor Garrard, previous to his election, was a minister in the Baptist Church, and a member at Cooper's Run Church, in Bourbon County. His secretary, appointed by him when he came into office, was Harry Toulman, who was a minister in the Unitarian Church, and a man of great erudition and talents. Garrard himself partook largely of Arian or Socinian sentiments, as did the pastor of Cooper's Run Church, and a majority of the members of that church imbibed the same sentiments.

James Garrard was born in the county of Stafford, Virginia, on the 14th of January, 1749. He engaged in the service of his country at a very early period of the Revolution. While in the service he was elected a member of the Virginia Legislature, where he took a decided and influential part in the passage of the famous act securing universal religious liberty.

He emigrated to Kentucky at a very early period, and was exposed to the perils and dangers of the times. He was frequently elected a member of the Legislature previous to his election twice as Governor. As a man he had few equals, and ever acted with prudence, firmness, and decision. He embraced religion at an early age, holding it in higher esteem than all else below the sun. He was a man of practical usefulness in his private intercourse, faithful in all things, kind and tender in his affections. He was a good husband, parent, neighbor, and master, and was universally beloved. He died at his residence in Mount Lebanon, Bourbon County, January 19, 1822, in the seventy-fourth year of his age. The Legislature of Kentucky, in December, 1822, erected a monument to his memory, upon which is inscribed the substance of what I have stated above.

The successor of Governor Garrard to the gubernatorial chair was Christopher Greenup, the third Governor of Kentucky. He was born about the year 1750 in the then colony of Virginia. He was one of the soldiers and heroes in the conflicts of the Revolution, and won no small share of the honor which crowned the triumph of our arms. He bore a part also in the bloody conflicts with the Indians in the first settlement of Kentucky. He freely exposed his life in the perils and dangers of that day and time.

After gaining considerable distinction in arms he settled permanently in Kentucky, and on the 4th of March, 1783, was sworn in as an attorney of the District Court of Kentucky, established by the act of the Virginia Legislature. On the 18th of March, 1785, he was appointed clerk of that court, which office he held during its existence. In 1792 he was elected a member of Congress, and served as such until the year 1797. After this he filled the office of clerk of the Senate of Kentucky until within a short time of his election as Governor, which occurred in August, 1804. After the expiration of his term as Governor, having filled the office with credit to himself and honor to the State, he was elected to the Legislature from Franklin County. In 1812 he acted as justice of the peace for that county. He served many years as a director of the old Bank of Kentucky, which was chartered in the year 1807. He died on the 27th of April, 1818, in the sixty-ninth year of his age. During his continuance in the executive chair he was scrupulously mindful of the public interest, faithful and prompt in the performance of every duty, and required the same of all who were under his control and influence. In his appointments to office he looked to the man, and judged for himself as to worthiness and qualifications, regardless of the number or character of the persons petitioning for the applicant. The varied, important, and respectable offices which he filled from the time of his youth is evidence indubitable of his popularity and qualifications.

The fourth individual who filled the gubernatorial chair of Kentucky was General Charles Scott, who was a distinguished officer in the conflict for independence. He was born in Cumberland County, Virginia, and served as a corporal in a volunteer company of militia in the campaign of 1755, which resulted in Braddock's defeat. Upon the breaking out of the Revolutionary War he raised the first company of volunteers south of James River that entered into actual service, and greatly distinguished himself. He was appointed by General Washington to the command of a regiment in the Continental line, and was with General Wayne at the storming of Stony Point. He was at Charleston when it surrendered to Sir Henry Clinton. After the termination of the war he came to Kentucky, and settled in Woodford County in the year 1785.

He was with General St. Clair in his defeat on the 4th of November, 1791, where six hundred men were killed in the space of an hour. He was with General Wilkinson when he conducted a corps of horsemen against the Indian towns on the Wabash, killed some of the warriors, and took a number of prisoners. In 1794 he commanded a portion of General Wayne's army at the battle of the Fallen Timbers, where the Indians were defeated and driven under the walls of the British fort. In 1808 he was elected to the office of Governor, and discharged its duties faithfully until 1812, when his term expired. He died about the year 1820, at a very advanced age. He was a man of strong natural endowments, but somewhat illiterate and rough in his manners. Many amusing anecdotes are related of him, especially during his canvass for Governor, of which our limits forbid a rehearsal. His opponent was the distinguished and highly-talented John Allen, who fell in the disastrous battle of the River Raisin. His regiment, in that battle, formed the left wing of the American force. As a lawyer, Colonel Allen ranked with the first men in his profession.

CHAPTER IV.

Isaac Shelby Elected Governor a Second Time—He Enters the Field in Person in the War of 1812—Defeat of Raisin—The Fall of John Allen at Raisin—General Dudley; his Defeat—Battle of Tippecanoe—Fall of Joseph H. Davies—Battle of Mississinaway—Fort Stephenson—Battle of Thames—Victory of New Orleans—Battle of Erie—Tecumseh—Proctor—Moravian Towns on the River Thames—Colonel Richard M. Johnson Wounded—Tecumseh Killed—Proctor Fled—General Jackson at New Orleans—George Madison Elected Governor—His Death—Gabriel Slaughter Acted as Governor—New Election Question—Governor Madison, Sketch of—John Pope—Sketch of Governor Slaughter—Independent Banks, Forty Odd Chartered—Twelve Months' Replevy Law—Commonwealth Bank Chartered—Party Names in Kentucky—Judge Clark's Decision—Summoned Before the Legislature—Denunciation of Court of Appeals—Their Firmness—Judges of the Court of Appeals Summoned Before Legislature—Victory for the Judges—Reorganizing Act Passed—Great Excitement—Robert Wickliffe Denounces Relief Party—New Court Organized—Both Courts Continued to Hold Sessions—Names of Parties at that Time—Array of Parties at that Time—Old Court Triumphant—General John Adair Elected Governor—His Opponents—General Adair, Sketch of—General Joseph Desha Elected Governor—A Sketch of his Life—New Party Names Assumed—Election Excitement in 1828—Metcalfe and Barry Opponents for Governor—Metcalfe Elected—His Administration—Breathitt Elected Governor over Buckner—Sketch of Breathitt—His First Public Speech—Removal of his Father to Kentucky.

Isaac Shelby was elected Governor of Kentucky, for the second time, at the commencement of the war of 1812 with Great Britain. He became a candidate with great reluctance; but the importunities of many influential friends demanded it of him, under the belief that the exigencies of the time at that particular crisis called for the services of just such a man. He yielded, and was elected upon terms highly gratifying to his feelings.

Governor Shelby, as has been stated before, distinguished himself in the war of the Revolution; also in the war with the Indians in the early settlement of Kentucky; and he was not less distinguished as a statesman of great prudence and foresight. The Legislature of 1812-13 passed a resolution requesting the Governor to assume in person the direction of the troops of the State, whenever, in his judgment, he thought such a step necessary. He, without hesitation, entered the field in person. The power and influence of his name acted like a spell upon the people, and four thousand men rallied to his standard in less than thirty days, and they reached the shore of Lake Erie, the camp of General Harrison, just as Commodore Perry was disembarking his prisoners taken in the naval battle on the lake. It may well be supposed that there was a high time of gratulation with the three generals there met, Perry, Harrison, and Shelby. I have before alluded to these matters in the sketch given of the life of Governor Shelby.

The war was begun the same year of Governor Shelby's election, and was brought to a close before the termination of his term of office, the history of which belongs with greater propriety to the United States than to any individual State. Kentucky distinguished herself in many battles in the Northwest and Southwest, and spilt her blood freely on every battlefield.

The disastrous news of the inglorious surrender of Hull was received in Kentucky with a burst of indignant fury, but it by no means diminished the ardor of the people. Seven thousand Kentuckians were already in the field, and one thousand five hundred were on the march to Detroit when the news of the surrender met them. Upon the receipt of this news Governor Shelby made a call for one thousand five hundred men to march against the Indian villages in Northern Illinois. The call was answered immediately with two thousand volunteers, under General Hopkins; but they finally returned home without any opportunity of encountering the enemy.

By the surrender of Hull we lost the Territory of Michigan, and consequently all control of the Indian tribes of the Northwest, and they poured themselves on our extended frontiers in great numbers. The American army was disastrously defeated at Raisin, and a number of the men cruelly massacred on the 22d of January, 1813. The brave John Allen fell in this battle, a victim of their cruelty. Four days previously the British were defeated at Frenchtown. On the 5th of May, 1813, eight hundred Kentuckians, under General Dudley, were either killed or taken prisoners. The battle of Tippecanoe was fought November 7, 1811, where Joseph H. Daviess and other distinguished Kentuckians fell. The battle of Mississinaway was fought in December, 1812. Fort Stephenson was besieged July 31, 1813; the victory of the Thames, October 5, 1813; and the victory of New Orleans, January 8, 1815. In all these battles Kentucky bore a most conspicuous part.

The naval battle on Lake Erie occurred on the 10th of September, 1813. The number of men in each squadron was nearly equal. The British had six vessels, and the Americans nine, but seven of the latter were gunboats. The British vessels carried sixty-three guns, and the American fifty-four. Most of the American guns were thirty-two and twenty-four pounders, while a majority of the British guns were nine, six, and four-pounders, with a few as high as twenty-four and eighteen pounders. The action began about 12 o'clock, and continued some two or three hours. The American loss was twenty-seven killed and ninety-six wounded. Perry's victory was complete. The fleet was surrounded, except two of their smallest vessels, which tried to escape. In this they failed, and the whole fleet of the enemy became the prize of their captors.

This splendid victory decided the fate of the campaign; it gave Harrison complete command of the lake, and the power to throw his forces into the rear of Proctor's position at Detroit and Malden. Proctor soon ascertained, however, that Harrison, with his regulars, and a strong reinforcement of Kentuckians under Shelby, were crossing the lake, and, comprehending their object, he quit his position and commenced a rapid retreat. At this crisis more than half the Indians in his employ deserted him. Tecumseh, at the head of one thousand, remained, and accompanied him upon the condition that the first favorable ground should be selected for a battle.

The horses of the Kentuckians were left on the American shore, under guard, in an ample grazing ground. Proctor's retreat was on the 24th of September. Our forces embarked on the 27th, and, crossing the lake, pursued rapidly, coming up with the enemy on the 5th of October near an old Moravian village on the banks of the river Thames, where a most decisive battle was fought and won. On the ground were about five hundred British regulars, and from one thousand to fifteen hundred Indians. Harrison's force, including the regulars and friendly Indians, was about three thousand five hundred.

The ground upon which the battle was fought was by far most favorable to the enemy. Harrison's line of battle was formed of five brigades; three in General Henry's division, Trotter's, King's, and Chiles's; and two in General Desha's division, Caldwell's and General James Allen's. Governor Shelby took his station just where the two lines intercepted. The mounted gun men were ordered to the charge. Colonel Johnson, finding that the whole of his regiment could not act with effect against the British, directed his brother to charge the English with one battalion, while he charged the Indians with the other. The charge upon the British was a complete success. The whole regiment threw down their arms and surrendered. The charge on the Indians proved alike successful. In this charge Colonel Johnson was wounded, and borne from the field before the close of the action. The Indians kept up a vigorous fire after the British had surrendered, but the fall of Tecumseh, together with the overwhelming force opposed to them, soon compelled them to flee. Proctor had fled early in the engagement, and eluded successful pursuit.

This battle was the close of hostilities in the Northwest, where Kentuckians acted the most conspicuous part; but continued in the eastern and southern borders, in which our State bore no part of consequence, except at New Orleans, which, as has been before stated, was the last battle of the war. Of this battle I have elsewhere given an account; suffice it to say that it was the greatest victory of the war, the British, with nearly double our force, having sustained a loss, according to the account of the American Inspector General, of about two thousand six hundred, whilst the loss in killed on the American side was only eight or nine. The most accurate account we are enabled to obtain of the British force shows that it was at least seven thousand eight hundred and ninety-three. They certainly had nine regiments of grenadiers, one of cavalry, a large body of marines, a corps of artillery, a corps of sappers, engineers, &c., whilst the whole force of the American army numbered precisely five thousand four hundred and ninety-three, rank and file, and some six hundred of them unarmed. The principal cause of our signal triumph on that occasion is mainly attributable to the superior tact and management of Jackson as a military man over Packingham, the commander of the British army. On Jackson's part were extraordinary firmness, vigor, prudence, caution, and unequaled activity. Every moment of the time which the tardiness of Packingham allowed was improved by Jackson with great activity and energy. Had Packingham after landing pressed on, as Bonaparte or Jackson would have done, he could have taken New Orleans easily; but, instead of that, he awaited some sixteen days for the arrival of his reinforcements before he commenced the attack. In the meantime, Jackson was reinforced by two thousand Kentuckians and a regiment of Louisianians; had dug ditches, made breastworks, and done everything else that wisdom could contrive, ingenuity invent, and energy and industry accomplish, to be fully prepared for the reception of the enemy, and the result was a complete triumph.

When this battle was fought, peace had actually been agreed upon at Ghent, of which we had not then been informed, and was soon afterwards ratified; and a war which had opened with disgrace terminated with glory.

Governor Shelby's second term of office having expired, George Madison, the sixth Governor of Kentucky, was duly elected as his successor in August, 1816, with Gabriel Slaughter as Lieutenant Governor, for the term of four years.

A very short time after his election Madison died, and the first great question which ever agitated the people of Kentucky since the adoption of the new Constitution was whether the Lieutenant Governor became Governor during the four years, or whether a new election could be ordered by the Legislature. After a very animated conflict the question was settled in favor of the Lieutenant Governor holding the office for and during the time for which the Governor had been elected. Since that time similar events have twice occurred in Kentucky under the same Constitution, and the same principle carried out; first, on the death of Governor Breathitt; secondly, on the death of Governor Clark; and lastly, under the present Constitution, upon the death of Governor J. L. Helm.

Governor Madison was born in Rockingham County, Virginia, in June, 1763. He was distinguished in arms as well as in the cabinet. He was but a boy when he first entered the ranks in our struggle for independence; he was also in many battles fought by the early settlers of Kentucky. At the head of a company he was wounded in St. Clair's Defeat in 1791; and was again wounded in 1792, in the attack by the Indians on the camp of Major John Adair.

He was a brave man; and it is said of him that his looks, his words, his whole demeanor designated him emphatically a soldier, and he ever stood ready to shed his blood, if need be, in his country's cause. His patriotism and zeal in behalf of his country knew no bounds. He had served two years in the war of the Revolution before his removal to Kentucky, and had been here but a short time before he was called upon to take part in the administration of the State. On the 7th of March, 1796, he was appointed by Governor Shelby as Auditor of Public Accounts, which office he filled for more than twenty years. He became so generally known, and was so universally popular, during this period, that there was not an office within the gift of the people of Kentucky that he could not easily have attained.

When a requisition was made in 1812 to aid in an expedition against Canada and the Indians of the Northwestern Territory, he accepted the office of major under Colonel John Allen, who had raised a volunteer regiment for that expedition, and was at the memorable battle of Raisin, and displayed remarkable courage and firmness. It was here that Colonel Allen and Captains Simpson, McCracken, Hickman, and a great number of other brave men fell. Madison was in command of the force that stood within the pickets, and exacted the terms of capitulation of Proctor, by which his men, and all the wounded, were to be protected from the violence of savage cruelty. In 1816, as before stated, Madison having resigned the office of Auditor, was elected Governor, but died about six weeks afterwards, the 14th of October, 1816, which sad event left an appalling gloom upon the whole people of the State.

As I have before stated, Colonel Gabriel Slaughter had been elected Lieutenant Governor, and upon the demise of Governor Madison succeeded him in the executive chair for the four years of Madison's term. He appointed John Pope as Secretary of State, an act at that time not acquiesced in heartily by the people, from the fact that he as Senator in Congress had opposed the late war with England. Mr. Pope, being regarded as the principal cause of the exciting debates which occurred in the Legislature for one or two sessions on the new election subject, finally resigned, and Slaughter for the balance of the term administered the government without any Secretary at all.

Governor Slaughter died at his residence in Mercer County, in 1830, at sixty-three years of age, and the Legislature, by joint resolution, ordered a marble monument to be erected to his memory on the spot where he was buried. He was a native of Virginia, and emigrated to Kentucky at an early period. Early in life he became a member of the Baptist denomination of Christians, and was a prominent and useful member of that society. He was frequently a member to its associate churches, and generally presided as moderator. He was a colonel at the battle of New Orleans of a regiment of Kentucky troops. General Jackson entertained a high respect for him as a soldier and patriot. He was a man of determined firmness; in this respect he resembled Jackson. On one occasion, while acting as president of a court-martial whose decision was not in accordance with the views of Jackson, the court were ordered to reverse their proceedings, but Slaughter declined to comply, saying, he knew his duty, and had performed it.

During the long wars of the French, together with our own war, the financial concerns of the civilized world were in great disorder. Gold and silver had been banished from circulation, and inflated paper currency had taken its place, and nominal prices of all commodities became greatly enhanced. At the return of peace, however, specie payments were resumed, and a consequent fall in the value of all commodities took place, the tendency of which was to bankrupt thousands.

About this time Kentucky chartered some forty independent banks, with an aggregate capital of $10,000,000, which by law they were permitted to redeem with the paper of the Bank of Kentucky instead of specie. At this time the Bank of Kentucky was in good credit, and had resumed specie payments. During the summer of 1818 the State was flooded with the paper of these independent banks; speculation, of course, ran high, and the pressure of debt soon became terrible. Most of these banks failed within the space of a year, and in two years there was scarcely one alive.

The Legislature of 1819-20, as a relief measure, passed a twelve months' replevy law. Still the cry was for more relief, so the Legislature of 1820-21 chartered the bank called the Bank of the Commonwealth. This bank was not required to redeem its notes in specie, though made receivable for all debts and taxes. Lands owned by Kentucky south of Tennessee River were pledged for their final redemption. If a creditor refused to receive this paper for his debt, the debtor could replevy two years. The paper of this new bank was poured out in great profusion, and it soon sank down to half its nominal value. This depreciated currency creditors had to take in payment of their whole debt, or else receive nothing at all for two years, and run the risk, besides, of new delays and the bankruptcy of securities.

The party names which existed in Kentucky at that time were called "Relief" and "Anti-Relief." Each side had advocates of the greatest and most distinguished men of the State. Among those on the Relief side were Rowan, Barry, Sharp, Bibb, T. B. Monroe, General James Allen, and others. On the Anti-Relief side were such men as Robert Wickliffe, B. Hardin, Crittenden, Robertson, Chilton, Allen, Brents, Buckner, Walker, Tompkins, and others.

The question of the power of the Legislature to pass such an act was soon before Judge Clark, of the Circuit Court, who promptly decided the act unconstitutional. So indignant were the Legislature at this presumption in Judge Clark, as they regarded it, that in 1822 he was summoned to appear before a called session of the Legislature, where violent efforts were made to intimidate him or drive him from office. The storm, however, was allayed, and Clark still retained his office.

Judge Clark's decision was soon sustained in a similar case, by Judge Blair of another circuit, which again aroused the inflammatory spirit of the Relief party; but all were awaiting with impatience the decision upon the question of the Court of Appeals of Kentucky, which tribunal was then occupied by John Boyle, William Owsley, and Benjamin Mills. These were all men of great purity of character, judicial experience, profound learning in the laws, and great firmness of purpose. The case came before them, of Lapsley and Brashear, at the fall term of 1823. The people of the State, at their previous election, by a large majority, had decided against the decisions of Clark and Blair, and had uttered terrible denunciations against the judges of the Court of Appeals, in advance, if they should dare to thwart their wishes. The judges maintained an unbroken silence until the proper time for them to act. When the time arrived they delivered their opinions seprately, and each concurred fully with the judges of the Circuit Court, that the act of the Legislature was in violation of the Constitution of the United States, and totally void. There is a clause in the Constitution which prohibits the States from passing any law impairing the obligations of contracts, which the judges regarded as conflicting with the act alluded to.

The limits of this chapter will not permit that I should enter into the reasoning of the judges upon the subject. Judges, under the Constitution, then held their offices during good behavior, and were removable only by impeachment or address; the latter case requiring two-thirds of the Legislature to remove them. The opinion of the court created immense sensation in Kentucky, and the canvass of 1824 was renewed with redoubled efforts, in hope to obtain a two-thirds vote of the Relief party, with a view to the removal of the judges. Desha, the Relief candidate for the office of Governor, and a large majority of the Legislature for Relief, were elected.

The Legislature met in December, and the three judges were summoned before them. They calmly assigned their reasons for the decision they had given, and were replied to by Rowan, Bibb, and Barry, all three men of distinguished talents. The vote was taken, and a constitutional majority not being obtained, the victory resulted for the judges.

As the Relief party could not remove the judges by either of the ways pointed out in the Constitution, viz., *impeachment* or *address*, not having a majority of two-thirds in either branch of the Legislature, yet they were so inflamed, and so determined in their purpose, as to resort to any means at all plausible for the accomplishment of their object; hence a bill was immediately introduced to repeal the act by which the Court of Appeals had been organized, and passing an act organizing the Court of Appeals anew. The bill was debated with the most intense excitement that ever occurred in a legislative hall before. Robert Wickliffe, Anti-Relief, denounced the opposite party with the most severe invective, as trampling upon the Constitution "deliberately, knowingly, and wickedly." John Rowan, one of the most distinguished and talented men of Kentucky, replied with boldness and equal severity.

The debate continued three days, and to a late hour each night. The galleries were crowded with spectators. The Governor and Lieutenant Governor were present on the occasion, and mingled on the floor with the members, displaying the most intense excitement. Great disorder prevailed, and the

Governor himself was heard to urge the calling of the previous question.

The bill was passed by a very large majority in the House of Representatives as well as in the Senate, was soon signed by the Governor, and became a law. A new court was soon organized, consisting of four judges, instead of three, as before. William T. Barry was Chief Justice; John Trimble, John Haggin, and Reginald Davidge were associated justices; Francis P. Blair was appointed clerk, and took forcible possession of the records. The Old Court, Boyle, Owsley, and Mills, denied the constitutionality of the reorganizing act, and continued to set as a Court of Appeals, and decide as usual such cases as were brought before them.

The names now by which the parties were distinguished were the Old and the New Courts. A great majority of the lawyers of Kentucky were of the Old Court party, and so also was a majority of the circuit judges, who recognized the Old Court as the true court, and took their cases before them, and judges obeyed their mandates as before. Some of the cases, however, were taken up to the New Court, and a few of the circuit judges obeyed their mandates exclusively. Never were the passions of men raised to a higher pitch of excitement than existed during the canvass for the Legislature of 1825. The result was a triumphant majority in the representation branch for the Old Court party, still, however, retaining a majority in the Senate of the New Court party.

In the canvass of 1826 both parties were arrayed for another exciting and final struggle. The Old Court party were triumphant this year in both branches of the Legislature, and when the Legislature met, the obnoxious reorganizing act was repealed, and the three old judges re-established in office as before, and their salaries were voted to them during the period of their illegal removal. Since that time all the acts of the New Court have been treated as a nullity.

To give an unbroken chain of the exciting incidents which attended the Relief and Anti-Relief, the Old and New Court questions, I have passed through the years of the administration of Adair and Desha.

We return now to the election of General John Adair in 1820, the seventh Governor of Kentucky, but the ninth term of the office; for it will be recollected that Garrard and Shelby each served two terms as Governor. General Adair's opponents for the office were Judge Logan, General Desha, and Colonel Butler, all men of great popularity and distinction.

General Adair was born in South Carolina, in the year 1757. At an early age he entered the army of the Revolution as a volunteer, was made a prisoner by the British, and treated with great cruelty and insult. In 1786 he came to Kentucky, and settled in Mercer County. He acted as Major, and was an efficient officer in the border war on the northwestern frontier, and had frequent engagements with the Indians. In November, 1792, he had one of the most desperate encounters with the Indians that ever occurred. It took place in Preble County, Ohio, where Eaton now stands.

Among the wounded in that battle were Lieutenant, afterwards Governor, George Madison, and Colonel Richard Taylor, the father of General Zachary Taylor, the hero of the Mexican war. The Indians on this occasion were commanded by the celebrated Little Turtle. In the winter of 1805-6, when General Adair was Register of the land office of Kentucky, Little Turtle passed through Frankfort on his way to Washington City, accompanied by Captain Wells, Indian Agent. General Adair called on him and had a pleasant conversation with him in regard to the battle, in the course of which Adair said that he attributed his (Little Turtle's) defeat to his having been taken by surprise; to which Little Turtle replied, that "a good general is never taken by surprise."

In 1807 General Adair became somewhat unpopular on account of his supposed connection with Burr in his treasonable enterprise; and he was regarded with an eye of some suspicion. He was at the time one of the leaders in Kentucky in what was called the Federal party. It was afterwards generally believed that his course in the Burr affair was predicated on the opinion that Burr's plans were approved by the Government, and only contemplated a war with Spain.

In 1813 he was aid to Governor Shelby, and was present at

the battle of the Thames. His name was honorably mentioned to the Government by his superior officers on that occasion. Governor Shelby afterwards appointed him Adjutant General of the State troops, with the brevet rank of Brigadier General, in which character he commanded the Kentuckians at the battle of New Orleans.

The paper controversy between Adair and Jackson, growing out of imputations cast by Jackson upon the conduct of the Kentucky troops, acquired for Adair greater notoriety and popularity in Kentucky than he had possessed for many years previously, and doubtless aided him materially in his election to the office of Governor in 1820.

General Adair was frequently a member of the State Legislature, and several times Speaker of that body. In 1825 he was elected to the United States Senate for one year, being an unexpired term. In 1831 he was elected to Congress, and served one term. In all situations which he filled, whether civil or military, he was faithful, and commanded the respect and confidence of his constituents. He was a brave soldier and an ardent patriot, and occupied high rank and prominence among the early pioneers of Kentucky. He died on the 19th day of May, 1840, at eighty-three years of age.

General Joseph Desha, who was defeated by General Adair in 1820, was elected to the gubernatorial chair in 1824, over Judge Christopher Tompkins, and was the eighth individual who had been elected to that office in Kentucky. He claimed to have descended from the Huguenots of France, whose paternal grandfather fled to this country in the seventeenth century to avoid the cruel persecutions of his sect. He was born the 9th of December, 1768, in the State of Pennsylvania. In 1781 his father emigrated to Kentucky, and in the following year he removed to Tennessee. In the year 1789 he married the daughter of Colonel Bledsoe, and in 1792 settled in Mason County, Kentucky.

He was a volunteer under General Wayne in 1794, and served in his campaign with distinction. Between the ages of fifteen and twenty-two he took an active part in many of the skirmishes and contests with the Indians. In one of these skirmishes he had two brothers shot and killed by his side. His many good qualities as a soldier and a citizen made him very popular with the people, and he represented the county of Mason several years in the Legislature previous to the year 1806. In 1816 he was elected to Congress, and, by re-election, continued a member of that body until 1819. Whilst in Congress he acted uniformly with the Republican party. He supported warmly the war of 1812, was commissioned a Major General in 1813, and commanded a division at the battle of the Thames.

It was during his administration that a wayward son of his was tried and finally convicted of the murder of Baker under most disgraceful circumstances, and whose life was saved through the clemency of his father as Governor. I suppose there are but few fathers who would not have acted the same way if similarly situated, yet Governor Desha was much censured for the act by many. He did not pardon his son until he had attempted a suicide, before the day designated for his execution, by cutting his throat.

At the expiration of Governor Desha's term of office he retired from public life to his farm in Harrison County, and died in Georgetown, Scott County, on the 11th of October, 1842.

The Old and New Court question being finally settled by the elections of 1826, and the obnoxious acts of the Legislature repealed by the Legislature of 1826-7, and the Old Court fully reinstated and the acts of the New Court declared a nullity, State politics, which had run so high, seemed now to be entirely abandoned, or rather absorbed in national politics. New parties were at once formed, and new names of those parties assumed.

In 1824 Adams had been elected President over Jackson, mainly through the influence of Henry Clay, in the House of Representatives, over the delegates from Kentucky and Missouri. Clay, having received the appointment of Secretary of State under Adams, was charged with bargain and intrigue for the office, and denounced as an apostate from the Republican principles. Adams was denounced as a Federalist, although he had acted with the Democratic party for more than twenty years previous to that time, and was a distinguished member of President Monroe's administration.

Although the New Court party had ostensibly acquiesced in the decision of the people, yet they seemed fully bent on obtaining the power and control of the State in another form. The old issues were laid aside, and the New Court party, with Amos Kendall, editor of the Argus, at its head, almost to a man opposed the administration of Adams, whilst the great mass of the Old Court party sustained the administration and Mr. Clay in the vote he had given for Adams. The New Court party now assumed the name of "Democratic Republicans," and the Old Court party that of "National Republicans." The contest, both at the State election in August, and the Presidential election in November, 1828, was attended with great warmth and bitterness, owing to the hate which existed in Kentucky towards New England since the war of 1812; and the unpopularity of Adams in the West, thrown into the scale with the military glory of Jackson, the latter preponderated, and Jackson was elected.

The result of the gubernatorial election the preceding August was different, although the strife, contention, and excitement which prevailed was equally intense. The National Republican party had selected as their standard-bearer for Governor, General Thomas Metcalfe, who commenced the world as a stone-mason, but had risen by his energy and the force of his native talents to great distinction. He was a member of that Congress which made Adams President. The opposite party selected Wm. T. Barry, late Chief Justice of the New Court, as their standard-bearer. Barry was beaten, but their party carried a majority of the Legislature and their Lieutenant Governor; and it was obvious that a large majority of the votes of Kentucky were in the ranks of the opposite party. In 1831 the scale turned; a majority of the Legislature preponderated against Jackson and in favor of those who had supported Adams, and Clay, at this session, was elected to the United States Senate.

General Thomas Metcalfe administered the government of

the State wisely and prudently for his term of four years, which expired in 1832. A short sketch of his life, compiled from Collins' History of Kentucky, is here given:

He was born the 20th day of March, 1780, in the county of Fauquier, State of Virginia. His parents were poor and humble, aspiring to no distinction, saving that of a good name and spotless reputation. At an early day he emigrated to Kentucky, and settled in Fayette County. The necessity, growing out of the poverty and misfortunes of his father and family, contributed in no small degree to stamp the character of young Metcalfe with the elements of greatness, which his natural industry and enterprise subsequently so fully developed. In his early youth he was sent to school only long enough to attain to moderate perfection in the then recognized rudiments of an English education, sufficient, however, to inspire an ardent love for knowledge. At the age of sixteen he was apprenticed to an older brother to learn the trade of a stone-mason. The hours unemployed by his work were devoted to books and to study. What to other boys was labor, was to him relaxation and repose.

At the age of nineteen his father died, leaving his mother and several children very poor, and dependent partially upon him for support. To enable him more effectually to render them the aid their circumstances required, his brother canceled his indentures and set him free. With energy he set about providing for his widowed mother and her orphaned children, a duty which he most faithfully performed.

In 1809 he made his first public speech. At that time difficulties with Spain were contemplated, and a requisition had been made upon the State for volunteers. The ardor and eloquence of his remarks on that occasion spread through the whole regiment and ardently animated the men, and an overflowing compliment of volunteers flocked to his standard. His expectations, however, were disappointed, as they had been on two previous occasions when he had raised men for the contemplated war, and he again betook himself to the labor of his trade. In 1812 he was elected a member of the

House of Representatives of Kentucky, where he served with worth and honor.

In 1813 he raised a company of volunteers, and was at the battle of Fort Meigs. He was stationed on the left flank of the line, on this side of the river, under Boswell, who defeated more than double his number of Indians. His intrepidity and gallantry on that occasion secured him the favorable notice of General Harrison, the commander-in-chief. While absent on the campaign of 1813, he was again elected to the Legislature, receiving the suffrage of every voter in the county but thirteen. He served in this body several years, and in 1818 was elected a member of Congress under circumstances most gratifying to his friends. He remained in Congress until 1827, when he received the nomination of the National Republican party for Governor, and was elected as before stated.

After the expiration of his term of service he retired to his farm in Nicholas County, but was soon recalled to public life. In 1834 he was elected to the Senate of Kentucky. In 1840 he was appointed President of the Board of Internal Improvements, the arduous and responsible duties of which he discharged most faithfully and honorably for a number of years. He was honored and beloved by all who ever knew him. In 1848 he was appointed to fill the unexpired term of Mr. Crittenden in the Senate of the United States. He boasted of his service as a stone-mason, and delighted in being called "Old Stone Hammer." He died at his farm in Nicholas County, Kentucky, on the 18th of August, 1855.

In 1832 the great contest of political parties was again renewed, with as great excitement and bitterness as had prevailed at any previous election. Jackson and Clay were the competitors for the Presidency. Judge R. A. Buckner, of Green County, was selected by the National Republican party, and John Breathitt, of Logan County, by the National Democrats, or Jackson party, for the office of Governor, to succeed Metcalfe. The most untiring efforts were made by both parties, but the election resulted in favor of Breathitt by a majority of about one thousand votes, which was extremely mortifying to Buckner as well as his friends. But defeat did not dispirit them. They immediately called a convention, and at once organized for the decisive conflict which was to come off in November between Jackson and Clay for the Presidency. The Jackson party also held a convention, and organized for the conflict. The time intervening was marked by tremendous exertions on both sides. The result was overwhelming in favor of the National or Clay party. The popular majority at the election in favor of the Clay party was over seven thousand, and it continued to be the dominant party of the State for many years after.

We have stated that Breathitt was elected Governor in August, 1832, being the twelfth Governor of Kentucky by succession of terms of that office. Governor Breathitt was a native of the State of Virginia, and was born on the 9th of November, 1786, near New London. His father removed from Virginia, and settled in Logan County in the year 1800, where he raised his family. John was the eldest of his father's children. His advantages of education were limited, but he made the best use of the means in his power, and by diligent attention to his books at an early age made himself a good surveyor. Before he was of full age he received the appointment of deputy surveyor of public lands, and in that capacity surveyed many townships in the State of Illinois, then a Territory of the United States. In early life he taught a country school, by which and surveying, which he still kept up, he soon acquired considerable property, especially in lands. He then commenced the study of law, under the direction of Judge Wallace, and was admitted to the bar as a qualified attorney in February, 1810.

His industry and capacity for business soon secured him a lucrative practice, and he advanced rapidly in public estimation. In 1810 he was elected a Representative of Logan County to the State Legislature, and was successively elected to that office several times. In 1828 he was elected Lieutenant Governor, and served his term of four years with dignity and propriety. In 1832 he was elected Governor, but died before the expiration of his official term, at the Governor's house in Frankfort, on the 21st of February, 1834.

CHAPTER V.

James Clark elected Governor—Sketch of his Life—Robert P. Letcher elected Governor—Sketch of his Life—William Owsley elected Governor—Sketch of his Life—John J. Crittenden elected Governor—Sketch of his Life—Sketch of James T. Morehead—Sketch of Charles A. Wickliffe—Beriah Magoffin elected Governor—Sketch of his Life—Acting Governor Robinson—Thomas E. Bramlette elected Governor—Sketch of his Life—John L. Helm elected Governor—Sketch of his Life—Mrs. Governor Helm—Ben. Hardin Helm—Hon. H. W. Bruce—Thomas Hays—John W. Stevenson acting Governor—Elected at Regular Election—Sketch of his Life—Successor of Thomas L. McCreery in U. S. Senate—Hon. P. H. Leslie, acting Governor until August Election, 1871, when Election takes place regularly.

James Clark was elected Governor of Kentucky at the August election in 1836, which was the thirteenth administrative term of said office. He was the first circuit judge who had the boldness to pronounce the Relief law unconstitutional, and was well worthy the honor conferred by his election to the gubernatorial chair, not only for his talents, but for the signal service he had rendered his country at a time when an attempt was made to sweep away, as with a tempest, the most conservative features of our Constitution.

Governor Clark was born in Bedford County, Virginia, in 1779, near the celebrated Peaks of Otter. His father, Robert Clark, emigrated to Kentucky at a very early period, and settled in Clark County. James received the principal part of his education under Dr. James Blythe, afterward Professor in Transylvania University. He studied law with his brother, Christian Clark, a very distinguished lawyer of Virginia, and returned to Kentucky and commenced the practice of his profession in Winchester, Clark County, in 1799. Soon afterward he set out in search of a more eligible situation, and traveled throughout the West, taking Vincennes and St.

Louis in his route; but failing to find a situation to suit his views, he returned to Winchester, and soon obtained an extensive practice.

At this period of his life he was several times elected a member of the Legislature, where he soon attained a high position and great influence. In 1810 he was appointed a judge of the Court of Appeals, and acted in that capacity about two years. In 1812 he was elected to Congress, and served from the 4th of March, 1813, until March, 1816. In 1817 he received an appointment as judge of the Circuit Court, which office he filled with great ability and general satisfaction to the public until he resigned in 1824. In May, 1823, he rendered his decision in regard to the Relief law, of which we have heretofore spoken. In 1825 he was elected to Congress to fill the vacancy occasioned by the appointment of Mr. Clay as Secretary of State of the United States, and he continued to represent the Fayette district in that body until 1831. In 1832 he was elected to the Senate of Kentucky, and was chosen Speaker in the place of Mr. Morehead, who was then acting as Governor in place of Breathitt, who had died.

Governor Clark died the 27th of August, 1839, in the sixtieth year of his age. He was of fine personal appearance, of cheerful and social disposition; an easy address and fascinating manner made him the life of every circle in which he mingled. He was full of fun, fond of anecdotes, and could tell a story with inimitable grace. He possessed those qualities well calculated to display the amiable traits of his character in their best light, and those stern and manly virtues which inspire confidence and command respect. His death was sensibly felt and universally deplored.

The fourteenth administrative term was occupied by Robert P. Letcher, who was elected in 1840 by a majority of about twenty-seven thousand votes over his opponent. General Harrison's majority over Van Buren, at the succeeding November election for the Presidency, greatly exceeded that of Letcher.

Governor Letcher was born in Goochland County, Virginia, received a good education, and adopted the profession of law.

He served a number of years as a member of the State Legislature, and at one time was elected Speaker of the House. He served as a member of Congress from 1823 to 1835, and as Governor from 1840 to 1844. In 1849 he was appointed Minister to Mexico.

He died in Frankfort, Kentucky, January 24, 1861. Governor Letcher was one of the most amusing and effective stump speakers I ever listened to. He had a fund of anecdotes always applicable to the matter in hand, which he told with such zest and humor as always to excite the risibility of even those of the most serious cast of mind. His administration as Governor was generally regarded as wise and prudent.

Judge Wm. Owsley filled the fifteenth administrative term of Governor, beating for that office Colonel William O. Butler, a highly distinguished and very popular gentleman. Governor Owsley was born in the State of Virginia, in the year 1782. In 1783 his father moved to the then county of Kentucky, and settled near where the town of Crab Orchard now stands, in Lincoln County, which was among the earliest border settlements in the western wilderness. The father of William Owsley had eleven children, and the Governor himself had ten or twelve, most of whom were daughters. William, the subject of this sketch, and his brother Joel, by their devotion to study, succeeded in getting a better education than was common for boys at that day. Joel studied medicine, and settled himself in Burksville, Cumberland County, where he did an extensive practice, accumulated a good deal of property, and raised a large and respectable family of children, some of whom are quite distinguished for their talents and business qualifications. Joel died within a year or two past at a good old age, honored and respected by all who knew him, as a physician, a neighbor, a friend to the poor, and above all, as a teacher in the Christian Church.

William Owsley taught for awhile a country school, and while thus engaged improved his education, and learned plain surveying, and became a deputy surveyor, and afterwards deputy sheriff of the county of which his father was high sheriff. Among the pupils of William while he taught school was a Miss Elizabeth Gill, and when he attained about twenty-one years of age it so turned out that William married his young and blooming scholar. They were of congenial dispositions and habits, and constituted a happy pair during their long lives.

While William was engaged in his early official pursuits, he attracted the attention of John Boyle, afterwards Chief Justice of Kentucky, who offered William the use of his library and the advantage of his instructions in the study of law, which were accepted, and, by perseverance and close application, young Owsley soon obtained license, and commenced practice in the county of Garrard. He succeeded well, and ranked high as a lawyer. He afterward represented Garrard several years in the Legislature, and became so favorably known as a legislator and lawyer, that in 1812, when he was only thirty-one years old, he was appointed by Governor Scott to the bench of the Court of Appeals as the colleague of Judge Boyle. Judge Owsley resigned this office in a short time, in consequence of the passage of a law reducing the number of judges of the court to three, but a vacancy occurring in 1813, he was immediately reappointed by Governor Shelby.

I have before stated that it was during the service of Boyle, Owsley, and Mills, on the Supreme Bench, that the controversy between the Old and the New Court parties was waged. The character of that momentous struggle will ever constitute a page of Kentucky history, and the virtues of the men who then rendered themselves conspicuous will be duly commemorated. Nothing less than the firmness, wisdom, and coolness of these judges could have saved the country in that time of dread and peril from anarchy, revolution, and ruin. It seems providential that such men were on the bench to save the State in that stormy trial.

In 1828 Judge Owsley resigned his office as judge, and retired to his farm in Garrard County. Some time after this he again represented Garrard County in the Legislature, but continued to practice law in his circuit, and also in the Court of Appeals. His business became so extensive in the courts at Frankfort, that he parceled out his farm among his children, and removed to Frankfort. Here he resided until 1843, when he purchased a splendid farm in Boyle County, and gave up his practice altogether. In 1844, as we have before stated, he was elected Governor by an overwhelming majority, getting more votes than were received by General Harrison in 1840. As Governor of the State he was distinguished for his devotion to the duties of the office, his faithful examination into the affairs of the State, particularly its public debt, and for his unshaken determination to bring every officer up to his duty, and to have the laws faithfully executed. The public debt was greatly diminished during his administrative term.

In person, Governor Owsley was tall and slender, six feet two inches in height, reserved in his disposition, and talked but little. He was proverbial for honesty, firmness, and impartiality. His manners were plain, simple, and purely republican; and he was ever the sturdy foe of all new-fangled fashions in social intercourse, and new notions in law and politics. He was between seventy-five and eighty years of age when he died.

The Honorable John J. Crittenden succeeded Owsley to the gubernatorial chair, being the sixteenth administrative term of the Government of Kentucky. He was born in the county of Woodford, within a few miles of Versailles, on the 10th day of September, 1786. His father was John Crittenden, an officer of the Revolution, a man of intelligence and great moral worth. He had four sons, all men of high distinction, viz: John, Thomas, Robert, and Henry. The three first were eminent as lawyers, and in public life, and the last, though a farmer, was frequently called to public stations. They were all brave and gallant as the sire from whom they descended; accomplished in mind and manners, men without fear and without reproach.

John J. Crittenden received as good an education as could be obtained in the schools of that day in Kentucky. He completed his education at Washington Academy and at the College of William and Mary, in Virginia. On his return home he commenced the study of the law in the office of that very distinguished jurist, George M. Bibb, and under his tuition he soon became thoroughly prepared for the practice of his profession. He commenced the practice in Russellville, in the midst of many brilliant competitors. All the honors of the profession were soon his, and he soon acquired a fame co-extensive with the nation. His oratory was hardly equaled, and seldom surpassed by any. He was elected first to the Legislature of Kentucky from the county of Logan in 1811, and the same honor was conferred upon him for six consecutive years.

In 1817 he was elected Speaker of the House of Representatives. So distinguished had he become that the Legislature of 1817 elected him to the United States Senate. As a member of that body he was hailed by the people as among the foremost of our orators, and as a fit colleague for Henry Clay himself, and one destined to take rank with our ablest statesmen.

In 1819 he removed to Frankfort, to be more convenient to the Federal and Supreme courts, where he had an extensive practice. In 1825 he was elected to the Legislature from Franklin County, in that memorable period of the Old and New Court controversy. He was one of the most prominent and most distinguished of the Old Court party. He was three times elected to the Legislature from the county of Franklin. In the session of 1829–30 he was chosen Speaker of the House of Representatives. In 1835 Mr. Crittenden was again sent to the Senate of the United States, and held the office by re-election until the coming in of the administration of General Harrison. By him he was appointed Attorney General of the United States, and the appointment was hailed by men of all parties as the most appropriate that could have been made.

The melancholy death of the President brought into power an administration that Mr. Crittenden did not altogether approve, consequently he resigned. A few months afterward (in 1842) he was again elected to the United States Senate, and was at that time the acknowledged leader of the Whig party. He was five times elected to the United States Senate by the Legislature of Kentucky, an honor of which perhaps no other citizen can boast. He was truly great upon every question that has been of sufficient importance to interest the public mind. He never shrank from public duty, but was always ready to defend his principles and opinions as became a man.

He was an ardent advocate of the war of 1812, and was a volunteer in the service of his country. He was aid to Gen. Ramsey in the expedition commanded by Gen. Hopkins, and was aid to Governor Shelby, and served in that capacity with distinguished gallantry at the battle of the Thames. In 1843 he was again elected to the United States Senate, but in 1848, having received the Whig nomination for Governor of Kentucky, he retired from the Senate and was elected Governor, which office he held until his appointment as Attorney General by the acting President, Fillmore. He was again elected to the United States Senate in 1855, for the term ending in 1861, and was, when he retired, the oldest member of that body. In 1860 he was elected a Representative of Kentucky to the thirty-seventh Congress, and died in Louisville, Kentucky, July 25, 1863.

The successor to the gubernatorial chair of Mr. Crittenden was Lazarus W. Powell, being the seventeenth administrative term of the Government of Kentucky. His administration was not distinguished by any very important event. He was prudent and regardful of the public interest. He was a very polite gentleman in common intercourse, and a very popular man. He ranked among the most distinguished at the bar in the circuit in which he practiced. He was born in Henderson County, Kentucky, October 6, 1812. He was over six feet high, and of fine personal appearance.

He graduated at St. Joseph's College, Bardstown, Kentucky, in 1833; studied law at Transylvania University, Lexington, Kentucky, and came to the bar in 1835, following his profession and carrying on a farm at the same time. In 1836 he was elected to the Kentucky Legislature, and was a Presidential elector in 1844; was elected Governor in 1851, and was elected Senator in Congress for the term commencing in 1859, serving on the committees of Judiciary, Pensions, and Printing. Governor Powell died some three or four years since.

In 1855, when Know-Nothingism was in the ascendant in Kentucky, Charles S. Morehead was elected Governor as the successor of Governor Powell, being the eighteenth administrative term of that office. Governor Morehead's administration was wise and prudent. He was a man of a high order of talents, of fine personal appearance, polite, affable, and very popular. He was born in Nelson County, Kentucky, in 1802. He adopted the profession of law, and after practicing it a few years was elected to the State Legislature, serving during 1828 and 1829. He was appointed Attorney General of Kentucky in 1832, which office he held five years. In 1838, 1839, and 1840 he was again returned to the Legislature, officiating as Speaker during the latter year; was re-elected and made Speaker in 1841; was again re-elected in 1842 and 1844, and for the third time chosen Speaker. He was a Representative in Congress from 1847 to 1851. In 1853 he was once more returned to the Legislature, and in 1855 elected Governor. He was for many years one of the most devoted friends of Henry Clay. In 1860 he was a delegate to the Peace Convention held in Washington. He died some few years since.

James T. Morehead was elected Lieutenant Governor at the same time Breathitt was elected Governor (1832), and after the death of Governor Breathitt, in 1834, he became Governor. He was born in Covington, Kentucky, May 24, 1797, studied law, and entered upon the practice in 1818. He served three years in the State Legislature before he was elected Lieutenant Governor. In 1837 he was again elected to the Legislature, and in 1838 was appointed President of the Board of Internal Improvements, which office he held until 1841, when he was elected to the United States Senate for the term of six years. He subsequently resumed the practice of his profession, and died at Covington, December 28, 1854.

Charles A. Wickliffe was elected Lieutenant Governor at the same time that James Clark was elected Governor (1836). On the death of Governor Clark, in 1839, he, under the Constitution of Kentucky, became the acting Governor, which office he filled with ability for the balance of the term for which Clark had been elected. He was born in Bardstown, the 8th of June, 1788, and was educated at the Bardstown Grammar School. He studied law, and attained a high position at the bar. In 1812 he was appointed and served as aide-de-camp to General Winlock, and during the same year was elected to the State Legislature, and re-elected the following year. He was at the battle of the Thames as aide-de-camp to General Caldwell; after which he was again elected to the Legislature, where he continued until 1823, when he was elected to Congress. He was four times re-elected to this position.

He was several times Chairman of the Committee on Public Lands. On his retirement from Congress, in 1833, he was again elected to the Legislature, and was elected Speaker the next year. In 1841 he was appointed Postmaster General by President Tyler. In 1845 he was sent by President Polk on a secret mission to Texas, to look after annexation. In 1849 he was a member of the Convention called to revise the State Constitution; and in 1861 he was once more elected a Representative to Congress, having previously occupied a seat in the Peace Convention in February of that year, and served to the close of the thirty-seventh Congress. He was also a delegate to the Chicago Convention of 1864.

Governor Wickliffe filled a large space in the political history of Kentucky. His father moved from Virginia to Kentucky in 1784, four years before the birth of Charles, who was the youngest of nine children. The distinguished Robert Wickliffe, of Fayette County, was the eldest of these children. Governor Wickliffe was in very bad health for several years before his death, and had entirely lost his sight. He died at Baltimore a few years since, over eighty years of age.

The nineteenth gubernatorial term of the office of Governor was occupied for the first two years by the Hon. Beriah Magoffin, a gentleman of high distinction, a lawyer and a farmer of prominence. His wife was a grand-daughter of Governor Shelby, the first Governor of Kentucky, who did the honors of the mansion during the two years Governor Magoffin remained in the office with propriety and admiration. The writer had the pleasure of being there several times during his administration, and enjoyed the hilarity of those occasions with great zest.

Governor Magoffin, in size and general appearance, always reminded me of the distinguished George D. Prentice. Like him, he was of sociable, genial manners, and the center of attraction at his levees. The late civil war coming up during his administration, and it appearing manifest that his predilections were altogether on the side of the South, the Union party, then the dominant party in Kentucky, became greatly disaffected towards him, and desired to get rid of him as Governor on the best terms possible, because, personally, there were no objections to him. He occupied the gubernatorial chair from 1859 to 1861, when, by some arrangement, I. F. Robinson, Speaker of the Senate, administered the government to the end of the term for which Governor Magoffin had been elected, to-wit, 1863, Governor Magoffin having resigned.

The acting Governor, Robinson, was distinguished in Kentucky as a lawyer and statesman of great urbanity, in all respects worthy, and deservedly popular. His administration, for the two years he administered the government, was wise, prudent, and universally approved by the dominant party.

At the regular election in August, 1863, Thomas E. Bramlette, of Adair County, Kentucky, was elected to succeed Magoffin in the gubernatorial chair, being the twentieth gubernatorial term of that office after the adoption of the first Constitution of Kentucky in 1792.

Biographies are the landmarks of past centuries, and make up a large portion of the history of the world. By reading Plutarch's lives of the most distinguished men of Greece and Rome we acquire a complete history of those times. By reading the lives of the signers of the Declaration of Independence and other distinguished men of that day, we acquire a full knowledge of those times in America; the cause, progress, and result of the Revolutionary War. The life of Napoleon Bonaparte is a history of France, and of the wars with other powers under his administration. So, also, is the life of General Washington a history of the United States and of the American Revolution; and I might say just the same thing of other men in numerous other countries. These reflections influence me to indulge much in biographical history, which is generally more interesting and more instructive than history of any other kind.

I have said that General Thomas E. Bramlette was the twentieth Governor of Kentucky, elected in 1863, and continuing through the term which ended in 1867. He administered the government faithfully and with general satisfaction, though his ultra exercise of the pardoning power during his administration was objected to by many.

Governor Bramlette was born at Elliott's Cross Roads, in Cumberland County, Kentucky (afterward Clinton County), in the year 1817. His father, A. S. Bramlette, represented his county for many years in the Legislature, and was twice elected Senator from his district, and proved himself a faithful member of that body.

Governor Bramlette acquired considerable distinction as a lawyer in the circuit in which he practiced. At twenty-four years of age he was elected to the Lower House of the General Assembly of Kentucky. He was appointed by Governor Crittenden Commonwealth's Attorney for his judicial district in 1848. He was a district elector on the Whig ticket in the Presidential contest between Pierce and Scott. He was afterwards nominated for Congress on the Whig ticket in his district, but was beaten by a small majority by the Hon. James S. Chrisman. In 1856 he was elected judge of his judicial district, which office he held until about the beginning of the late civil war. Resigning, he raised a regiment under the United States Government, and commanded the regiment so raised until July, 1862, when he retired from the army. In the spring of 1863 the President of the United States (Mr. Lincoln) appointed him to the position of United States Attorney for the district, which office he filled for a short time, and until he received the nomination of the Union party of Kentucky for the office of Governor of the State. His opponent in this race was the Hon. Charles A. Wickliffe, the Democratic candidate. Governor Bramlette filled the office to which he had been elected to the full end of his term (September, 1867).

On account of the extreme sickness of Governor Helm, his inauguration took place at his home. Governor Bramlette and other distinguished gentlemen were present on the occasion. Governor Bramlette delivered a valedictory address on that occasion highly creditable to himself and to the honor of Kentucky. After the termination of his official term as Governor he removed to Louisville, where he is now engaged in the practice of the law.

The successor of Governor Bramlette to the gubernatorial chair was the Hon. John L. Helm, being the twenty-first gubernatorial term. Governor Helm was born on the 4th day of July, 1802, in Hardin County, Kentucky. The birth day of this great nation was his birth-day, and he ever remembered it with burning enthusiasm. He was the eldest son of George B. Helm, a native of Virginia, and one among the first settlers of the State of Kentucky. His mother's name was Rebecca Larue. His grandfather, Thomas Helm, came from Prince William County, Virginia, in the year 1780, in company with Henry Floyd, William and Benjamin Pope.

After remaining about a year at the Falls (now Louisville), and having during that time lost by death four of his children, he determined to seek a more healthy locality, and removed to the vicinity of Elizabethtown. At this place he erected a fort for the protection of his family against the incursions of marauding savages, and soon became the owner of the land upon which the fort was situated, about two miles distant from Elizabethtown.

Here he continued to reside until his death, which occurred about fifty years ago, and at the family burying-ground on this farm he was buried. Governor Helm in after years became the owner of this farm, now called "Helm Place," and continued to reside there to his death. The father of Governor Helm died while on a trip to Texas, about the year 1821 or 1822, leaving John L. the eldest of a large family of children, a mere boy, upon whom was devolved the charge of that family. At sixteen years of age Governor Helm commenced writing in the clerk's office of the Hardin Circuit Court, of which Samuel Haycraft, who still survives, was then, and for many years afterward, clerk. At twenty-one years of age he was licensed to practice law.

He soon gained eminence and a commanding position at the bar, which he ever afterward retained. His first official position was that of County Attorney for Meade County, though he resided in Hardin County, there being no resident lawyer in Meade. During the pendency of the Old and New Court question, a history of which I have heretofore given, Governor Helm defended the position of the Old Court party with decided and marked ability.

Governor Helm was first elected to the Legislature of Kentucky at the August election, 1826. From that period up to 1844 he served in that body eleven years, six years of that time as its presiding officer, and with distinguished ability. After this he was elected to the Kentucky Senate, and at the expiration of his four years' service he was elected Lieutenant Governor with Crittenden, on the Whig ticket. Upon Crittenden's appointment to the office of Attorney General in Mr. Fillmore's Cabinet he became the acting Governor. The duties of that position were discharged by him with zeal and ability, and he rendered the State very efficient service.

Upon the expiration of his term of service as acting Governor he retired to private life, devoting his attention to his farm and profession. He was not long permitted to enjoy the sweets of retirement. He was soon afterward elected President of the Louisville and Nashville Railroad, then in process of construction, and which had been almost abandoned by its friends as a failure. Governor Helm overcame many difficulties apparently insurmountable, and was still President of the road when the first train ran through from Louisville to Nashville.

In 1865 he was again called from his retirement and elected

to the Kentucky Senate, and in August, when his term was but half expired, he, then in the sixty-fifth year of his age, was elected Governor of the State. He was elected on the 7th of August, inaugurated at his home on the 3d of September, being then very sick, died on the 8th, and was buried on the 10th at the family burying-ground at Helm Place. He gave satisfactory evidence that he fully trusted in Christ, the Redeemer. Mrs. Governor Helm was the daughter of the distinguished Benjamin Hardin, of Bardstown. She bore to the Governor twelve children, several of whom have died.

Ben. Hardin Helm, his eldest son, was a Brigadier General in the Confederate army. He was a good lawyer and a truly brave man, and won high reputation as a soldier. He had his horse shot under him, was himself badly wounded at Baton Rouge, and was finally killed on the 20th of September, 1862, at the head of his brigade on the bloody field of Chickamauga. He left a widow and three children. George Helm, another son of the Governor, was a lawyer also, and commenced practice at Memphis, Tennessee, where he died in 1858. One of his daughters married the Hon. H. W. Bruce, a member of the Confederate States Congress, and now Circuit Judge of the ninth judicial district. Another of his daughters was the wife of Major Thomas Hays, an officer of high standing in the Confederate States service. Of his twelve children, about eight are now living. The widow still survives, the beloved of her children and of all who ever knew her.

John W. Stevenson, having been elected on the ticket with Governor Helm as Lieutenant Governor, consequently became the acting Governor until the next regular election, which occurred August, 1868, when he was elected the twenty-second Governor of Kentucky for the balance of the term for which Governor Helm had been elected. Governor Stevenson was born in Richmond, Virginia, and graduated at the University of that State. After preparing himself for the profession of the law, he settled in Covington, Kentucky, in 1841, where he soon took high rank in the practice of his profession.

He served in the State Legislature in 1845–46–47, and was elected a member of the State Constitutional Convention in

1849, and took a leading part. He was a member of the Democratic National Conventions of 1849, 1852, and 1856. He was twice Senatorial elector, and was one of the three Commissioners appointed to revise the Civil and Criminal Code of Kentucky. He was elected also from the Covington District a Representative to the thirty-fifth Congress, and was a member of the Committee on Elections. He was elected also to the thirty-sixth Congress, in which he served on the same committee.

He was the nominee of the Democratic Convention of 1867 for Lieutenant Governor, as before stated, and in 1868 elected Governor by a majority of nearly ninety thousand votes over his opponent, Colonel Sidney Barnes. At the session of the Legislature 1869–70 he was elected United States Senator, to succeed the Hon. Thomas L. McCreery to that office, and resigned the chair as Governor the 1st of February, 1871, when his place was filled by Hon. P. H. Leslie, Speaker of the Senate, and Senator from the Barren County District.

CHAPTER VI.

The Antiquities, Curiosities, Minerals, &c., of Adair County—Of Barren County—Of Boone County—Of Bourbon County—of Bracken County—Of Bullitt County—Of Carroll County—Of Clinton County—Of Cumberland County—Of Edmonson County—Of Grayson County—Of Green County—Of Greenup County—Of Garrard County—Of Hancock County—Of Hart County—Of Henry County—Of Kenton County—Of Larue County—Of Laurel County—Of Lewis County—Of Lincoln County—Of Meade County—Of Mercer County—Of McCracken County—Of Montgomery County—Of Nicholas County—Of Nelson County—Of Owen County—Of Pendleton County—Of Rockcastle County—Of Union County—Of Woodford County—Of Warren County—Of Whitley County.

Near the Sulphur Lick in Allen County, on Bay's Fork of Big Barren River, the following words are cut in the bark of a beech tree: "James McCall dined here on his way to Natchez, June 10, 1770." About nine miles from Scottsville, on the lands of S. E. Carpenter, there is inscribed on a large beech tree, "Ichabod Clark, mill site, 1779;" and on the other side, "Too sick to get over."

There are a number of caves in the county. In 1844 two shells were found in one of these caves, one about eighteen inches long, which had been sawed in the middle, with a hole in the end by which to hang it up; the other answers the purpose of a water vessel, having a bowl in the end. In the west end of the county, between Scottsville and Bowlinggreen, are the remarkable remains of an ancient fortification, belonging to a people unknown, and presenting one of the strongest military positions in the world. At this place Drake's Creek makes a horse-shoe bend, running for the distance of a mile, and returning within thirty feet of the commencement of the bend. The partition which divides the channel of the creek at this point is solid limestone, thirty feet thick at the base, two hundred yards in length, forty feet high, and six feet wide at the top. The top is level, and covered with small cedar trees. The area included within the bend of the creek contains about two hundred acres of land. The top of this is leveled, and forms a square area of about three acres, which is inclosed with walls and a ditch. The walls even to this day are about three feet high around the whole circuit of the fort. In the rear of the fort many small mounds are still perceptible. Tall cliffs intercept all access from the opposite banks of the stream; and the fort can only be approached by the narrow causeway, which renders the fort impregnable.

At the west side of the pass is another mound forty feet in circumference and four feet high. Upon excavating this mound a stone coffin was dug up, two and a half feet long, one foot deep, with a stone covering. Upon opening the coffin the arms and thigh bones of an infant were found in it; other bones were also found of much larger dimensions. Human bones of most extraordinary size have been exhumed from mounds in the county; the thigh bones from eight to ten inches longer than the race of men now inhabiting the country.

In Barren County there are a great number of mineral springs. The most famous is one now in Metcalfe, formerly Barren, on the east fork of Little Barren River, which flows off in a considerable branch, and is believed to be the largest stream of mineral water in all the Green River country. There are several springs within a few miles of Glasgow, which are considered quite beneficial to invalids. Several wells in the county have been bored in the last few years which have yielded petroleum in paying quantities.

The following inscription on a beech tree on the east fork of the south branch of Little Barren River may be seen: "James McCall, of Mecklenburg County, North Carolina, June 8, 1770;" and several initials of other names.

There are quite a number of mounds in the county; the most remarkable are at the mouth of Peter's Creek, on Big Barren River. Twelve miles southwest of Glasgow, on the pike leading to Nashville, are a number of small mounds, all very much of the same size and shape, two or three feet high, of oval form, about fifty yards apart, forming a circle four or five hundred yards in circumference. About the center of the circle a large mound is situated, twenty or thirty feet high, and ninety or one hundred feet in diameter. About a hundred yards outside of the circle is another mound, about the size of the one within. On these mounds trees are growing five feet in diameter. There are other mounds near by which contain bones, teeth, and hair of human beings in a perfect state of preservation. These bones are found in graves three feet long, from one to one and a half feet wide, and lined with flat stones.

There are several caves within four or five miles of Glasgow, in which bones have been found, one of which seemed to be the upper part of a skull, scalloped on the edges, and carved on the outside. It was large enough to be used as a spoon, though it might have been intended for an ornament.

Petersburg, in Boone County, is situated on an aboriginal burying-ground. In digging cellars for houses earthenware vessels have been found, as also Indian utensils of stone, curiously carved. Near that place are the remains of ancient fortifications. An embankment or breastwork, about four feet high, is still visible, extending from the Ohio River to Taylor's Creek, including an area of about twenty-five acres of land.

Twelve miles west of Burlington is a singular chasm in a hill, forming a split or zigzag avenue through it from the lowland on the Ohio River to Woolper Creek. The north side of the chasm is a perpendicular wall of rock seventy or eighty feet high, composed of pebble stones.

The celebrated Big Bone Lick is situated in this county, twelve miles west of Burlington, and one and a half miles east of the Ohio River. The lick is in a valley which contains about one hundred acres. The valley is surrounded by hills of unequal elevation, the highest altitude on the west side being some five hundred feet. The lick spreads over an area of about ten acres. There is no account of this lick being visited previous to the year 1773. That year it was visited by James Douglass, of Virginia, who found upon the surface of the ground large numbers of the bones of the Mastodon or Mammoth, and the Arctic Elephant. The last of these bones were removed some eighty years ago, but since that period a number have been exhumed from beneath the soil, which at times has been assiduously dug up and searched as if seeking for hidden treasures. Some of the teeth of those large animals weighed ten pounds; and some of the tusks which were dug up were eleven feet long and six or seven inches in diameter. Some of the thigh bones were five feet in length. The ribs were equally long, and three or four inches broad. Mr. Douglass used the ribs for tent poles when he first visited the lick.

The first collection of these fossil remains was made by Dr. Goforth in 1803, who in 1806 intrusted them to an English traveler by the name of Thomas Ashe, to be exhibited in Europe, but when he got to England he sold them for a large sum, and pocketed the money. The next collection was made by order of Mr. Jefferson, whilst he was President of the American Philosophical Society, in the year 1805, and was divided between that society and the French naturalist, Mr. Canier. A third collection was made in 1819 by the Western Museum Society. A fourth collection was made by Mr. Finnell, which was sold to a Mr. Graves for $2,000, and taken by him to the Eastern States and there sold for $5,000.

The springs at this place were much frequented at one time for their medical virtues, but for many years past no accommodation for visitors has been provided.

There is a salt spring in Bourbon County, in the Cambridge neighborhood, said to be more strongly impregnated than the waters of the Blue Licks. Sulphur and chalybeate springs are common in this county. Lead ore has occasionally been found in small quantities; also an inferior species of iron ore.

About a mile below the town of Paris is an ancient ditch. It crosses a narrow neck of Stoner Creek, where the creek makes a great bend, leaving in the bend an area of about fifty acres of land. Within the bend is a large mound, in which human bones have been found. Outside of the ditch, on the top of the cliff of the creek, is another large mound. This mound is said by an old settler to be one of a chain of mounds that extended quite across the country in a northwest by west direction. In these mounds coals have been occasionally found a little below the surface; also human bones, stone hatchets, spears, arrow points, and a peculiar kind of ware.

Near the junction of Stoner and Hinkstone forks of Licking, six miles north of Paris, is an ancient circular fortification, with embrasures at the cardinal points. This is situated on low ground, subject to overflow. When or by whom made is beyond conjecture.

Three miles further up the Hinkstone is a similar fortification, with two mounds, one within and the other without the circle. Stone axes, hatchets, chisels, dirks, flint spears, and arrow points, also a hatchet of iron corroded with rust, have been found here. Indian graves are found also. It is believed by many, from manifest indications, that the time was when Bourbon County had a native Indian population.

The vestiges of a large Indian town are still perceptible near where Pretty Run enters into Strodes' Creek. A variety of ornaments have been found here, such as bears' tusks and claws, with holes drilled through them. Stone medals, shells, fragments of vases with handles, stone axes, and implements of warfare have been found in profusion. It seems evident that this town had a tragic end. In every direction bones and teeth corresponding with every age have been discovered just beneath the surface of the soil, some lying across each other within the foundations of their huts, but more numerously in the bottom below the site of the town, where, perhaps, the tide of battle rolled. In excavating a place for a building in this town some years ago, some large bones were found fifteen feet below the surface, in a fissure between two rocks, not as large as the Mammoth, but larger than any known species of living animals on this continent.

Five miles below Paris, on Stoner, a cave has been discovered which contained a number of skeletons in a good state of preservation. These were probably some of the Indians killed at the siege of Hinkston's Station, which was the last fight in Bourbon County with the Indians of which we have any account.

Augusta, the county seat of Bracken County, is situated in a bottom of the Ohio River, and was a large burying-ground of the ancients. Wherever dirt is turned up human bones are sure to be found. They have been found in great numbers, and of great size, everywhere between the mouths of Bracken and Locust creeks, a distance of about a mile and a half. When General John Payne dug his cellar, one hundred and ten skeletons were taken up in the space of sixty by seventy feet. They were numbered by the skulls which were found. His garden was a burying-ground, was full of bones, and, as he says, the richest ground he ever saw. The skeletons were of all sizes, from seven feet long to the infant.

We are lost in conjecture who these people were. There is no tradition that any town was ever located here, or that any battle was ever fought near this place. General Payne found in his garden many arrow-heads, and earthen ware of clay and pounded muscle. Some of the largest trees of the forest were growing over these remains when the land was cleared in 1792.

In Bullitt County there were a number of forts and stations, particularly in the neighborhood of the salt works. The names of the first forts were called Nonsense. These forts and stations were the scenes of a number of conflicts with the Indians, who resorted to the licks to hunt game and make salt. On Cahill's Knob, near the licks, on one occasion, the Indians whipped to death an old man whom they caught while he was chopping wood for the salt works. The first salt ever made in Kentucky was made at Bullitt's salt works.

From five hundred to one thousand men have often been collected at this place, engaged in the various branches of salt-making, buying, selling, &c., and guarding the salt-making, whilst at that time Louisville, Lexington, and a few other places could only boast of a few hovels, and the buffalo slept securely where the capital of Kentucky now stands.

About eight miles below the mouth of the Rolling Fork of

Salt River, in Bullitt County, was one of the hardest fought battles with the Indians of which we have any record, in which the whites were finally defeated, being greatly overpowered by numbers. The enemy, however, lost more than half of their men.

In Carroll County there are a number of mounds, but generally of a small size. On the second bank of the Ohio River, about a fourth of a mile from the Kentucky River, there are the remains of a fortification of a circular form, situated on level ground, and about one hundred and twenty feet in diameter. About two miles from the mouth of the Kentucky River there are also the remains of what must have been a very formidable fortification on an eligible point, and of quadrangular form. The embankment of the fortification is evidently of artificial construction, and must have been made at great labor and expense. Its area is about an acre. The paths or roads leading to the water were visible a few years ago, and are, perhaps, yet so.

In 1837 one of the numerous small mounds found in that county was examined, and the skull and thigh bones of a human being of very large frame was found; also a silver snuff box in the shape of an infant's shoe. On another mound or hill, a short distance from the Kentucky River, in opening a stone quarry, the jaw-bone and a large number of human teeth were found. About four miles from Carrollton, on the Muddy Fork of White Run, in the bed of the creek, on a limestone rock, is the form of a human being in a sitting posture, and near by is the form of one lying on his back, six feet long, and distinctly marked.

In Christian County there are several very interesting curiosities. Two of the forks of Little River sink and disappear entirely in the earth for many miles, when they emerge and flow on as before. About twelve miles from Hopkinsville is what is called the Pilot Rock. It is about two hundred feet high. The summit is level and covers about half an acre of ground, which affords some wild growth and shrubbery. This rock attracts great attention, and is visited by a large number of persons. Its most elevated summit can be reached without great difficulty, and affords a fine view of the surrounding country for many miles.

About twenty miles from Hopkinsville, in the northern extremity of the county, is a somewhat singular curiosity in the shape of a natural bridge, but it is not so large as the celebrated Rock Bridge of Virginia. The bridge crosses a deep ravine, is thirty feet in height, with a magnificent arch and a span of sixty feet. The surface is level, and the general width about five feet.

On the west fork of Red River, near the block-house built by John Montgomery and James Davis in 1785, is a large cave. They and their families would frequently hide within it to avoid the attacks of marauding Indians.

Poplar Mountain, in Clinton County, a spur of the Cumberland Mountains, penetrates the county to its center, making a beautiful curve, and the valley in the curve is called Stockton's Valley, of the most fertile limestone land. The elevation of this mountain above the valley is from one thousand to one thousand five hundred feet. Coal, in abundance and of the best quality, is found in the mountain in strata of about four feet.

On the top of this mountain, about four miles from Albany, there are three chalybeate springs, which have been visited a great deal for the last twenty-five or thirty years, and have proved of great benefit to invalids. An extensive view of the surrounding country may be had from this mountain. The springs are about twelve miles from the Cumberland River; but of a clear morning, it is said, the stream may be traced by the eye from the top of this mountain for a distance of an hundred miles. On Indian Creek, three miles from the mountain springs, there is a perpendicular fall of ninety feet. Besides, coal and iron ore abound in the country, and it is said that Plaster of Paris has been discovered in the hills.

The American oil well is situated in Cumberland County, about two and a half miles from Burksville. The well is situated immediately on the bank of Little Renix Creek, about half a mile from where it enters Cumberland River. At the time of its development, in the year 1830, it was considered one of the greatest curiosities and wonders of Kentucky. While some men were boring for salt water, after penetrating about one hundred and seventy-five feet through a solid rock, they struck a vein of oil, which suddenly spouted up to the height of fifty feet above the surface. It continued to this height for several days. The oil thus thrown up ran into Renix Creek, thence into the Cumberland, covering the surface of the water for several miles, and, upon being ignited, presented the grand spectacle of a river on fire. The flames covered the surface of the river for many miles, reached to the tops of the tallest trees on the banks of the river, and continued until the supply of oil was entirely exhausted.

The writer was at the well a few days after the burning ceased, and remembers that it was in the month of April, and that the leaves upon the tallest trees along the banks of the Renix and the Cumberland were so scorched as to kill them. The salt-borers were greatly disappointed, and the well was neglected for some time, until it was discovered that the oil possessed valuable medicinal qualities. It was afterwards bottled up in large quantities, and extensively sold in nearly all the States of the Union and in Europe.

The Rock House, in Cumberland County, is regarded as a great natural curiosity. It is situated not very far from Creelsboro, in Russell County. It is a lofty arch of solid rock, forty feet in height, some sixty feet in breadth, with a tall cliff overhanging it. In high stages of water a portion of the river rushes through the aperture with great violence down a channel worn into the rock, and pours into the river again about one and a half miles below. In ordinary stages of water the arch, or what is generally termed the Rock House, is perfectly dry.

Not far from the oil well, at the junction of Big and Little Renix creeks, there is a beautiful cataract of some fifteen or twenty feet fall, it being in the waters of the latter stream. At the point where these streams empty into the Cumberland there was, in the first settlement of the country, a battle between the whites and Indians, in which the whites were victorious. The rock-bound graves of the Indians may yet be seen upon the ground. Other battles were fought in Cumberland, which formed a part of Green County until 1798, but the particulars can not be gathered at this late day.

During the great oil excitement in Kentucky four or five years ago, a great many oil wells were developed on the Cumberland River and its tributaries, affording more oil than any other wells which had been developed anywhere else in the State.

Grayson County abounds more in mineral waters than almost any other county of the State. There are in the county a great number of white sulphur springs. Four or five miles from Litchfield, the county seat of Grayson, is situated what is called the Grayson Springs. It is a watering-place of considerable note. With the hotel and cottages some two or three hundred persons, perhaps a greater number, can be comfortably accommodated. Within a little valley, less than half an acre in extent, are an immense number of springs, some of them more strongly impregnated with sulphur, it is said, than any other springs in the United States. Some of them are very cold, and others very warm. It is said that many remarkable cures have been effected by the use of the waters.

One of the natural curiosities of Edmonson County is Dismal Rock, a perpendicular rock one hundred and sixty-three feet high, on Dismal Creek. Near the town of Brownsville is a cave, not very extended, but quite large at the opening or entrance into the cliff of Green River. To the mouth of this cave Green River sometimes rises; and in the cave is a large tree, somewhat imbedded in the sand, which, when the writer visited it some thirty years ago, seemed to be perfectly petrified, especially the bark portion. The writer broke off several pieces nearly as large as his hand, which he has still preserved in his cabinet of curiosities to this day.

The writer also visited another curiosity of Edmonson County, at the same time, called Indian Hill, situated about a mile from the town of Brownsville. This hill is circular at the base, and one mile in circumference. Its altitude is eighty-four feet perpendicular, and is only accessible on one side, and that to those on foot. The remains of a fortification are yet very visible around the brow, and a number of mounds and burial places are scattered over the area. A spring of fine water issues from the rock near the surface. When the writer visited it the whole of the area was covered with timber, some of the trees being very large. From this hill a delightful view of the surrounding country is had.

In this same county the greatest wonder of the world is situated—a wonder that has attracted visitors from nearly every part of the habitable globe, and no one who has ever visited it returned from it disappointed. I mean the Mammoth Cave, a visit to which impresses every beholder with astonishment and awe. There have been many elaborate descriptions given of this great cave, some one of which has been seen by almost every one who feels any interest in the wonderful. I shall, therefore, on the present occasion, only attempt an outline view.

The mouth of this cave is within half a mile of Green River, about twelve miles from Brownsville, the county seat, and equidistant from the cities of Louisville and Nashville (about ninety miles from each place). About two hundred yards from the cave the hotel is situated, a large edifice, two hundred feet long by forty-five feet wide, with piazzas sixteen feet wide extending the whole length of the building, above and below.

In approaching the mouth of the cave the first thing that attracts attention is a rush of cold air issuing from the cave. Going into the cave, you descend some rude steps of stone for about thirty feet, which brings you under the arch, and just before you is a small stream of water falling from the face of the rock and disappearing in a deep pit.

A hundred feet further, and you reach the door, set in a rough stone wall. Passing through this door you reach a narrow passage, and descending gradually along the passage a short distance you arrive at the great vestibule of the cave. This hall is of oval shape, two hundred feet in length by one hundred and fifty feet wide, roof flat and level, sixty feet high, and looking almost as smooth as plastering. Two passages at the opposite extremities open into it, each running a straight course at right angles to each other, five hundred or six hundred feet long by one hundred feet wide. The passage to the right is called Audubon Avenue; the other, the beginning of the main cavern itself.

At a remote period this chamber seems to have been used as a cemetery, as there have been disinterred many large skeletons of a race of people doubtless long since passed away from earth. In viewing this part of the cave the mind is impressed with a sense of vastness, solitude, and grandeur indescribable.

Leaving this ante-chamber by an opening on the right, you enter the Audubon Avenue, which is more than a mile long, some sixty feet high, and as many wide. Near the termination of this avenue is a natural well, twenty-five feet deep, containing the purest water. The little bat-room cave is on the left as you pass, and about three hundred yards from the great vestibule. This branch is remarkable for its pit, two hundred and eighty feet deep, and its being the resort in winter of an immense number of bats, which hang upon the wall in a torpid state till spring opens.

Returning to the vestibule, at right angles to the little bat-room, you enter the grand gallery or main cavern. This is a vast tunnel, extending for many miles, averaging fifty feet in width and as many high. In a quarter of a mile you reach what is called the Kentucky Cliffs, and descending gradually about twenty feet, enter what is called the Church, the ceiling of which is sixty-three feet high, and the church itself one hundred feet in diameter. Here is a natural-looking pulpit. Eight or ten feet above the pulpit, and immediately behind it is the organ loft, sufficiently capacious for a large choir. In this great temple of nature religious service is frequently performed, and with the slightest effort of the speaker he can be heard by the largest congregation.

Leaving the Church you are brought to the ruins of the old saltpetre works, leaching vats, pump-frames, &c. About thirty feet above you see a large cave, which is called Gothic Avenue, which you reach by a flight of stairs. This avenue is forty feet wide and fifteen feet high, and two miles long, the ceiling in many places as smooth as if plastered. Elevated above the floor a few feet, in a recess on the left, two mummies were found in the year 1813, in a good state of preservation. In 1814 a mummy was also found in Audubon Avenue by some miners, and concealed, but in 1840 was recovered, though much injured and broken by the weights which had been placed upon it.

In the Gothic Avenue there are a number of stalagmite pillars, reaching from the floor to the ceiling, extending the entire length of the hall. The Devil's Armchair is a large stalagmite column, in the center of which is a comfortable seat. Near the foot of the chair is a small basin of sulphur water. Napoleon's Breastworks, the Elephant's Head, and Lovers' Leap are also in this avenue. Immediately below the Lovers' Leap you enter a chasm in the rock three feet wide and fifty feet high, which leads to the lower branch of the Gothic Avenue.

At the entrance of this lower branch is a large flat rock called Gatewood's Dining Table, to the right of which is the Cooling Tub, from which a stream flows into the Flint Pit. You next pass Napoleon's Dome, the Cinder Banks, Crystal Pool, Salts Cave, and enter on Arnett's Dome. In the wall of this dome is a beautiful waterfall, passing off by a small channel into the Cistern.

Returning from Gothic Avenue to the main cave, at the stairs is situated the Ball-room. Here is an orchestra fifteen feet high, which could accommodate one hundred musicians. Next you arrive at Willie's Spring, then pass Well Cave, Rocky Cave, and arrive at the Giant's Coffin. Beyond the coffin the cave makes a large bend, and then resumes its general course. Opposite this point is the Sick-room Cave, and beyond this is a row of cabins for consumptive patients. The atmosphere of the cave is always temperate and pure. Next you reach the Star Chamber. The ceiling here is very high, and one, in looking up, cannot but imagine that he sees the stars of the firmament. You enter next the Salts Room. In this room are the Indian houses under the rocks. In this neighborhood are the Black Chambers. Next is the Humble Chute, which is the entrance to the Solitary Chambers. Here you have to crawl on your hands and knees for some fifteen or twenty feet. In this branch is the Fairy Grotto.

Returning from this point, you re-enter the main cave at the cataract, and come next to the Chief City or Temple. This is an immense vault, covering an area of two acres, which is covered by a dome of solid rock one hundred and twenty feet high.

A narrow passage behind the Giant's Coffin leads to a circular room one hundred feet in diameter, called the Wooden Bowl; this bowl is the vestibule of the Deserted Chambers. On the right are the Steeps of Time. Descending about twenty feet you enter the Deserted Chambers. At Richardson's Spring the imprint of moccasins and children's feet of some bygone age are to be seen. In this branch are the Covered Pit and Gorin's Dome, a solid rock two hundred feet high. The Bottomless Pit terminates the Deserted Chambers.

Beyond this pit is the Winding Way, and Pensacola Avenue, which averages fifty feet in width and thirty feet high. Next is Bunyan's Way, which leads to the river. Descending gradually a few feet you enter a tunnel fifteen feet wide, and soon reach the Great Crossings, where two great caves cross. Near this is the Pineapple Bush. The Winding Way is one hundred and five feet long, eighteen inches wide, and from three to seven feet deep. At its termination is Relief Hall, which terminates at River Hall. Here two roads are presented, the one to the left leads to the Dead Sea and the Rivers, and that to the right to Bacon Chamber, Bandits' Hall, the Mammoth Dome, &c. Proceeding to the left a short distance, by the aid of lights you look down a precipice upon a sheet of water eighty feet below, which is called the Dead Sea.

At the foot of the slope you travel, you arrive at the River Styx, black and deep, and overarched with rocks. Having passed the Styx, you reach the River Lethe. Descending this a quarter of a mile you arrive at a level and lofty hall called the Great Walk, which stretches to the bank of the Echo. The Echo is wide and deep enough to float a steamer of the largest class. This river is three-fourths of a mile long. In this river the eyeless fish are caught; there is nothing resembling an eye about them.

Beyond the Echo there is a walk of four miles to Cleaveland Avenue, passing through Elghor, Silliman's Avenue, and Wellington's Gallery, to the ladder which leads up to St. Mary's Vineyard. One hundred feet further you reach the base of the hill of the Holy Sepulcher. In this avenue are situated Cleaveland's Cabinet, the Rocky Mountains, Croghan's Hall, Serena's Arbor, &c. There is in this cave another avenue more than three miles long, lofty and wide, and at its termination a hall said to be larger than any in the cave.

In the western part of Green County, on Brush Creek, and extending into the counties of Larue and Hart, are immense quantities of iron ore of good quality. A number of years ago, forges and furnaces were in extensive operation in this quarter. There were two forges and a furnace on Brush Creek, and a very extensive furnace on Linn Camp, just over the line of Green, in Hart County. A mile or two lower down Linn Camp was a very extensive powder-mill establishment, which manufactured great quantities of powder during the war of 1812, and for many years afterwards.

There were several ancient fortifications in Green County, which the writer often visited in his youth, the remains of which have nearly disappeared by the cultivation of the soil, the most extensive of which was on Pittman's Creek, two and a half miles from Greensburg, near Pittman's old station, at what is called the Narrows. The creek makes a bend at this point, including in its area some two hundred acres of land, coming around so near that in the narrows, or neck of the bend, there was but little more than room enough for a wagon to pass safely, great precipices being on either side of the neck.

Just beyond this neck were three fortifications, and a mound four or five feet high, in which human bones were found at an early day, of different sizes. Within the remains of the fortifications were several trees of large size, which grew there, no doubt, after their abandonment. In 1826 Doctor N. H. Arnold cut a channel or canal through this neck and erected a mill at that point, which has been in operation ever since.

On the top of the cliff, outside of the curve of the creek, and about three-fourths of a mile from the fortifications, was situated Pittman's Station, one of the earliest settlements in the Green River country. Another station was situated on Green River where Greensburg now stands. It is said that the court-house was built upon the very spot where the station was situated. Another station, called Shank Painter, or Skagg's Station, was situated where the small village of Summersville now stands, six miles northwest of Greensburg. Another was situated on Little Barren River, about ten miles southwest of Greensburg.

In the year 1770 a company called the Long Hunters, the leader of which was Colonel James Knox, encamped some time near where Mount Gilead Meeting House now stands, ten miles east of Greensburg, on the road leading to Columbia. Some two miles nearer Greensburg, on the same road, was Gray's Station, erected about the year 1790, for the protection of the early settlers in that neighborhood.

There are quite a number of caves in Green County, but few, however, of great magnitude. The largest is at Greensburg, the mouth of which is within the limits of the town. It admits of access a distance of six hundred yards, has an average width of about ten feet, and an average height of about eight. In the early settlement of the town a human skeleton was found in a recess of the wall of this cave, about which an outer wall of stone had been built with human hands. The ceiling of the cave is of solid rock, and a portion of it sufficiently dry and smooth to admit the tracing of your name with the smoke of a candle. There are no stalagmites or formations of any kind in the cave from the drippings. Just at the point where access stops in the cave is a fine spring of the purest water, which is supposed to be the source of the town springs. Hence it has always been called the cave spring.

This spring is large, and would afford an abundant supply of water for a large city.

A few hundred yards below Greensburg the cliffs of Green River are very high. In a valley between the residence of Mr. A. B. Nibbs and the town three fine springs break out within a few yards of each other, and uniting their waters pour over the projecting cliff, about one hundred yards from their source, and fall a distance of about sixty feet, resembling a heavy rain. It is a place of great resort in the summer time for bathing, and is called the Drip.

Some two hundred yards below this point, nearly at the top of the cliff, and three or four hundred feet above the bed of the river, is a small cave, in the solid rock, from which issues a bold spring of as fine water as ever ran out of the earth. There is a winding path which leads to it from the top of the cliff, but a misstep might precipitate one to the river, a distance of three or four hundred feet, almost perpendicular. It is from this spring that the family of Mr. Nibbs is supplied with drinking water.

In the western portion of Green County are many large springs, breaking out of the cliffs of Brush Creek, and if that portion of country enjoyed the facilities which railroads afford it would doubtless become one of the greatest manufacturing portions of the State. For many years the Green Spring Furnace, for the manufacture of pig metal and castings, was propelled and carried on by a big spring issuing from a cliff of Brush Creek; so also was a spinning factory, from a similar stream, both of which have ceased operations.

There are, however, several mills for the manufacture of flour, &c., and two carding machines, with corn mills attached, propelled by springs of a similar character. In the south part of the county, on Little Barren River, is a large flouring mill and carding machine, propelled by a spring of the same kind.

About two and a half miles from Greensburg, on the Columbia road, is a very noted spring called the Blowing Spring, from the fact that there is a continual strong current of air issuing from the cave out of which the spring runs. There is a large steam flouring and saw mill within forty yards of the mouth of the cave, and a large distillery being constructed, for all which this spring will supply water in superabundance.

In Green County there are doubtless more springs of pure water than are to be found in any quarter of the globe in the same extent of country. There is scarcely a farm but what has numerous springs of the best and purest water; and there are numerous sulphur springs, also, in different parts of the county, and a sulphur well, in the heart of the town, of superior quality. The county of Green is not mountainous, but generally hilly or slightly undulating, and nearly all susceptible of cultivation. Considering its extent, it is one of the finest tobacco-growing counties in the State.

On the north bank of Green River, four miles east of Greensburg, is a noted well, which, for more than forty years, on account of its curiosity, has attracted a great number of visitors. The well was dug in 1828 by Mr. Samuel White, who soon afterward removed to Jackson County, Missouri, and died. It is usually known by the name of the Burning Well. When first bored, this well discharged oil and gas in great quantities, but no one in the vicinity knew what to make of it, or what to think of it; and the disagreeable smell which issued from it for a time annoyed the whole neighborhood. It was believed to be of no use, and it was concluded to fill up the well, which they succeeded in doing so far as to prevent the flow of oil, but did not diminish the extraordinary flow of gas.

Dr. Wright, a celebrated chemist and geologist, declares the gas to be produced from petroleum. The discharge of the gas is not confined to the well, but can be found at many points in the river bottom. The inflammatory quality of the gas was first discovered by accident. Mr. White, or some one of his family, had gone to the well one night with a lighted candle, when the gas took fire and suddenly blazed up as high as the tree tops. Every beholder was struck with wonder and astonishment.

The blaze gradually fell back, and they took hogsheads of water and set them around so as to have large quantities to throw on the fire at once; but with every effort made they were unable to extinguish it. It burned in a large volume, as large as a hogshead, the flames extending from three to six feet above the ground; and after burning for months showed no diminution in heat, force, or size, except when the earth cracked, and falling in, smothered out some of the blaze. It has an odor resembling rotten eggs, or coal oil, and is so strong that it can be smelled, at times, ten or twelve miles. When not burning, water makes its appearance within five or six feet of the top, the cavity being ten or twelve feet across.

The water is in a continual turmoil, as if a dozen kettles were boiling, as the gas rushes through it. The gas can also be seen bubbling up through the water at the mouth of the lagoon and the edge of the river, and if set on fire burns with a bright blaze until smothered out with mud and earth. During the great oil excitement a few years ago, notwithstanding the abounding indications of petroleum oil at this place, wells were bored to the depth of several hundred feet, but without reaching oil in any paying quantities.

Three miles west of Columbia, Adair County, on the road leading to Greensburg, near Russell Creek, in a great bend of the creek, are two large mounds, through one of which the road was cut many years ago, at which time human bones were found. These mounds are not so high now as to prevent cultivation, and fine corn is growing upon them the present year (1870).

On the farm of Wm. Todd, Esq., about two miles from Columbia, on the road leading to Milltown, and on the south side of Pettie's Fork, is quite a remarkable cave. A running stream of the purest water issues from the cave, supposed to originate at its extreme end, where there is a good spring, half a mile distant from the mouth. The stream from the spring is supposed to run under the floor or main bed of the cave, and does not make its appearance until it arrives within about thirty feet of its mouth.

In entering the cave, you go up this stream the distance above stated, when you ascend steps, or a stairway, about ten feet, when you enter the main channel. Proceeding through the cave, you arrive at a number of rooms, both on the right and left. At the distance of about one hundred feet from where you enter the main channel you arrive at a large room, situated on your right. It is of a circular form, and about twenty feet high to the ceiling. In this room is a pool of water, a mound of stone about three feet square, and near to this mound is a large round stone about the size of a tobacco hogshead. Its appearance in such a place is as unaccountable as those rocks of immense magnitude which are sometimes found on the prairies of Illinois, entirely detached, and miles distant from any quarry. Mineralogists denominate them "boulders," but they are usually called by the inhabitants "lost rocks." They are a species of granite, of roundish form, and lie upon the surface, or are but slightly embedded in the soil. By mounting either the mound or round rock in this room of the cave you can reach the ceiling, which seems lined with thin sheets of rock about the thickness of sole leather, and beating upon them with your knuckle makes a sound very much like that of a drum, though the cadence of the tone is different on different sheets. These sheets of thin rock have very much the appearance of curtains. Passing this room, at no great distance you arrive at another room, in which there is an excellent sulphur spring. Most of the rooms in the cave are very much beautified by the formations from the drippings, which are white, very numerous, and look like icicles. Whilst the army was encamped between the cave and Columbia during the late civil war, the cave was very much visited by both the officers and soldiers, who carried away a great quantity of these formations, detracting thereby from the beauty of some of the rooms of the cave.

In Greenup County there is one of the largest and most beautiful fortifications to be found in Kentucky. It embraces in its area about ten acres of ground. There are four entrances to the fort, which is square, one on each side; then there are two wings to the fort, one at the north entrance, and one at the south—the one on the north extending three-fourths of a mile to the Ohio River; the one on the south a half mile, extending to a tributary of the Ohio. The walls around are constructed of earth, twelve feet broad on the top, thirty at the bottom, and ten feet high. The entrances are twelve feet wide; the wings six feet high; the ground within a level plain, and covered with trees of the largest class, beech, sugar-tree, poplar, &c The walls are covered with trees also. It is certainly a great mystery who constructed this fortification, or when it was done. It was doubtless done a hundred years or more before any white man trod its soil.

There is standing on the bank of the river at Riverton, Greenup County, an old apple tree, which tradition says was planted by Daniel Boone, more than half a century ago, when he was on a visit to his brother, Jesse Boone, who had lived on the farm now known as Riverton. In the old graveyard, near by, the remains of the mother of Daniel Boone are believed to be buried, and also the grandfather of General J. B. Hood, the Confederate officer. In digging the foundation for a new store recently, at Mt. Olivet, the workmen discovered two posts about four feet in length, and about seven feet apart, standing perpendicularly in the ground, and five or six feet below the surface. At the foot of one of these posts was a large square rock, on which was inscribed, in plain, but roughly carved letters, D. B., 1775. The posts, on exposure to the air, at once crumbled to dust. It is probable these initials were made by Daniel Boone, as he spent a considerable portion of his time in that neighborhood years ago.

About four miles above Hawesville, the county seat of Hancock County, and three-fourths of a mile from the Ohio River, is a natural fortification, being a circular table of land, surrounded on all sides by a cliff from fifty to one hundred and twenty-five feet high, generally projecting at the top, and impossible of ascent except in one place. By a little work in digging it could be rendered impregnable.

About five miles above Hawesville, on the Ohio River, there is a mound, or burial place of the dead. It has never been explored. That portion around the fortification is covered with bones. An internal examination of the mound has never been made, but, externally, no other bones have been found except those of human beings. Issuing from a large rock, about one hundred yards from the fortification, is a spring which discharges bituminous matter, similar in smell to common tar. It is seven or eight miles from this to Tar Spring, in Breckinridge County.

In Hart County there are a number of caves, sinks, springs, &c. About three and a half miles from Munfordville, the county seat, there is a remarkable spring, resembling very much the ebb and flow of the ocean tides. A short distance below the mill-dam in the stream, at certain hours in the day, the water rises to the height of twelve or fifteen inches above its ordinary level, flows over the dam for some time, and then falls to its usual stand. The flood occurs about the hour of twelve o'clock each day, and is perfectly uniform in the time of its ebb and flow.

Six miles east of Munfordville, in the level barrens, is a hole in the earth, circular in form, sixty or seventy feet in diameter, of a funnel shape for twenty-five or thirty feet, when the diameter is diminished to ten or twelve feet. Below this point it has never been explored, and sinks to an unknown depth. On throwing a stone into this hole or sink, its ring as it strikes the sides gradually dies away without being heard to strike any bottom. It is supposed that visitors have thrown more than a hundred cart-loads of rock into it.

Six or seven miles northeast of Munfordville is what is called the Frenchman's Knob, which obtained its name from a Frenchman having been killed upon it. Near the top of this knob is a hole or sink, which has been explored two hundred and seventy-five feet by letting a man down by ropes. There are also a number of caves in the county from a half to two miles in length, but they excite little attention, from the fact that they are in the neighborhood of the Mammoth Cave. There is a large spring in the river bottom at Munfordville, which supplies the town with all the water used by it, which, so far as known, is bottomless. Several attempts, by the assistance of ropes, have been made to find bottom, but it was not discovered. When Green River is very high the spring is overflown.

In Larue County, about a mile above Hodgensville, the county seat, on the south side of Nolin Creek, is a knoll about thirty feet above the level of the creek, containing about two acres of ground, the top of which is level, and a comfortable house has been erected upon it. It was upon this knoll that Benjamin Lynn and his comrades encamped, who were perhaps the earliest pioneers of that immediate neighborhood. On a hunting excursion from that camp Lynn got lost, from which circumstance the creek took the name of No-lynn. The companions of Lynn went in search of him, and traveling a south course about fifteen miles found where he had encamped on a creek, and from that circumstance the creek was called Lynn Camp. This creek lies in what is now Hart County.

There was a fort erected by one Philip Phillips within about one-fourth of a mile of this knoll about the year 1780 or 1781, where the first settlement of the county was made. Phillips was a surveyor from the State of Pennsylvania.

On the Big South Fork of Nolin, about five miles from Hodgensville, there are several mounds, two of which being opened were found to contain human bones, beads of ivory or bone, and a quantity of sea shells. Near the mounds appear to be the remains of a fortification or town, and within the area has been found the image of a bird, cut out of a rock, with several holes drilled through it.

On a bluff of the Rolling Fork is to be seen a stone wall, three or four feet high, extending across the level land from cliff to cliff, and at the bend of the creek must have constituted an impregnable fortress. The cliff is about two hundred feet high, and so precipitous that an invading army could not scale it if there was any show of resistance.

In Laurel County there are the remains of some old Indian towns, as also vessels that are supposed to have been used for cooking purposes. Other implements have also been found. A quantity of iron ore has been discovered, and there are some appearances of lead. The water power of the county is unsurpassed by almost any county in the State. Boone's old trace ran through this county, and passed immediately over the spot where the court-house now stands. There are several fine chalybeate springs in the county, and coal in great abundance.

In Lewis County there is a celebrated watering-place called Esculapia, or Sulphur Springs, affording comfortable accommodations for two hundred persons or more. There are two springs, one chalybeate, the other white sulphur, and the waters are said to be superior to those of a similar kind in Virginia.

Near Vanceburg is a large quarry of slatestone; also a quarry of limestone, the stone of the latter containing some fifty or sixty per cent of magnesia. A few miles above Vanceburg great quantities of sandstone and alum-rock are found; and near by is a large copperas bed, from which the people of the vicinity supply themselves. Within a mile is a large blue clay bank, suitable for stoneware, &c.

In the locality of the Knob Licks, Lincoln County, is a curiosity of some note. There are several detached hills, some of them having large hollows, owing to the decomposition of the slate formation. These hills are destitute of vegetation. The greatest height of these knobs is two hundred feet, whilst the base of some are one hundred and fifty yards in diameter.

In Meade County are several groves and caves in which human bones have been found. In a cave near Brandenburg, the county-seat, the skull of a grown person was found. There are quite a number of knobs in this county of considerable notoriety, and we mention Indian Hill, on Otter Creek, Jennie's Knob, Bee Knob, Buck Grove, Jackey's Grove, Hill Grove, and Hog Back Grove. These places lie almost in a range, and extend down the river from the mouth of Salt River to the mouth of Sinking Creek, a distance of forty miles by land and eighty miles by the river.

Where Hardin, Breckinridge, and Meade counties corner is a village containing thirty or forty families, called Big Spring, which derives its name from a big spring that bursts forth near the center of the village. It flows for two or three hundred yards in a stream of sufficient size to turn a mill, when it sinks beneath the surface and disappears altogether. This village incorporates within its bounds a portion of the three counties above named.

The Harrodsburg Springs, of Mercer County, was formerly

the most fashionable watering-place in the State of Kentucky, and was a delightful summer resort, not only for health, but for pleasure also. Dr. Christopher Graham was its last owner as a watering-place, and spared neither pains nor expense in improving it. Some fifteen or twenty years ago Dr. Graham sold the place to the General Government as a residence or hospital for invalid soldiers, since which time it has not been resorted to as a watering-place.

The scenery of the Kentucky and Dix rivers is among the grandest and most picturesque in the United States for imposing effects. Towering cliffs, rising many hundred feet above the shore, with perpendicular walls, overpower the beholder with the majesty of nature's works.

There were two ancient towns or fortifications in Mercer County, both situated on Salt River, one about four miles above Harrodsburg. It contains a mound some twelve feet high, filled with human bones and crockery-ware, and is traversed with ditches. The other ruins are about one and a half miles above. There is no mound at this place; only the elevations of earth as dug out of the ditches. The form of each place is quadrangular.

Near Salt River, muscle-shells, conglomerated into large lumps of rock, exist. They are generally found about two feet below the surface. One of these was found on the farm where General Robert B. McAfee lived and died.

Colonel Daniel Boone spent the winter of 1769–70 in a cave on the waters of Shawnee, in Mercer County. A tree marked with his name stood near the head of the cave.

As celebrated a place as almost any other in the State is the Blue Lick Springs, in Nicholas County. It was here, in the early settlement of Kentucky, that one of the most bloody battles occurred that was ever fought with the Indians, which at the time shrouded Kentucky in mourning on account of the many brave and distinguished citizens who fell. The fatal battle was fought on the 18th of August, 1782. It was at this point in early times that a supply of salt was procured for the people, though at great labor and expense. It has now become one of the favorite and most fashionable resorts as a watering-place in all the west. It is situated on Licking River, about two hundred yards from the banks of the stream. The main building is six hundred and seventy feet in length, and three stories high, surrounded by galleries eighteen hundred feet in extent. The Blue Lick water has become a valuable article of commerce, and thousands of barrels are exported annually to foreign countries. It was in a fight near this place that Colonel Boone was a second time taken prisoner by the Indians.

In Owen County are some remarkable places. Among them the Jump Off, a perpendicular precipice on the Kentucky River, one hundred feet high or more, with a hollow passing through its center fully wide enough for a wagon road. The Point of Rocks on Cedar Creek is a beautiful and romantic spot, where a big rock, seventy-five feet high, overhangs a place in the creek called Deep Hole, to which no bottom has ever been found, and which abounds in fish of the finest kind. Pond Branch flows out of a valley supposed once to have been the bed of the Kentucky River. It is about one and a half miles from Lock and Dam No. 3. The water of the stream empties itself into the river by two outlets, forming a mountain island, two and a half miles long, and one and a half wide in its broadest part.

In Pendleton County the remains of an ancient fortification are yet visible near the town of Falmouth, midway between the two rivers, near the junction, and extending up both streams. It is a regular circle in form, with four entrances or openings, opposite each other, and corresponding with the points of the compass. Trees, from two and a half to three feet in diameter, were standing on the embankment years ago, which proves conclusively that the fortification is very ancient. Every height and hill surrounding the junction of the rivers for miles around are crowded with Indian graves, or small mounds, evidencing clearly that a bloody warfare once prevailed here between a people occupying the ground and an invading enemy.

In Rockcastle County are numerous banks of bituminous coal, which have never been opened to any extent, on account of obstructed navigation in Rockcastle River. In the bed of the river are very large rocks, which are supposed to have broken loose from the cliffs at some period and tumbled into the bed of the river, produced, perhaps, by some powerful concussion of the earth. Rockcastle River is about seventy-five miles long from its source to its mouth, and is lined all along with these banks of bituminous coal. There are numerous saltpetre caves among the hills of Rockcastle, from which great quantities of powder were manufactured during the war of 1812. Big Cave, eight miles from Mt. Vernon, extending through a spur of the mountains called Big Hill, is about six hundred yards in length. The arch is from ten to twenty feet high. Large rooms branch off several hundred yards in length, and the end of one has not been reached. Some of the rooms cover an area of several acres. There is a bold, running stream of water in the cave. Carts and wagons pass through from one side of the mountain to the other without difficulty. The way is level and straight, and oxen are taught to pass through in perfect darkness, without a driver. There are several mineral springs in the county. Boone's old trace to Boonesborough led through this county.

Union County abounds in mineral springs. A white sulphur spring, five miles from Morganfield, has been well-improved, and is quite a popular watering-place. The other springs of most notoriety are chalybeate, and the water is of fine quality. About eight miles from Morganfield is a large flat rock, with a number of deeply indented impressions of the naked foot of human beings, of all sizes; also plain footprints of the dog. About three miles from Caseyville is what is called the Anvil Rock, which closely resembles the blacksmith's anvil. It is about fifty feet high, twenty in width, and two feet thick, with a spur like the horn of an anvil. It is a solitary rock, standing upon level bottom-land. How it was placed there, in an erect position, is a wonderful mystery. There is also a hill in the center of an extended river-bottom three-fourths of a mile long, and half a mile wide, and eighty or one hundred feet in height. There is also a very extensive cave in this county which has only been partially explored, in which a number of human bones have been found. On Highland Creek there is a tar or oil spring, from which tar, or oil, flows in considerable quantities.

The greatest curiosity of Woodford County is a large cave spring. It is situated on the southern border of the town of Versailles, the county-seat, and about one hundred yards from the court-house. The spring, which is of clear, crystal water, issues from an abrupt break, on gradually descending ground, and flows off in a stream sufficiently large to afford water for a grist-mill. This cave runs under the town; and immediately over the cave, in front of the court-house, a public well has been dug, which affords, at all seasons, an inexhaustible supply of water.

In Warren County caves are very numerous. There is one about six miles northeast of Bowlinggreen, with a perpendicular descent of about thirty or forty feet. At the bottom are vast quantities of human bones. About three miles south of Bowlinggreen, on the Nashville turnpike, in level barrens, is the Cave Mill. A creek breaks up from the ground, runs about two hundred yards, and disappears in a cave, and after a course under ground of one and a half miles, again appears and runs into Barren River. Immediately under the roof of the cave is a grist-mill and carding-machine, with no covering but the arch of the rock above. Directly over the mill the turnpike runs.

There are a great number of mounds in this county, some of them quite large, all containing human bones. In one of them was found a smooth, round, well-polished flint, weighing the fourth of a pound, as if intended, apparently, for a four ounce weight. Near Bowlinggreen, on the north bank of the river, are a great many ancient graves, some of them with a row of stones, set on edge, around them. These graves, with a large mound on which tall trees are growing, are included within the remains of an old earth-built fort. Some ancient relics were found here in 1838, one of them in the shape of a bowl, composed of earth and pounded shells. It seems to have been burnt or dried in the sun, and is of a dark color.

Two others found were composed of the same materials, but of lighter color, and shaped like a flat-bottomed candlestick.

Situated on a bluff, on the south side of Green River, about twelve miles from Bowlinggreen, is an old fort, inaccessible except at one corner. The hill is level on the top, with overhanging cliffs some thirty feet high. Near the center of the hill is situated the old fort, which seems to have been erected with stone and earth. The area of the fort is about seven acres. From the fort, for the distance of more than a mile, extends a line of mounds, diminishing in size as they recede from the fort. There are other ancient works in this county which have not been examined.

Eight miles east of Bowlinggreen, in the open barrens, is a sink, fifty yards wide, and one hundred yards in length. It is called Wolf Sink, from the circumstance of a wolf having gone into it to feed upon a horse which had fallen in, and there died, being unable to get out. It is about one hundred and fifty feet deep, with large trees growing in it.

McFadden's Old Station is four miles above Bowlinggreen, on Barren River. On the north side of the river, three miles from Bowlinggreen, many inscriptions are to be found upon the beech trees, indicating that a camp had been there for some ten or twelve days; the dates under the names extending from the 13th to the 23d of June, 1775. It is conjectured by some to be the camp of the Long Hunters. The highest of the names on one tree was nine feet, and the lowest four feet from the ground, there being thirteen names, as follows: J. Newell, E. Bulger, J. Hite, V. Harman, J. Jackman, W. Buchanan, A. Bowman, J. Drake, O. Nall, H. Skaggs, J. Bowman, Thomas Slaughter, J. Todd. There are a number of names on other trees close by, some bearing the dates June 14th, June 15th, June 17th, and others June 23d. On another tree, about fifty yards off, appear two names, one bearing the date of 1779, the other 1796.

One of the most remarkable objects in Whitley County is the Falls of Cumberland River, about fourteen miles from Williamsburg, the county-seat. The river here is precipitated over a fall of sixty-three feet perpendicular. The roar of the falling waters, on a clear morning, may be heard many miles. Behind the sheet of water is a cave in the surface of the rock, and a person can go almost across the river by this passage. It is in the shape of an arch, formed by the rock on one side and by the falling waters on the other. The scenery in the neighborhood is wonderfully romantic. The hills and mountains rise upon each other like clouds upon the horizon.

Before the settlement of Kentucky by the whites, Drennon's Lick, in Henry County, was a valuable hunting-ground for the Indians. Deer and other game resorted to this Lick in great numbers. For many years, during the watering season, it has been much resorted to by invalids and seekers of pleasure. It is a medicinal spring of black and salt sulphur.

About five miles from Madisonville, in the county of Hopkins, on a high and rocky hill, are the remains of an ancient fortification. An area of about ten acres of ground is walled with stone. By whom it was built, or when, is unknown to any one at this day.

In Kenton County, on a farm owned by Mr. Ellison Williams, a companion of Daniel Boone, is a well formerly known and called the Hygeian well, once kept as a watering-place, but never a place of great resort. A weak sulphur spring, situated four miles from Covington, called the Lettonian Spring, has become a place of considerable resort, especially to the citizens of Covington.

Mr. M. Swing, of Covington, Kentucky, one of the oldest residents, has in his possession a snuff-box carved from the horn of an ox, and bearing the date of 1782. It was made by Colonel William Prichard, a young hunter in the dark and bloody days of Kentucky, and in one of the principal forts erected by Daniel Boone. The fort was situated at the mouth of the Licking River, opposite Cincinnati, where Covington now stands, which was then a dreary wilderness. Young Prichard, with a few soldiers and hunters, was at the time besieged in the fort by the Indians, and to while away the time during the siege, when not on duty, he carved this box, covering it with devices and emblems of the time. On the bottom is the date 1782. On each of the sides are Masonic emblems—the All-seeing eye, &c., the coat-of-arms of England, and other devices. On the lid is a representation of a Colonial hunter, with knee-breeches, queue, &c., taking aim with an old flint-lock gun at a startled deer, while in the distance are lying around specimens of the hunter's skill. The box was once captured by a noted Indian chief, and was regarded as a great curiosity by the Indians. It was afterward found on his dead body by the hunter who killed him. It is kept as an heirloom, having already descended through five generations, and is esteemed by the present possessor of tenfold more value than its weight in gold.

Three miles from the town of Barboursville, on the north bank of Cumberland River, are the remains of an ancient fortress, surrounded by a ditch enclosing about four acres of ground.

The Knob Licks, of Lincoln County, are numbered among the curiosities of Kentucky. The greatest height of these knobs is about two hundred feet, and the base of the highest some four hundred feet in diameter. These knobs are intersected with ravines, and destitute of vegetation.

In McCracken County silver ore in small quantities is said to have been found, and it is believed that lead ore abounds in this county.

At Mount Sterling, Montgomery County, was situated a considerable mound, from which the place derives its name. At the first settlement of this place there were trees growing on this mound as large as any in the surrounding forest. The mound was dug down some twenty-five years ago or more, and, interspersed with the human bones which were dug up, were found also many curious things, among which were two breast-plates, one of copper, and one of queensware, each about the size of a man's hand; large beads were found also, some of copper and others of ivory; also copper bracelets.

About five miles from Mount Sterling is another mound, near to what appears to have been an ancient intrenchment of square form. On the eastern side appears to have been a gateway, some twenty feet in width, and leading to a spring some thirty yards off. When the county was first settled by the whites trees were growing in the intrenchment and on the banks as large as any in the forest which surrounded it.

In Garrard County, some twelve miles from the county-seat, on Paint Lick Creek, an area of ground of about ten acres is deeply indented with marks resembling the tracks of wagon wheels. They are yet plainly visible, and have been so ever since the settlement of the country by the whites, a period of more than eighty years. The place bears the name of White Lick.

In Nelson County there is stated to be a natural tunnel, of circular form, several feet in diameter. It begins at the eastern and terminates at the western declivity of the eminence on which the town of Bardstown, the county-seat, is situated.

CHAPTER VII.

Centennial Celebration at Camp Knox; Great Crowd in Attendance; Bountiful Repast; Speaking on the Occasion—Long Hunters, Visit of—Colonel James Knox—Doctor Walker—Christopher Gist—George Croughan—Colonel James Smith—John Findley—General George Washington visits Kentucky; Account of same—Boone and Knox—James Stewart—Green River—Friendship of an Indian—Mount Gilead—Skin-house Branch—Return of Long Hunters—Immense Immigration—Surveyors in the Country—Earliest Settlers in Green, Names of—Cane Creek Fort—Indian Annoyances—Colonel William Whitley—Nickajack Towns; their Capture—Troubles ended in Southern Kentucky—Long Hunters revisit Kentucky—Encampment near Bowlinggreen—Names Cut upon Beech Trees—William Skaggs, Incidents of; his Death.

On the 4th day of July, 1870, a centennial celebration took place at Camp Knox, in Green County, of the first settlement of a *camp* ever established by the white man in all Southern Kentucky. A vast crowd of people had assembled on the occasion, young and old, male and female. The Masonic fraternity also turned out in great numbers, some five or six lodges of the county of Green and adjoining counties being represented, and leading in the grand procession. A bountiful repast had been provided for the assembled crowd, tastily spread upon long tables quadrangularly arranged, of which all partook to their heart's content when the speaking was concluded.

The writer on that occasion, by the particular request of the committee of invitation, had the honor of being one of the speakers, and as the subject of his remarks furnished some incidents intimately connected with the history of Kentucky. We give them here, omitting the portion relating to the day upon which the celebration took place, and so memorable in the history of our nation as a free and independent people.

He said: "The next incident of history which we propose to speak of as being worthy of commemoration, is the visit and encampment of a party called the Long Hunters, headed by Colonel James Knox, who, one hundred years ago, here, on this branch, which for sometimes afterward was known and called by the name of Skin-house Branch, and on this very ground where we now all stand in the enjoyment of such peace and great hilarity, pitched their tents. I have made considerable research of late into the history of the first settlement of Kentucky, but have nowhere been able to find any very detailed account of the career of Colonel James Knox in Kentucky.

"We know that Dr. Walker visited the northeastern portion of Kentucky as early as 1750; and that Christopher Gist was sent out by what was called the Ohio Company on an exploring expedition in the year 1751, and descended the Ohio River to the Falls, where Louisville is now situated. In 1765 Colonel George Croughan, a British officer, descended the Ohio from Fort Pitt to a point below the Wabash, where he was encountered and taken prisoner by the Indians. In 1766 Colonel James Smith visited Kentucky; and in 1767 it was visited by John Findley, on a trading expedition. All these visits were obscure, and of but little importance. Somewhere between 1767 and 1770 General George Washington made a visit to Kentucky on a surveying expedition, and made surveys in what are now Greenup and Lawrence counties for one John Fry. The patent for these lands was issued by the Crown of Great Britain in 1772. Upon the beginning corner of one of those surveys General Washington cut the initials of his own name. One of the surveys was on Big Sandy River, and the other on Little Sandy. We have no very satisfactory account of this visit. We learn, however, from his will, made in the year 1790, that he owned five thousand acres of land in Kentucky, on Rough Creek, and that he disposed of the same by the will alluded to, valuing said lands at $10,000, or $2 per acre, and regarded it as being more valuable on account of the abundance of iron ore upon it. But the visits of Colonel Daniel Boone's party in 1769, and of Colonel

James Knox in 1770, were the first that were at all worthy of note or attention. Boone remained in the country about two years, traveling the northern and middle regions, and giving them considerable attention. The party under Knox came a year later, but remained two years also. Boone's party was frequently harrassed by the Indians, and Boone himself taken prisoner; but he soon afterward made his escape and returned to his company, narrowly escaping with his life. One of his companions, by the name of James Stewart, was killed in a skirmish with the Indians. Knox's party, however, sustained no loss of which we have any account. It consisted of about forty stout hunters, from New River, Holston, and Clinch River, who united for an expedition west of the Cumberland Mountains. Nine of the company, led by Knox, reached the country south of the Kentucky River, and became acquainted with Green River and the lower part of the Cumberland, and from the time they were absent they obtained the name of Long Hunters. We learn from some of the descendants of the Long Hunters that when they reached this section the expedition numbered twenty-two men, with four horses, which carried their baggage and supplies. After crossing the Cumberland Mountains they moved in a southern direction until they came to Dix River. Proceeding on their journey, one or two of the hunters being in advance of the rest, met suddenly and unexpectedly in the forest a solitary Indian, who was at once recognized, they having seen him before at the lead mines on the Holston. The Indian was pleased at finding himself recognized, became very familiar, and gave the hunters, it is said, such directions as enabled them to find what is now called Green River. He told them that after crossing a certain number of ridges and streams of water, they would come to a river running west; crossing this river, and keeping it on their right, they would come to a valley called the Beech Woods, where they would find game in great abundance. They pursued the directions given by the Indian, and found all that he had told them to be true. Arriving in the valley of Beech Woods, they at once established the camp, on the very spot where the Christian Church at Mt. Gilead

10

now stands, near the branch now known as Skin-house Branch. The camp established here was the headquarters of the company, and from which frequent hunting excursions were made. Returning to camp, they would deposit in a house, or pen, they had built at this place, the skins of the animals they had killed, such as buffalo, elk, bear, deer, &c., until the house was literally filled. About this time the incursions of the Indians made it dangerous for them to remain longer; they consequently left. Upon their return to the place, three or four years afterward, they found that the skins had all molded and rotted, they having become exposed to the weather by the twisting and curling of the bark with which the house had been covered. Hence the name given to the branch, Skinhouse, which ripples by it.

"Upon the return of Knox to the western settlements of Virginia, he was enabled to give so satisfactory an account of the country he had so thoroughly explored, its salubriousness, inexhaustible fertility, &c., that in a short time emigration began to pour in; and in less than two years after his return to Virginia a number of surveyors were in the country, some of them locating the bounty lands which had been given to the Virginia troops by the British Crown for services rendered in the war with the French. Some of the earliest settlers of Green and Adair counties were located in this valley, all men of the highest character. To name such as are now remembered were Major James Blain, Captain George Spears, Captain William McKnabb, Colonel Jesse Gray, Archibald Skaggs, James Harris, Samuel Workman, John Moore, Colonel Robert Haskins, Colonel Daniel Trabue, Stephen Trabue, Henry Hatcher, Joshua Atkinson, Joseph Burton, Robert Ball, Mrs. Elizabeth Trabue and daughters, Rev. Elijah Summers, William and Edmund Willis, Jeremiah Ingram, Absalom Atkinson, John, William, and Robert Caldwell, William and John Hancock, Benjamin Brewster, James Edrington, John Cabaniss, and others. For the protection of the families of this valley Jesse Gray and others of the pioneers established a fort on Cane Creek, about a mile and a half from this place, about two hundred yards from the creek, near an excellent spring, on the land now owned by Alfred Anderson, and about two hundred yards from where the Greensburg and Columbia road crosses said creek. This fort was called Gray's Station, and was of great advantage to the settlers, who were enabled, with less fear of molestation by the Indians, to clear their lands, raise their corn and other supplies for the emigrants who were now continually coming in.

"To Colonel James Knox, and the Long Hunters under his command; to Colonel Jesse Gray, &c., are the people of Kentucky indebted in no small degree for the happiness and prosperity which we this day enjoy.

"In the years 1792, 1793, and 1794 the Indians south of the Tennessee River gave great annoyance, and made frequent inroads upon the southern and southwestern portions of Kentucky, even as high up in the State as the Crab Orchard, Logan's, and McKinney's stations. To put an end to this, Colonel William Whitley conducted an expedition against their towns, the principal of which was called Nickajack. In making this expedition he passed by the way of Gray's Station, and was joined by Gray and others. Gray acted as a spy in the expedition. In Tennessee Whitley was joined by Major Orr, and the two corps, amounting to six or seven hundred men, rendezvoused at Nashville. The Indians were taken greatly by surprise, and in the battle which ensued were defeated with great loss of life.

"This expedition ended the troubles in Southern Kentucky with the Indians; and here we are to-day, 'under our own vine and fig tree, allowed to worship the God and father of our spirits, according to the dictates of our own consciences, and no one to molest us or make us afraid.' In the midst of the very forest where the cruel and savage Indian roamed and wild beasts abounded, and on the very spot where Colonel Knox established his camp a hundred years ago, two large churches, one of brick and the other of wood, lift their spires, and from their altars on every Sabbath day the holy incense of prayer ascends to heaven.

"On the very spot where a hundred years ago the hunters of Camp Knox had naught on earth to eat for the sustenance of life but wild meat, jerked or roasted before the fire on a forked stick, and that perhaps without salt, the thousands here assembled are enjoying in superabundance, and to their hearts' content, food and viands which the appetite of even the most fastidious would crave. It is to the men of a hundred years ago that we are all indebted for the liberty, the prosperity, and happiness which we now enjoy in so pre-eminent a degree.

"The Long Hunters were again in Kentucky in the year 1775, and there are strong indications that they encamped on Barren River, about three miles from Bowlinggreen. On the north side of the river, on a conspicuous beech tree, are engraved the names of thirteen persons, handsomely cut in the bark. The names stand in the following order, beginning with the highest: J. Neaville, E. Bulger, J. Hite, V. Harman, J. Jackman, A. Bowman, J. Drake, N. Nall, H. Skaggs, J. Bowman, Thos. Slaughter, J. Todd. The date is thus given: '1775, June the 13th.' On another tree near by is the name of Wm. Buchanan, June 14th, 1775; and on the opposite side of the same tree, the name of J. Todd, June 17th, 1775. There is also another tree near by with the names of J. Drake and Isaac Hite, each with the date June 15th, 1775, and above the names, the date June 23d, 1775. These dates, from the 13th to the 23d, prove that the party encamped at that place at least ten days.

"Some of the descendants of Henry Skaggs, one of the Long Hunters, still reside in Green County. William Skaggs, a near relative of Henry, was personally well-known to your speaker, and has related many incidents to him connected with the early settlement of Green County, one of which I will relate.

"He and his companions, at a very early period, occupied a fort near Little Barren River, about ten miles from where Greensburg now stands. Being scarce of food on one occasion he started out alone to hunt for game, and had not proceeded far before he heard, as he thought, the yelping of a turkey. He neared the place from whence the sound came, and suddenly discovered an Indian, with gun in hand, standing behind a fallen-down tree. He was himself discovered by the Indian about the same time. Skaggs immediately sprang behind a tree, the Indian at the same time lying down behind the fallen tree. They remained in their respective situations for several hours, each afraid to leave for fear of being shot by the other. Skaggs several times observed the Indian raise himself high enough to look toward him from behind the log, and leveling his gun in that direction determined to shoot at him the next time he raised his head above the log. An opportunity soon occurred, when Skaggs fired, shooting the Indian in the forehead, and killing him. He was afraid to approach the place, however, for a considerable time, and not until he felt fully assured he had killed the Indian. Finally, approaching the place and finding the Indian dead, he dragged him to a tree close by, and leaned him in a sitting posture against it. He was never at the place afterwards; and, said the old man, in relating the affair to me, 'his bones may be there yet for ought I know.'

"William Skaggs died on Big Brush Creek, in Green County, in August, 1852, at a very advanced age, not far from ninety; and has at this day in Green County a greater number of descendants than any other man that now lives or ever lived in the county."

CHAPTER VIII.

Counties of Kentucky; When Formed; County-seats—Population and Increase—First Constitution of Kentucky—Where Convention was Held—Names of the Members and Counties Represented—Frankfort the Seat of Government—Convention met in 1799 to form New, or Second Constitution—Members Composing that Body and Counties Represented—Third Constitution Ratified 11th of June, 1850—Counties Represented—The Congress of 1776, which Declared Independence—Its Author—Declaration—States Represented and Names of Members—Confederation of the Thirteen Original States; Ratification of—States Represented and Names of Members—Names of Presidents and Vice Presidents of United States—Date of Adoption of United States Constitution—When Ratified by the Several States—Electors of Presidents, &c., of United States in Kentucky from her Admission—Their Names and who they Voted for—Population of Kentucky, with Increased per cent. from 1820 to 1870—Speakers of House of Representatives of United States from Kentucky—Presidents of the Senate—Chaplains of United States Senate and House of Representatives.

We give in tabular form the present counties of Kentucky, and when formed, with the name of county-seats, population in 1860 and 1870, and increase of population:

COUNTIES.	When Formed...	COUNTY-SEATS.	Population. 1860.	Population. 1870.	Increase..
Adair	1801	Columbia	9,509	11,107	1,598
Allen	1815	Scottsville	9,187	10,246	1,059
Anderson	1827	Lawrenceburg	7,404	5,491	....
Ballard	1842	Blandville	8,692	12,577	3,885
Barren	1798	Glasgow	16,665	17,783	1,118
Bath	1811	Owingsville	12,113	8,291	....
Boone	1798	Burlington	11,196	10,696	....
Bourbon	1785	Paris	14,860	14,862	2
Boyd		Cattlettsburg	6,044	....	....
Boyle	1841	Danville	9,304	9,516	212
Bracken	1796	Brooksville	11,021	11,509	488
Breathitt	1888	Jackson	4,980	7,445	2,465
Breckinridge	1799	Hardinsburg	13,236	13,418	182

HISTORY OF KENTUCKY.

COUNTIES.	When Formed.	COUNTY-SEATS.	Population. 1860.	Population. 1870.	Increase.
Bullitt	1796	Shepherdsville	7,289	7,282	....
Butler	1810	Morgantown	7,927	9,452	1,525
Caldwell	1809	Princeton	9,318	10,829	1,511
Calloway	1821	Murray	9,915	....	....
Campbell	1794	Alexandria	20,909	24,000	23,091
Carroll	1837	Carrollton	6,579	6,189	....
Carter	1837	Grayson	8,516	7,484	....
Casey	1806	Liberty	6,406	8,890	2,484
Christian	1796	Hopkinsville	21,627	24,000	2,373
Clarke	1792	Winchester	11,484	10,882	....
Clay	1806	Manchester	6,652	....	....
Clinton	1835	Albany	5,781	6,536	755
Crittenden	1841	Marion	8,996	9,386	390
Cumberland	1798	Burksville	7,340	7,691	351
Daviess	1815	Owensboro	15,519	20,564	5,045
Edmonson	1825	Brownsville	4,665	6,460	....
Elliott	1869	Martinsburg	....	4,333	....
Estill	1808	Irvine	6,886	9,201	2,315
Fayette	1780	Lexington	22,599	26,696	4,097
Fleming	1798	Flemingsburg	12,489	12,992	503
Floyd	1799	Prestonsburg	6,388	7,877	1,489
Franklin	1794	Frankfort	12,694	15,301	2,707
Fulton	1845	Hickman	5,317	6,165	848
Gallatin	1798	Warsaw	5,056	5,075	19
Garrard	1793	Lancaster	10,581	10,378	....
Grant	1820	Williamstown	8,356	9,529	1,173
Graves	1823	Mayfield	16,233	19,003	2,770
Grayson	1810	Litchfield	7,982	11,577	3,595
Green	1792	Greensburg	8,806	9,380	574
Greenup	1803	Greenupsburg	8,760	11,463	3,703
Hancock	1829	Hawesville	6,218	6,591	373
Hardin	1792	Elizabethtown	15,189	15,706	517
Harlan	1819	Mt. Pleasant	5,494	4,436	....
Harrison	1793	Cynthiana	13,779	12,886	....
Hart	1819	Munfordville	10,348	13,690	3,342
Henderson	1798	Henderson	14,262	18,545	3,283
Henry	1798	Newcastle	11,949	11,074	....
Hickman	1821	Clinton	7,008	8,453	1,445
Hopkins	1806	Madisonville	11,875	13,828	1,953
Jackson	......	Cloverbottom	3,087	4,547	1,460
Jefferson	1780	Louisville	89,404	118,935	29,531
Jessamine	1798	Nicholasville	9,465	8,640	....
Johnson	1843	Paintville	5,306	7,509	2,203
Josh. Bell	1867	Cumberland Ford	....	3,731	....
Kenton	1839	Covington	25,467	37,135	12,668
Knox	1799	Barbourville	7,707	8,297	590
Larue	1843	Hodgensville	6,891	8,275	1,384
Laurel	1825	London	5,488	5,919	431
Lawrence	1821	Louisa	7,601	8,497	896
Letcher	1842	Brashersville	3,904	5,608	1,704
Lee	1870	Proctor	....	3,055	....
Lewis	1806	Clarksburg	8,361	....	....
Lincoln	1780	Stanford	10,647	10,951	304

COUNTIES.	When Formed.	COUNTY-SEATS.	Population. 1860.	Population. 1870.	Increase.
Livingston	1798	Smithland	7,213	8,000	5,787
Logan	1792	Russellville	19,021	20,230	1,209
Lyon		Eddyville	5,307	6,281	974
Martin	1870	Warfield	....	....	....
McCracken	1824	Paducah	10,360	13,989	3,629
Madison	1785	Richmond	17,207	19,560	2,353
Magoffin		Salliersburg	3,485	4,685	1,200
Marion	1834	Lebanon	12,593	13,634	1,041
Marshall	1841	Benton	6,982	9,458	2,476
Mason	1789	Maysville	18,222	18,245	23
McLean		Calhoun	6,144	7,610	1,466
Meade	1823	Brandenburg	8,898	6,488	....
Mercer	1785	Harrodsburg	13,701	13,194	....
Menifee	1869		....	3,742	....
Metcalfe		Edmunton	6,745	7,935	1,190
Monroe	1820	Tompkinsville	8,551	9,231	680
Montgomery	1796	Mount Sterling	7,859	7,557	....
Morgan	1822	West Liberty	9,287	5,976	....
Muhlenburg	1798	Greenville	10,725	12,638	1,913
Nelson	1781	Bardstown	15,799	14,817	....
Nicholas	1799	Carlisle	11,630	9,130	....
Ohio	1798	Hartford	12,209	15,682	3,473
Oldham	1823	Lagrange	7,283	9,027	1,744
Owen	1819	Owenton	12,719	14,309	1,590
Owsley	1842	Booneville	5,335	3,894	....
Pendleton	1798	Falmouth	10,443	14,024	3,581
Perry	1820	Hazard	3,950	4,277	327
Pike	1821	Pikeville	7,384	9,562	2,178
Powell	1851	Stanton	2,257	2,599	342
Pulaski	1798	Somerset	17,201	17,630	429
Rockcastle	1810	Mount Vernon	5,343	7,147	1,804
Robertson		Mount Olivet	....	5,411	....
Rowan		Morehead	2,282	3,471	1,199
Russell	1825	Jamestown	6,024	5,811	....
Scott	1792	Georgetown	14,417	11,616	....
Shelby	1792	Shelbyville	16,433	15,733	....
Simpson	1819	Franklin	8,146	9,253	1,107
Spencer	1824	Taylorsville	6,188	5,957	....
Taylor	1848	Campbellsville	7,481	8,057	576
Todd	1819	Elkton	11,575	12,611	1,036
Trigg	1820	Cadiz	11,051	13,686	2,635
Trimble	1836	Bedford	5,880	5,478	....
Union	1811	Morganfield	12,791	13,639	848
Warren	1796	Bowlinggreen	17,320	....	....
Washington	1792	Springfield	11,575	12,468	....
Wayne	1800	Monticello	10,259	10,600	341
Webster		Dixon	7,533	10,953	3,320
Whitley	1818	Williamsburg	7,762	8,638	876
Wolfe		Hazelgreen	....	3,640	....
Woodford	1788	Versailles	11,219	8,240	....

Showing an increase in ten years of 277,011.

The first Constitution of Kentucky was formed, as has before been stated, in the year 1792. At that time there were only nine counties in the State. The Convention was held at Danville, Mercer County, where all previous conventions of importance had been held. Among the members of that Convention, even at so early a date, were some of the most talented men in the United States. The following are the names of those who composed the Convention and the counties they represented, some forty-five in all:

County of Fayette—Hubbard Taylor, Thomas Lewis, George S. Smith, Robert Fryer, and James Crawford.

County of Jefferson—Richard Taylor, John Campbell, Alexander S. Bullitt, Benjamin Sebastian, and Robert Breckinridge.

County of Bourbon—John Edwards, James Garrard, James Smith, John McKenny, and Benjamin Harrison.

County of Nelson—William Keen, Matthew Walton, Cuthbert Harrison, Joseph Hobbs.

County of Madison—Charles Kavendor, Higgerson Grubbs, Thomas Clay, Thomas Kenedy, Joseph Kenedy.

County of Mercer—Samuel Taylor, Jacob Froman, George Nicholas, David Rice, and Samuel McDowell.

County of Lincoln—Benjamin Logan, John Bailey, Isaac Shelby, Benedict Sayre, and William Montgomery.

County of Woodford—John Watkins, Richard Young, William Steele, Caleb Wallace, and Robert Johnston.

County of Mason—George Lewis, Miles W. Conway, Thomas Waring, Robert Rankin, John Wilson.

Samuel McDowell, of Mercer County, was President of the Convention, and Thomas Todd, Clerk.

Frankfort, the county-seat of Franklin County, having been established as the seat of government of Kentucky, the second Convention to frame a new Constitution, or rather to remodel the first, was held at that place August 17, 1799. There were at that time in the State of Kentucky twenty-five counties, sixteen new counties having been formed since the adoption of the first Constitution. The members who composed this Convention were not less talented than those of the former.

Alexander Bullitt, of Jefferson County, was chosen President.

The members were as follows, viz:

From Bourbon County—John Allen, Charles Smith, Robert Wilmot, James Duncan, William Griffith, Nathaniel Rogers.

Bracken—Phillip Buckner.

Campbell—Thomas Sanford.

Clarke—Robert Clarke, R. Hickman, William Sudduth.

Christian—Young Edwing.

Fayette—John Breckinridge, John McDowell, John Bell, H. Harrison, B. Thruston, Walter Carr.

Franklin—Henry Innis, John Logan.

Fleming—George Stockton.

Garrard—William M. Bledsoe.

Green—William Casey.

Harrison—Henry Coleman, William E. Boswell.

Jefferson—Alexander S. Bullitt, Richard Taylor.

Jessamine—John Price.

Lincoln—William Logan, N. Huston.

Logan—John Bailey, Reuben Ewing.

Mason—Philemon Thomas, Thomas Marshall, Jr., Joshua Baker.

Mercer—Peter Brunner, John Adair, Thomas Allen, Samuel Taylor.

Madison—Green Clay, Thomas Clay, William Irvine.

Montgomery—Jilson Payne.

Nelson—John Rowan, Richard Prather, Nicholas Minor.

Shelby—Benjamin Logan, Abraham Owen.

Scott—William Henry, Robert Johnson.

Woodford—Caleb Wallace, Wm. Steele.

Washington—Felix Grundy, Robert Abell.

Warren—Alexander Davidson—in all fifty-seven members.

The present, or third Constitution of Kentucky, usually denominated the New Constitution, was signed and ratified at Frankfort, the seat of government, on the 11th day of June, 1850. James Guthrie was President of the Convention, Thos.

J. Helm, Secretary, and Thos. D. Tilford, Assistant Secretary. At this time there were one hundred counties in the State, and one hundred members of the Convention, as follows:

Adair—Nathan Gaither.
Allen—George W. Mansfield.
Anderson—George W. Kavanaugh.
Ballard and McCracken—Richard D. Goblson.
Barren—John T. Rodgers, Robert D. Maupin.
Bath—James N. Nesbit.
Boone—Charles Chambers.
Bourbon—G. W. Williams, Richard H. Hanson.
Breathitt and Morgan—John Hargis.
Boyle—Albert G. Talbott.
Bracken—William C. Marshall.
Breckinridge—Daniel J. Stephens.
Bullitt—William R. Thompson.
Butler and Edmonson—Vincent S. Hay.
Caldwell—Willis B. Machen.
Calloway and Marshall—Edward Curd.
Campbell—Ira Root.
Carroll and Gallatin—John T. Robinson.
Carter and Lawrence—Thomas J. Hood.
Casey—Jesse Coffey.
Christian—John D. Morris, Ninian E. Gray.
Clarke—Andrew Hood.
Clay, Letcher, and Perry—James H. Garrard.
Cumberland and Clinton—Michael L. Stoner.
Crittenden—Henry R. D. Coleman.
Daviess—Phillip Triplett.
Estill and Owsley—Luther Brawner.
Fayette—James Dudley, Robert N. Wickliffe.
Fleming—William W. Blair.
Floyd, Pike, and Johnson—James M. Lackey.
Franklin—Thomas N. Lindsey.
Grant—William Hendrix.
Graves—Richard L. Mayes.
Grayson—John J. Thurman.
Green—Thomas W. Lisle.

Greenup—Henry B. Pollard.
Hardin—Thomas D. Brown, James W. Stone.
Harrison—Hugh Newell, Lucius Desha.
Hart—Benjamin Copeland.
Henderson—Archibald Dixon.
Henry—Elijah F. Nuttall.
Hickman and Fulton—Thomas James.
Hopkins—William Bradley.
Jefferson—David Merriwether, William C. Bullitt.
Jessamine—Alexander K. Marshall.
Kenton—John W. Stephenson.
Knox and Harlan—Silas Woodson.
Larue—James P. Hamilton.
Laurel and Rockcastle—Jonathan Newcum.
Lewis—Larkin J. Proctor.
Lincoln—John L. Ballinger.
Livingston—William Cowper.
Logan—William K. Bowling, James W. Irwin.
Louisville City—James Rudd, William Preston.
Madison—Squire Turner, William Chenault.
Marion—Green Forrest.
Mason—Peter Lashbrooke, John D. Taylor.
Meade—Thomas J. Gough.
Mercer—Thomas P. Moore.
Monroe—John S. Barlow.
Montgomery—Richard Apperson.
Muhlenburg—Alfred M. Jackson.
Nelson—Ben. Hardin, Charles A. Wickliffe.
Nicholas—Benjamin F. Edwards.
Owen—Howard Todd.
Ohio and Hancock—John H. McHenry.
Pendleton—John Wheeler.
Pulaski—James D. Allcorn.
Russell—Nathan McClure.
Scott—William Johnson.
Simpson—Beverly L. Clarke.
Shelby—Andrew S. White, George W. Johnston.
Spencer—Mark E. Huston.

Taylor—William N. Marshall.
Todd—Francis M. Bristow.
Trigg—Alfred Boyd.
Trimble—Wesley J. Wright.
Union—Ignatius A. Spalding.
Warren—Chasteen T. Dunavan.
Wayne—James S. Chrisman.
Whitley—Thomas Rockhold.
Woodford—John L. Waller.
Washington—Charles Cooper Kelly.

THE GENERAL GOVERNMENT.

On the 8th day of June, 1776, the Congress of the United Colonies of America, being then in session, took up the subject of their independency of Great Britain. On Tuesday, the 11th day of June, a committee was appointed by Congress to prepare the Declaration. The members chosen for this purpose were Thomas Jefferson, John Adams, Benjamin Franklin, Roger Sherman, and R. R. Livingston.

On Thursday, the 4th of July, the committee made report, through Mr. Harrison, of Virginia, that they had agreed to a Declaration, which, being read, was agreed to. The credit of the authorship of that unequaled instrument and grand production is awarded to the chairman of the committee, Thomas Jefferson. The sentiments which it contained are too familiar to every one to make it necessary to insert it here. The concluding paragraph of that instrument is as follows:

"We, therefore, the representatives of the United States of America, in General Congress assembled, appealing to the Supreme Judge of the world for the rectitude of our intentions, do, in the name and by the authority of the good people of these Colonies, solemnly publish and declare, That these United Colonies are, and of right ought to be, FREE AND INDEPENDENT STATES; that they are absolved from all allegiance to the British crown, and that all political connexion between them and the State of Great Britain is, and ought to be, totally dissolved; and that, as FREE AND INDEPENDENT STATES, they have full power to levy war, conclude peace, contract alliances, establish commerce, and to do all other acts and things which INDEPENDENT STATES may of right do. And for the support of this declaration, and with a firm reliance on the protection of DIVINE PROVIDENCE, we mutually pledge to each other our lives, our fortunes, and our sacred honor."

The Declaration was then, by order of Congress, engrossed, and signed by the President and the Representatives of the several States, thirteen in number.

JOHN HANCOCK.

New Hampshire.—Josiah Bartlett, William Whipple, Matthew Thornton.

Massachusetts Bay.—Samuel Adams, John Adams, Robert Treat Payne, Elbridge Gerry.

Rhode Island.—Stephen Hopkins, William Ellery.

Connecticut.—Roger Sherman, Samuel Huntingdon, William Williams, Oliver Wolcott.

New York.—William Floyd, Philip Livingston, Francis Lewis, Lewis Morris.

New Jersey—Richard Stockton, John Witherspoon, Francis Hopkinson, John Hart, Abraham Clark.

Pennsylvania.—Robert Morris, Benjamin Rush, Benjamin Franklin, John Morton, George Clymer, James Smith, George Taylor, James Wilson, George Ross.

Delaware.—Cæsar Rodney, George Read, Thomas McKean.

Maryland.—Samuel Chase, William Paca, Thomas Stone, Charles Carroll, of Carrollton.

Virginia.—George Wythe, Richard Henry Lee, Thomas Jefferson, Benjamin Harrison, Thomas Nelson, Jr., Francis Lightfoot Lee, Carter Braxton.

North Carolina.—William Hooper, Joseph Hewes, John Penn.

South Carolina.—Edward Rutledge, Thomas Hayward, Jr., Thomas Lynch, Jr., Arthur Middleton.

Georgia.—Button Gwinnett, Lyman Hall, George Walton.

Articles of Confederation were agreed to by the thirteen original States above named, on the 15th day of November, 1777, and were ratified by eight States on the 9th of July, 1778; and, finally, by all the States on the 1st of March, 1781. The

Articles of Confederation continued in force until the formation and adoption of the Constitution of the United States, in 1787, when was formed a more perfect Union for the security of liberty to ourselves and our posterity. The Government of the United States went into operation under that Constitution in 1789. The names of the delegates to the Convention from the several States who signed that instrument are as follows, viz:

GEORGE WASHINGTON,
President and Deputy from Virginia.

New Hampshire.—John Langdon, Nicholas Gilman.
Massachusetts.—Nathaniel Gorham, Rufus King.
Connecticut.—William Samuel Johnson, Roger Sherman.
New York.—Alexander Hamilton.
New Jersey.—Wil. Livingston, William Patterson, David Brearley, Jonathan Dayton.
Pennsylvania.—Benjamin Franklin, Robert Morris, Thomas Fitzsimons, James Wilson, Thomas Mifflin, George Clymer, Jared Ingersoll, Gouv. Morris.
Delaware.—George Read, John Dickinson, Iaco. Broom, Gunning Bedford, Jr., Richard Bassett.
Maryland.—James McHenry, Daniel Carroll, Dan. or St. Thomas Jenifer.
Virginia.—John Blair, James Madison, Jr.
North Carolina.—William Blount, Hu. Williamson, Richard Dobbs Spraight.
South Carolina.—J. Rutledge, Charles Pinckney, Charles Cotesworth Pinckney, Pierce Butler.
Georgia.—William Few, Abr. Baldwin.

Attest: WILLIAM JACKSON, Sec'y.

The Presidents and Vice Presidents of the United States from the adoption of the Constitution to the present time have been as follows:

PRESIDENTS.

George Washington, of Virginia; served two terms; born in 1732; inaugurated at fifty-seven years of age; died the 14th of December, 1799, sixty-eight years old.

John Adams, of Massachusetts; served one term; born 1735; inaugurated at sixty-two years of age; died the 4th of July, 1826, ninety-one years old.

Thomas Jefferson, of Virginia; served two terms; born 1743; inaugurated at fifty-eight years of age; died July 4th, 1826, eighty-three years old.

James Madison, of Virginia; served two terms; born in 1751; inaugurated at fifty-eight years of age; died June 28th, 1836, eighty-five years old.

James Monroe, of Virginia; served two terms; born in 1758; inaugurated at fifty-eight years of age; died July 4th, 1831, seventy-two years old.

John Quincy Adams, of Massachusetts; served one term; born in 1767; inaugurated at fifty-eight years of age; died February 23d, 1848, eighty years old.

Andrew Jackson, of Tennessee; served two terms; born in 1767; inaugurated at sixty-two years of age; died June 8th, 1845, seventy-eight years old.

Martin Van Buren, of New York; served one term; born in 1782; inaugurated at fifty-five years of age; died July 24th, 1862, seventy-nine years old.

William Henry Harrison, of Ohio; elected for one term; born in 1773; inaugurated at sixty-eight years of age; died April 4th, 1841, sixty-eight years old.

John Tyler, of Virginia; served the balance of Harrison's term; born in 1790; inaugurated at fifty-one years of age; died January 17th, 1862, seventy-two years old.

James K. Polk, of Tennessee; served one term; born in 1795; inaugurated at forty-nine years of age; died June 15th, 1849, fifty-four years old.

Zachary Taylor, of Louisiana; elected for one term; born in 1784; inaugurated at sixty-five years of age; died July 9th, 1850, sixty-six years old.

Millard Fillmore, of New York; born in 1800; served the balance of Taylor's term; inaugurated at fifty years of age; seventy years old, and yet survives.

Franklin Pierce, of New Hampshire; served one term; born

in 1804; inaugurated at forty-nine years of age; died October 8th, 1869, sixty-five years old.

James Buchanan, of Pennsylvania; served one term; born in 1791; inaugurated at sixty-five years of age; died June 1st, 1868, seventy-seven years old.

Abraham Lincoln, of Illinois; elected two terms; born in 1809; inaugurated at fifty-two years of age; was assassinated at a theater in Washington City the 15th of April, 1865, early in the second term of his office; fifty-six years old.

Andrew Johnson, of Tennessee; served the balance of Lincoln's term; born in 1808; inaugurated at fifty-seven years of age; is now sixty-two years of age, and still survives.

Ulysses S. Grant, of Illinois; elected as the successor of Johnson; born in 1822; inaugurated at forty-seven years of age; now fifty years old, and is the present incumbent of the office, whose term expires in 1872.

VICE PRESIDENTS

John Adams, served two terms; installed in 1789 and 1793.

Thomas Jefferson served one term; installed in 1797.

Aaron Burr served one term; installed in 1801.

George Clinton served two terms; installed in 1805 and 1809, and died during second term.

Elbridge Gerry served one term; installed in 1813, and died in office.

Daniel D. Tompkins served two terms; installed in 1817 and 1821.

John C. Calhoun served two terms; installed in 1825 and 1829.

Martin Van Buren served one term; installed in 1833.

Richard M. Johnson served one term; installed in 1837.

John Tyler served part of one term; installed in 1841.

George M. Dallas served one term; installed in 1845.

Millard Fillmore served part of one term; installed in 1849.

William R. King served one term; installed in 1853, and died in office.

J. C. Breckinridge served one term; installed in 1857.

Hannibal Hamlin served one term; installed in 1861.

Andrew Johnson served part of one term; installed in 1865.
Schuyler Colfax, present incumbent, installed in 1869.

The following are the names of the Presidents of the Continental Congress, from 1774 to 1788, inclusive, viz:
Peyton Randolph, of Virginia, September 5, 1774.
Henry Middleton, of South Carolina, October 22, 1774.
Peyton Randolph, of Virginia, May 10, 1775.
John Hancock, of Massachusetts, May 24, 1775.
Henry Laurens, of South Carolina, November 1, 1777.
John Jay, of New York, December 10, 1778.
Samuel Huntington, of Connecticut, September 28, 1779.
Thomas McKean, of Delaware, July 10, 1781.
John Hanson, of Maryland, November 5, 1781.
Elias Boudinot, of New Jersey, November 4, 1782.
Thomas Mifflin, of Pennsylvania, November 3, 1783.
Richard Henry Lee, of Virginia, November 30, 1784.
Nathaniel Gorham, of Massachusetts, June 6, 1786.
Arthur St. Clair, of Pennsylvania, February 2, 1787.
Cyrus Griffin, of Virginia, January 22d, 1788.

The Constitution of the United States was adopted, as we have before stated, on the 17th of September, 1787, and was ratified by the several States as follows:
By Delaware, December 7, 1787.
By Pennsylvania, December 12, 1787.
By New Jersey, December 18, 1787.
By Georgia, January 2, 1788.
By Connecticut, January 9, 1788.
By Massachusetts, February 6, 1788.
By Maryland, April 28, 1788.
By South Carolina, May 23, 1788.
By New Hampshire, June 21, 1788.
By Virginia, June 26, 1788.
By New York, July 26, 1788.
By North Carolina, November 21, 1789.
By Rhode Island, May 29, 1790.

ELECTORS OF PRESIDENT AND VICE PRESIDENT IN KENTUCKY, FROM THE TIME OF HER ADMISSION INTO THE UNION AS A SEPARATE STATE.

At the first election under the Constitution, Kentucky, as a State, had no voice. George Washington was elected, by a unanimous vote of the Electors, President of the United States, and John Adams Vice President by a plurality of one vote over all other of his opponents. The Constitution then provided that he who received the highest electoral vote should be President, and the next highest Vice President. But at the fourth Presidential election, in 1801, Thomas Jefferson and Aaron Burr having each received an equal number of votes, the choice devolved upon the House of Representatives. The House having balloted at intervals for seven consecutive days, on the afternoon of the 17th day of February, 1802, on the 36th ballot, Thomas Jefferson was declared duly elected President of the United States. This result was occasioned by Delaware and South Carolina voting blank, while the votes of Vermont and Maryland were given for Mr. Jefferson. The Vice Presidency, as a matter of course, devolved on Aaron Burr.

After this, the Constitution was so amended as to provide that Electors, in casting their votes, should vote for President and Vice President separately, so as to avoid in future a recurrence of the difficulty.

At the second Presidential election, 1793, George Washington was again unanimously elected President, and John Adams re-elected Vice-President by a plurality of votes. The Electors for Kentucky that year were R. C. Anderson, Charles Scott, Benjamin Logan, and Notley Conn, who voted for George Washington for President and Thomas Jefferson for Vice President, which were the only votes cast for Jefferson in that election, even Virginia voting for George Clinton, of New York.

At the third Presidential election, 1797, John Adams was elected President, having received seventy-one of the one hundred and forty electoral votes, and Thomas Jefferson, Vice-President, he having received sixty-eight votes, the next highest number. The Electors for Kentucky that year were Stephen Ormsby, Caleb Wallace, Isaac Shelby, and John Coburn, all of whom cast their votes for Thomas Jefferson and Aaron Burr.

At the fourth Presidential election, 1801, Thomas Jefferson was elected President and Aaron Burr Vice President. The Electors for Kentucky that year were John Coburn, Charles Scott, John Pope, and Isaac Shelby, all of whom cast their votes for Jefferson and Burr.

At the fifth Presidential election, 1805, Thomas Jefferson was re-elected President and George Clinton Vice President. The Electors for Kentucky that year were Charles Scott, Isaac Shelby, John Coburn, Ninian Edwards, Hubbard Taylor, Joseph Lewis, William Irvine, and William Roberts, all of whom cast their votes for Jefferson and Clinton.

At the sixth Presidential election, 1809, James Madison was elected President and George Clinton Vice President. The Electors for Kentucky that year were Samuel Hopkins, Charles Scott, William Logan, Robert Trimble, Matthew Walton, Hubbard Taylor, Robert Ewing, and Christopher Greenup, all of whom cast their votes for Madison and Clinton.

At the seventh Presidential election, 1813, James Madison was re-elected President and Elbridge Gerry Vice President. The Electors for Kentucky that year were Robert Ewing, William Irvine, William Casey, Robert Mosby, Samuel Murrell, Hubbard Taylor, Samuel Caldwell, Duvall Payne, Richard Taylor, Walker Baylor, William Logan, and T. D. Owings, all of whom voted for Madison and Gerry.

At the eighth Presidential election, 1817, James Monroe was elected President and Daniel D. Tompkins Vice President. The Electors for Kentucky that year were Duval Payne, Richard Taylor, Hubbard Taylor, William Logan, Robert Trimble, Alexander Adair, Thomas Bodley, Samuel Caldwell, Willis A. Lee, Samuel Murrell, William Irvine, and Robert Ewing, all of whom cast their votes for Monroe and Tompkins.

At the ninth Presidential election, 1821, James Monroe and

Daniel D. Tompkins were re-elected a second term to the same offices. The Electors for Kentucky that year were Samuel Murrell, Martin B. Hardin, E. M. Ewing, Willis A. Lee, Samuel Caldwell, James Johnson, John E. King, Jesse Blidsoe, John Pope, Thomas Bodley, Richard Taylor, and Hubbard Taylor, all of whom cast their votes for Monroe and Tompkins.

At the tenth Presidential election, 1825, John Quincy Adams was elected President and John C. Calhoun Vice President. The election of the President in this instance devolved on the House of Representatives, no one of the aspirants at the time having received a majority of all the electoral votes cast. The candidates were Adams, Jackson, Crawford, and Clay. The result was the election of Adams. The Electors for Kentucky that year were J. R. Underwood, Richard Taylor, John E. King, Joseph Allen, Andrew McLean, W. Moore, Young Ewing, Thomas Bodley, Benjamin Letcher, D. Payne, James Smiley, J. J. Crittenden, Joshua Fry, and H. Taylor. The Electoral College of Kentucky cast her entire vote for Henry Clay for President, and seven voted for John C. Calhoun for Vice President and seven for Nathan Sanford.

At the eleventh Presidential election, 1829, Andrew Jackson was elected President and John C. Calhoun Vice President. The Electors for Kentucky that year were Thomas S. Slaughter, Reuben Munday, Matthew Lyon, Benjamin Chapeze, Edmund Watkins, John Younger, Nathan Gaither, John Sterrett, Tunstall Quarles, Benjamin Taylor, Robert J. Ward, Richard French, Tandy Allen, and Thompson Ward. The entire electoral vote of Kentucky was cast for Jackson and Calhoun.

At the twelfth Presidential election, 1833, Andrew Jackson was re-elected President and Martin Van Buren Vice President. The Electors for Kentucky that year were Joseph Eve, Alney McLean, Ben. Hardin, W. K. Wall, M. P. Marshall, J. L. Hickman, M. V. Thompson, William Owsley, Burr Harrison, Thomas Chilton, John J. Marshall, D. S. Patton, E. M. Ewing, Martin Beatty, and Thompson M. Ewing. The electoral vote of Kentucky was cast for Henry Clay for President and John Sargent for Vice President.

At the thirteenth Presidential election, 1837, Martin Van Buren was elected President and Richard M. Johnson Vice President. The Electors for Kentucky that year were Burr Harrison, Thomas P. Wilson, Henry Daniel, William E. Wall, Philip Triplett, Robert Wickliffe, D. S. Patton, Thomas Metcalfe, E. Rumsey, M. P. Marshall, Richard A. Buckner, J. F. Ballinger, Christopher Tompkins, Robert P. Letcher, and Martin Beatty. The entire vote of Kentucky was cast for William Henry Harrison for President and Francis Granger for Vice President.

At the fourteenth election of President, 1841, William Henry Harrison was elected President and John Tyler Vice President. The Electors for President that year for Kentucky were Richard A. Buckner, Charles G. Wintersmith, James T. Morehead, Thomas W. Riley, Robert Patterson, William H. Field, Iredell Hart, Daniel Breck, James W. Irwin, R. H. Menefee, B. Y. Owsley, M. P. Marshall, James Harlan, A. Beatty, and W. W. Southgate. The entire electoral vote of Kentucky was cast for Harrison and Tyler.

At the fifteenth Presidential election, 1845, James K. Polk was elected President and George M. Dallas Vice President. The Electors for Kentucky that year were Philip Triplett, Green Adams, B. M. Crenshaw, W. W. Southgate, Ben. Hardin, W. R. Grigsby, Jo. R. Underwood, W. J. Graham, R. A. Patterson, Leslie Combs, John Kincaid, and L. W. Andrews. The entire electoral vote was cast for Henry Clay for President and Theodore Frelinghuysen for Vice President.

At the sixteenth Presidential election, 1849, Zachary Taylor was elected President and Millard Fillmore Vice President. The electors for Kentucky that year were Archibald Dixon, M. V. Thompson, L. Lindsay, J. L. Johnson, F. E. McLean, William Chenault, Thomas W. Lisle, M. D. McHenry, B. R. Young, Leslie Combs, A. Trumbo, and W. C. Marshall. The entire electoral vote of Kentucky was cast for Taylor and Fillmore.

At the seventeenth Presidential election, 1853, Franklin

Pierce was elected President and William R. King Vice President. The Electors for Kentucky that year were Joshua F. Bell, Chas. S. Morehead, L. Anderson, J. S. McFarland, John G. Rogers, Thomas E. Bramlette, John L. Helm, C. F. Burnam, Thomas F. Marshall, S. J. Rodman, L. M. Cox, and Thomas B. Stephenson. The vote of Kentucky was cast for Winfield Scott and William A. Graham.

At the eighteenth Presidential election, 1857, James Buchanan was elected President and John C. Breckinridge Vice President. The Electors for Kentucky that year were Elijah Hise, J. A. Finn, J. W. Stephenson, Timoleon Cravens, J. T. Hawkins, B. Magoffin, George W. Williams, Ben. F. Rice, William D. Reed, R. W. Woolley, R. H. Stanton, and Hiram Kelsey. The vote of Kentucky was cast for Millard Fillmore and A. J. Donelson.

At the nineteenth Presidential election, 1861, Abraham Lincoln was elected President and Hannibal Hamlin Vice President. The Electors for Kentucky that year were W. H. Wadsworth, E. L. Vanwinkle, Q. Q. Quigley, S. A. Seavell, William Sampson, W. A. Hoskins, Phil. Lee, William M. Fulkerson, William C. Bullock, John M. Harlan, John B. Huston, and W. S. Rankin, who cast the vote of Kentucky for John Bell for President and Edward Everett for Vice President.

At the twentieth Presidential election, 1865, Abraham Lincoln was re-elected President and Andrew Johnson Vice President. The Electors for Kentucky were Frank Wolford, Thomas F. Marshall, T. A. Duke, B. C. Ritter, T. C. Winfrey, J. P. Barbour, W. F. Bullock, A. H. Ward, George S. Shanklin, W. A. Hoskins, and Harrison Taylor, who cast the vote of Kentucky for George B. M'Clellan for President and George H. Pendleton for Vice President.

At the twenty-first Presidential election, 1869, Ulysses S. Grant was elected President and Schuyler Colfax Vice President. The Electors for Kentucky in that year were Jesse D. Bright, Frank Wolford, J. M. Bigger, A. K. Bradley, W. W. Bush, A. H. Field, Boyd Winchester, A. B. Chambers, George W. Craddock, Harrison Cockrill, and John M. Rice, who cast the vote of Kentucky for Horatio Seymour for President and F. P. Blair for Vice President.

The Speakers of the House of Representatives of the Congress of the United States from the State of Kentucky, since her admission into the Union as a separate State, are as follows, viz:

12th Congress,			Henry Clay,	1811 and 1812.
13th "		first session,	"	1813.
14th "			"	1815 and 1816.
15th "			"	1817 and 1818.
16th "		first session,	"	1819.
18th "			"	1823 and 1824.
27th "			John White,	1841 and 1842.
32d "			Lynn Boyd,	1851 and 1852.
33d "			"	1853 and 1854.

The Presidents of the Senate of the United States during the same period, being Vice Presidents, are as follows:

From the 25th to 26th Congress inclusive, Richard M. Johnson, 1836, 1837, 1838. and 1839.

From the 35th to 36th Congress, inclusive, John C. Breckinridge, 1857, 1858, 1859, and 1860.

Kentucky has furnished two Presidents *pro tem.* of the Senate, viz: John Brown, 1803, and John Pope, 1810. Also one Clerk to the House of Representatives: Thomas Dougherty, who served from January, 1815, to December, 1822. Also one Chaplain to the United States Senate: J. Breckinridge, of the Presbyterian Church, and two to the House of Representatives: J. Breckinridge, of the Presbyterian Church, and Henry B. Bascom, of the Methodist Episcopal Church.

POPULATION OF KENTUCKY.

The population of Kentucky with the increase per cent. from 1820 to 1870, is as follows:

Year.	Population.	Increase per cent.
1820. - -	564,135	- - 38.82
1830. -	687,917	- 21.00
1840. - -	779,828	- - 13.36

Year.	Population.	Increase per cent.
1850.	982,405	25.09
1860.	1,155,684	17.64
1870.	1,320,407	14.25

The increased population of Kentucky has not been as great in the last ten years as we might reasonably have expected when we consider the vast amount of land within her bounds and the great extent of her mineral wealth. Whilst her increase has been but a little more than fourteen per cent., Missouri has increased forty-two per cent. and Illinois forty-seven per cent., and the new States and Territories in still a much larger proportion.

The greatest increase of the population of Kentucky has been in the cities. The counties which exhibit the greatest ratio of increase are Ballard, Butler, Campbell, Daviess, Estill, Grant, Grayson, Hancock, Henderson, Hickman, Jefferson, Kenton, Letcher, McCracken, Madison, Marshall, Ohio, Pendleton, and Pike.

Jefferson County increased 58,325 in the last twenty years, whilst the increase of the city of Louisville in the same time was 56,564. While the increase of Fayette County in twenty years was only 177, the city of Lexington increased from 7,920 to 14,856. In the same length of time, Clarke County has lost 801 in population, Harrison 187, Jessamine 1,611, Mason 217, Mercer 922, Scott 2,439, Owen 3,865, Shelby 1,362, and Woodford 4,183. Anderson, Barren, Bath, Boone, Bracken, Caldwell, Fleming, Gallatin, Henry, Montgomery, Morgan, Nicholas, Spencer, Trimble, and Washington have lost in population, and all the other counties except those above specified have increased at a low rate.

Kentucky is naturally rich in the fertility of her lands and in the abundance of her minerals, but fails to attract population in many parts in consequence of a lack of the means of communication which rivers and railroads are sure to afford. Upon an examination of the map of Kentucky, it may be seen, that, where manufactures and improvements exist to great extent, the population has increased; otherwise, the population has decreased.

CHAPTER IX.

Historical Sketches of the Leading Denominations of Christians in the State of Kentucky, including the Catholic, Baptist, Presbyterian, Episcopalian, Methodist, Cumberland Presbyterian, Christian, &c., with Brief Biographical Notices of the most Distinguished among the Pioneers.

ROMAN CATHOLIC CHURCH.

Doctor Hart and William Coomes are mentioned as the first Catholic emigrants to Kentucky. They emigrated from Maryland in 1775, and settled at Harrodsburg Station. Doctor Hart engaged in the practice of medicine, and the wife of Mr. Coomes opened a school for children; so that the first practicing physician and the first school-teacher in Kentucky, of which we have any account, were Roman Catholics.

Hart and Coomes, after remaining at Harrodsburg a few years, removed with their families to Bardstown. Previous to their removal they were as actively engaged as any others at the station in repelling Indian invasions; and Mr. Coomes, especially, in the memorable siege by the Indians of 1776-77, acted a conspicuous part.

In 1785 a large colony of Catholics emigrated from Maryland, and settled chiefly on Pottinger's Creek, some twelve or fifteen miles from Bardstown. With this colony were the Haydens and Lancasters. In the spring of 1786 another colony from Maryland, led by James Rapier, settled in the same neighborhood. In 1787 Thomas Hill and Philip Miles brought out another band, followed in 1788 by Robert Abell and his friends; and in 1790-91 Benedict Spalding and Leonard Hamilton came out with their families and connexions, and settled on the Rolling Fork, in what is now Marion County.

As early as 1787 there were some fifty Catholic families in

Kentucky; but there was no clergyman among them. About this time application was made to the very Reverend John Carroll, of Baltimore, the ecclesiastical superior of all the Catholics in the United States, who sent them as their first pastor the Rev. Mr. Whelan, an Irish priest. He administered to their spiritual wants until the spring of 1790, when he returned to Maryland.

Three years elapsed before another pastor came. In 1793 Bishop Carroll sent out the Rev. Stephen Theodore Baden. He is represented as a very learned, zealous, and most excellent man. He labored with unremitting zeal among the Catholics of Kentucky for nearly forty years, and until he wore himself down by his extraordinary exertions in his errand of mercy. He estimated the number of Catholic families in Kentucky at the time of his arrival at about three hundred, but there was no church in the whole State. From that period the Catholic population increased rapidly, many churches erected, and schools established.

In 1797 another zealous Catholic missionary arrived in the State, the Rev. M. Fournier, a native of France; and, two years later, the Rev. M. Salmon, also a Frenchman. Their labors were of short duration. Mr. Salmon was killed by a fall from his horse, near Bardstown, on the 9th of November, 1799, and Mr. Fournier died soon after, on the Rolling Fork, from the rupture of a blood-vessel. The same year, to supply their places, Bishop Carroll sent out the Rev. Mr. Thayer, a native of New England, and previously a minister in Boston of the Congregational Church, who, upon joining the Catholics, was promoted to the ministry in that church also. He remained in the State from 1799 to 1803, and, upon his departure, the Rev. Mr. Baden was again left alone for the space of about two years.

In 1805 the Rev. Charles Rininck, a native of Belgium, who had been compelled to leave Europe on account of the disturbances occasioned by the French Revolution, arrived in Kentucky. He was a man of great activity and zeal, was disheartened at no difficulties, traveled a great deal, and accomplished much good. He labored incessantly, both bodily and mentally, for twenty years, and died in the year 1824 while on a missionary excursion to the State of Missouri. He erected in Kentucky ten Catholic churches, in the building of which he often worked with his own hands. For many years he had charge of six large congregations, besides a great number of minor stations scattered over the whole State. He delighted to visit the poor, and children and servants were the special objects of his pastoral care and solicitude. He was the founder, in the year 1812, of that highly distinguished and justly celebrated institution of the sisterhood at Loretto. It is situated in what is now Marion County, and has prospered wonderfully from the beginning. It has a great many branch establishments, both in Kentucky and Missouri, all of which have female schools attached to them.

In the spring of 1806 a band of Catholics came to Kentucky as missionaries, all of whom were of the order of St. Dominic, and established themselves at St. Rose's, near Springfield. Among them were the Rev. Edward Fenwick, Thomas Wilson, William Raymond Tuite, and R. Auger. They labored with great zeal and efficiency. A theological seminary and college for young men were connected with their institution. About a mile from St. Rose a flourishing female institution was soon afterward established, called St. Magdalene, conducted by the Sisters of the Third Order of St. Dominic.

It was not until the year 1811 that the first bishop arrived in Kentucky, the Right Reverend Doctor Flaget, who had been consecrated in Baltimore by Bishop Carroll. He was regarded as an excellent and admirable man, loved by everybody who became acquainted with him. It is said of him that he had no enemy. He reared quite a number of benevolent and literary institutions in Kentucky during the period of his long life.

Among the companions of Bishop Flaget when he took up his permanent abode in Kentucky were the Rev. B. M. David and the Rev. G. J. Chabrat. The latter was the first priest ordained by Bishop Flaget in Kentucky. The Rev. Mr. David was consecrated bishop in the newly dedicated Cathedral of Bardstown on the 15th of August, 1819, and died the

12th of July, 1841, in the eighty-first year of his age. He was the founder of the Theological Seminary of Bardstown, and of the order of Sisters of Charity in Kentucky.

Among the most zealous and efficient clergymen of their day were the Rev. William Byrne, who founded St. Mary's College in Marion County, and the Rev. G. A. M. Elder, the founder of St. Joseph's College in Bardstown. The former was an Irishman, and the latter a native Kentuckian. Both of these institutions are still flourishing, and have been of immense advantage to the cause of education in Kentucky. Both these institutions were ordained together, in the Cathedral of Bardstown, on the 18th of September, 1819, by Bishop David. The Rev. Wm. Byrne died of cholera, at St. Mary's College, the 5th of June, 1833, and the Rev. Mr. Elder died at St. Joseph's College, of an affection of the heart, on the 28th of September, 1838. Both died in the institutions which they had respectively reared, and which they left behind as their sepulchral monuments.

Bishop John McGill, the major part of whose ministerial life was spent in the city of Louisville, died at Richmond, Virginia, at the age of sixty-two years, about the 1st of January, 1872. He was born in Philadelphia in 1809. His parents moved to Bardstown when he was a child. He studied law in Bardstown, and practiced his profession several years in New Orleans; but afterward returned to Bardstown and studied theology. He was ordained a priest after the stated term, and appointed pastor of the Cathedral, and was at the same time editor of the Catholic Guardian. He was a forcible writer and logical preacher.

Archbishop Martin John Spalding, lately deceased at Baltimore, a truly great and good man, was also a native of Kentucky, and spent here the larger portion of his ecclesiastical labors. He was born near Calvary, in Marion County, in the year 1811, and at the time of his death (February, 1872) was in the sixty-second year of his age. He has many distinguished relations in Kentucky who survive him. Two of his brothers, the Hon. Richard Spalding, of Lebanon, and the Hon. Ignatius Spalding, of Union County, are members of the present

General Assembly of Kentucky; and Rev. J. Lancaster Spalding, of the city of Louisville, is a nephew. He was also a brother of Father Ben. Spalding, who lost his life in the year 1866, by a fire which broke out at the Cathedral, on Fifth Street, in the city of Louisville.

Archbishop Spalding began the studies which were to prepare him for the ministry at St. Mary's College, in Marion County, under Father Byrne, and subsequently took a four year course at the College of Rome, where he acquitted himself with distinguished honors. He was ordained priest on the 13th of August, 1834, in the twenty-third year of his age, twenty-four being the required age, and for this purpose he received a special dispensation from the Pope, Gregory XVI. On returning home he officiated as pastor of St. Joseph's, at Bardstown, and at the same time was a teacher in the college. Here he remained until he was appointed to the Cathedral in the city of Louisville, with Bishops Reynolds and McGill, in the year 1844. While here he engaged arduously in both literary and ecclesiastical labors. In 1848 he was consecrated Associate Bishop of Louisville with Bishop Flaget, and became Bishop after the death of the latter. In this capacity he remained until the 6th of May, 1864, when he was transferred to the Archiepiscopal See of Baltimore. It was during the last few weeks of his life that he was attacked with a bronchial affection, followed by a sympathetic derangement of the stomach, which superinduced dropsy, resulting in his death.

Archbishop Spalding stood among the first in the esteem of his church, and was one of the most eloquent pulpit orators of the United States. His literary works were numerous, among them The Evidences of Catholicity, Review of D'Aubigne's History of the Reformation, Sketches of Kentucky Life, and his Life of Bishop Flaget. He was the apostolic delegate of the Pope to the last Plenary Council at Baltimore in 1866, and took a prominent part in the proceedings of the Ecumenical Council of the Vatican, and was one of the Committee "*De Fide.*" He advocated with earnestness and honesty the doctrine of Papal Infallibility.

I have no data by which to ascertain the number of Roman Catholics in Kentucky. They are, however, very numerous in many portions of the State. Their schools, academies, and colleges are numerous also. Their college of greatest note in Kentucky is St. Joseph's, located at Bardstown, Nelson County. This institution was founded in 1819, and was for many years the most prosperous institution of the kind in the State. Many distinguished men of Kentucky received their education at this institution. Rev. P. De Fraine is the present President, assisted by eight professors and instructors. The number of pupils at this time is about eighty. The expenses of tuition per annum is about $150. There are several other schools of high repute in this place.

I have gathered the following statistics of the Roman Catholic Church, viz:

The total number of members of the Sacred College is seventy; but there are at present but fifty-three, not including two reserved *in petto*, that is in secrecy; leaving fifteen vacancies. Of the fifty-three, twelve were made cardinals by Pope Gregory the XVI., and all the rest by Pope Pius the IX. The present Most Holy Father, Pope Pius the IX., was born at Sinigaglia, May 13th, 1792; reserved *in petto* December 23d, 1839; published Cardinal Priest the 14th of December, 1840; elected Pope the 16th of June, 1846, and crowned five days afterward. The cardinals are thus divided: Cardinal bishops, five; cardinal priests, forty-one; cardinal deacons, seven. In nationality there are thirty-nine Italians, five French, four Germans, three Spaniards, one Spanish American, and one Irish. The patriarchs, archbishops, and bishops number nine hundred and fifty-three; vacant sees, one hundred and fifty-seven; total, eleven hundred and ten. In the United States there are seven archbishoprics, viz: New York, Baltimore, Cincinnati, St. Louis, New Orleans, San Francisco, and Oregon City. There are forty-seven bishoprics; vicariates apostolic, six. The dioceses are divided among seven provinces, a number of States belonging to each province. In the bishoprics above named, Kentucky is embraced in the province of Cincinnati.

There are no archbishops residing in Kentucky, and only

two bishops, viz: William McCloskey, D. D., Louisville, and A. M. Toebbe, D. D., Covington.

HISTORICAL SKETCH OF THE BAPTIST CHURCH.

There were Baptists among the earliest pioneer settlers of Kentucky. As early as 1776 William Hickman, Sr., was laboring in Kentucky as a minister. He was on a tour of observation at the time, and after a stay of only a few months returned to Virginia. After remaining there for eight years he came back to Kentucky and made it his permanent home, laboring faithfully in the field for more than fifty years. He traveled extensively, often in the most distant and exposed settlements, frequently at the peril of his life. He was about six feet high, of slender form, and, in the language of Elder John Taylor, "walked as straight as a palm tree," even in the most advanced years of his life. His deportment was stern and grave. His style of preaching was plain and solemn, and operated with great force on the consciences of his hearers. He was for a great number of years pastor of the church of Elkhorn. It is believed that he baptized as many, perhaps more persons, than any other minister who ever labored in the State.

In 1779 John Taylor, Joseph Reding, Lewis Lunsford, and several other ministers visited Kentucky, but owing to the constant alarms from Indian depredations there seemed to be but little interest manifested for religion, and but few opportunities for preaching. Their principal object was, however, to see the country, with a view to future settlement. These ministers all soon returned to Virginia, except Reding, but at a later period some of them returned and took up their permanent residence in Kentucky.

In 1780 a great number of Baptists removed to Kentucky from Virginia, but it was not until 1781 that the first church was organized, which was called Gilbert's Creek Church. When Lewis Craig came from Virginia, most of his very large church there came with him. They were constituted when they started, and were an organized church on the road and transacted business as such. They settled at Craig's Station, on Gilbert's Creek, a few miles from where Lancaster (Garrard County) now stands.

In 1782 other churches were constituted, one in Severn's Valley, where Elizabethtown (Hardin County) is situated; another on Nolin, in what is now Larue County; and another at Cedar Creek, in Nelson County.

In 1783 the church at South Elkhorn, five miles from Lexington, was organized, and was for forty years one of the most prosperous in the State.

After the close of the Revolutionary War a flood of Baptists poured into Kentucky from Virginia, and churches began to spring up everywhere in the State, even yet while savage depredations were frequent and the times perilous. It was no uncommon thing for men to go to church with their guns in hand to guard against surprise from the Indians.

In 1785 three associations were organized, viz: Elkhorn, Salem, and South Kentucky. These embraced the entire State. These associations, which embraced at first only three or four churches each, increased rapidly; so that in 1790 there were forty-two churches, three thousand one hundred and five members, forty-two ordained ministers, and twenty-one licentiates. Among the ministers of that day were John Gano, Ambrose Dudley, John Taylor, Lewis Craig, William Hickman, Joseph Reding, William E. Waller, Augustine Eastin, Moses Bledsoe, John Rice, Elijah Craig, and William Marshall, all acknowledged to be men of piety, great energy of character, and well-balanced intellects. A fourth association was constituted in 1798 out of Elkhorn Association, called Bracken.

In 1799, what is known as the great revival in Kentucky commenced, and continued through several years. Accessions to all the churches in the State at that period were very great, and especially so to the Baptist Church.

In 1802 North Bend Association was organized. The same year South Kentucky Association was divided, making two associations instead of one, calling one the North District and the other the South District Association.

Long Run Association was organized in 1803. The Green

River Association, lying in what is now Warren, Barren, Green, and Adair counties was organized in 1800, about the beginning of the great revival in that quarter of the State. The first year of its existence there were added to the church more than one thousand members. In 1804 it contained thirty-eight churches, and, the territory being large, it was thought good policy to divide it into three bodies. The middle portion of the churches retained the old name; the northern portion was organized under the name of Russell's Creek Association; and the southern portion, Stockton's Valley Association.

In 1801 the Regular and Separate Baptists united upon terms previously agreed upon, since which time they have been called United Baptists.

From 1802 to 1812, there were several schisms and divisions in the Baptist Church. One party was led off by James Garrard, a Baptist minister of great influence, who had been elected Governor of Kentucky in 1796, and Augustine Eastin, another gentleman of talents and influence; but that party soon died away. About the same time another popular minister by the name of John Bailey led off a small party from the South District Association, and, obtaining no countenance from the General Union Association, they assumed the name of the South Kentucky Association of Separate Baptists. In 1804 a number of ministers went off on the subject of slavery. They are known in the records by the name of Emancipators. They withdrew from the General Union of Baptists in 1807, formed an association of their own, and were quite numerous at first, but they soon dwindled away, and no vestige of them remains. In 1809 there was a great schism in the Elkhorn Association, which originated in a difficulty between Jacob Creath and a member of his church about a negro trade. The result was that several ministers and churches withdrew from Elkhorn Association, and organized the Licking Association of Separate Baptists.

There were no more schisms in the Baptist Church worth recording until about the year 1829, when one was begun and carried on by Alexander Campbell. This was by far the greatest schism that ever occurred in the church; but still the

Baptists retained their usual ratio to the population of the State, which was about one to twenty of its inhabitants. In 1832, when the storm of this schism had spent its fury, they had thirty-three associations in Kentucky, four hundred and eighty-four churches, two hundred and thirty-six ordained ministers, and thirty-four thousand one hundred and twenty-four members. Their increase since then has been unprecedented; in the succeeding ten years they had doubled their numbers.

We have spoken of William Hickman as the first preacher in Kentucky, but Lewis Craig was the founder of the first worshiping assembly. He distinguished himself greatly in Virginia before he came to Kentucky. He was several times imprisoned in that State for preaching the gospel. As he, with others arrested at the same time, passed through the streets of Fredericksburg, on their way to prison, they struck up and sung those familiar lines, "Broad is the road that leads to death," &c. While in prison Mr. Craig preached through the grates to large crowds, and was the means of doing much good. He was in the gospel ministry about sixty years, and died at the age of eighty-seven years.

John Taylor was also a very efficient preacher, and made himself very useful. He itinerated for ten years after he first came to Kentucky, with great profit to the cause in which he was so zealously engaged. It was his custom to visit six or eight associations every year. He died in the eighty-second year of his age.

John Gano, a native of New Jersey, settled in Kentucky in 1787, and was one of the most eminent ministers of his day. He spent many years as an itinerant, traveling from New England to Georgia. He was a pastor in the city of New York for twenty-five years. During the Revolutionary War he was chaplain to the army, and greatly encouraged the soldiers in those perilous times.

I have mentioned these few names as examples of the high moral worth and talents of the pioneer Baptist ministry of Kentucky. The same could be said of many of their compeers, a sketch of whom the limits of our work will not conveniently allow. I now add, in conclusion, that there is at this time in Kentucky (1870) one General Association of Baptists and forty-four District Associations; three hundred ministers, five hundred churches, and a membership of about one hundred thousand. They have two large colleges of high reputation, one at Georgetown, the other at Bethel; also twelve female high schools. They have now but little if any division in their church, and are nearly all known as United or Missionary Baptists.

The Baptist denomination in this country, embracing all its shades and forms of opinion, numbers 1,503,630 communicants, over whom are placed 9,553 ministers, connected with 783 associations. The number of Baptist churches is 18,605, nearly twice the number of the Baptist ministry.

HISTORICAL SKETCH OF THE PRESBYTERIAN CHURCH.

The first Presbyterian minister who ever crossed the mountains was the Rev. David Rice, who emigrated to Kentucky in the year 1783, and who immediately on his arrival set about gathering the scattered Presbyterians into regular congregations. Three churches were soon organized; one at Danville, another at Cane Run, and another at the forks of Dix's River. Mr. Rice was followed the next year by the Rev. Adam Rankin, who gathered together the church at Lexington, and the Rev. James Crawford, who settled at Walnut Hill. In the year 1786 the Rev. Thomas Craighead and the Rev. Andrew McClure were added to the number. Shortly after this these ministers organized themselves into a Presbytery, under the name of Transylvania. The above named ministers all came from the State of Virginia, except Mr. Craighead, who was from North Carolina.

Transylvania Presbytery met for the first time October 17th, 1786, in the court-house in Danville. Mr. Rice presided as moderator by the appointment of the General Assembly, and Mr. McClure acted as clerk. The ministers present on that occasion were David Rice, Adam Rankin, Andrew McClure, James Crawford, and Zerah Templin. The ruling elders present, representing as many churches, were Richard Steele, David Gray, John Bovel, Joseph Reed, and Jeremiah Frame. By this time there had been twelve churches organized in Kentucky, viz: Cane Run, Concord, Danville, Forks of Dix River, New Providence, Mount Zion, Mount Pisgah, Salem, Walnut Hill, Hopewell, Paint Lick, Jessamine Creek, Whitley's Station, and Crab Orchard.

The number of Presbyterians in Kentucky by the year 1802 justified the erection of a Synod, and accordingly on Tuesday, the 14th of October of that year, the first Synod was held in Lexington in the Presbyterian Church. Mr. Rice preached the opening sermon, and was elected moderator, and Mr. Marshall clerk. Thirty members were present, of whom seventeen were ministers. The number of ministers then within the bounds of the Synod was thirty-seven, including the three Presbyteries, Transylvania, Washington (in Ohio), and West Lexington. During the session Cumberland Presbytery was formed from Transylvania, embracing the southern part of Kentucky and a portion of Tennessee. The Synod at that time embraced all the settled portion of the country west of the mountains.

In 1814, the limits of the Synod were reduced by the erection of the Synod of Ohio, and was again reduced in 1817 by the erection of the Synod of Tennessee; after which the Synod of Kentucky was confined to the bounds of the State.

The Rev. David Rice may justly be regarded as the founder of Presbyterianism in Kentucky. He was born in Hanover County, Virginia, the 20th of December, 1733, the same county which gave birth to that elegant orator and statesman, Henry Clay. Father Rice, by which name he was familiarly known, was about one year the junior of Gen. George Washington. He was converted to religion under the preaching of the distinguished President Edwards, and studied theology under the Rev. John Todd. He took a warm and zealous part in the war of the Revolution, and often harangued the people at country-meetings in regard to their grievances. When he came to Kentucky he was in the fiftieth year of his age. He was an active minister of the gospel. Besides organizing a number of churches, he greatly advanced the cause of education in Kentucky. He was the first teacher in Transylvania Seminary, and for several years chairman of the Board of Trustees; but when that institution was removed to Lexington, and had fallen under deistical influence, he took an active part in raising up a rival in the Kentucky Academy. He was a member of the convention which met at Danville in 1792 to form the first Constitution for the State of Kentucky, and exerted his influence in that convention for the insertion of an article in that instrument providing for the gradual emancipation of slavery in Kentucky, in which he failed of success. By his will he emancipated his own slaves, the younger ones to be free when they attained the age of twenty-three years. His will is on record in the office of the Green County Court.

Previous to Mr. Rice's arrival in Kentucky marriages were uniformly celebrated by justices of the peace, but after that period the services of a minister were always procured on such occasions when possible. On the 3d of June, 1784, he married a couple at McAfee's Station, and on the next day preached the funeral of Mr. James McCann, Sr., the first sermon ever preached on the banks of Salt River.

Mr. Rice was a man of sound judgment, of conservative disposition, and of very exemplary deportment. His talents were of a plain, practical cast; his manner solemn and impressive. In person he was tall and slender, and very active in his movements, even in advanced age. He died in Green County on the 18th of June, 1816, in the eighty-third year of his age, having removed to that county some twenty years previous to his death; and lies buried on the farm now owned by Brice Edwards, Esq., about eleven miles from Greensburg, south of Green River. No stone marks the resting place of the body of this good man.

The Rev. Thomas B. Craighead was a native of North Carolina, and arrived in Kentucky three years after the arrival of Mr. Rice, and was immediately called to the pastoral charge of Shiloh Congregation, in Sumner County, Tennessee. Here he soon became somewhat unpopular on account of suspicions that he favored Pelagianism. The Synod of 1805 appointed a commission to investigate the report of his unsoundness. The investigation resulted in the suspension of Mr. Craighead from the ministry. He made several ineffectual efforts to have the suspension removed, but without effect, until the year 1824, when he made such a vindication of himself as to explain his views to the satisfaction of the General Assembly, which restored him to the ministry. Shortly after this period he died, in Nashville, at the age of about seventy-five years. Previous to his death, for some time, he suffered the misfortune not only of blindness but of poverty also. Mr. Craighead was tall and spare, and about six feet high. He excelled, it is said, as an extemporaneous orator, being of that character which captivates and carries away the hearer in spite of himself. The Hon. John Breckinridge said of him that his discourses made a more lasting impression upon the memory than those of any other man he had ever heard.

The Rev. Andrew McClure, who removed to Kentucky with Mr. Craighead, organized the Salem and Paris churches, and in 1789 took charge of the latter, where he remained until he died in 1793, in the thirty-ninth year of his age.

The Rev. Adam Rankin came from Augusta County, Virginia, in 1784, and settled in Lexington. He immediately became pastor of Mount Zion Church, and subsequently of Pisgah Church, situated about eight miles southwest of Lexington. In 1792 he separated from the Presbyterian Church on account of psalmody, carrying with him a majority of his congregation, and retained possession of the church edifice at Lexington. The portion adhering to the Presbyterian communion erected a new building, to the pastoral charge of which the Rev. James Welch was called in 1795.

The Rev. Robert Marshall came from Ireland to America in the twelfth year of his age, and at sixteen years of age he joined the army of the Revolution. He was in six general engagements, in one of which he narrowly escaped with his life, a bullet grazing his locks. He was licensed by Red Stone Presbytery, and was ordained, in 1793, pastor of Bethel and Blue Spring churches. He was an active leader in the great revival of 1800. In 1803 he embraced the views of the New

Lights; but, convinced of his error seven years afterward, returned to the old church, and in 1812 was reinstated in the pastoral charge of Bethel Church, where he continued until his death, which occurred in 1833, at the age of seventy-three years. His preaching was said to be clear, logical, systematic, calm, and persuasive, except when he attempted to rouse and impress his audience; then he was vehement, and even startling, in his language and manner.

The Rev. Carey H. Allen was ordained pastor of Paint Lick Church on the 11th of October, 1794. He was an eloquent speaker, of great zeal and popularity, and always succeeded in impressing his audience favorably. He died of consumption the 5th day of August, 1795, after a ministry of less than two years. He was a mirthful, pleasant companion, occasionally eccentric. The following incident is related of him while on his way to Kentucky. He stopped for the night where a company of young persons had assembled to dance. They invited him to join them, and no denial would be taken. He was assigned a partner and led out upon the floor, when suddenly he called upon the musician to stop. "My habit is," he said, "when I engage in any business that I am not accustomed to, first to ask the blessing of God upon it. With your permission, therefore, we will ask the blessings of God upon what we are about to do." He accordingly dropped on his knees and poured forth an impressive prayer; then, rising to his feet, followed the prayer with a powerful exhortation. So unexpected an interruption astonished the company and held them spell-bound. The burning words of the speaker sunk into their very souls, and found an echo in their consciences. Many of them burst into tears, and besought him to tell them what they must do to be saved. He continued in the neighborhood several days, and many hopeful conversions were the result of his efforts.

Rev. John P. Campbell, M. D., was regarded as one of the most brilliant of Presbyterian preachers. He was born in Augusta County, Virginia, in 1767, came to Kentucky with his father in 1781, and graduated at Hampden Sidney College in 1790. In 1792 he was licensed to preach, and was at once associated with his preceptor (Dr. Hoge) as co-pastor of Lexington, Oxford, New Monmouth, and Timber Ridge congregations. In 1795 he took up his residence in Kentucky, and his first charge was the churches of Smyrna and Flemingsburg, though he exercised his ministry at Danville, Nicholasville, Versailles, Lexington, Chilicothe, Ohio, and many other places. In the year 1811 he officiated as chaplain to the Kentucky Legislature. He was an accurate and well-read theologian, while his published writings were numerous and regarded as able. He was the author of Strictures on Stone's Letters on the Atonement; Essays on Justification; Letters to Craighead; A Sermon on Christian Baptism; The Pelagian Detected; A Reply to Craighead; An Answer to Jones; and a Review of Robinson's History of Baptism. He was married three times, leaving a family of nine children at his death. He died the 4th of November, 1814, in the vicinity of Chilicothe, Ohio, aged fifty-three years.

The Rev. Samuel Rannells was born in Hampshire County, Virginia, December 10th, 1765, licensed to preach in 1794, and visited Kentucky as a missionary in the spring of 1795. He was ordained over the churches of Paris and Stonermouth in 1796, which charge he retained until his death, which occurred the 24th of March, 1817, in the fifty-second year of his age. He was said to be a man of eminent purity, exemplary conduct, and respectable talents, gifted in prayer, and a zealous minister.

Rev. Robert Stewart came to Kentucky in 1798, and was soon after appointed professor of languages in Transylvania University, but resigned the following year. In 1803 he preached to the church at Salem. In 1804 he took charge of Walnut Hill Church, which he retained for nearly forty years, and was esteemed by all who knew him as a good man. He lived to a very old age, and long after most of his old companions in the ministry had gone to their rest.

Rev. Robert Wilson came to Kentucky as a missionary in 1798. He married and settled in Washington, Mason County, where he remained until his death, October 31st, 1822, in the fiftieth year of his age. He was remarkable during his whole life for his active, humble, and devoted piety; and his labors were greatly blessed, especially in his own flock. He organized the churches of Augusta and Maysville, and was of great advantage to the churches at Smyrna and Flemingsburg, they being in a languishing condition a long time for the want of a pastor.

Rev. John Lyle was born in Rockbridge County, Virginia, the 20th of October, 1769, licensed to preach in 1795, and came to Kentucky as a missionary in 1797. In 1800 he took charge of Salem Church, where he remained several years. He subsequently established one of the most flourishing female schools in Paris, and had from one hundred and fifty to two hundred pupils in attendance. He declined teaching in 1809, but continued his ministerial labors until 1825, in which year he died, on the 22d of July. He was a man of sound judgment and studious habits; and was an earnest, faithful, feeling, and sensible minister. There were many converted under his ministrations.

Rev. Archibald Cameron was a very distinguished preacher of Kentucky. He was a native of Scotland, but came to America when he was very young. He was of good parentage, and the youngest of six children. He was born in 1770 or 1771, moved from Monongahela River to Kentucky in 1781, and settled within six miles of Bardstown, at the foot of what is now called Cameron's Knob. At the age of fifteen he was at the school of Dr. James Priestly, at Bardstown. Among his companions at school were John Rowan, Felix Grundy, John Pope, John Allen, and others who became distinguished in after life. After this Mr. Cameron went to Transylvania University, and became a very accomplished scholar. At nineteen years of age he professed religion, and joined the Presbyterian Church at Bardstown. He studied theology with the Rev. David Rice, and was licensed to preach February 14, 1795, by Transylvania Presbytery. He preached at many points in Nelson, Shelby, and Jefferson counties, and was ordained and installed June 2d, 1796, over the churches at Akron and Fox Run, in Shelby. He preached a great deal, and his labors were spread over a circuit of more than forty miles. A number of churches were planted and built up by him, and great accessions were made to them under his ministrations. He was their pastor for more than forty years.

Mr. Cameron was a man of great intellect, combining strength, originality, and discrimination. His discourses were always systematic, instructive, and practical; also eloquent and impressive, and he was generally regarded as the ablest man in the Synod. He was the author of many published writings of high repute. He died the 4th of December, 1836. During his last illness he was sustained by the spirit of that gospel which with so much faithfulness and success he had preached to his fellow-men.

Rev. James Welch came from Virginia, and was ordained pastor of the churches at Lexington and Georgetown in the year 1796. He continued in this charge until 1804, when he was obliged to practice medicine to support his family. In 1799 he was appointed professor of ancient languages in the Transylvania University, which station he filled for several years. Of the date of his death I am not informed.

Rev. Matthew Houston, Rev. John Dunlavy, and Rev. Richard McNemar, all of whom came to Kentucky about the close of the last century, left the Presbyterian Church and joined the Shakers, a sect that was instituted in America in the year 1774. The head of this sect, or party, was a woman by the name of Ann Lee, (or Leese, as some say). They assert that she is the woman spoken of in the 12th chapter of Revelation; that she speaks seventy-two tongues unintelligible to the living; but she converses with the dead, and they understand her language. They say further, that she is the mother of all the elect, and that she travails for the whole world; and that no blessing can descend to any one except through her. The three ministers above mentioned were respectable and highly educated, otherwise they could not have been Presbyterian ministers; and why, or how, they could have been led away with such absurdities, is unaccountably strange.

The primary principles of this sect (the Shakers) are "faith, hope, honesty, continence, innocence, simplicity, meekness, prudence, patience, thankfulness, and charity." A virgin life is strictly believed to be essential to a true follower of Christ; only the children of the world marry and are given in marriage. They say a true believer's union is spiritual, and needs no fleshy support. Their parentage is spiritual, and produces no fleshy offspring. Their inheritance is spiritual, and cannot be controlled by human laws. Their temporal property, which is necessary for the support of the body while in life, is regulated by a sacred compact. By mutual agreement it is consecrated to religious uses, for the benefit of the whole body, and descends to their spiritual heirs. They say the first gospel dispensation appeared in the male, in the person of Jesus Christ. The second gospel dispensation was manifested in the female, and is the second appearing of Christ in the person of Ann Lee, in which appearing the woman as well as the man is restored to her proper lot and order in the new creation. They do not believe that death is the closing scene of man's probation for eternity. The doctrine of a probationary state beyond the grave was taught by Mother Ann Lee, the spiritual head and founder of the sect. Confession, they say, is the only method whereby one can be cleansed from his sins. Those who have no opportunity in this world of embracing the gospel of Christ's second appearing in the female will have it offered to them in the next, with the other dogmas of their faith; but awful will be the sentence of those souls who, having the privilege, reject it in this world; and they alone of all God's creatures are forever and eternally lost who, having once embraced Shakerism, turn away and become reprobates.

The Shakers believe in a dual God: "A Father, the fountain of wisdom and power, and a Mother, fountain of goodness and love." They believe in direct divine communication—the revelation from the first parents of all souls not only to the man Jesus as the first-born of humanity in the male line, eighteen hundred years ago, but also to the woman Ann Lee, the first-born of humanity in the female line in modern times. Equal suffrage and equal participation in the government of an order founded by a woman is recognized.

The ministers live in a house by themselves. The power vested in them is absolute. They make all the appointments;

each succeeding minister is appointed by his predecessor. They claim the true apostolic succession or "holy anointing" from Mother Ann Lee, and the first fathers and mothers in the church, which is the Millennial Church. Every member has access to the confessional at all times, but there is one day in the year especially set apart as a season of fasting and confession. It is invariably appointed for a Sabbath day, and occurs about the thanksgiving period in the New England States. The ordinary services are dispensed with on this day, which makes the day appear very long, to the younger portion of their community especially. While the world's people are feasting on thanksgiving fare, they are ruminating on the bitter food of reflection.

For social purposes there is a "retiring-house," which is occupied evenings and Sundays by the brethren and sisters. Here are the sitting-rooms, wherein to wait till all descend together, and in order to the dining-hall. The sleeping apartments are in the same building, situated on either side of long corridors. The rooms to the right as you enter are devoted to the use of the brethren; the opposite ones belong to the sisters. Four or five persons occupy the same suite, which consists of the sleeping-room, leading to a clothes-room and bath-room. Shaker neatness and cleanliness are proverbial.

On Sunday, Tuesday, and Friday evenings, an hour is devoted to a union meeting. Then the brethren and sisters living in opposite apartments meet for conversation. Each sex sits in a long row, facing the other, about five feet apart. Anecdotes are related, and poetry is repeated, provided it is original, or by another believer; for "world's poetry" is tabooed, lest it might contain sentiments of love. New songs which have been sent by other societies are learned, and visitors discussed, and perhaps criticised by a young brother or sister, who are sharply reproved by their seniors as not competent to pass judgment; but stocks, bonds, real estate, the Gold Board, and politics are especially forbidden. In the large hall, above the refectories, evening services are held on Wednesday, Thursday, and Saturday evenings of every week, and on stormy Sundays, when the meeting-house is not opened. The foregoing account of the Shakers is compiled from the statement of a lady who was a Shakeress for fifteen years.

Rev. Joseph P. Howe came from North Carolina in 1794, and was ordained over the churches at Mount Sterling and Springfield in July, 1795. He prayed and sang well, and acted a very conspicuous part in the great revival in Kentucky about the beginning of the present century. He died in the year 1830.

The Rev. John Howe, a younger brother of the Rev. Joseph P. Howe, was first installed pastor of the churches of Beaver Creek and Little Barren in April, 1798, which relation he sustained for some few years. He became pastor of the church at Greensburg, Green County, about the year 1805, and remained at this place a year or two, conducting a school, in the meantime, with marked success. On the county-court order-book the following entry is made March 25th, 1805: "It is ordered that the Rev. John Howe and his scholars have the east jury-room of the court-house for school purposes, and James Allen, Wm. Barret, and Daniel White gave bond of indemnity against damages." How long he remained preaching and teaching at this place the writer cannot, at this late period, ascertain; but he returned afterward to his former residence in Barren County, and remained there until the year 1812, when he again returned to Green, purchased a farm of one hundred acres of land near Greensburg, where he continued to reside until the fall of 1845. During that period of thirty-three years he preached, and at least two-thirds of the time taught school in New Athens Seminary, at Greensburg. The greater part of that time he had charge of three congregations—Greensburg, Bethel, and Ebenezer. Never were people more devoted to a minister than were the people of these several congregations to him. He was a very learned man, especially in the classics, and very popular as a teacher. His school was always as full as he could wish, and sometimes a great deal more so. When such was the case and he could not well manage it himself, the writer assisted him, and was the only assistant he ever employed whilst teaching in Greensburg. Many leading men in after life were pupils of his school, some of them from distant counties, and a few even from distant States. To name some of them, the companions of the writer at this school, were Judge A. W. Graham and Voltair Loving, of Bowlinggreen; Judge Barnett, of Green; Judge Richard A. Buckner, now of Lexington; Judge Burr H. Emerson, now of Missouri; Doctors Sterrett, Briggs, and Barclay, of Bowlinggreen; Dr. Lewis Barret, of Munfordville, now deceased; Dr. Richard F. Barret, late professor in the Medical School of St. Louis; Dr. Isaac Burnett, a distinguished physician of Western Kentucky; Dr. John D. Winstone, now of Nashville; Dr. Wm. L. Howe; Dr. James J. Allen, who died in Jackson, Mississippi; Dr. John Rowan Allen, now of Memphis, Tenn.; Hon. Henry Grider, of Bowlinggreen, now deceased; Hon. Aylett Buckner, lately deceased; Rev. John Howe Brown, now of Springfield, Illinois, for a great number of years pastor of the church at Richmond, Ky., and principal of a Female High School, and afterward for many years pastor of McCord Church, Lexington, Ky.; Rev. Martin Baker, of the Cumberland Presbyterian Church; Rev. David F. Dickinson, of the Methodist Church, now of Illinois; Rev. Wm. Scott, of Bloomfield, Ky., of the Presbyterian Church; Rev. Richard Howe Allen, at present pastor of the oldest church in Philadelphia; Hon. Hiram Rountree, of Hillsborough, Illinois. Many lawyers of eminence, viz: Wm. T. Willis, who was killed at the battle of Buena Vista; Benj. G. Burks, who died in Texas; Samuel J. Cook, now living in Arkansas; Arthur P. Buckner, who died in Mississippi; John McFerran, Cornelius Burnett, and Joseph Hardin, all deceased; Napoleon B. Burks, president of a literary institution in Texas; besides a number of others which space will not allow me to mention.

Mr. Howe's wife, a most estimable lady, formerly a Miss Wallace, having died in 1842, and his youngest and only single daughter having married a Mr. Reuben Creel, who had determined to remove to Missouri, the old gentleman concluded to accompany him, and with that view, in the fall of 1845, being then about seventy-five years old, sold out his farm and went to Missouri, settling in Pettus County, near the town of Otterville, in the same neighborhood of some of his children, who had gone there many years previously. Here he continued to reside until his death, which occurred twelve years afterward.

He was born the 31st of December, 1769, in North Carolina, and came to Kentucky in 1794. He removed to Missouri in 1845, and died in 1857, in the eighty-eighth year of his age. I never knew him to be sick during my acquaintance with him, a period of about thirty-five years. He was about five feet ten inches high; active and slightly corpulent; walked erect and with a quick step at seventy-five years of age, when I last saw him. He was never known to have a personal difficulty with any one; amiable in his disposition, sociable in conversation, firm, unyielding and undeviating in his religious principles. He had no enemies even among those who differed with him in religious sentiments. His whole life was devoted to preaching and teaching. He engaged in no secular pursuits. Even his farm received but little of his attention, being carried on exclusively by the few negroes which he owned. He was a kind husband and an indulgent father and master. Within the year preceding his death he became quite doted, and did not recognize at times his most intimate friends and acquaintances. But few of his writings were ever published. I have seen several of his published sermons, delivered on funeral occasions—one on the occasion of the death of Gen. James Allen's first wife, another on the occasion of the death of the writer's first wife. Both of these were admirable productions. He was never known in my day to read a sermon, or even to use skeletons or notes. His sermons were plain, sensible and convincing, without pathos. It was but seldom that his discourses had the effect to move to tears. On one occasion, however, I remember to have heard a lady, a member of his congregation, shout like a Methodist, which occurrence so moved upon the whole congregation that there was scarcely a dry eye in the house. The inward emotions of his own heart were often made manifest by the silent trickling tear upon his own face.

Rev. James Blythe was born in North Carolina in 1765; came to Kentucky as a licentiate in 1791; in 1793 was ordained pastor of Pisgah and Clear Creek churches, and continued as pastor or stated supply for these churches some forty years. He took an active part in the establishment of the Kentucky Academy, and when, in 1798, that institution was merged into Transylvania University, he was appointed professor of mathematics, natural philosophy, astronomy, and geography; and when Mr. Moore resigned, he fulfilled the duties of president of that institution for some twelve or fifteen years. When, in 1818, Dr. Holley was elected president of the institution, Dr. Blythe was transferred to the chair of chemistry in the Medical Department, which situation he retained until 1831. After this he was appointed president of Hanover College, Indiana, where he died in 1842, in the seventy-seventh year of his age.

Rev. James McCord was born in Baltimore in 1785, and was brought to Lexington at five years of age. He had a liberal education, and commenced reading law with the Hon. Henry Clay at an early age. Becoming pious he devoted himself to the ministry, and was the first pastor of the Second Presbyterian Church, of Lexington, in 1815, which situation he filled for four years, and then moved to Paris. His published writings were numerous, among them two volumes of his sermons. He was a man of great intellect and remarkable brilliancy. His successors in the Second, or McCord Church, as it was afterward called, were able and eloquent men also— the Rev. John Breckinridge in 1823, Rev. John C. Young in 1829, and the Rev. John H. Brown in 1844. That pulpit has always been well-filled, even to the present time, with ministers of the best ability. Mr. McCord died in the year 1820.

Rev. Gideon Blackburn was one of the most eloquent divines of his day in Kentucky. He encountered many difficulties in early life, being left an orphan at eleven years of age; but he surmounted them all and became a proficient scholar. It was his misfortune to lose a patrimonial estate of about $20,000. He obtained a situation in a saw-mill for a while, and four months he labored as a surveyor, frequently sleeping in a canebrake, to avoid the Indians, with no other covering than a blanket. He received his pay for surveying in horses, which he took to Maryland and sold for $1,500, which enabled him to pay all his debts and take him through Dickinson College. In 1803, when he was thirty-one years old, he was appointed by the General Assembly missionary to the Cherokee Indians. In 1827 he was appointed president of Center College, which situation he filled for three years, and was succeeded by the Rev. Dr. Young. The last years of his life were spent in Illinois, where he died.

Revs. James McFarland and David Nelson were both preachers of a high order of talent. The former died in 1828, whilst pastor of the church in Paris. The latter died in Illinois in the year 1844.

Rev. Thomas Cleland was of the second generation of pioneer preachers in Kentucky. Revs. David Rice, Zerah Templin, Robert Marshall, and their fellow-laborers in the Presbyterian Church, were older than he. So were Wm. Hickman, Lewis Craig, and John Gano, among the Baptists, and Francis Poythress, Benjamin Ogden, and James Haw, among the Methodists, though nearly all of these were alive when he commenced the ministry. He was cotemporary, however, among the Presbyterians, with Carey H. Allen, John P. Campbell, John Lyle, Robert Stewart, Archibald Cameron, and some others, being a few years younger than any of them. He survived them all. Other distinguished men in other professions were his cotemporaries also—Henry Clay, Felix Grundy, Joseph H. Davis, John Boyle, John Rowan, John Pope, Wm. T. Barry, Benjamin Mills, and Benjamin Hardin—the three latter were younger, and the former older than he. Dr. Cleland was in the ministry fifty-five years, commencing in 1803, and terminating with his death in 1858. He participated actively in the revival, and was quite efficient as an exhorter some two years before his licensure to preach. After his licensure he made many missionary tours, and effected much good, visiting places which had never before been visited by Presbyterian preachers. He held the first Presbyterian meeting that was ever held in Wayne County, Kentucky, and also the first at Vincennes, Indiana. Mr. Cleland came to Kentucky with his father in the year 1789, and was then but eleven years old. They lived at first on a place belonging to Colonel Richard Taylor, the father of General Zach. Taylor, in a cabin in the edge of a dense canebrake, and Wm. Hancock and Zach. Taylor were his playmates. Mr. Cleland was designed at first by his father for the profession of the law, and with that view every opportunity which his father could possibly afford was embraced for the bestowment of a good education upon him. On the 1st day of January, 1795, then in the eighteenth year of his age, accompanied by his father, he came to Greensburg with the view of learning Latin and Greek under the instruction of General James Allen, who was a highly educated young lawyer and clerk of the county and Quarter Session Court, and boarded with John C. Allen, Esq., the brother of James. He remained here some nine months, reciting his lessons in the clerk's office, and in that short period attained unprecedented proficiency, having read all the Latin authors in use in those days, amounting to nine books, from Corderias to Ovid inclusive. He also committed to memory several lengthy orations, Cicero against Veres, Cataline, &c. After this he went to school some eighteen months at the Kentucky Academy, at Pisgah, Woodford County. When he was in the twenty-second year of his age he went to Transylvania University, at Lexington, to complete his education, but the time he intended to spend there was cut short, first by the death of his mother, and then of his father, which events occurred in the year 1799. These events changed the course of his future life. He had some religious impressions at an early period of life, but it was during his residence at Greensburg that his conscience was greatly quickened. It was here he first saw and heard the Rev. John Howe, who had just been licensed to preach, and with whom he was greatly pleased. He saw at this place also the Rev. Samuel Findley, who, in passing, preached several sermons, which he heard with pleasure and delight. About this time he often retired to the woods, and kneeled down in some deep sink-hole to pray, unobserved by any but God. Mr. Cleland was born the 22d of May, 1778, in Fairfax County, Virginia, and died at his residence, near New Providence Meeting-house, in Mercer County, January 31st, 1858, just fifty-eight years to a day after the death of his mother. Mr. Cleland was married within the bounds of New Providence Church, of which he was afterward pastor, on the 22d day of October, 1801, to Miss Margaret Armstrong, a most estimable lady in all regards. She died the 24th of April, 1854. The first sermon he ever preached after licensure was at the house of Robert Caldwell, in Mercer County. His text was "Come thou, and thy house, into the Ark." His early preaching was at Springfield and Hardin's Creek, now Lebanon. In 1803 the Rev. Samuel B. Robinson, at that time pastor of the churches of Cane Run and New Providence, organized a church called Union, some eight or ten miles above Lebanon, consisting of a Mr. Copeland and wife and seven others. Under the ministrations of Mr. Cleland there were thirty more added to the church that year. In October, 1804, Mr. Cleland was ordained pastor of this church, which about that time numbered one hundred members.

Before the establishment of theological seminaries, Mr. Cleland's house became, in the language of one, "the school of the prophets." The following young men were students of divinity under his supervision, viz: Nathan H. Hall, John R. Moreland, James C. Barnes, Charles Phillips, Samuel Wilson, John H. Brown, Wm. Dixon, Robert L. Mafee, Wm. H. Forsythe, Robert Hamilton, David Todd, Robert Caldwell, F. R. Gray, Joshua H. Wilson, and G. Moore, most of whom are still living, and nearly all of them highly distinguished as preachers. John H. Brown married a daughter of Mr. Cleland, and two of his sons, both still living, are ministers also of the Presbyterian Church. After spending twenty-three years of his most active life in Washington County, he moved to Mercer County to take charge of New Providence Church in 1813, and on the 31st of March he also took charge of the Cane Run Church, shortly before under the care of the Rev. Samuel B. Robinson for a space of ten years. Mr. Cleland continued to preach once a month at Union for three years after his removal from that neighborhood. About 1815 commenced Mr. Cleland's literary labors, which were numerous. There were two very able productions from his pen published previous to that date, and after that date some twenty odd, a list of which would occupy more space than we can conveniently allow, extending through a period of near forty years. The 10th of July, 1822, he received from Transylvania University the honorary degree of D. D. At that time Dr. Blythe was the only D. D. in Kentucky. Mr. Cleland received this honor with great reluctance. On account of his health he was compelled to give up his pastoral charges some three or four years before his death, and died in the eightieth year of his age, beloved by all who ever knew him.

Mr. Cleland was an able, eloquent, and popular preacher, and enjoyed more extensive usefulness than almost any other man. He had extraordinary control over the sympathetic feelings of his hearers. Under his melting appeals entire congregations have often been seen weeping, sometimes to sob, and even to cry aloud. His preaching was full of pathos, not alarming, but moving and persuasive, and made his hearers feel. He never read his sermons. The Rev. Mr. Barnes said of his preaching, "that it was instructive to the ignorant, encouraging to the timid, and edifying to the believer."

Rev. John Breckinridge was a son of the Hon. John Breckinridge, of whom we have heretofore spoken, and was born on North Elkhorn, in Fayette County, on the 4th of July, 1797, and died in the forty-fourth year of his age, August 4, 1841, at the same place. He was deprived by death of his father when he was but nine years old. His distinguished brother, J. Cabell Breckinridge, was his guardian, by whom he was principally reared. He attended the best schools Kentucky afforded, and completed his education at Princeton, New Jersey, where he graduated with great distinction in the year 1818. He was designed for the law, but becoming a subject of divine grace while at Princeton, joined the Presbyterian Church, and at once determined to devote himself to the gospel ministry, and after spending several years more at Princeton as a student of theology, and part of the time as a teacher in the college, he was licensed and ordained a minister of Jesus Christ. In 1822 he was Chaplain of the House of Representatives in Congress. In 1823 he became pastor of the McCord Church in Lexington. In 1826 he removed to Baltimore, as co-partner of the late Dr. Glendy, and afterward was sole pastor of the Second Presbyterian Church of that city. In 1831 he removed to Philadelphia as Secretary and General Agent of the Board of Education of the Presbyterian Church. In 1836 he was elected professor in the theological seminary at Princeton. Upon the organization of the Board of Missions of the Presbyterian Church he was elected Secretary and General Agent, and continued at the head of the operations of that board from 1833 to 1840. At the period of his death he was the pastor elect of the University of Oglethorpe, Georgia. He was as universally known, loved, and admired as any minister of the gospel possibly could be. His talents were of the highest order. He was highly distinguished in the attainments of his profession, and none excelled him as a pulpit orator. So greatly was he admired and loved, that calls and invitations to churches, colleges, &c., were continually pressed upon him from every quarter of the country. In personal appearance he was of middle stature, finely formed, and possessed of great strength and activity. He was twice married. His second wife and one child, and three children by his first marriage, survived him.

Rev. Samuel B. Robinson was the predecessor of Mr. Cleland at Providence and Cane Run churches, and was ordained as pastor of these churches October 23, 1801. He came from Harrison County to Mercer, and lived on a plantation near Harrodsburg, purchased for his benefit. The great revival continued in his church until the year 1805, and so great had the membership and congregation become, that the church building about that time was greatly enlarged. Mr. Robinson was generally admired as a preacher at that day. He was warm and ardent in his devotional exercises, and was regarded as an excellent Christian; but many of his congregation became negligent in paying him his salary, in consequence of which he left them and removed to Columbia, Adair County, Kentucky, in the year 1812, where he continued to reside for many years, having the care of the church at that place, and I believe the church at Shiloh also, a few miles from the town. He often preached at Ebenezer Church, in Green County, and always assisted the Rev. John Howe at Greensburg on sacramental occasions. His first wife having died, he married, though quite advanced in years, a lady near Lebanon, and went there to live, and continued to reside there until his death. He is the grandfather of the Rev. Mr. Cheek, of Danville.

Robert J. Breckinridge having lately died, and being justly regarded as one of the master spirits of the age in whatever light he may be viewed, I deem it a duty indispensable to give a synopsis, at least, of his life and character:

He was the seventh child and fourth son of the eminently distinguished politician, statesman, and lawyer, John Breckinridge, whose history I have heretofore given. He was born at Cabell Dale, Fayette County, Kentucky, on the 8th day of March, 1800. Through his ancestry on both his father's and his mother's side he brings an unbroken Protestant lineage from the Reformation, and his ancestors took part in the memorable defense of Londonderry in the seventeenth century. He received his education in Kentucky, until he was sixteen years old. His teachers were Thompson, Wilson, O'Harra, and Brock, all well-known in central Kentucky as such at that period. When in his seventeenth year he followed his brother John, whose history I have also given, to Princeton College, New Jersey, where his brother Cabell graduated a few years previously. He remained at Princeton two years, and then spent one winter at Yale College; thence he went to Union College, New York, where he graduated under the presidency of the great Dr. Nott in 1819. In the summer of 1820 he returned to Kentucky, and resided with his mother until his marriage, the 11th of March, 1823. During this period his time was occupied in reading law, writing for the press, managing the business of his mother, and acting as administrator of his father's large estate, from which alone one of the most important lawsuits ever tried in any of our courts originated. The suit was with the Hon. Robert Wickliffe, whose history I have heretofore given. In 1824 he commenced the practice of law in Lexington as a partner of the late Charleton Hunt. He took an active part in the politics of that day, was an Old Court man, and was elected to the Legislature on that ticket in 1824 from Fayette County. He took a prominent part in shaping the legislation which quieted the State, and settled the controversy then existing, which at one time threatened seriously civil war. He was returned to the Legislature again in 1826, also in 1827 and 1828. With the winter of 1828 ended his career as a politician and statesman. Making a profession of religion, he joined the Presbyterian Church under the pastorage of his nephew-in-law, the Rev. J. C. Young. After this he moved his membership to Mt. Horeb, near his own farm in Fayette County, and was chosen a ruling elder in that church. As elder of the church he sat in the General Assembly which met in Cincinnati in 1831. Early in life he became hostile to negro slavery, and an advocate of gradual emancipation. He also favored the passage of a law to prohibit the carrying of the mails on Sunday; and in the summer of 1831 became an independent candidate for the Legislature, but perceiving that his views, though he had argued the question ably, were not likely to be adopted by the people of his county, he withdrew from the canvass on the morning of the election. In the spring of 1832 he was licensed to preach the gospel by West Lexington Presbytery. Immediately after this he removed with his family to Princeton for private instruction, and to attend the lectures of Sir Archibald Alexander. While at Princeton he was called to the Second Presbyterian Church, Baltimore, previously occupied by his distinguished brother John. Here he soon became engaged in a heated controversy with the Catholics, and though warned to expect personal violence he did not cease his attacks upon them. He also opposed the Universalists, and engaged heartily in the advocacy of temperance, and did not forget in the meantime the advocacy of his anti-slavery principles. He commenced here, too, a thorough evangelization of the city of Baltimore and the State of Maryland. He made himself while at Baltimore a thorough Hebrew scholar, and learned to read the French, German, and Italian languages. He was on the side of the Old School party in the great controversy which divided the Presbyterian Church some thirty odd years ago, and was the author of some of the great papers which rent the Church. In the General Assembly of 1837 he was the acknowledged leader of the Old School party. He was the principal contributor by his writings in 1835 to the religious and literary magazine established in Baltimore by himself and the Rev. Andrew B. Cross; also of the "Spirit of the Nineteenth Century." In the fall of 1836, accompanied by his wife, he made a trip to Europe, and remained about a year. In Glasgow, Scotland, occurred his famous debate on slavery with George Thompson, followed by his more noted letter to Dr. Wardlow on the same subject. Upon his return from Europe he resumed his labors at Baltimore, preaching, lecturing, and writing. In 1841 he was Moderator of the General Assembly. His wife died in 1845, after which he accepted the presidency of Jefferson College, at Cannonsburg, Pennsylvania. In 1847 he returned to Kentucky, and accepted the pastorate of the First Presbyterian Church at Lexington, Kentucky, where he remained until 1853, when he accepted a professorship in Danville Theological Seminary, founded by his efforts mainly, which he held until 1869. After that time he resided in Danville as a private citizen.

In the fall of 1847 he was appointed by Governor Owsley, Superintendent of Public Instruction, and became the author of the school law that gave the State an efficient system of common schools. He held this position until 1854, having been elected to it by the people in 1850. After the adoption of the new Constitution, Mr. Breckinridge was the candidate of the emancipation party in 1849 for the Constitutional Convention, but was defeated, as he thought, through the hesitancy of Mr. Clay to sanction the movement. The debates of that year were high, and no defender of slavery dared meet Mr. Breckinridge.

When the secession cloud began to rise in Kentucky he came forward boldly for the Union, and spoke earnest and determined words for it. His Fast Day Sermon at Lexington, in 1861, on that subject, was more widely published and read than anything before or since from him. He opposed with great vehemence the late Declaration and Testimony party of the Synod of Kentucky. Since 1869 he has taken no active part in the affairs of Church and State, but being in feeble health, waited for the summons to rest from his labors and enter upon his reward.

His reputation as a good theologian has been established both at home and in Europe by two volumes published by him, one entitled "The Knowledge of God Objectively Considered," and the other "The Knowledge of God Subjectively Considered." A third volume, "A Defense of Revealed Truth from all Attacks of Unbelievers," is left in an incomplete condition. In 1837 he published "Travels in Europe" in two volumes. His great lecture upon the "Internal Evidences of Christianity" is published in "University of Virginia Lectures upon Evidences of Christianity." Dr. Breckinridge was a very extensive writer, and were his writings, theological, political, moral, and historical collected, would make a dozen or more large volumes. His power as a speaker was great, and his eloquence captivating. He spoke with earnestness and great solemnity. His knowledge of scriptures was thorough and minute. He was noted for the tender love he bore for his children, and the sweetness of his family intercourse. His mind was richly stored with knowledge from ancient and modern times, gathered from all fields, history, science, and language. His manners were thoroughly polite, kind, and dignified. He took great interest in farming, and was a careful breeder of fine stock. He departed this life the 27th day of December, 1871, in the seventy-second year of his age, leaving a large estate, which he had inherited and husbanded well, as a heritage to his descendants. The wife, a most estimable lady, who survives him, is his third one. He leaves, also, seven children. His life was one of labor and good deeds. This generation has known no abler, truer, or more worthy man than Robert Jefferson Breckinridge. Jefferson was added to his name at the special request of President Jefferson.

The age in which Dr. Breckinridge lived produced no mind that we thought superior to that of Dr. Breckinridge. At a very early age he established himself as the best stump orator of the State—superior by the clearness of his thought, force, and vividness of his expression. As a lawyer, even to his last years, his opinion was sought by those most distinguished in the intricacies of the profession. As a theologian, his works will have a lasting effect. As a preacher, he had no superior. As an emancipationist, and as a Union man, he ever grappled as a Christian, and not as a politician; and as soon as these questions became settled he abandoned the discussion. What would have been the effect upon the future had Dr. Breckinridge allowed his name to have been placed upon the national ticket with Mr. Lincoln in 1864 as the Republican candidate, which was greatly and generally desired, we can not form an opinion. That he declined the honor was regretted by a great number who witnessed the administration of Andrew Johnson, whose nomination and election Dr. Breckinridge is reported to have opposed to the last; and after events proved the justness of his opposition.

A few years ago the Presbyterian Church became politically divided—one party is called the General Assembly party, the other the Declaration and Testimony party. There is no difference, however, as I perceive, in their religious sentiments, and it is to be hoped that their difficulties will be settled at no distant day, and that they may again become united. I give below the status of the parties respectively, as reported in the proceedings of their General Assemblies for 1870:

General Assembly Party.		Declaration and Testimony Party.		Total.
Ministers	51	Ministers	80	131
Licentiates	4	Licentiates	6	10
Candidates	6	Candidates	8	14
Churches	126	Churches	130	256
Communicants	5,510	Communicants	4,609	10,119

HISTORICAL SKETCH OF THE PROTESTANT EPISCOPAL CHURCH.

Kentucky was first settled by emigrants from Virginia and North Carolina, and as both of these were Royal colonies, wherein the Episcopal Church was not only greatly favored by the laws, but where rectors, clergy, and large landholders were nearly all Episcopalians, it would be reasonable to expect that a very large proportion of the emigrants would have been members of that church. It was not so, however, owing to the fact that the hardship of first settlements, and fear of Indian hostilities, restrained all but the poorer and more adventurous portion of the people from venturing upon so hazardous an enterprise, and very few of those belonged to the Episcopal Church. It so happened, however, that the Henderson Colony, from North Carolina, were mostly Episcopalians, and brought with them a clergyman, the Rev. Mr. Lisle (in Collin's History of Kentucky his name is spelled Lithe), and it is on the authority, probably, of the speech of Governor Morehead's oration, that the first public service for the worship of Almighty God in Kentucky, on the Lord's Day, was under the shadow of a forest oak at Boonesboro, with the use of the Episcopal Prayer Book.

The Revolution brought about the disestablishment of the Episcopal Church in these colonies. The effect upon the Virginia clergy, who were by no means remarkable for disinterested devotion to their sacred calling, was immediate and very startling. Deprived of their incomes, and threatened with the confiscation of their glebes, a large number of their best educated and aspiring men at once abandoned their calling, and sought a living in other learned professions, or by teaching or farming. By this time the fame of the rich wild lands of Kentucky had reached Virginia; the severer hardships of the pioneers had been overcome, Indian hostilities had ceased, and henceforth among the emigrants were many substantial, adventurous farmers, and some young aspiring professional men. Some of these were Presbyterians, and a very few, here and there, Episcopalians. An impoverished but highly educated class of clergymen, ready to avoid or escape the opprobrium of turning their backs upon their sacred profession, accompanied these emigrants, and, it is believed, in rather disproportionate numbers.

Bishop B. B. Smith some years ago, by diligent inquiry, obtained the names of six clergymen, who, having been educated in this country, had gone to England for Holy Orders, the mother country having persistently refused to send bishops, though frequent petitions were forwarded for that purpose. Of these six, three at least rose to no inconsiderable eminence in their newly chosen professions. Bishop Smith had seen the letters of orders of Judge Sebastian, of Dr. Chambers, of Bardstown, and of Dr. Gant, of Louisville. The Rev. Mr. Elliott, of Franklin, never renounced his office, but is believed to have exercised it but seldom. The same is true of the Rev. Mr. Crawford, of Shelby. Little is known of the Rev. Mr. Johnson, of Nelson. Not one of these took any part in organizing a parish, or in endeavoring to revive a church whose prospects for the future they no doubt regarded as absolutely hopeless.

All these years the few scattered Episcopalians were being slowly, and in some cases very reluctantly, swallowed up by the more numerous bodies around them. No effort anywhere appears of a parochial organization, or of any effort to obtain the services of a clergyman from over the mountains.

Somewhere between 1800 and 1810 two clergymen, apparently uncalled and unsought for, made their appearance—the Rev. Mr. Kavenaugh, in Henderson, where he soon afterward died; and Rev. Mr. James Moore, at Lexington, where, for some years, he held the distinguished position of President of Transylvania University. He was the first minister of the Episcopal Church of the United States who permanently located in Kentucky. He emigrated to the State in 1792 from Virginia, and was at that time a candidate for the ministry in the Presbyterian Church. His trial sermons not being sustained by the Transylvania Presbytery, Mr. Moore became displeased with what he considered rigorous treatment, and in 1794 sought refuge in the Episcopal Church. Soon afterward he became the first rector of Christ's Church in Lexington. He was appointed to the presidency of the University in the year 1798, and was professor of logic, metaphysics, moral philosophy, and belles-lettres. Under his control this institution enjoyed a good degree of prosperity. He was distinguished for sound learning, devoted piety, courteous manners, and liberal hospitality. It is believed that Mr. Kavenaugh had also been a Presbyterian minister.

The Rev. John Lisle, or Lythe, as he is called in Collin's History, of the Episcopal Church or Church of England, was in Kentucky when Colonel Henderson established his proprietary government in 1775, and was a delegate from the Harrodsburg Station to the Legislative Assembly. This Assembly met the 23d of May, 1775. The records of that Assembly show that Mr. Lythe brought in a bill to "prevent profane swearing and Sabbath-breaking." After being read the first time it was recommitted to a committee composed of Lythe, Todd, and Harrod, to make amendments. Mr. Lythe was also one of the committee appointed to draw up a contract between the proprietors and the people of the colony. The day succeeding the adjournment of the Assembly "divine service," as the journal records, "was performed by the Rev. Mr. Lythe, of the Church of England," and it was under the shade of an elm tree this service was performed. But little is known of Mr. Lythe, except what the legislative proceedings of Transylvania show. He officiated as chaplain, and his name appears upon several important committees, which show that he was a man of some note. What became of him afterward seems not to be known at this remote day.

Kavenaugh and Moore both, it is believed, sought for Episcopal ordination, either at the hands of Bishop White or Bishop Madison, soon after the Episcopal Church had obtained from England the consecration of a bishop for Pennsylvania and Virginia.

About this time a new era dawned upon the Church in Kentucky. A missionary spirit at the East inclined the young men entering the Church to seek out fields of usefulness in the far West; and at Lexington efforts were made to secure the services of some one to succeed the Rev. Mr. Moore in his position as rector of Christ Church. The Rev. John Ward was really the first who infused an earnest church life into any parish in Kentucky. The Rev. Mr. Shaw soon made his appearance in Louisville, and began, though with far less success, a like work. The Rev. Mr. Burgess, a nephew of the Rev. Mr. Ward, soon followed him to Kentucky, but his life and ministry were very short, and so also were those of the Rev. Mr. Osgood, in Henderson, who after several years succeeded the Rev. Mr. Kavenaugh. Thus the two first ministers of that place lie buried there.

We are now approaching the period when were really laid the foundations of the Protestant Episcopal Church in the diocese of Kentucky. In 1820 the Rev. George Chapman succeeded the Rev. John Ward, who had removed to St. Louis, where he accomplished the same great and good work of a parochial organization that he had done in Lexington. It was not until toward the close of Dr. Chapman's ten year rectorship, that indications of growth elsewhere began to manifest themselves. The Rev. David C. Page had imparted new life to Christ Church, Louisville. At Danville the materials for the formation of a parish had been collected during occasional visits from Dr. Chapman. A desire was felt at Henderson for the renewal of church services. But above all, church life had been largely infused into the dioceses of Connecticut, Pennsylvania, and Virginia; and indeed, since 1810, into the whole Church on the Atlantic slope.

This spirit became so strong in 1829, that the Rt. Rev. Thos. C. Brownell, Bishop of Connecticut, was sent upon a missionary tour to Kentucky, and to the regions beyond, even to the shores of the Gulf of Mexico. He held the first confirmations ever administered in Kentucky. A large number were confirmed in Lexington, and not a few in Louisville. The clergymen were aroused to new exertions, and a few zealous laymen animated with new hopes that the old Church might live again. Earlier that same year a very deep impression was made by a visit from that remarkable man, Bishop Ravenscroft, of North Carolina, whose majestic presence and impassioned eloquence have left memories which can never be effaced.

The wise counsels of these bishops led to the calling of the first convention of the clergy and laity of the diocese, and to its permanent organization. After the organization of this diocese, in 1831, the Rt. Rev. Wm. Meade, D. D., made still a more thorough visitation of it, entering at Maysville and terminating at Hopkinsville. The warmth with which he was everywhere received by emigrants from the Old Dominion, of every religious denomination, was very marked; and at his suggestion the first steps were taken which led, the next year, to the election of its first bishop.

In 1830 the Rev. Dr. Chapman resigned his position as rector of Christ Church, Lexington, and was succeeded by the Rev. B. B. Smith, D. D., now one of the Rt. Rev. Bishops of the United States.

At the Convention of 1832 the diocese had the requisite number of clergy to entitle it to the choice of a bishop, which fell upon the Rev. Benjamin Bosworth Smith, rector of Christ Church, Lexington, whose consecration took place the following October, in St. Paul's Church, in the city of New York. At that time, including the bishop, there were in the diocese six clergymen, and six organized parishes: Louisville, Lexington, Danville, Paris, Henderson, and Hopkinsville, only two of which, Louisville and Lexington, had completed edifices, and there was one incomplete at Danville. Lexington, the mother church, had nearly one hundred communicants—as many as in all the other churches combined. Including a few scattered abroad, it is probable that the whole number of communicants in the diocese did not exceed two hundred. From this period the growth of the Church, though by no means rapid, has been steady and uninterrupted. As yet it is confined chiefly to cities and county towns, and has hardly penetrated at all into rural districts. It is doubtful whether a single parish is mainly supported by those who derive their income from the cultivation of the soil.

In the course of thirty years, the expansion of the Church over so large a territory, the increased and more urgent calls for missionary work in all parts of the diocese, together with the increasing years of the first bishop, led to various plans for the election of an assistant bishop, which resulted, in the fall of

1867, in the consecration of the Rt. Rev. George D. Cummins, D. D., who entered at once upon his arduous duties in several places with marked success, so that in 1870 the church edifices had increased to thirty-five, the number of clergy, including the two bishops, to forty-five, and of communicants there were three thousand five hundred, of whom, in eight churches in Louisville, were one thousand two hundred and fifty. The increase in all other respects has been about in the same proportion. Meantime, the anti-revolutionary prejudice against the Church has almost entirely died away. Doctrinal preaching of a bitter and controversial character happily belongs to the past. A generous and comprehensive spirit of charity warms the heart of the younger clergy of all denominations, and to the utter exclusion of party politics from all Episcopal pulpits. All these things combined, inspire the hope that the growth of the Protestant Episcopal Church in Kentucky will proportionably be much greater during the next fifty years than it has been during the last forty.

I omitted to mention in its proper place, that during the visit of Bishop Ravenscroft to Lexington, in the summer of 1829, was the first occasion of confirmation being administered in the diocese. It is not known under what circumstances the bishop was invited to visit Lexington, but the impression made there by his majestic presence, his eloquence, and great number confirmed by him on that occasion, will never be forgotten.

The Rev. Benjamin O. Peers, of the Episcopal Church, became quite distinguished in Kentucky, not only for his devotion to the cause of general education, but for his learning and ardent piety also. He was first a member of the Presbyterian Church, and studied theology at Princeton; but after completing his course in that institution he connected himself with the Episcopal Church, and located in Lexington, where he established the Eclectic Institute, which became one the most valuable institutions of learning in the West.

He spent much time, labor, and money in the cause of common school education, and contributed by his untiring efforts, more, perhaps, than any other man in Kentucky, in arousing public attention to the importance of the subject, and bringing about our present common school system. Mr. Peers was distinguished also as a writer of no inconsiderable celebrity. His work on Christian Education appears to have been his favorite of his published works. Mr. Peers, while at the head of the Eclectic Institute, was chosen president of Transylvania University, which position he accepted contrary to the advice of many of his friends, and held the position but for a short period. At the time of his death, in 1842, he was editor of the Episcopal Sunday School Magazine at New York, and also editor of the Sunday School publication of the Church. Mr. Peers was born in London County, Virginia, in the year 1800. His father, Valentine Peers, moved to Kentucky in 1803, when Benjamin was only three years old, and was a soldier of the Revolutionary War. Benjamin received the first rudiments of an academical education in the Bourbon Academy, and completed his scholastic course at Transylvania University, under the administration of Dr. Holley. He died at Louisville in 1842.

We should not omit a more particular notice of so important a character as that of Bishop Smith, of Kentucky. He, as we have before stated, was chosen the first Bishop of Kentucky at the Convention held in the year 1832, the diocese, previous to that time, not having the requisite number of clergy to entitle it to the choice of a bishop.

The now Rt. Rev. Benjamin Bosworth Smith was born in Bristol, Rhode Island, June 13, 1794; graduated at Brown University, Providence, Rhode Island, September, 1816; was admitted to the Holy Order of Deacons in the Protestant Episcopal Church, in St. Michael's Church, Bristol, Rhode Island, on the 17th of April, 1817, by the Rt. Rev. Alexander Veits Griswold, Bishop of the Eastern Diocese, which at that time included the whole of New England, except Connecticut, and Presbyter in St Michael's Church, Marblehead, Massachusetts, of which he was then minister.

During most of 1820 and 1821 Bishop Smith was rector of St. George's Church, Accomack County, Virginia, and in 1822 and 1823 of the parishes of Jefferson County, Virginia, including Charlestown, Shepherdstown, and Harper's Ferry.

From 1823 to 1828 he was rector of St. Stephen's Church, Middleburg, Vermont.

From 1828 to 1830 he was rector of a mission in Philadelphia, afterward Grace Church, and editor of the Episcopal Recorder, the larger of the only two Episcopal papers at that time in the country. In 1830 he was called to be rector of Christ Church, Lexington, resigning in 1837. In the infancy of the common school system in Kentucky, he served as superintendent in 1839 and 1840, and in that time visited and lectured in seventy-six counties out of ninety-one in the State at that time. In 1841 he removed to Katorama, near Louisville; in 1850 he removed into the city, and in 1867 to Frankfort, his present place of residence, and is now in the seventy-seventh year of his age.

Bishop Smith is now (1872) the presiding bishop of the Protestant Episcopal Church in the United States, obtained by seniority, he being by a few moments the oldest in the episcopacy. He was consecrated at the same time with Bishops McIlvaine, Meade, and others, he being the first upon whom the hands of the consecrating prelates were laid, which, consequently, gave him precedence.

The Rt. Rev. George D. Cummins was elected Assistant Bishop of the Diocese of Kentucky, June 1st, 1866, and is generally regarded as one of the most able and eloquent ministers of the Episcopal Church of Kentucky. We have but seldom noticed particularly any of the ministers of the different churches of Kentucky who are still living, except such names as have become particularly distinguished for their talents. Bishop Cummins ranks with ministers of the highest order of talents in any of the churches. He was born in Kent County, Delaware, on the 11th of December, 1822; he is consequently forty-nine years of age since the 11th of last December. He graduated at Dickinson College, Pa., in 1841, and the degree of D. D. was conferred upon him by Princeton College in 1856. He was ordained deacon in the Episcopal Church in 1845, and presbyter in 1847. He became the rector of Christ Church, Norfolk, Virginia, in 1847; in 1853, rector of St. James Church, Richmond, Virginia; in 1855, rector of Trinity Church, Washington City; in 1858, rector St. Peter's Church, Baltimore, and in 1863, rector of Trinity Church, Chicago. As before stated, he was elected assistant bishop in 1866, and on the 15th of November, 1866, was consecrated to that office in Christ Church, Louisville, Kentucky.

HISTORICAL SKETCH OF THE METHODIST EPISCOPAL CHURCH.

From the best information, James Haw and Benjamin Ogden were the first traveling preachers appointed to labor in Kentucky. At that time there were no regular societies in existence in Kentucky, and these two men were the first regular itinerant ministers who were sent here under the control of the Methodist Episcopal Church. This was in the year 1786. They were the first in Kentucky to collect the scattered Methodist emigrants and organize them into societies; and in the year aforesaid the first Methodist Church was organized by Benjamin Ogden, in the cabin of Thomas Stephenson, who lived about two and a half miles from Washington, in Mason County.

The appointments to Kentucky for the year 1787 were James Haw, elder; Thomas Williamson and Wilson Lee; Cumberland, Benjamin Ogden. The number in society at the close of that year was ninety whites. The appointments for 1788 in Kentucky were: Francis Poythress and James Haw, elders; Lexington Circuit, Thomas Williamson, Peter Massie, and Benjamin Snelling; Cumberland, D. Combs and B. McHenry; Danville, Wilson Lee. The number of membership at the close of this year was four hundred and seventy-nine whites and sixty-four colored. Lexington Circuit embraced the northern part of the State, Cumberland the lower part and a good portion of the State of Tennessee, and Danville Circuit the center of the State south of the Kentucky River.

In 1789 the number of ministers sent to Kentucky, and the arrangements of the circuits, remained the same. In the summer and fall of 1789 and spring of 1790 there were great revivals in the Church, and its numercial strength was nearly doubled. At the close of the year there were one thousand and thirty-seven whites and fifty-one colored.

On the 26th of April, 1790, at Masterson's Station, five miles from Lexington, Conference was held for the first time in Kentucky, and was the first Conference attended in the West by Bishop Asbury. At the close of the Conference at Charleston, South Carolina, the Bishop left to meet the Kentucky Conference, accompanied by his traveling companion, Hope Hull. The difficulties and hardships he was subjected to in making the trip nearly prostrated him; yet in his journal he says: "My soul has been blessed among these people, and I am exceedingly pleased with them, and would not for all the place have been prevented in this visit." In this Conference there were but twelve preachers. The appointments made at this Conference for the ensuing year were: F. Poythress, presiding elder; Lexington Circuit, Henry Birchett and David Haggard; Limestone Circuit, S. Tucker and J. Lillard; Danville Circuit, Thomas Williamson and Stephen Brooks; Madison Circuit, B. McHenry and Benjamin Snelling; Cumberland Circuit, Wilson Lee, James Haw, and Peter Massie.

The foregoing names, with Bishop Asbury, constituted the first Conference held in Kentucky, two years before her admission into the Union as a sovereign and independent State.

Francis Asbury, the presiding bishop, stands pre-eminent among that hardy and adventurous band. He landed from England on the shores of America on the 27th of October, 1771, and from that hour to the day of his death he labored unceasingly for the cause in which his whole heart was engaged. Perhaps no man since the settlement of the United States has traveled more extensively or effected a greater amount of good. He traveled and preached along the sea-board from Maine to Georgia, and from the Atlantic to the utmost extent of civilization in the West. His journal states that on one occasion he traveled five hundred miles in the space of nine days. Fifty miles was no uncommon day's journey for him, and often, for many days together, the bare earth was his bed. He spent fifty-five years in the ministry, the last forty-five of which were spent in America, and died on the 21st day of

March, 1816, leaving a name unsullied, and deep foot-prints in the sands of time, which can never be effaced whilst Methodism endures.

Francis Poythress, who had only been admitted into the traveling connection about two years before at Baltimore, was sent to Kentucky in 1788 in the capacity of an elder. As a preacher at that day he was excelled by very few. It is said of him that he had a clear, musical voice and a superior knowledge of the Scriptures. Bishop Asbury said of him in 1790, in a note made in his journal: "Brother Poythress is much alive to God, and that sermons anointed with the spirit of God and baptized in the blood of the Lamb will always burn as fire in dry stubble." He continued to travel mainly in Kentucky until the spring of 1800, when he was appointed by the Baltimore General Conference to a very large district in North Carolina. So great were the draughts on his mind during the labors of this summer that he became partially deranged. In the fall of that year he returned to his sisters in Kentucky, near Nicholasville, where he remained a confirmed lunatic until his death.

Henry Birchett was only five or six years in the ministry before his death. He was born in Brunswick County, Virginia, and left ease, safety, and prosperity for the sake of his Master's cause, and freely offered himself for four years' service in the dangerous stations of Kentucky and Cumberland. He was a man of great meekness, love, and labors, made himself very useful during his short career, and was highly esteemed by all who became acquainted with him. He died in Cumberland Circuit, in great peace, in 1794.

David Haggard came out from Virginia with Birchett, and was his colleague on the Lexington Circuit in 1790, and traveled a few years with great acceptability. He finally went off with the O'Kelley party, and, returning to the East, died in connection with the New Lights.

James Haw entered the traveling connection at a Conference held in Sussex County, Virginia, in 1782, and was appointed in 1786 as one of the first two ministers to labor in Kentucky. Here he continued until 1791, when he settled in Sumner

County, Tennessee. In 1795 he joined O'Kelley's party. In 1800 he attached himself to the Presbyterian Church, and when the Cumberland Presbyterians separated from the mother Church he joined in with them, and died in that connection, a few years afterward, at his residence in Sumner County.

Peter Massie entered the connection in 1789, and labored faithfully in the ministry for upward of three years, riding successively the Danville, Cumberland, and Limestone circuits. He died suddenly, as was his desire, at Hodge's Station, five miles south of Nashville. He fell from his seat and expired the 19th of December, 1791, and was the first to fall in the service on the western waters.

Samuel Tucker was appointed by the Baltimore Conference in 1790 to the Limestone Circuit in Kentucky, and descending the Ohio River on the way to the work assigned him, the boat in which he was descending was attacked by the Indians and most of the crew killed. Mr. Tucker was seriously wounded, but was enabled to reach Limestone (now Maysville) where he died of his wounds. He was buried in the cemetery at Maysville, but the exact spot is unknown.

Benjamin Snelling was admitted into connection and set to travel the Limestone Circuit in 1788. He continued in Kentucky a short time, when he returned to the East. After remaining there for some time, he returned to Kentucky, and settled in Bath County, where he finally died.

Joseph Lillard was born near Harrodsburg, Kentucky. He was admitted to the traveling connection at the first Conference held in Kentucky, and appointed to Limestone Circuit. He traveled but a few years, when he died near Harrodsburg in a local relation.

Barnabas McHenry was regarded as one of the old apostles of Methodism from the fact that he attached himself to that Church in its infancy in the United States. He joined the traveling connection in 1787, and in 1788 was sent to the Cumberland Circuit. He labored in various circuits in Kentucky for eight years, when, on account of his bad health, he located. He was re-admitted in 1819, but in 1821 was returned superannuated. .This relation he sustained until his death, which occurred the 16th of June, 1833, of cholera. He was fond of the doctrines of the Church, and delighted in teaching them to others. He lived in the enjoyment of the blessing of sanctification, and died in peace.

Wilson Lee was admitted into the traveling connection in the year 1784, at twenty-three years of age, and in 1787 was sent to labor in Kentucky, where he continued faithfully, and with great acceptability, until 1792. He was then transferred to the East, where he continued in the field until his death, which occurred in Anne Arundel County, Maryland, on the 11th of October, 1804, from the rupture of a blood vessel. He professed the sanctifying grace of God. His life and conversation illustrated the religion he professed. He had great fervency of spirit and energy in the ministry. He often hazarded his life on the frontier stations, which he filled throughout Kentucky. He rode from fort to fort, and from station to station, often without any guide or protection.

Benjamin Ogden was born in New Jersey, in 1764, and embraced religion when he was twenty years old. In early life he was a soldier in the war of the Revolution. In 1786 he united with the traveling connection, and as a missionary received his first appointment to Kentucky, together with James Haw. In 1788 he located on account of his health, and did not re-enter the traveling connection again until 1817; but his health soon gave way once more, and he ceased the connection again, but resumed the itineracy in 1824, and continued an effective man until 1827. He was then placed on the superannuated list, where he remained until his death, which occurred in 1824, after a long life of labor and toil in the gospel, expiring, it is said, in all the calmness and confidence of faith and hope, and went to his reward.

There were a number of other Methodist preachers in Kentucky at a very early period of scarcely less note than those I have named, whose history space in this work will not allow me to sketch in detail. John Page was admitted into the traveling connection of Kentucky in 1791, Benjamin Northcott in 1792, James O'Gull and John Ray in 1791. William

Burke was appointed to the Green Circuit, in the Western territory, in 1792. He volunteered for the work in Kentucky the 13th of April, 1793, and attended the Conference held at Masterson's on the 6th of May, 1793, and was appointed first to the Danville Circuit. He was a faithful, efficient, and laborious itinerant. He continued to travel various circuits in different States until the year 1808, when he was placed on the supernumerary relation, and appointed to Lexington Circuit. In 1809 he was appointed to Green River District, where he continued until October 1, 1811, when he was sent to the work in Ohio. In 1812 he lost his voice entirely, owing, it was believed, to over-exertion in preaching, and occupied a supernumerary relation for several years. As a preacher he was regarded among the first in his day. His good memory was stored richly with Bible truths, and his superior acquaintance with human nature enabled him to adapt his sermons to the various character of his hearers with better effect than almost any other preacher of his time. His great courage and high moral purpose made him not only fearless but effective in planting the Gospel of Christ in this wilderness country. He was born on the 13th of January, 1770, in Loudon County, Virginia. Of the precise date of his death the writer is not informed.

I should not close these accounts of early Methodism in Kentucky without mentioning the name of William McKendree, who, as remarked by one, "was like an illuminated torch sent down for awhile from the upper sanctuary to burn in the golden candlesticks of God's house on earth." His first visit to Kentucky was in the fall of 1800, with Bishop Asbury and Whatcott, from the Virginia Conference, and attended the Conference held this year in Kentucky, at Bethel, at which time he was appointed presiding elder for all the Western country. He traveled over that immense scope of country until its division into three parts, two years afterward. He remained presiding elder of the Kentucky District for three years more, when he was appointed to the Cumberland District in the fall of 1806, where he continued until 1808, when, at the General Conference held in Baltimore that year, he was elected bishop, and in that relation continued for twenty-five years, and until his death, which occurred in 1833. A few years before his death the writer saw him in Greensburg. He was very old then, and preached but seldom. A young man, whose name is not remembered, accompanied him, and preached in the Methodist Church. His effort on that occasion was rather poor, and what rendered his sermon less interesting was the peculiarity of his voice and utterance. Bishop McKendree sat in the pulpit with him, and offered up a most sensible and fervent prayer at the conclusion of the service. The writer could but admire the venerable appearance and neatness of the old bishop. His dress was black cloth, short breeches, with knee buckles, black stockings, shoes with large silver buckles, broad-brimmed hat, and black cravat. His appearance, with his solemn, humble Christian bearing, commanded the reverence and esteem of all who saw him. Judging from his appearance at that time he must have been near eighty years of age. He was in Kentucky during the great revival that we have several times mentioned, and was a witness to the great outpouring of the spirit of God on many occasions, although there were many extravagances and irregularities at some of the meetings of those times among all denominations, such as what were called jerks, barks, &c.

The statistics of Methodism show that from the beginning, in 1786, her march has been steady and onward, and the increase in numbers surprisingly great from that day to this. At the close of the year 1787 there were but ninety Methodists in Kentucky. At the close of the year 1788 there were four hundred and seventy-nine whites and sixty-four colored. At the close of the year 1789 there were one thousand and thirty-seven whites and fifty-one colored. Within the limits of the Kentucky Conference there were in the year

1800	1,626	whites and	115	colored	members.
1810	5,513	"	243	"	"
1820	11,887	"	1,119	"	"
1830	22,074	"	4,682	"	"
1840	30,939	"	6,321	"	"

The exact returns for 1850 and 1860 are not in possession of the writer, but the increase at those periods was about in the same ratio as at the periods above stated.

The general minutes for 1870 show in the two Conferences of the State as follows: Kentucky Conference, 90 traveling preachers; 7 superannuated, and 114 local; total, 211 preachers. In the Louisville Conference, 103 traveling preachers; 8 superannuated; 186 local; total, 297 preachers. White members of the Church in Kentucky Conference, 17,313; colored, 225; total, 17,538 members. Louisville Conference, white members, 25,398; colored, 262; total, 25,660; total preachers and members of the Methodist Episcopal Church of Kentucky, 43,706. The number of infants baptized the conference year 1870 in Kentucky Conference, 304; Louisville Conference, 655; total, 959; Sunday Schools in Kentucky Conference, 130; Louisville Conference, 175; total, 305; Sunday School teachers in Kentucky Conference, 947; in Louisville Conference, 1,135; total, 2,082; Sunday Schools in Kentucky Conference, 6,216; in Louisville Conference, 9,449; total, 15,665 There are now thirty-five annual Conferences in connection with the Methodist Church of the United States, to which belong 10 bishops, 2,725 traveling preachers, 187 superannuated preachers, and, besides these, 4,714 local preachers. The connection has 6,173 Sunday Schools, with 42,505 teachers and 282,467 scholars.

The number of communicants on the rolls of the different evangelical churches of the United States is estimated at 5,400,000, which is about one-seventh of the entire population of the land. Methodism has the reputation of being the most pushing corps in the great evangelical army. Between Methodism and Presbyterianism there is believed to be more substantial harmony of feeling and operation than between any other two denominations. The various branches of these two denominations united, present communion rolls of over 3,000,000 names, leaving out of the estimate the children they have at Sabbath Schools and the families and children under their influence.

HISTORICAL SKETCH OF THE CUMBERLAND PRESBYTERIAN CHURCH.

This Church constituted themselves a Presbytery separate from the general Presbyterian Church and Kentucky Synod on the 10th day of February, 1810. About the beginning of the present century there was a remarkable revival of religion in Kentucky among all denominations, but especially with the Presbyterians. This revival continued through several years, and has ever since been distinguished as the "Great Revival." Many new congregations were soon formed, insomuch as to be impracticable to accommodate them all with licensed or ordained ministers. The necessity for supplies appearing evident, it was proposed to the preachers engaged in the revival to choose from the laity men whose gifts and piety would justify such a step, and encourage them to prepare for the ministry, though they might not have a classical education. The proposition was acceded to, and several persons were selected. They were encouraged to improve their talent by exhortation, and also to prepare written discourses, to be exhibited at the next Transylvania Presbytery as specimens of their ability. The discourses produced were well-approved, but the persons producing them were not then received as candidates, but were directed to prepare other discourses for the next Presbytery. The next Presbytery decided in favor of the proposed plan, and proceeded to license three men to preach the gospel, viz: Alexander Anderson, Finis Ewing, and Samuel King, as probationers. Two of the three men thus licensed had no knowledge at all of the dead languages, but, under all the circumstances, the Presbytery thought they would not be out of the line of duty in promoting them to the work of the ministry. A considerable number of the members of the Presbytery, however, were still very much opposed to the measure, entered their protest, and wrote to Synod. About this time Transylvania Presbytery was divided, and Cumberland Presbytery created out of it. In this Presbytery there was always a majority in favor of licensing men to preach "who were apt to teach, and sound in the faith," though they might not possess a liberal education. That Presbytery, therefore, from time to time, licensed men of this description to preach. The Synod finally took the matter in hand, and appointed a Commission to meet in the bounds of Cumberland Presbytery, and directed the members, licentiates, &c., to meet the Commission, which many of them did. The principal charges against the Presbytery were: 1st. Licensing men to preach who had not been examined on the languages. 2d. That those men who had been licensed had only been required to adopt the Confession of Faith partially. The reasoning offered by the second party not being satisfactory to the Commission, they demanded that all the young men should be given up to them for re-examination. This proposition was refused by the Presbytery. The young men then being summoned to submit, and refusing, the Commission proceeded solemnly to prohibit them all, whether learned, or less learned, from preaching or ministering any more as Presbyterians. A majority of the Presbytery were summoned to appear before the next Synod to answer for not surrendering their young men, and also to be examined themselves on doctrines. The Presbytery being conscious that the Commission had acted illegally, determined to petition the General Assembly. The first decision of the General Assembly appeared somewhat favorable, and encouraged them to believe that their grievances would eventually be redressed. They therefore waited and petitioned, until they became convinced by an act of the General Assembly that they justified the action of the Synod in the course they had pursued. After another fruitless application to Synod, three of the ordained ministers of Cumberland Presbytery, in good standing and of acknowledged piety, viz: Samuel McAdow, Finis Ewing, and Samuel King, constituted themselves into a separate Presbytery. They had their meeting at the house of said McAdow on the 4th of February, 1810, in Dickson County, Tennessee, and then and there agreed and determined to constitute a Presbytery, to be known by the name of the Cumberland Presbytery, on the following conditions, viz: That all candidates for the ministry before licensure, and all licentiates before ordination, are to receive and adopt the Confession of Faith and Discipline of the Presbyterian Church, except the idea of fatality that seems to be taught under the mysterious doctrine of predestination; but such as can adopt the Confession without such exception shall not be required to make any. Moreover, that all licentiates before ordination shall be required to undergo an examination in English grammar, geography, astronomy, natural and moral philosophy, and church history.

They then proceed to set forth the doctrine of their new organization in six articles, in order that their tenets, or the distinctive features of their faith, may not be misunderstood. In regard to literary qualifications for the ministry they do not undervalue it, but regard it as a hand-maid to the useful work. Their discipline is Presbyterian. Their congregations are governed by Church Sessions, Presbyteries, and a Synod, to be called the Cumberland Synod. They are tenacious of their presbyterial form of church government especially, because it is congenial with the republican form of government established by these United States. They continue to observe a custom which was introduced during the great revival of 1800, that of encamping on the ground at their communions for four days and nights.

Thus was begun and carried on that organization called Cumberland Presbyterians, by which great good has been effected in every community where it has existed. Their ministers have not been idlers in the vineyard of their Heavenly Master, but their humble labors have been crowned and blessed of God, which is manifestly proven by the fact that thousands upon thousands have flocked to the standard of the Cross under the ministrations of their ministers, and have proven to the world by their orderly walk and conversation that they are truly followers of the " meek and lowly Jesus." The labors, self-denial, and sacrifices of their early ministers were exceedingly great. They were remarkable for their bold, manly, and impressive eloquence, and untiring zeal. With indomitable perseverance, and without worldly compensation, they performed an important part in converting the wilderness into a fruitful field. It was at the camp-ground near Greensburg, more than forty years ago, that the distinguished Presbyterian minister, John H. Brown, then a wayward youth, and a great number of others, were brought to see the error of their ways, and to experience that religion which has characterized their lives ever since. This was effected under the preaching of the Barnetts, two very efficient preachers of the Cumberland Presbyterian order, who resided at the time in southwestern Kentucky.

There are now in Kentucky seven Presbyteries in the Cumberland Presbyterian Synod of Kentucky (1870), to-wit: Anderson, Cumberland, Davies, Kentucky, Logan, Ohio, Princeton.

The number of ministers, licentiates, candidates for the ministry, and churches in Kentucky, are as follows, viz:

PRESBYTERIES.	Ministers.	Licentiates.	Candidates.	Churches.
Anderson	15	2	6	27
Cumberland	10	6	..	26
Davies	9	..	..	28
Kentucky	12	7	9	24
Logan	21	7	3	38
Ohio	12	5	..	24
Princeton	8	4	1	23
Total	87	31	19	190

From the foregoing it appears that there are ministers, licentiates, and candidates, 137; churches, 190; number of communicants (1870), 11,400.

HISTORICAL SKETCH OF THE CHRISTIAN CHURCH.

Among the great number of worthy and talented men who co-operated in the grand enterprise of the establishment of what is called the Christian Church on a permanent basis, Alexander Campbell stands conspicuous, and did more for its accomplishment than perhaps any other man in the United States. Others preceded him in repudiating human creeds, and in adopting the Bible alone as the only rule of faith and practice for the followers of the Lord Jesus Christ. He, however, was the master-spirit in exciting investigation, overturning prejudices, and setting the Church to work in its proper sphere. He was born about the year 1787 or 1788, in the county of Down, in the north of Ireland. At fourteen years of age he went to Scotland to complete his education for the Presbyterian ministry. At the age of about twenty-one he came to America with his father, Elder Thomas Campbell, who lived to a very old age. He early became convinced in his mind that infant sprinkling was not in accordance with the Bible, and was forthwith baptized by immersion upon a profession of his faith. Prosecuting his enquiries he changed his mind in regard to many other notions he had imbibed, and which he got to believe were unscriptural. So he nobly resolved that he would "sacrifice everything for the truth, but the truth for nothing." He says that he had scarcely commenced to make sermons before he discovered that the religion of the Testament was one thing, and that of any sect with which he was acquainted was another. He betook himself to the occupation of a farmer for a number of years, and labored during that time, on every Lord's Day, to separate the truth from what he considered the traditions of men. In 1816 he was solicited by influential Baptists, both in New York and Philadelphia, to settle in one of those cities, but he declined upon the ground that he did not believe the Churches in either of those places would submit to the views which he entertained, and he did not wish to produce any division among them. It was about the year 1823 that he had the celebrated debate with Wm. McCalla, of the Presbyterian Church. In August of that year he commenced the publication of a monthly pamphlet, called the "Christian Baptist," the principal object of which was to lay a foundation for the union of all Christians throughout the world. In the debate with McCalla, alluded to, Mr. Campbell contended that baptism was a divine institution, designed for putting the legitimate subject of it in actual possession of the remission of his sins.

It was not until about 1827 that baptism for the remission of sins seems to have become much agitated. In that year Walter Scott and John Secrest began to preach in the Mahoning Association, in Ohio, the doctrine of remission as recorded in Acts, Chapter II., verse 38. The preaching of these men produced a powerful effect, and during the last six months of the year Elder Secrest immersed, with his own hand, five hundred and thirty persons for the remission of sins. How many were immersed by Scott is not precisely known, but the number was very great. The Mahoning Association of that year employed Elder Scott to preach the whole of his time within the boundary of that Association. The results of this appointment were triumphant. There were soon afterward found in Kentucky, as well as in Ohio, many able advocates of the same views of Scott, who disconnected themselves from the Baptist Church, or else were driven out, and compelled to establish separate churches, that they might enjoy the liberty wherewith Christ had made them free.

In 1830 Mr. Campbell commenced the publication of the "Millenial Harbinger." This periodical, with some other publications of a similar character commenced about that time, together with a number of able preachers advocating the same doctrine, spread the principles of this reformation with unprecedented rapidity. At a general meeting of the Christian Churches in Kentucky, held at Harrodsburg, in May, 1834, an agent was appointed to visit the churches and ascertain the number of members, &c., and report the result at the next general meeting. That report shows even at that early period that there were in the State at that time three hundred and eighty congregations, with an aggregate number of thirty-three thousand eight hundred and thirty members, and about one hundred and ninety-five preachers, including evangelist and local. From the best estimate that can be made, the churches now number four hundred and fifty; preachers, evangelist and local, three hundred; and members, about sixty thousand.

The churches are unanimous in repudiating all human creeds, as also all ecclesiastical organizations bearing any other name than that of Christians or Disciples of Christ. They regard the sum total of human duty "to believe what God says, and to do what He commands." When the believer obeys God's commands, then they say they have a right to appropriate God's promises, and only then. The penitent believer

15

must confess Christ before men, and from the heart bow to his authority, and be baptized in obedience to his command; then he can appropriate to himself all the promises that are made to baptized believers; but even then has no right to hope for a continuance of divine favors, except so far as he makes it the business of his life to know the will of God, and to do it in all things.

Barton W. Stone, another distinguished man, who died in this communion, ranked high as a scholar, a gentleman, and a Christian, yet in the course of his life was regarded as somewhat devious and erratic in his religious notions and opinions. In 1832, however, a union took place between the friends of Stone and those of Alexander Campbell, from which period to his death there seemed to be a perfect agreement in the doctrine promulgated by each. In 1843 Mr. Stone says himself, "I saw no distinctive feature in the doctrine that Alexander Campbell preached and that which we had preached for many years, except on baptism for the remission of sins; even this I had once received and taught, but had strangely let it go from my mind till Brother Campbell revived it afresh."

Mr. Stone was born in Maryland, on the 24th day of December, 1772. His father having died, his mother removed to what was called the backwoods of Virginia in 1779, and settled near Dan River, in Pittsylvania County. Here he went to school some four or five years, and became quite a proficient scholar for his age. In 1790 he entered Guilford College, North Carolina, with a determined resolution to acquire an education, intending at that time to qualify himself for the profession of the law, but while attending that school he embraced religion, joined the Presbyterian Church, and turned his thoughts to the ministry. In 1793 he commenced the study of divinity under Wm. Hodge, of Orange County, North Carolina, and in April, 1796, he was licensed by Orange Presbytery to preach. He soon afterward came west, preaching at various points on the route to Knoxville, Nashville, and so on to Bourbon County, Kentucky. About the close of this year he settled in the bounds of Cane Ridge and Concord congregations. He labored with great acceptance and success. In 1798 he became the settled pastor of these congregations. Early in 1801 the great revival commenced in Tennessee and southern Kentucky, under the labors of James McGready and other Presbyterian ministers. Mr. Stone hastened to a great Presbyterian camp-meeting in Logan County, Kentucky, where he witnessed for the first time those strange exercises of falling, jerking, dancing, &c. Filled with the spirit of the revival, he returned immediately to his congregations. A series of meetings took place after his return. He preached much, and dwelt with great emphasis on the universality of the gospel. These strange exercises also made their appearance in his congregations. Different denominations united; the work spread in all directions; party creeds and names seemed buried in Christian love and union. The great Cane Ridge camp-meeting commenced in August of that year, and lasted six or seven days. Twenty or thirty thousand persons were supposed to be present, coming from Ohio and other remote parts. The salvation of sinners seemed to be the object of all. It was about this time that Robert Marshall, John Dunlavy, Richard McNemar, B. W. Stone, and John Thompson, all Presbyterian preachers and members of the Synod of Kentucky, renounced Calvinism, and taught everywhere they went that Christ died for all; that the divine testimony was sufficient to produce faith; that the spirit was received through faith, and not in order to faith. McNemar was soon taken under dealings by the Presbytery of Springfield, Ohio; and the case finally came before the Synod of Lexington, Kentucky, in September, 1803. As soon as it was discovered that the decision of Synod would be against McNemar, the five ministers above named withdrew from the jurisdiction of that body, and constituted themselves into a Presbytery, which they called the Springfield Presbytery. About a year afterward they took upon themselves the name of Christians, and threw overboard what they considered as man-made creeds. From this period Stone dates the reformation which has progressed with such rapidity to the present day. Soon after their withdrawal from the Synod, they were joined by Matthew Houston and David Purviance.

In 1805 Houston, McNemar, and Dunlavy joined the Shakers, an account of which I have given under the head of the Presbyterian Church. In 1807 Marshall and Thompson returned to the Presbyterian Church. Although Mr. Stone repudiated the orthodox views on the subject of the Trinity, sonship, and atonement, yet he did not acknowledge the sentiments continually charged by his opponents. In the near prospect of death, he averred that he had never regarded Christ as a created being. He died on the 9th of November, 1844, in the triumph of faith, beloved and regretted by all who knew him.

Among a great many others of the Baptists, that good man, John T. Johnson (brother of the distinguished soldier and statesman, Richard M. Johnson), embraced and advocated the teaching of Alexander Campbell. This was about the year 1831. About that time he became a conductor of a pamphlet called the Christian Messenger; and it was about the beginning of 1832 that a perfect union was effected with the followers of Campbell, Stone, Johnson, &c.

There have been differences of opinion as to what is the real name of this body of Christians. By some they are called Campbellites; by others, Disciples; but the title they claim for themselves is simply that of "Christians;" and they found their claim on the fact, as they say, that they copy after, as nearly as possible, the primitive Christian churches that were under the personal direction of the apostles. They, as I have stated before, have no creed but the Bible; no government, save congregational. The sacrament is usually administered at the close of service, every Sunday forenoon, and the communion is open. They deny the charge of Unitarianism, and make much of the divinity of Christ and his atonement. Their distinctive feature in regard to those who, par excellence, claim to be orthodox, consists, as one has said, "in the order and importance of baptism by immersion. One says, faith, repentance, and pardon; the other says, faith, repentance, *baptism*, and pardon."

Since about 1831, or 1832, this body has grown to be one of the largest in the West, and especially one of the largest in Kentucky, with a very extensive literature, and a large number of able men. The number of their communicants in the State of Kentucky alone, in 1870, is said to be 90,000, being an increase of 15,000 in three years. The number of communicants in the United States is said to be not less than 800,000, and of preachers 2,000. As to the number of preachers in Kentucky the writer is uninformed. No denomination of Christians within our knowledge, of the same years from their beginning, number so many communicants, ministers, churches, schools, academies, seminaries, colleges, universities, weekly, monthly, and quarterly publications, as they. They have under their control in Kentucky the Kentucky University at Lexington, Jefferson College at Jeffersontown, Eminence College at Eminence, Daughters College at Harrodsburg, Lexington College at Lexington, Madison Family Institute at Richmond, Patterson Institute at Middletown, Flemingsburg Academy at Flemingsburg, and May's Lick Academy at May's Lick.

MORMONISM, OR LATTER DAY SAINTS.

The following sketch of Mormonism is taken from the diary of the writer, written nearly thirty years ago, on his return from a visit to Illinois and Missouri:

At St. Louis, June 17th, 11 o'clock, we again embarked upon the water on board the iron boat, Valley Forge, bound for Louisville. The boat was heavily freighted, and had a great number of passengers. On the morning of Sunday, June 18th, we began to ascend the beautiful Ohio, which separates Kentucky from Illinois.

On board the boat was a Mormon preacher, whose name was Lorin Farr. He was direct from the city of Nauvoo, Hancock County, Illinois. He was about twenty-three years of age, a little under average size, of good appearance, unassuming manners, and good natural sense, without the polish of education. He was on his way to Massachusetts (from whence he had emigrated a few years previously) with the view of assisting and conducting to the city of Nauvoo a number of individuals who had embraced the Mormon religion. That day it became generally known on the boat that there was a Mormon preacher aboard, and a general desire prevailed with the passengers to have him preach. He was approached upon the subject and at once assented; and the passengers being soon all seated in the main cabin, he proceeded to discourse as follows:

"I am aware, my friends, of the reports of an unfavorable character and the prejudices which exist against the Mormon community. They have, as all must allow, been greatly persecuted. This, however, is no more than might be expected. Christ and the apostles were greatly persecuted, and how can we expect to be free from it. Now let it be distinctly understood that I appear before you at this time, not as the advocate of Jo. Smith, or of any other Mormon, but of the Mormon doctrine. I preach against the doctrine of none, but stand upon my own tub, and am willing that others may do the same. I desire that all should know and believe the Bible. We hold its precepts and truths as sacred as any people in the world, and would on no account detract from it in the smallest particular.

"As the foundation of the few remarks which, at your request, I have been induced to make at this time, I will read from the 6th verse to the 12th, inclusive, of the 1st chapter of Gallatians:

"'6. I marvel that ye are so soon removed from him that called you into the grace of Christ unto another gospel:

"'7. Which is not another; but there be some that trouble you, and would pervert the gospel of Christ.

"'8. But though we, or an angel from heaven, preach any other gospel unto you than that which we have preached unto you, let him be accursed.

"'9. As we said before, so say I now again, If any *man* preach any other gospel unto you than that ye have received, let him be accursed.

"'10. For do I now persuade men, or God? or do I seek to please men? for if I yet pleased men, I should not be the servant of Christ.

" ' 11. But I certify you, brethren, that the gospel which was preached of me, is not after man.

" ' 12. For I neither received it of man, neither was I taught it, but by the revelation of Jesus Christ.'

"I would now inquire, what was the gospel that Paul and the other apostles preached? You remember they were commissioned to go out and preach the gospel, and certain signs were to follow those who believed. Look, if you please, at the last chapter of Mark, beginning at the 15th verse:

" ' 15. And he said unto them, Go ye into all the world, and preach the gospel to every creature.

" ' 16. He that believeth, and is baptized, shall be saved; but he that believeth not shall be damned.

" ' 17. And these signs shall follow them that believe: In my name shall they cast out devils; they shall speak with new tongues;

" ' 18. They shall take up serpents; and if they drink any deadly thing, it shall not hurt them; they shall lay hands on the sick, and they shall recover.

" ' 19. So then, after the Lord had spoken unto them, he was received up into heaven, and sat on the right hand of God.

" ' 20. And they went forth, and preached everywhere, the Lord working with them, and confirming the word with signs following. Amen.'

"You may here, then, learn the difference between Mormons and other denominations professing Christianity. We believe that to obtain salvation, the signs which I have enumerated from the Bible must follow the believer. You know that on the day of Penticost they spoke with new tongues, &c. It is also necessary to salvation that you repent and be baptized, and the promise is unto you and unto your children, &c. I know that different opinions prevail as to the mode of baptism, and I am only astonished that there should be a contrariety of sentiment upon the subject among any enlightened people. As for the Mormons, they believe that the only proper mode is by immersion. This was the way Christ was baptized, as is evident from the fact that he went down into the water, and came up straightway out of the water; otherwise it is not a birth, or being born. We are commanded, then, first to believe, then to repent, and then to be baptized, which last brings forcibly to our memories the death, burial, and resurrection of the Saviour. Read upon this subject the VI. Chapter of Romans:

"'3. Know ye not, that so many of us as were baptized into Jesus Christ were baptized into his death.

"'4. Therefore we are buried with him by baptism into death; that like as Christ was raised up from the dead by the glory of the Father, even so we should walk in newness of life.

"'5. For if we have been planted together in the likeness of his death, we shall be also in the likeness of his resurrection:

"'6. Knowing this, that our old man is crucified with him, that the body of sin might be destroyed, that henceforth we should not serve sin.

"'7. For he that is dead, is freed from sin.'

"Now, planting means to cover up. When you hear an individual say that a thing is planted, you know at once that it is covered up with earth or something else. If, therefore, you plant corn or any other seed, you cover it up; and if you be yourself planted in the likeness of Christ, like him you must be covered up, or immersed in the liquid grave. This is the first step into the Kingdom of God. The Bible is the starting point, and it is that to which we must apply all along our way. Creeds are abominable. Mormons have nothing to do with them; they are the work of men, and often of very designing men. The Bible is a better rule, the safest, the surest, and the most infallible rule. So far as regards arts and sciences, I concede this to be an enlightened age of the world; but in regard to the true knowledge of God it is lamentably a dark age. There has been great apostacy from the Church of Christ, and especially in the mode of baptism practiced by many at this day professing Christianity. I am at a loss to conceive how any intelligent mind can read the story of Phillip and the eunuch, and doubt that immersion was the mode then practiced. There is but one Lord, one faith, and one baptism, which baptism, in my feeble way, I have discoursed about, and which you must adopt if you would walk in obedience to the commands of Christ. After this you must receive the Holy Ghost by the laying on of hands. In proof of which, read the XIX. Chapter of Acts, beginning at the 1st verse:

"'1. And it came to pass, that while Apollos was at Corinth, Paul having passed through the upper coasts, came to Ephesus; and finding certain disciples,

"'2. He said unto them, Have ye received the Holy Ghost since ye believed? And they said unto him, We have not so much as heard whether there be any Holy Ghost.

"'3. And he said unto them, Unto what then were ye baptized? And they said, Unto John's baptism.

"'4. Then said Paul, John verily baptized with the baptism of repentance, saying unto the people, That they should believe on him which should come after him, that is, on Christ Jesus.

"'5. When they heard this, they were baptized in the name of the Lord Jesus.

"'6. And when Paul had laid his hands upon them, the Holy Ghost came on them; and they spake with tongues, and prophesied.

"'7. And all the men were about twelve.'

"It will not do to confine the laying on of hands to the ordination of priests, ministers, &c. It is equally applicable to others as to them. It might with the same propriety be contended, that faith, repentance, &c., should be confined to priests and ministers only, which, as all would concede, is preposterous."

Having made the foregoing remarks, he then proceeded to say: "That there is not a more persecuted set of beings in the world than these people called Mormons; and this persecution proceeds in a great degree from erroneous apprehensions and false reports concerning them. Nine-tenths of all that is said against them is untrue, not only as regards their morality and general conduct, but in regard also to their belief and the doctrines which they teach. I own we have had men among us, men of whom we would gladly rid ourselves, and so has every community, but do not condemn a whole community because of some unworthy members. I know we have good men among us—men as far above anything mean or dishonorable as any set of men in the world, and who are as far from entertaining many of the opinions and beliefs attributed to them as the persons are who make the charges; but our rule is, and it would be a good one for others to pursue, to condemn no creed until we know what it is." Thus having spoken, he closed with an appropriate prayer.

At the conclusion of the prayer, a stranger in the congregation arose, and expressing himself with vehemence and apparently with great emotion, remarked, that he did not gainsay anything the preacher had said in regard to the Scriptures, nor what he had said in regard to this being a dark age; nay, when he reflected how many hundreds of the ignorant of our race had been made the dupes of such a scamp and villain as Jo. Smith, he was strongly inclined to believe with the preacher that this indeed and in truth must be a dark age, and that if any man upon top of the earth deserved the halter more than any other, that man was Jo. Smith. The gentleman having seated himself, the Mormon again arose, and replied as follows: "The gentleman just seated acted the part he had seen and heard others play before in regard to the Mormons. Because he had formed a poor estimate of Jo. Smith, of course all the Mormons must necessarily be a trifling, ignorant, and deluded set. Now, if the gentleman had looked at the matter properly, or even considered what he was saying himself, it would have saved him a deal of that passion which he has so clearly manifested on this occasion. He says he does not gainsay or deny the doctrines I have preached, or rather what I have said in regard to the Scriptures, nor does he deny this being a dark age of the world; then there is no issue between us about which we ought to contend; for the gentleman will remember that, in all my remarks, I never mentioned Jo. Smith's name once, except to say that I was not his advocate. Jo. Smith was not in my thoughts, nor do I arise now to eulogize or defend him, nor condemn him, or the gentleman, or any one else; my object was merely, by the particular request of these people, to say something about the peculiarities or doctrines of the Mormons, and to give some of the reasons upon which their belief is founded; and although the gentleman has not disagreed with me in anything I have said, yet he attempts to answer me by a tirade of abuse against Jo. Smith. Sir, I have nothing to say on this occasion for or against Jo. Smith, but for the Mormon doctrine I am an advocate, and will defend it with my best abilities on all proper occasions."

Thus ended the sermon of Lorin Farr, and his controversy with the stranger. The writer has never sought or availed himself of any other means of acquiring a knowledge of the doctrines or tenets of the Mormons, and gives the foregoing account rather as a matter of curiosity, and with the belief, also, that it embraces truly the sentiments of the Mormon people.

CHAPTER X.

Henry Clay, Sketch of his Life—John Breckinridge, Sketch of—Mrs. Breckinridge—George Nicholas, Sketch of—Chilton Allan—Samuel Hanson—Joseph H. Daviess—Richard C. Anderson, Jr.—Wm. T. Barry—Solomon P. Sharp—George M. Bibb—Humphrey Marshall—Jesse Bledsoe—Harry Innis—George Robertson—John Speed Smith—John B. Thurston—David Trimble—John White—Henry Grider—James Harlan—Judge William McClung—Alexander D. Orr—John Coburn—John T. Johnson—Robert P. Henry—Thomas Chilton—James B. Clay—Thomas Corwin—Martin D. Hardin—James S. Jackson—Wm. P. Duval—Joshua H. Jewett—Francis Johnson—Sherrod Williams—Elijah Hise—James Guthrie—John Boyle—Daniel Breck—F. M. Bristow—Presley Ewing—Henry C. Burnett—Thomas J. Helm—Joshua F. Bell—John Calhoon—Beverly L. Clark—Albert G. Haws—James Love—Richard H. Menifee—Stephen Ormsby—Wm. Wright Southgate—General Leslie Combs—William J. Graves—Archibald Dixon—Thomas P. Moore—Richard French—Benjamin Tobin—General Samuel Hopkins—Captain William Hubbell—General Jefferson Davis—President Abraham Lincoln—William Mitchell—Colonel Acquilla Whitaker—James S. Whitaker—Richard T. Whitaker—Christopher Graham, M. D.

HENRY CLAY.

The life, letters, and speeches of Henry Clay have been published in several volumes, and are in the hands of many. Scarcely any man ever attained higher distinction than he, not only as a civilian, but as a statesman, orator, diplomatist, and patriot. His fame was wide-spread and unbounded; not a civilized nation on earth, perhaps, to whom his fame was unknown. An honester man, or one more devoted to the best interest of his country, perhaps never lived. Born with no other heritage than poverty, he attained that distinction to which he arrived by the force of his own talents alone; his native genius, assisted by the ardor of his exertions, effected it; and the malice of his enemies could never tear it from him, nor even blot the page of that history which records it.

Mr. Clay had only received a common school education when he entered the office of the clerk of the court of Chancery at Richmond as a copyist. He commenced the study of the law at nineteen years of age, and shortly afterward removed to Lexington, Kentucky.

Mr. Clay was born in Hanover County, Virginia, on the 12th of April, 1777. He was admitted to the bar at Lexington in 1799, and very soon obtained an extensive practice. He began his political career by taking an active part in the election of delegates to frame a new Constitution for Kentucky in 1799. He was elected a Representative of Fayette County to the Legislature of Kentucky for the first time in 1803, and in 1806 was appointed the successor of General John Adair, who had resigned, to the Senate of the United States for the remainder of the term. In 1807 he was again elected to the Legislature of Kentucky, and was chosen Speaker. It was in 1808 that the duel occurred between him and Humphrey Marshall. In 1809 he was again elected to the United States Senate for the unexpired term of Mr. Thurston, resigned. In 1811 he was elected a member of the House of Representatives in Congress, and was chosen Speaker of that body, and was five times re-elected in that body to the same office. He was an advocate of the war with Great Britain; and the national spirit was greatly aroused and awakened to resist her aggressions by his eloquence. In 1814 he was appointed one of the Commissioners to negotiate a treaty of peace at Ghent. After his return from this mission he was again elected to Congress, and in 1818 delivered his famous speech on the subject of recognizing the independence of the South American Republics. It was this year also that he advocated with such power the national system of internal improvements. A monument of stone, inscribed with his name, was erected on the National Road to commemorate his services in behalf of that improvement.

In 1819-20 he exerted himself for the establishment of protection of American industry. He also rendered essential services in the adjustment of the Missouri Compromise question. These questions being settled, he retired from Congress to attend to his private affairs. In 1823 he was again elected to Congress, and re-elected Speaker. It was during this session he exerted himself in support of the independence of Greece. He was Secretary of State under the Presidency of John Quincy Adams. The attack made by John Randolph on Mr. Clay during this administration led to the duel between these distinguished men, which terminated, however, without bloodshed.

In 1831 Mr. Clay was again elected to the United States Senate, where he commenced his labors in favor of the tariff. Soon after his re appearance in the Senate he was unanimously nominated for President of the United States, but was defeated by the re-election of General Jackson. In 1836 he was again elected to the United States Senate, where he remained until 1842, when he resigned, and took his final leave of that body as he supposed.

In 1839 he was before the Convention again for the nomination for the Presidency, when General Harrison was selected as the candidate, who was elected over Van Buren by an overwhelming majority. In 1844 he again received the nomination for President, but was defeated by the election of James K. Polk.

After this he remained in retirement until 1849, when he was again elected to the Senate of the United States, where he devoted all his energies to the measures known as the Compromise Acts. His efforts during this session greatly impaired his strength and health, and he went to New Orleans and Havana, but received no permanent improvement in this respect, and returned to Congress. Being unable to participate in the active duties of the Senate, he resigned his seat, to take effect upon the 6th of September, 1852.

Mr. Clay was greatly interested in the success of the Colonization Society, and was for a long time one of its most efficient officers, and also its President. He died at Washington City, June 29th, 1852, at a little over seventy-five years of age, honored and respected not only by his own country, but by the civilized nations of the earth.

JOHN BRECKINRIDGE.

John Breckinridge was one of the most distinguished lawyers and statesmen of Kentucky, and his name is intimately connected with its history. He was born in Augusta County, Virginia, adjoining the town of Staunton, on the 2d day of December, 1760. His ancestors came from Ireland, and early in the last century to Virginia, and were of what was called the Scotch-Irish descent. His grandfathers, on both his father's and mother's side, lie buried in Tinkling Spring Cemetery, Augusta County, Virginia. His father died in Bottetourt County, Virginia, whither he removed when the subject of this sketch was only eleven years old.

Mr. Breckinridge was highly educated, without other aid than books, except about two years spent at the college of William and Mary in Virginia. He quit this college at about nineteen years of age, and was immediately elected a member of the House of Burgesses of Virginia from Bottetourt County, without any knowledge on his part of what was in agitation. On account of his youth his election was twice set aside, and it was only on the third return, and that, too, against his remonstrances, that he took his seat. From this period to his death he lived only as a lawyer and a statesman.

His wife was Mary Hopkins Cabell, of Buckingham County, Virginia, whom he married in 1785, and settled in Albemarle, where he practiced law until 1793. In the spring of that year he removed to Kentucky, and settled in Lexington, near to which place, at "Cabell's Dale," he resided till his death, which occurred the 14th of December, 1806, having just completed his forty-sixth year.

Mr. Breckinridge was regarded as profoundly learned as a lawyer, and highly gifted as a public speaker. He was honest in all his engagements, and exact in all his professional duties. His private character was without reproach; and he eminently deserved the distinction which he attained. He attained great popularity, and had a most controlling influence in every deliberative body in which he was at any time a participant. He occupied a commanding position as a statesman the greater part of his life, and took part in all the great questions of the day, whether of a local or public nature. The Constitution of 1799 was more the work of his hands than of any other single man, and the molding of the most important laws of the Commonwealth, which stand upon our statute book to this day, were mainly the labor of his hand. He was in his day the leading statesman in all the West, and the acknowledged leader of the old Democratic party which came into power with Jefferson, of whom Mr. Breckinridge was a devoted friend, both personally and politically, and held the office of Attorney General under his administration. The famed resolutions of 1798, asserting the principles of the Democratic party, and making the first great movement against the alien and sedition laws, were the production of his hands.

Several of Mr. Breckinridge's sons arrived at great distinction in the community—Robert C. Breckinridge as a Presbyterian divine, and John Cabell Breckinridge as an eminent lawyer. The latter was the father of the distinguished John C. Breckinridge, late Vice President of the United States, afterward elected to the United States Senate, and in the war of the rebellion of 1861 took a leading part as a Confederate general.

The subject of this sketch is said to have been of very noble appearance, tall, slender, and muscular, with gray eyes and brown hair; grave and silent in ordinary intercourse, but courteous and gentle in his manners, and greatly beloved by all who ever knew him.

GEORGE NICHOLAS.

George Nicholas, an eminent lawyer of Virginia, came to Kentucky just before she was admitted into the Union as a sovereign State, and was one of the most prominent members of the Convention which formed the first Constitution of Kentucky. He was a colonel for some years during the Revolutionary War. Previous to his emigration to Kentucky he was a very prominent member of the Virginia Convention, and was a zealous advocate for the adoption of the Federal Constitution. He had the confidence of the people of Kentucky in an eminent degree, and influenced to a considerable extent the course taken by Kentucky in politics in the contest of 1798. His moral sentiments were utterly opposed to the practice of duelling. This was clearly indicated in a letter written by him to A. S. Bullitt, in 1792, in answer to the inquiry of Bullitt whether he (Nicholas) expected any further satisfaction from him.

Colonel Nicholas was the preceptor of many students of law who attained the highest rank in their profession. Among the most distinguished were Rowan, Grundy, Pope, Talbot, etc. Colonel Nicholas died in 1799, between fifty and sixty years of age.

CHILTON ALLAN.

Chilton Allan was born on the 6th day of April, 1786, in the county of Albemarle, in the State of Virginia. His father, Archibald Allan, died while Chilton was an infant, and his mother, a woman remarkable for her good sense and forethought, removed to Kentucky in 1797. At that period the means of education even to the rich in this new country were limited, and especially so to those in humble circumstances. The subject of this sketch was, for the most part, engaged in industrial pursuits to procure means of subsistence and an education, having opportunities of only a few months in the year to attend country schools. While a boy, an incident occurred that excited in him new hopes, and awakened new exertions of mind. Having gone to the shop of a country shoemaker to procure a pair of shoes, he discovered among the scraps upon the floor an old book, which, upon taking it up, he found to be the Life of Franklin, a book he had never seen before, and on looking over several pages he became so interested that he immediately made a bargain for its purchase. He opened it at the part of the book in which Franklin's first appearance in Philadelphia is described, being unknown, possessed of but one Dutch dollar, &c. This made such an impression on his mind as to give him the first aspirations for knowledge. He read the book over, and over again, until he became so enamored with its contents as often to embrace it, and to sleep with it under his pillow; and to the day of his death he regarded Franklin as the greatest man America had ever produced. His family and friends, when he was about fifteen years of age, concluded that it would be prudent that he should learn some useful occupation as a means of future support; and he was accordingly placed in an excellent family to learn the trade of a wheelwright, where he continued the stipulated term of three years. He acquired the business with such aptitude, and was so good a boy, that after the first year he was allowed to retain for himself all he could make over what was considered full work for an experienced workman. Under this arrangement, during the last two years of his apprenticeship, he made three dollars and fifty cents every week for his own use, which enabled him amply to provide himself with books and other necessaries. He devoted part of the night and Sundays to reading, having no taste for sports of boys of his age, and being naturally fond of solitude he went on Sundays to the forests to read, and was in the habit there, without any special motive, of making speeches to the trees and the winds.

These three years of his life he ever remembered with the greatest pleasure. No ill-feeling, unkindness, or word of reproach was ever manifested by any member of the family toward him, and he never regretted the manner in which this portion of his life was occupied, believing that industry, with intervals for reading, afforded more solid means for the acquisitions of practical knowledge than was to be found in the schools of that day.

At the end of this servitude as an apprentice he had arrived at eighteen years of age, and all the property he possessed was a horse, at that time regarded as a fine one. The first act of his uncontrolled mind, after finishing his trade, was to give his horse to the Rev. John Lysle, a Presbyterian clergyman and teacher of eminence, for a year's board and tuition in his justly celebrated school. The time and the means before him seemed so short, and being naturally of a feeble constitution, his grasping efforts and the toil of study he imposed upon himself made his health give way. His teacher being fully persuaded in his own mind that this result was attributable alone to intense study and close application to books, advised him to lay them aside, and told him he must die soon if he did not.

This announcement from his excellent and venerable teacher prostrated all his hopes in the very morning of his life. Greatly depressed in feeling he quit the school, unable at that time either to study or work. After some considerable time, however, still distressed with that inquietude that ever attends the mind having no fixed object in view, by the advice of friends he went to the Olympian Springs, where in a few weeks he experienced the most rapid recovery. Having been accustomed from childhood to private study, he again devoted himself to self-instruction. While thus engaged it came in his way to form an intimate acquaintance with the late Governor Clark, who offered him the use of his law library.

While a student of law in the town of Winchester a circumstance occurred which gave him the first practical illustration of the liberality of our institutions. One Saturday evening, taking a walk for exercise, he saw a crowd of men in the suburbs, and curiosity attracting him thither he discovered that a gentleman of long residence in the town, and a lawyer by profession, had taken much pains to raise a company of light infantry, with a view to its command, and the company had assembled that evening to elect their officers. While looking on as a spectator he was approached by several gentlemen in succession, who solicited him to stand as a candidate for the captaincy. This was so unexpected, and seemed so unfit and even ludicrous to his own mind, that he regarded it as a joke, and merely answered with a smile. These approaches were soon repeated by others, and finally he was approached by a friend in whom he had unbounded confidence, whose entreaties he could not resist, and he yielded passively, and without taking time to weigh the consequences. The vote was taken, and he was elected by a vote nearly unanimous, only five or six out of the whole company dissenting. His commission from the Governor was soon received, and he now, for the first time, began to reflect upon the subject, and came to the conclusion in his own mind that he had been too precipitate in yielding his assent. He had been elected to an office of the duties of which he knew nothing; his exposure at the first muster, then a month off, he feared would be the consequence. In this dilemma he thought of an expedient, which he immediately carried into effect. He went to a workshop, and made sixty small blocks of wood, with square ends, to stand erect upon the table, making one side to indicate the front. He then procured a gun, and the treatise of Baron Steuben on military tactics, the book then in use. Thus prepared, he went to his room and placed his blocks on the table in a form to represent his company in single lines, then taking the book and looking at the words of command, by reiterated efforts moved his wooden men through all the evolutions of a company muster. In the same manner, with the gun and book, he learned the manual exercise, so that by the first muster he was able to go through without any manifest blunder. He managed to procure a box of muskets for his company, and they were soon brought to a good state of discipline.

The duties of his office interfering considerably with his studies, he some time afterward sent his resignation to the company at a time when from indisposition he was unable to attend the muster, but he was again elected to the command, and thereby almost forced to retain the office.

In the month of August, 1808, he obtained license, was admitted to the bar, and obtained a lucrative business in the very beginning of his professional career. The first time he attended a court of an adjoining county he received the appointment of Commonwealth's Attorney. The first year of his practice he made in fees seven hundred and sixty-five dollars, which more than enabled him to discharge the debts he had contracted while a student; for although without property he had no difficulty in obtaining credit.

Our courts at that early day were fine schools in which to acquire the art of speaking. Free discussion was allowed, as well of the law as the facts, before the juries. Every question was discussed. There was more speaking then at a single term than there is now in a whole year. Readiness as a speaker was as sure a means of reputation at the bar as a profound knowledge of the law is at this time.

Mr. Allan's professional business so increased as soon to possess him, pecuniarily, with a competency. As soon as he was eligible to a seat in the Legislature (in 1811) he was elected a Representative in that body by the people of Clark County by a handsome majority over respectable opposition.

With the exception of a few years he continued in the Legislature until the coming on of the celebrated Old and New Court controversy, which made so prominent a figure in the history of Kentucky. I have elsewhere given a full history of this controversy, which brought the people of the State to the very brink of civil strife. It was in this memorable part of the history of Kentucky that Mr. Allan had first an opportunity of exhibiting his profound knowledge of the structure of the American Government, and of coming into the favorable notice of the people of the whole State. During the pendency of this controversy he was transferred from the House of Representatives by the people of his district to the Senate of Kentucky, and that without opposition. He made there the first speech that was made in either house against what was called the Reorganizing Act. This speech, and several others he made on the same subject, went through several editions in pamphlet form by the voluntary act of the people of different parts of the State. They tended more to enlighten the minds of the people on that question than perhaps the speeches of any other man. He continued from year to year, during the pendency of that controversy, to speak and write in favor of what he considered the constitutional rights of the people. For the real question involved in the contest was, whether the rights of the people were based on stable organic law, or depended on the ever-shifting majorities that ruled the Legislature. At last he had the satisfaction to pen with his own hand the law which put down the New Court, and restored the constitutional Old Court to the undisputed exercise of its duties.

The experience of the violence of unchecked majorities made such a profound impression on his mind in favor of an independent judiciary, that he viewed with the deepest regret the late changes in the constitutions of several of the States, by which the judges were made elective. Previous to the last Convention in Kentucky to remodel the Constitution he wrote five essays on the subject, maintaining with great ability, that under an elective judiciary, in high party times, the minority has no safe protection.

After the expiration of his senatorial term a convention of the people of his county offered him the nomination for re-election, which he declined, and returned to the duties of his profession, in which he continued until 1829, when he was again returned to the Legislature. In 1831, without consulting him, he was announced in the Lexington papers as a candidate for Congress, and was elected by a very large majority over his opponent, receiving several hundred more votes than the usual strength of his party. In 1833 he was re-elected to Congress without opposition, and in 1835 again elected over an opponent of great popularity and influence. At the close of this term of service he voluntarily retired to private life. Of his speeches in Congress, those on the removal of the deposits, the division of the proceeds of the sales of the public lands among the States, internal improvements, a review of President Jackson's administration, the retrenchment of public expenditures, the pension law, and the tariff, attracted most notice. Many of his speeches were widely circulated, from the fact that they were subscribed for by members of Congress from different States and sent home to their constituents as valuable documents. He brought to the consideration of Congress the propriety of conferring upon the old States, for educational purposes, as much of the public lands as had been given to the new; and after his retirement from Congress he often expressed his surprise that the old States did not yet make effort to enforce the justice of this claim. At the head of a select committee, he was the author of a report on the pension law, which was an able document, and obtained a wide circulation.

The chief personal satisfaction that Mr. Allan enjoyed in Congress was the opportunity afforded him of becoming acquainted with the master minds of the nation, both houses of Congress at that time being distinguished for the large number of great men which they contained.

When he returned from Congress in 1837, without application he was offered the presidency of the Board of Internal Improvements of the State. The system of internal improvements had been enacted in his absence, and when he accepted the office he was unacquainted with the provisions of the law on that subject. On examination he found, to his surprise, that the Board was invested with more real power than had ever been conferred on any body of men in the State. In order to get the bills through, the Legislature had made appropriations on the widest scale for improvements in all parts of the State, with the proviso that the money should not be expended unless in the judgment of the Board the improvement ought to be made. Upon an estimate it was found that the Board had discretion over contracts involving an expenditure of more than a million of dollars. The Board consisted of three members besides the president, residing in different parts of the State, who were seldom all present at any meeting. The chief responsibility devolved on the president, whose duty it was to be always present, and to give checks for money.

The old friends of the president, Mr. Allan, came from all parts of the country, claiming their respective appropriations. At that time the highest honors of the State in time to come were associated with his name in common conversation. Temptation for electioneering on so large a scale has seldom been presented to any man—means so ample to gratify the people under the warrant of law, and when a refusal, to the minds of anxious applicants, seemed a violation of law. Thus situated, on taking a view of the whole ground, Mr. Allan called a meeting of the Board, and told them he was convinced, from the condition of the currency and the banks of the United States, that there would in the course of the year be a general suspension of specie payments, and a real turn in the monetary affairs of the whole nation. That if the public works submitted to their discretion should be placed under contract, that it would, in his opinion, involve the loss of the present means of the State, and that it would then be out of their power to have them completed. That for himself he had come to the determination to make no new contract, and that unless the Board would give a pledge to sustain him he would resign his office. The Board gave the pledge.

In a few months afterward there did occur a general suspension of specie payments by the banks, and the State, by his course, was saved from a debt, that might have been contracted, of twelve hundred thousand dollars. He held this office a year, when he resigned, and remained in private life until the year 1842, when there arose another cry for relief laws. To meet this crisis his old constituents again sent him to the Legislature, where he used his zealous exertions in helping to defeat a property law, and what was called a safety fund bank charter, without specie capital. The difficulties then pressing the people soon passed away, and even those who had been most indebted were gratified that relief laws had not been again resorted to.

Mr. Allan acquired his opinions from the standard writers of the Washington school, and always, with unwavering confidence, adhered to them. In public life he ever acted on the belief that there was no popularity worth possessing that was not gained in the cause of truth; that even in point of policy, the steady adherence to the principles on which depended the permanent good of the country was more sure of ultimate success than the bending to each successive breeze of public excitement; that all assumed character, not acted with the zeal of conviction on the theater of life, was a counterfeit upon nature, and would soon depreciate in the public esteem. He denounced in unmeasured terms the fatal scheme that sought to involve the United States in foreign alliances and wars, and maintained that the only rational expectation of improvement in the institutions of the other nations must be founded on the hope of gradual improvement and the reform of abuses, and not on war and sudden revolution; that free government is a science that must be learned, as other branches of knowledge, by the slow developments of time; that all history, as well as the experience of the present age, demonstrates the total incapacity of people who have derived their ideas, habits, and morals from the double despotism of church and state, either to understand or to reduce to successful practice such a government as ours; that it would be just as impossible by war and sudden revolution to communicate to such a people the knowledge of the science of free government, as it would be by such means to teach them astronomy or any other science; that history furnishes no example of such a people having ever come to the enjoyment of a rational liberty by mere successful war; that the American Revolution furnishes no exception to the general rule, because our people had been educated for previous ages in the school and in the enjoyment of liberty—a science they understood as well before as after the Revolution, which was not undertaken in search of new rights, but in defense of old ones from the encroachment of unconstitutional power; that all the real liberty the world ever enjoyed was brought to light, as was ours, by the improvement of the human mind in the school of progressive ages; that all the revolutions by war, even among the most enlightened people of continental Europe, from the year 1789, have been mere contests among leaders for absolute power, the result of all which has been that the people of France, by universal suffrage, have voted themselves a Dictator to save their property from the hands of robbers, and their throats from the daggers of anarchy; that while the reasoning faculties of man are of slow growth, his passions are developed with the rapidity of instinct, and, consequently, the nations of the world have for the most part been governed by their passions and seldom by their reason; that each nation, owing to the circumstances under which it was formed, is subject to be governed by some peculiar enthusiasm. The origin of our people, their history, their prosperity, their individual vanity, and national glory, all stand associated in their minds with the idea of human liberty. Hence the ease with which our enthusiasm, connected with the rights of man, can be made to blaze across the world. A noble enthusiasm, if guided by reason, may perpetuate American liberty. Enthusiasm is the force that moves the world of mankind. Misguided, it is the power by which ambitious men have bound the world in chains. Our peculiar national enthusiasm, diverted from its appropriate object, our own liberty, and misguided by its application to foreign nations, has, in various forms, been the scourge of our land from the year 1789, when it required all the influence of Washington to keep us out of the fires of the French Revolution which desolated Europe. That while our enthusiasm for foreign nations has been of no assistance to any people, it has been chiefly excited for political capital and applied to domestic use. That the only real assistance in the power of the United States to furnish to the progress of rational liberty in the world is by example, literature, intercourse, commerce, peace, and kindness; that it will require our anxious and sleepless vigilance to preserve our own liberties from discord and foreign intrusion. That while we indulge the hope of seeing our institutions spread over the world, we should ever have before our minds the danger that the words anarchy and despotism will be transferred to America. That there are more than five in the old world, for one in the new, whose interest it is to come here; and now, when space is annihilated by steam, and the nations brought into proximity, the despots of the earth go to the surplus, generous, and depraved part of the population and say to them—go, take their ballot box, and through it seize the property of America, reduce all to anarchy, and drive the nations to seek shelter under despotism, a task you have already performed in Europe. A cheap mode of conquest. The tax-payers say to the millions of paupers who live on the public charge—go and relieve us of the burden of your support. The property-holders say to all clans of robbers and thieves—go and relieve us of your depredations. Hunger says to millions—go, satisfy the cravings of your appetite. The Pope and the priests of all sects say to their countless followers—go and erect the true banner of the cross under a Western sun, on the ruins of the temples of revolted heretics. That when these facts are flashing their terrible warning in our faces, instead of the question of intervention, the question should be—Lord, what shall we do to save the religion Jesus Christ and the politics of George

Washington from misguided enthusiasm and the rude shock of the foreign world, ripened for mischief by the corruption of ages?

SAMUEL HANSON.

Samuel Hanson, of Clark County, Kentucky, was born in May, 1786, and died in February, 1858, at the age of nearly seventy-two years. His birth-place was in the State of Maryland, and he studied law in the District of Columbia. He was one of the most learned and accurate of his profession. He understood and practiced the system of pleading with great success. He was frequently a member in both branches of the Kentucky Legislature. Rodger Hanson was his son, who took an active part in the war of the Rebellion as a general on the Confederate side. He was a talented and brave man, ambitious of fame, and died valiantly fighting for the cause he had espoused with great ardor.

JOSEPH H. DAVIESS.

Colonel Joseph Hamilton Daviess stood in the foremost rank of the legal profession in Kentucky. He was born in Bedford County, Virginia, on the 4th of March, 1774. His parents were natives of Virginia, but removed to Kentucky in 1779, when Joseph was only five years old, and settled in the vicinity of Danville. At the age of eleven years Joseph was sent to a grammar school taught by a Mr. Worley, where he continued about two years, making considerable progress in the English and the Latin languages. He afterward made considerable advancement in the Greek language in a school taught by a Dr. Brooks. He evinced unusual capacity for learning, and was always at the head of his class. He was particularly remarkable for his talent in declamation and public speaking. There being no colleges in the country, he next attended the school of Dr. Culbertson, where he completed his knowledge of the Greek language.

In the autumn of 1792, Joseph, then in the eighteenth year of his age, volunteered his services under Major Adair, acting under Government orders, to guard the transportation of provisions to the forts north of the Ohio River. During this service the company was surprised one morning by a large body of Indians rushing upon them in camp, killing and wounding some fifteen of their men, and capturing and carrying away some two hundred of their horses. Young Daviess, discovering his horse tied to a tree within the Indian lines some distance off, resolved to have him at all hazards. He accordingly ran and cut him loose, and brought him back amid a shower of balls. Daviess was the only one of the company who saved his captured horse, and he narrowly escaped with his life, a ball passing through his coat, vest, and cutting off a small piece of his shirt. After a service of about six months he returned home and reviewed his classical studies. He then came to the conclusion to study law, and entered the office of Colonel George Nicholas, who had a higher reputation as a lawyer at that day than any other man in Kentucky.

The class of students which he entered consisted of young men, who all subsequently distinguished themselves not only as lawyers but as statesmen also, of the highest order of talent. They were Isham Talbott, Jesse Bledsoe, William Garrard, Felix Grundy, William Blackbourne, John Pope, John Rowan, William Stuart, and Thomas D. Owings.

So high was the regard of Nicholas for young Daviess, and such was his confidence in him, that at his death, which occurred a few years afterward, he appointed him one of his executors.

Mr. Daviess commenced the practice of the law in June, 1795, and in August was admitted to the bar of the Court of Appeals. In his first cause the renowned George Nicholas, his preceptor, was his antagonist, and in the result obtained a signal triumph over him. Daviess settled at Danville, where one of the district courts of Kentucky had been established, and at once commanded a large business in all the courts in which he practiced. When the circuit court system was established, having received the appointment of United States Attorney for the State of Kentucky, he removed to Frankfort to be more convenient to the Federal Court and Court of Appeals, both of which held their sessions there. This year

(1801–2) he went to Washington City to argue the celebrated cause of Wilson against Mason in the Supreme Court of the United States, and was the first western lawyer who ever appeared in that Court. His speech on that occasion is said to have excited the highest admiration of both the bench and the bar.

In 1803 he married Miss Anne Marshall, a sister of the Chief Justice of the United States. Mr. Daviess had acquired a large property in lands in the region of what is now Daviess County, and, after remaining a few years at Frankfort, removed to Owensboro the better to attend to his interests in that region of country.

In 1808 he removed to Lexington, resumed the practice of the law, and was soon almost overwhelmed with the business of his profession. I have heretofore noticed fully the part he acted as United States Attorney in the prosecution of Aaron Burr for treason, which supercedes the propriety of mentioning it here.

In the fall of 1811 Colonel Daviess entered the army, under Harrison, in the campaign against the Indians on the Wabash. He was appointed to the command of major in that campaign. On the 7th of November, 1811, was fought the celebrated battle of Tippecanoe, where he fell in a charge against the Indians which had been made at his own solicitation. He survived about seven hours, and died about midnight of that day, possessing to the last full command of his faculties.

Colonel Daviess was of athletic and vigorous form, near six feet high, commanding and impressive in his personal appearance—courteous to his friends, but repulsive in the extreme to those whom he disliked. As an orator he had no superior in Kentucky; and it was said of him by some of the best judges in the State, that he was the most impressive speaker they ever heard. The announcement of his death was a shock upon the public mind throughout the State. He was about thirty-five years of age at his death.

RICHARD C. ANDERSON, JR.

Richard C. Anderson, Jr., was born in Louisville on the 4th

day of August, 1788. He was named for his father, who served with gallantry as an officer throughout the Revolutionary War. His mother was a sister of the celebrated George Rodgers Clark. Mr. Anderson was educated at William and Mary College, and studied law with Judge Tucker, of Virginia. Upon his return to Kentucky he commenced the practice of the law, and soon attained a high stand in his profession. He commenced his political career as a Representative of his county in the State Legislature, in which body he served several years with great distinction. In 1817 he was elected to Congress, where he continued four years. His speeches in that body reflected great honor on his character as an orator and statesman. In 1822 he declined a re-election to Congress, but again entered the Legislature of his own State, and was chosen Speaker of the House. He presided over that body with ability, and was regarded by many as a perfect model of a presiding officer. In 1823 Mr. Anderson was appointed by President Monroe as Minister Plenipotentiary to the Republic of Columbia, by which country he was received with every demonstration of honor and respect. In 1824 he negotiated the treaty between the two Republics, which was ratified by the administration among its last acts. In 1825 he lost his wife, when he returned to Kentucky for a short time to place his children with his friends, but revisited Bogota in October of that year, where he remained until July, 1826, when, under instructions of President Adams, he repaired to Porto Bello to join Mr. Sergeant, who, together with himself, had been appointed to the Congress to be assembled at Panama. On his way to the place of his embarkation he was taken sick at the village of Turbaco, where he died on the 24th of July, 1826. In this mission he was succeeded by General William H. Harrison. It was often said of Mr. Anderson, that a better man than he never lived. In private life he was without a vice, and without reproach in all his public life. He died at thirty-six years of age.

WILLIAM T. BARRY.

William T. Barry was born in Fairfax County, Virginia, the

18th of March, 1780. He was regarded as a man of great moral worth, had many admiring and devoted friends, and but few, if any, personal enemies. He was a man of a high order of talent, with a mind well-cultivated. He figured largely in the political questions which agitated Kentucky at intervals, and was especially conspicuous during the pendency of what was called the "Old and New Court question." He removed to Lexington early in life, where he continued to reside until 1829, when he removed to Washington City and constituted a part of President Jackson's cabinet.

Major Barry was eminent as a lawyer, able as an advocate, and admired as an orator; taken altogether, he had but few superiors in the State. A number of his old friends and fellow-citizens of Lexington have erected a monument to his memory, which stands in the public square of the city of Lexington. He was emphatically a man of the people, and enjoyed great popularity. He was early called to occupy places in the Legislature of the State, and in 1820 was elected Lieutenant Governor. After the declaration of the war of 1812 he was one of the most vigorous advocates in Kentucky for its prosecution. Major Barry was one of the aids of Governor Shelby in the campaign of 1813 against the British and their savage allies for their brutal massacre at Raisin and Fort Meigs, the glorious result of which campaign has heretofore been particularly noticed. The courage and good conduct of Major Barry during that campaign secured for him the approbation of his commander and the affection of his brother soldiers.

Major Barry was the head and leader of what was called the Democratic party from 1825 to the time of his removal to Washington. In 1828 he canvassed the State as a candidate for Governor, but was defeated by a majority of less than seven hundred votes, yet he lost nothing in reputation by the contest, but doubtless aided greatly in promoting the triumph of the Democratic party at the November election following, when General Jackson obtained the vote of Kentucky by a majority of nearly eight thousand votes.

Major Barry, under the appointment of President Jackson, held the office of Postmaster General several years, when his health became greatly impaired. In the hope to retrieve his health, and at the same time not deprive the country of his valuable services, General Jackson appointed him in 1835 Ambassador to Spain. He sailed for his destination by the way of Liverpool; but on his arrival at that city was too unwell to proceed further. He shortly afterward died, and there, now, rest his remains.

SOLOMON P. SHARP.

The subject of this sketch was born in the State of Virginia, of humble parents. His father was a gallant soldier of the Revolution, and assisted in obtaining the memorable victory of King's Mountain. When the war was over he moved from Washington County, Virginia, first to the neighborhood of Nashville, Tennessee, and a short time afterward to the vicinity of Russellville, Kentucky. Solomon was a small child at that time.

Colonel Sharp gained admittance to the bar at the early age of nineteen; and relying solely on his own energies, without fortune or influential friends, he soon attained to high standing in his profession, and became engaged in an extensive and lucrative practice. He had no superior in all the Green River country for his age. His style of speech was conversational; in debate he was plain, concise, and logical; and he was an impressive and successful lawyer. As soon as by age eligible to a seat in the Legislature he was elected a member of the House of Representatives, where he displayed at once a high order of talent. He was repeatedly re-elected a member of that body, and until by the general voice of his district he was transferred to the Congress of the United States. In this body he served for two successive terms, and ranked among the most eminent politicians of the day. He was held in high estimation by one of the most distinguished statesmen of the United States, the Hon. John C. Calhoun, of South Carolina, and was his room-mate, and with him supported with zeal the administration of Mr. Madison. Mr. Calhoun regarded him as the ablest man of his age who had ever crossed the mountains. After his service in Congress he removed from Bowlinggreen to Frankfort, that he might be more convenient to the Supreme Court of the State, and the Federal Court of the District of Kentucky. He devoted himself assiduously to the practice of the law, and obtained an extensive practice. About this time he married the daughter of Colonel John M. Scott, of Frankfort, a most estimable lady.

He was appointed by Governor Adair to the important office of Attorney General, the duties of which office he discharged with great ability, and with entire satisfaction to the country.

In the very midst of his usefulness to the country, and in the 38th year of his age, he was assassinated at his own house, in Frankfort, on the Sunday night before the first Monday in November, 1825, being the night preceding the convention of the Legislature of which Colonel Sharp had been elected a member from the county of Franklin.

Jereboam O. Beauchamp, of Simpson County, Kentucky, was soon afterward arrested on the charge of being the murderer, and was tried, condemned, and executed for the crime. Previous to the execution his wife, formerly a Miss Cook, of Bowlinggreen, remained in jail with him, and on the night preceding the day appointed for his execution they both took laudanum with suicidal intentions; but having failed in producing the effect desired, they each attempted to cut their own throats with an old case knife which they had procured, in the accomplishment of which Mrs. Beauchamp succeeded; but Mr. Beauchamp, though badly wounded about the throat, producing a great flow of blood and consequent debility, was taken to the gallows and publicly executed.

The two (Beauchamp and his wife) were taken by their friends from thence to Bloomfield, Kentucky, and deposited in the same grave, occupying the same coffin, enfolded in each other's arms. Beauchamp had but a short time before the assassination occurred been married to Miss Cook, and she, as it is said, only consented to the alliance under the promise of Beauchamp that he would kill Sharp for alleged wrongs on his part toward her during his residence at Bowlinggreen.

GEORGE M. BIBB.

George M. Bibb was born in the State of Virginia in the year 1772, and graduated at Princeton College in 1792. He emigrated to Kentucky when young, studied law, rose rapidly in his profession, and was soon regarded as one of the ablest lawyers in the State. On account of his great legal attainments, solid judgment, and powers of reasoning already developed, he was selected by the Legislature of Kentucky to defend the occupying claimant laws against the State of Virginia before the Supreme Court of the United States. This trust he discharged with great ability, and satisfactorily to the people of Kentucky.

Judge Bibb took a very active part in the politics of Kentucky about the time of the reorganization of the Court of Appeals, and during the session of the Legislature of 1824–5. He was on the New Court side of that question, which was so fearfully agitated for several years, and a few other lawyers of great distinction, Rowan, Barry, and some others, coincided with his views on that subject; but an overwhelming majority of both the bar and the bench were on the other side, denominated the "Old Court party." After the people of the State had become fully enlightened on that question, the New Court party, though successful for a time, were finally signally defeated, the Old Court restored, and the acts of the New Court, of which Mr. Bibb was an uncompromising advocate, declared nugatory.

As soon as a *quietus* had been given to this agitating question, Mr. Boyle, who was Chief Justice of the Old Court, resigned his seat upon the bench, and Mr. Bibb, the great champion of the Relief and New Court party, was immediately appointed by the Relief Governor, Desha, then in power, his successor, which appointment was ratified by the Senate.

Judge Bibb was a Justice, and twice Chief Justice of the Court of Appeals of Kentucky, and was two years State Senator. He was twice a Senator in the Congress of the United States. The first time he served from 1811 to 1814; the second time, from 1829 to 1835. Upon his retirement from the Senate he was appointed Chancellor of the Chancery Court of the city of Louisville, in which situation he fully sustained his high character as a judge. He continued in this office until 1844, when he was appointed by President Tyler Secretary of the Treasury of the United States. After the inauguration of President Polk, he continued to reside in Washington City, and practiced law in the Supreme Court of the United States and in the courts of the District of Columbia. He also acted as an assistant in the office of the Attorney General of the United States. He died in Georgetown, D. C., the 14th of April, 1859.

HUMPHREY MARSHALL.

Humphrey Marshall was one of the earliest pioneers to Kentucky, having come here in 1780. He soon assumed a conspicuous position among the public men of the State, and was what was called a Federalist, to the fullest extent, in all the principles of that party. He was an active participant in all the political contests agitated in Kentucky at that day. He had a commanding force of character and brilliant talents, still great prejudice was excited against him on account of his political opinions, which were offensive to the masses of Kentucky. He was a member of the Convention of 1787, which assembled at Danville preliminary to the formation of a Constitution for the State. He was for many years a member of great influence in the Legislature of Kentucky, and was a Senator in Congress from 1795 to 1801.

The first history of Kentucky ever published was by Mr. Marshall. His personal prejudices are often interlarded in the work, which rendered it objectionable to many, but, taken altogether, it was a good and valuable work, and one which I read with great pleasure soon after its publication in 1824 or 1825, but have not been able to secure one since my present undertaking to write a similar work commenced. I could, doubtless, have derived great advantage from its reperusal.

It was in 1808 that the bloodless duel occurred between Mr. Marshall and Mr. Clay. Two of Mr. Marshall's sons became quite distinguished as jurists and lawyers—Thomas A. Marshall, late of the Court of Appeals, and the late John J. Marshall, of Louisville, late Judge of the Circuit Court. Mr. Marshall died in Lexington, some twenty-five years ago, or more, at a very advanced age.

JESSE BLEDSOE.

Jesse Bledsoe was at one time a distinguished advocate and jurist, and early in his career filled several important stations. He had but few superiors as a classical scholar, and he took great pleasure while he lived in reading the Grecian orators and poets in the original tongue. He was born in Culpepper County, Virginia, on the 6th day of April, 1776. When a boy hardly grown he emigrated to Kentucky with an elder brother, and completed his education at Transylvania University. After finishing his collegiate course he studied law, and became eminent in the profession. He was often a member of the Legislature, representing first Fayette and afterward Bourbon, having lived in both counties. He was Secretary of State under Governor Scott. He was United States Senator from 1813 to 1815, filling an unexpired term. He was a judge of the Circuit Court in the Lexington District, and while holding that position was appointed to the professorship of law in Transylvania University. After filling these situations for five or six years, he resigned both, and resumed the practice of the law. He removed to Mississippi in 1833, and from thence went to Texas in 1835 or 1836, and died near Nacogdoches, on the 30th of June, 1837, being sixty-one years old.

HARRY INNIS.

The Hon. Harry Innis was born in Caroline County, Virginia, in 1752. His father was an Episcopal minister, and a native of Scotland. President Madison and Innis were schoolmates. In 1776-7 Mr. Innis was employed by the Committee of Safety of Virginia to superintend the working of Chipel's lead mines, to procure a necessary supply of that article for the Revolutionary contest. He was elected by the Legislature of Virginia a commissioner to settle unpatented land claims in the year 1779, and in 1783 that body elected him one of the judges of the Supreme Court for the District of Kentucky. On the 3d of November of that year, in conjunction with Judges Wallace and McDowell, the court was commenced and held at Crow's Station, near the town of Danville. In 1787, that same body elected him Attorney General for the District of Kentucky, in the place of Walker Daniel, who had been killed by the Indians. He continued in this office until 1787, when he was appointed Judge of the Court of the United States for the Kentucky District, which office he held at the time of his death, which occurred in 1816. When Kentucky became an independent State in 1792, he was offered the office of Chief Justice, but declined it. He was president of the first electoral college for the choice of Governor and Lieutenant Governor of Kentucky. He was one of the members of the local board of war for the Western country. No man at that day stood in higher esteem than Judge Innis, who performed every trust confided to him with fidelity and ability. He was an especial favorite of Washington, and repeatedly received his thanks for the manner in which he performed high trusts confided to him. Judge Innis was twice married. The Hon. John J. Crittenden married one of the daughters of his second marriage. Judge Innis's widow survived him some thirty or forty years.

GEORGE ROBERTSON.

But few men in Kentucky have attained higher standing or greater eminence as a statesman, lawyer, and jurist, than the subject of this sketch; but he, according to the course of nature, must very soon end his earthly career. He is now eighty-one years of age, was a few months since stricken with paralysis, is closely confined to his bed, and it is believed can survive but a very short time. In this work I have given biographical sketches of but few persons who are still living, but the pre-eminence of Judge Robertson, and the intimate association of his name with the most important events connected with our history as a State for nearly three score years, demands imperiously that he should be particularly noticed.

The father of George Robertson, with his wife, emigrated

to Kentucky at a very early period in 1779, and settled at what is called Gordon's Station, during what was known as "the hard winter." Near this place he built a house for his family residence, which was regarded as the finest house in the whole State of Kentucky at that day. He was a man of great popularity, distinguished for his morality, and of strong natural mind. In June, 1788, he was elected and attended the Virginia Federal Convention, which met at Richmond, and having been also elected a member of the Legislature, he remained there during the ensuing year, and in December of that year removed to Kentucky. He was elected the first sheriff of Mercer County, under the Constitution of 1792, and died in the year 1802. His wife, whose name was Margaret, survived him forty-four years, and died at a very advanced age, at her son-in-law's, Governor Letcher, at Frankfort, in the year 1846. George Robertson was the youngest son of these parents. In 1804 he entered the school of Joshua Fry, where he studied the Latin and French languages. In 1805 he entered Transylvania University, where he remained until August, 1806. Being disappointed in his expectations of going to Princeton College, he entered a classical school at Lancaster, conducted by the Rev. Samuel Findly, where he remained some six months as a pupil, and afterward was an assistant teacher for about the same space of time. After this, he devoted a year or two to miscellaneous reading, when in 1808 he went to Frankfort, and studied law with Martin D. Hardin for a very short time, when he returned to reside with his brother-in-law, Samuel McKee, a very eminent lawyer of Kentucky, and for many years a member of Congress. He continued to read law until 1809, when he obtained license to practice from Boyle and Wallace of the Court of Appeals. He was married in 1809, at nineteen years of age, to a daughter of Dr. Bainbridge, of Lancaster, sixteen years of age. They were both poor at the time of their marriage. By the time he attained twenty-one years of age he had obtained an extensive practice. In 1816, being then only twenty-six years old, he was elected to Congress, and was twice re-elected afterward, without opposition. He resigned the last year of his service to resume the practice of his profession. While in Congress he was appointed on the most important committees of the House. He was the author of the bill to establish the territorial government of Arkansas. He was the author of the present system of selling public lands. After his retirement from Congress he was tendered by Governor Adair the appointment of Attorney General, and also the judgeship of the Fayette Circuit Court. About the same time he was offered by the authorities a law professorship in Transylvania University, but he declined them all, preferring to continue his practice as a lawyer to secure a competence for his family. In 1822 the relief questions in Kentucky, of which I have before spoken, were greatly agitated, and Mr. Robertson was prevailed upon to become a candidate for the Legislature, to which he was elected, and in which he remained until the final settlement of the question in 1826-7. In 1823 he was made Speaker of the House, and was re-elected at each succeeding session whilst he remained, except the year 1824. During the period he remained in the Legislature he wrote and spoke much, and was regarded at that time as possessing one of the most masterly intellects in the State. He was the author of the celebrated protest of the anti-relief party of 1824. He was also the author of the manifesto of the majority at the session of 1825-26. His speeches, widely circulated at that time, were deep in thought, forcible, argumentative, and exhibited a profound knowledge of the Constitution and the laws.

Judge Robertson was not a seeker of offices, though they were frequently offered him and their acceptance declined. He was offered the governorship of Arkansas by President Monroe. R. C. Anderson, Minister to Bogota, expressed a desire that he should fill his place. The Mission to Columbia was also offered him. He was tendered also by Mr. Adams, in 1828, the Mission to Peru, none of which were accepted. Under Governor Metcalfe he accepted, for a short time, the Secretaryship. He was confirmed Judge of the Court of Appeals upon the rejection of Mills and Owsley's nomination to that position, and was afterward commissioned Chief Justice of that court, which position he held until April, 1843, when he resigned to pursue his profession of the law. He had few equals as a jurist. He was for many years professor of constitutional law in Transylvania University. He is one of the judges of the Court of Appeals of Kentucky at the present time (1871.)

Judge Robertson was born in Mercer County, Kentucky, November 18, 1790, and is consequently now in the eighty-first year of his age. The honorary degree of LL. D. has been conferred on him by the colleges at Danville and Augusta. The day will doubtless come when his writings, speeches, addresses, and law lectures will be collected and published for the benefit of his countrymen everywhere. The authorized reports of the decisions of the Court of Appeals are monuments to his ability as a judge during a period of many years.

JOHN SPEED SMITH.

John Speed Smith was born in Jessamine County, Kentucky, the 31st day of July, 1792. He was a soldier under General Harrison, and participated in the bloody battle of Tippecanoe. He was aide-de-camp to General Harrison at the battle of the Thames in 1813. In 1819 he was elected to the Legislature of Kentucky, and was a Representative in Congress from Kentucky from 1821 to 1823. In 1827 he was again elected to the State Legislature, and made Speaker of the House. Subsequent to this he served several terms in both the House and Senate. He was appointed United States Attorney for the District of Kentucky by President Jackson. Previous to that, under the administration of J. Q. Adams, he was appointed by the President Secretary of Legation to the United States mission sent to the South American Congress, which was to assemble at Tacubaya. In 1839 he was appointed by the Legislature of Kentucky one of the Commissioners to Ohio to obtain the passage of a law for the protection of the slave property of Kentucky, which mission was altogether successful. He was Superintendent of Public Works in Kentucky several years, and died in Madison County, Ky., June 6th, 1854.

Colonel Smith was regarded as one of the most prominent men in the State as a politician, possessing great talents and influence. His son, Green Clay Smith, has become quite a prominent man in Kentucky since the death of his father, filling many important civil and military offices.

JOHN B. THURSTON.

John B. Thurston was born in Virginia, in 1757. He studied law, and after the completion of his studies emigrated to Kentucky. In 1805 he was elected to the United States Senate from Kentucky. He subsequently became a judge of the Circuit Court of Kentucky, in which position he continued until his death, which occurred at Washington City, on the 30th of August, 1845.

DAVID TRIMBLE.

David Trimble was born in Frederick County, Virginia, about 1782, and received his education at William and Mary College. He studied law, and came to Kentucky about the year 1803. He served in two campaigns under General Harrison in the war of 1812. He was elected a member of Congress from Kentucky in 1817, and served in that body five consecutive terms, ten years without interruption. He was highly esteemed for the integrity of his principles and the fidelity with which he discharged his public duties. He engaged extensively in the iron manufacture and in agriculture after his retirement from Congress, and contributed greatly to the development of the resources of the State. He died at Trimble's Furnace, October 26th, 1842.

JOHN WHITE.

John White was regarded as a man of talents and high attainments. He was born in the year 1805. At thirty years of age he was elected to Congress from Kentucky, and served in that body three consecutive terms—one as Speaker. He was Judge of the Nineteenth Judicial District at the time of his death, which occurred at Richmond, Kentucky, by suicide, September 22d, 1845. No cause was known for the rash act.

HENRY GRIDER.

Colonel Henry Grider was born in Garrard County, Kentucky, on the 16th of July, 1796. Having received a desultory education, he finished at Greensburg, Kentucky, under the instruction of the Rev. John Howe, at New Athens Seminary, which was under the charge of Mr. Howe for a great number of years. Colonel Grider was about twenty-two years of age at the time he quit that school. Judge Asher W. Graham attended the same school at the same time, and was about the same age of Colonel Grider. They were both from Bowlinggreen, Kentucky. Two more amiable and exemplary young men never lived. After leaving the school at Greensburg they both commenced the study of the law at Bowlinggreen, in which profession they both soon distinguished themselves. Graham was exalted to the judgeship of the Court of Appeals, and was afterward, for many years, a judge of the Circuit Court, which position he filled at the time of his death, which occurred a few years since.

Colonel Grider rendered his first public service in the army as a private in the war of 1812, and served with Shelby in his campaign to Canada. In 1827 he was elected to the Legislature of Kentucky, as also in 1831; and in 1833 to the Senate of Kentucky, where he served four years. He was a Representative in Congress from 1843 to 1847, and was also re-elected to the Thirty-seventh Congress, serving on the committees on Revolutionary Claims and on Mileage. He was re-elected to the Thirty-eighth Congress, and was a member of the Committee on Territories. He died soon afterward, on his farm in Warren County, at the age of about seventy years.

JAMES HARLAN.

Hon. James Harlan was born in Mercer County, Kentucky, June 22d, 1800. He received a good English education by the time he was seventeen years of age, when he employed himself in mercantile pursuits. He was thus engaged until twenty-one years of age, when he commenced the study of the law, and was admitted to the bar in 1823. In 1829 he was appointed Commonwealth's Attorney for the district in which he resided, and served in that capacity four years. In 1835 he was elected to Congress, re-elected in 1837, and was chairman of the committee for investigating defalcations. From 1840 to 1844 he was Secretary of State under Governor Letcher. In 1845 he was elected to the House of Representatives of Kentucky; and in 1850 he was appointed Attorney General, which office he held until his death, which occurred at Frankfort, February 18th, 1863.

Mr. Harlan attained a high stand at the bar as a lawyer, and obtained a very extensive practice in the Court of Appeals and in the other courts of Frankfort. His son, General John M. Harlan, now of the city of Louisville, is regarded as one of the great men of Kentucky, and has arisen already to high distinction as a lawyer. He acted with great credit to himself as a general on the Federal side of the late Rebellion.

JUDGE WM. M'CLUNG.

Judge William McClung was among the earliest settlers of Kentucky, and one among its most prominent citizens. But few men in Kentucky took a more active part in advancing the interests of the first settlers. He was particularly distinguished for his high attainments as a lawyer. He was for a great number of years a judge, first of the District Court, and afterward of the Circuit courts. He was a man of unswerving integrity, just and generous. His wife was a sister of the distinguished Chief Justice Marshall, who lived many years after the death of her husband, and to a very advanced age.

Judge McClung was filling the office of judge at the time of his death. He settled in Mason County, where he continued to reside until his death.

John A. McClung, of Mason County, and Colonel Alexander McClung, who removed to the State of Mississippi, both men of no inconsiderable distinction, were the sons of Judge McClung. The writer is uninformed as to the date of Judge McClung's death

ALEXANDER D. ORR.

Colonel Alexander D. Orr was an early settler in Kentucky, was a man in good circumstances, and of great popularity.

He was elected a member of the Legislature at the first election under the first Constitution of Kentucky, and, with John Brown and John Edwards, was one of the first members of Congress from Kentucky after it was admitted into the Union as a State. He continued in office three consecutive terms. He was a man of commanding person, and a polished gentleman. He died some thirty odd years ago. It is said of him that he built the first brick house ever erected in the county of Mason.

JOHN COBURN.

Judge John Coburn was born in the city of Philadelphia, but I think studied law with the distinguished Luther Martin, of Baltimore. It was under his advice, however, that he emigrated to Kentucky as early as 1784. He commenced business in Lexington as a merchant, and never practiced law in Kentucky. In this business he was very successful. About ten years afterward he removed to Mason County, and associated himself with Dr. Bazil Duke in the mercantile business, but was soon afterward appointed Judge of the District Court of Mason County; and, upon the reorganization of the courts, he became Judge of the Circuit Court, in which situation he continued until the year 1805. He was offered by President Jefferson the judgeship of the territory of Michigan, which he declined, but afterward accepted the judgeship of Orleans, holding his courts in St. Louis. In 1809 he resigned this office, and during the war of 1812 was appointed by Mr. Madison Collector of the Revenue for the Fourth District of Kentucky. This was the last office of public employment he ever held.

Judge Coburn's merits were early known and duly appreciated in Kentucky. A few months after his arrival in Kentucky he was elected a member of the convention which met at Danville, in 1785, to take preliminary steps to procure the admission of Kentucky into the Union. In 1796 he was one of the commissioners to settle the boundary line between Virginia and Kentucky. The citizens of St. Louis regretted much the resignation of Judge Coburn as judge of the territory, and urged him most strongly to relinquish the idea. In 1813 he was appointed by Governor Shelby one of his military family, which position he held only for a short time. It was mainly through his instrumentality that the Congress of the United States appropriated a thousand acres of land to the old pioneer, Daniel Boone, of whom Judge Coburn was a very devoted friend. He was a leading Democrat in politics, and an accomplished writer. In 1800 he was most favorably spoken of in connection with the office of United States Senator, but he relinquished his pretensions in favor of his friend, not less distinguished than himself, the Hon. John Breckinridge. Judge Coburn was born in 1762 or 1763, and died in 1823.

JOHN T. JOHNSON.

John T. Johnson was a brother of the distinguished statesman and soldier, Col. Richard M. Johnson. He attained greater eminence as a lawyer than his brother Richard, and was at one time a judge of the Court of Appeals of Kentucky. He was a Representative in the Congress of the United States two consecutive terms, from 1821 to 1825. After this he gave himself exclusively to the work of the Gospel, and was a preacher in what is denominated the Christian Church for nearly thirty years previous to his death. He was regarded as one of the leaders of this denomination of Christians, and preached with great power and success. Scores were added to this church under his ministrations. He died the 18th of December, 1857, in Lexington, Missouri.

ROBERT P. HENRY.

Robert P. Henry was born in Scott County, November 24, 1788, and graduated at Transylvania University, at Lexington, Kentucky. He studied law with Henry Clay, and was admitted to the bar in 1809, being then just twenty-one years of age. That same year he served as Commonwealth's Attorney for his district. He was aide-de-camp to his father, General William Henry, in the war of 1812. After this he settled in Christian County, where he practiced law, and became prosecuting attorney for that district. He was a director of what was called the Commonwealth's Bank, at Princeton. He was elected to Congress, and served from 1823 to 1827, and was a member of the Committee of Roads and Canals; and it was through his instrumentality that the first appropriation ever granted by Congress for the improvement of the Mississippi River was made. He declined the judgeship of the Court of Appeals offered him while in Congress. Before the expiration of his term in Congress he was taken sick of fever, and died the 25th of August, 1826, at the age of thirty-eight years.

THOMAS CHILTON.

Thomas Chilton, bearing the name of his father, the Rev. Thomas Chilton, who was a minister of note in the church which was denominated "Separate Baptists," was decidedly a man of talents. He had a fair education, and commenced preaching the gospel when quite a young man, but afterward abandoned it for the law, and practiced the profession some years in Elizabethtown with considerable success, competing with Ex-Governor Helm, Ex-Governor Wickliffe, Judge Churchill, Hardin, Tobin, and others. At one session of the Legislature he was elected clerk of the Senate. After that he was elected to Congress, and served from 1827 to 1831, and again from 1833 to 1835. Some time after this Mr. Chilton betook himself to preaching again, and removed to Alabama, where he both preached and practiced law, as I have been informed, until his death, which occurred some few years afterward. At the bar and on the stump Mr. Chilton, as a speaker, was interesting, and his style agreeable; but in the pulpit his manner was entirely changed. He spoke in a sort of sing-song tone peculiar to many ministers of the church to which he belonged. I have often heard him at the bar and on the stump, and always with pleasure; and when I afterward heard him in the pulpit I could but be astonished at the change.

JAMES B. CLAY.

James B. Clay, the son of the Hon. Henry Clay, and a man who had held several important positions in the history of our country, deserves to be mentioned. He was born in the city of

Washington, November 9, 1817, and received a classical education at Transylvania University. At the age of fifteen he went to Boston, where he spent two years in a counting-house. From Boston he emigrated to St. Louis, Missouri, then a city of only eight thousand inhabitants, and settled upon a farm. About the age of twenty-one he returned to Kentucky, and after spending two years in the manufacturing business, he graduated at the law school at Lexington, and practiced as the partner of his father until 1849.

During that year President Taylor appointed him Charge d'Affairs to Lisbon ; and having returned home by order of the Government, he was mentioned by name in President Fillmore's Message of 1850. He again took up his residence in Missouri, but returned to Kentucky in 1853, after the death of his father, and became proprietor of Ashland. He was elected to Congress in 1857, serving one term, and was one of the Committee of Foreign Relations. He was a member of the Peace Convention of 1861 to Washington, and died at Montreal, in Canada January 26th, 1864.

THOMAS CORWIN.

Thomas Corwin, so famous as a politician and statesman of the State of Ohio, was born, educated, and commenced the practice of the law in Kentucky. He was born in Bourbon County, Kentucky, of humble and unpretending parentage, on the 29th of July, 1794, and came to the bar in 1817. Having settled in Ohio, at the age of twenty-three he was elected a member of the Legislature of that State, and in 1831 a Representative in Congress from the Warren District. He continued a member of the House until 1840, when in October of that year he was elected Governor of Ohio, which office he held for two years. The Whigs, having a majority in the Legislature of Ohio in 1845, elected Mr. Corwin United States Senator, which office he held until his appointment by President Fillmore, in 1850, as Secretary of the Treasury. He took a very high stand in Congress as an advocate of Whig principles. His speeches at the bar, as well as on the stump, were eloquent and effective. In 1858 he was again elected a Representative in Congress, and during that year a volume of his speeches were published. He was again elected to the Thirty-seventh Congress, and during his term was appointed by President Lincoln Minister to Mexico, and died a few years afterward.

MARTIN D. HARDIN.

Martin D. Hardin was a man of superior intellect, and as a lawyer had but few superiors in the United States. He was educated at Transylvania Seminary, and practiced his profession at Frankfort with great success. He was the son of Col. John Hardin, of Washington County, and the father of the Hon. John J. Hardin who fell in the battle of Buena Vista, February, 1847. Mr. Hardin served several years in the Kentucky Legislature, was Secretary of State under Governor Shelby, and in 1817 was appointed by Governor Slaughter to the Senate of the United States, serving but one session. He served in the Northwestern Army in the war of 1812 as a major in the regiment of Colonel John Allen, and proved himself a brave and efficient officer. He was born on the Monongahela River, in Western Pennsylvania, on the 21st of June, 1780, and died in Franklin County, October 8, 1823, at forty-three years of age.

JAMES S. JACKSON.

General James S. Jackson was born in Madison County, Ky., studied law, and was regarded as a man of talents. He served as a captain of volunteers in the Mexican War. In 1861 he was elected a member of the House of Representatives of the Thirty-seventh Congress; but while the Rebellion was progressing he recruited a regiment of Kentucky cavalry, and was subsequently appointed a Brigadier General. He was killed at the battle of Perryville, in 1862, valiantly fighting in the service of his country.

WILLIAM P. DUVAL.

Governor William P. Duvall was born in Virginia in 1784, but in early life came to Kentucky, where he studied and practiced law. He was a Representative in Congress one term, from 1813 to 1815. In 1822 he was appointed by President Monroe Governor of Florida, and was re-appointed to the same office under the administrations of both Adams and Jackson. In 1848 he removed to Texas. Some six years afterward, on the 19th of March, 1854, he died in Washington City, at the age of about seventy.

JOSHUA H. JEWETT.

We know but little of Mr. Jewett. The writer of this sketch saw him frequently during his residence at Elizabethtown, Ky. He was a high-toned gentleman, and of respectable talents. He was born in Maryland, and in that State studied law. Removing to Kentucky, he practiced in competition with some of the leading lawyers of the State. He was born on the 13th of September, 1812. He was twice elected to the House of Representatives in Congress from the Elizabethtown district, and while there served as chairman of the Committee on Invalid Pensions. Mr. Jewett died a few years ago, at Elizabethtown, Kentucky, where his family resides. He was greatly afflicted in the latter part of his life with sore eyes, which finally, if not entirely, deprived him of sight. He was a man of fine personal appearance, of social disposition, and beloved by his acquaintances. His death was deeply lamented.

FRANCIS JOHNSON.

Hon. Francis Johnson, more familiarly known as Frank Johnson, was an eminent lawyer of Kentucky. He was born in Caroline County, Virginia. For three terms, or for six consecutive years, he was a Representative in Congress from Kentucky, and was an active, vigilant, and efficient member. He was one of those who, with Mr. Clay, contributed most to the defeat of General Jackson for the Presidency in 1824. He was the principal counsel for John U. Waring in his celebrated trial at Frankfort, in 1838 or 1839, for the murder of Thos. Q. Richardson, in whose acquittal he was successful. Benjamin G. Burks, late of Greensburg, Ky., was also for the defence in that case.

SHERROD WILLIAMS.

Mr. Sherrod Williams was born in Pulaski County, Kentucky, but removed to Wayne County when a boy. He was of the humbler walks of life. Commencing life poor, his education was quite limited, but by habits of industry in early youth, with great energy and indomitable perseverance, he soon acquired a fund of knowledge. At about the age of fifteen years he placed himself under the instruction of a gentleman at Monticello, Wayne County, to learn the trade of a brickmaker. After remaining some time at this business he engaged in the study of the law; and in the course of a short time he obtained license, and commenced practice with considerable success. About this time he married an estimable lady of high standing and good family, of Wayne County, a sister of the Hon. Frank Stone, Napoleon B., and Shelby Stone; but their dispositions were incongruous, and family jars were often the consequence.

Mr. Williams became greatly interested in politics during the pendency of the "Old and New Court question," and was an efficient advocate of the Old Court side, and soon rendered himself prominent as a politician. In 1829, at twenty-five years of age, he was elected a Representative from Wayne in the Legislature of Kentucky. The writer had a fair opportunity of becoming well acquainted with him. They were not only members of the same body, but they were roommates, and, being about the same age, became particularly intimate, each enjoying the confidence of the other in a high degree. Mr. Williams was several times afterward returned a member of the House of Representatives from Wayne, and was nearly always in his place and attentive to the interests of his constituents. In 1835 he was elected to Congress, and by re-election served for six consecutive years, occupying quite a high stand in this body. Mr. Williams's usefulness was greatly impaired afterward by the too frequent intemperate use of alcohol. Some years since he removed to one of the Southern States, where he died. Mr. Williams was a social, companionable, kind-hearted man, of fine address, and in personal appearance far above mediocrity.

ELIJAH HISE.

The Hon. Elijah Hise was a lawyer, jurist, and statesman of eminence and great distinction in Kentucky. He was born in Allegheny County, Pennsylvania, in 1801, and was of German descent. His parents moved to Kentucky and settled in Logan County when the subject of this sketch was a mere boy. Studious habits he adopted early, and stored his mind with useful knowledge. He chose the profession of law, and commenced the practice in Russellville, the bar of which at that time was attended by some of the ablest lawyers in Kentucky. Mr. Hise, though young, soon became distinguished as a lawyer, obtained a lucrative practice, and amassed before his death considerable wealth. In politics he was a devoted and uncompromising Jackson man, a sentiment to which the people of Logan at that day were very much opposed; and in 1828, being a candidate for a seat in the Representative branch of the Legislature, he was defeated, but not so badly beaten as to become discouraged; for the succeeding year he was again a candidate, and was successful, notwithstanding the predominancy of party against him. The writer had the honor of serving with him in that body, and of becoming intimately acquainted with him. He was a man of some eccentricities of character, but decidedly a man of talents. He was devoted to his friends, but exceedingly bitter in his remarks about those whom he did not like. In argument he was often exceedingly sarcastic, as well as forcible and convincing. During the session of the Legislature alluded to, the writer introduced a bill to repeal the law which allowed pay to the owners of slaves executed for the commission of crime. Mr. Hise was my coadjutor in the advocacy of the passage of that bill in opposition to the distinguished James Guthrie, who opposed with great power its repeal. Mr. Hise's speech on that occasion was one of great ability, and to it, mainly, was attributable the passage of the bill in the House; but it was defeated in the Senate by a small majority. Mr. Hise was several years a judge of the Court of Appeals, by appointment first, and then by election. Some years afterward he was elected a member of Congress, which position he held at the time of his death, which occurred three or four years since by suicide. The occurrence produced a shock, especially in the community where he was best known. He was a man of considerable wealth, holding a high position in public confidence at the time, leaving an affectionate wife and many relatives and friends to mourn his loss. Judge Hise had no children. I would gladly have extended this sketch, but have been furnished with no data other than what my personal acquaintance and my own recollection afforded.

JAMES GUTHRIE.

When the writer was a member of the Legislature of Kentucky in the year 1829-30, he took the pains to ascertain and preserve in alphabetical order the names, occupation, and birth-place of every member of that body. For information in this regard I am indebted alone to that document in respect to many distinguished individuals whose lives I have endeavored to sketch, and who have passed away from all transitory scenes. Among them the name of the Honorable James Guthrie appears. He was born in Nelson County, Kentucky, in the year 1792, and was thirty-seven years old at the session alluded to. He was chairman of the same committee to which the writer belonged, " the Committee of Courts of Justice," to which more business was referred than any other committee of the House during that session. Mr. Guthrie proved himself to be, during that session, one of the most working and efficient members of the body.

Mr. Guthrie started in life with but scanty means; studied law in Bardstown, and commenced the practice in Shepherdsville, Bullitt County. After remaining there a short time he removed to Louisville, where he soon afterward married a Miss Prather, an estimable lady of great wealth, residing in that city. Her fortune experienced no deterioration under the management and control of so excellent a financier as Mr. Guthrie ever proved to be; but, on the contrary, he continued to amass as long as he lived, and at his death was regarded as possessing more wealth than perhaps any other man in the State. Mr. Guthrie did more by legislation, and otherwise, to build up the city of Louisville than any other one of her citizens. He was always president or a leading member of some of the most important councils or incorporated companies of the city, and exercised greater influence in those bodies than any other individual belonging to them. He was for a long time president of the Louisville and Nashville Railroad, president of the Louisville and Frankfort Railroad, director in the Bank of Kentucky, and a director in many other banks and insurance companies. Mr. Guthrie was repeatedly a member of both branches of the Kentucky Legislature. He was president of the convention which formed the last Constitution of Kentucky, Secretary of the Treasury of the United States during the administration of James Buchanan, and lastly, Senator in the Congress of the United States. Soon after the commencement of his term of service he was taken sick, and was confined at home until his death, which occurred a year or two since, at about the age of seventy-five. Mr. Guthrie was in health of robust form, over six feet in height, and of fine personal appearance. His carriage indicated but little elasticity of action, his gait being slow and rather awkward. His speeches were sensible, but his manner not captivating.

JOHN BOYLE.

Judge Boyle was a native of Kentucky, and liberally educated. He studied law, and became eminent in his profession. He was was for a long time Judge of the Court of Appeals of Kentucky, and Chief Justice of the State. He was a Representative in Congress for three consecutive terms, from 1803 to 1809. After this he was appointed Governor of Illinois Territory. He was appointed by President Adams Judge of the United States District Court for Kentucky, in which situation he continued until his death, a period of about eight years. He died the 28th of January, 1834.

DANIEL BRECK.

The subject of this sketch died a few months since, at Richmond, Kentucky, at an advanced age. He was born near

Boston, Massachusetts, in the year 1788. He graduated at Dartmouth College in 1812. Having studied law he removed to Kentucky in 1814, where he soon afterward commenced the practice. The first public position ever held by him in this State was that of judge of a county court. In 1824 he was elected to the State Legislature, and served in that body five years by re-election. From 1835 to 1843 he was president of the Richmond Branch of the Bank of Kentucky. In 1840 he was a presidential elector; and in 1843 was appointed Judge of the Court of Appeals. He was a Representative in Congress from 1849 to 1851, and was on the Committee of Manufacture. The degree of LL. D. was conferred upon him by the Transylvania University in 1843. He attained the title of colonel in the militia service. After the expiration of his term in Congress he resumed the office of president of the Richmond Branch Bank.

F. M. BRISTOW.

The Hon. F. M. Bristow was born near Nicholasville, Jessamine County, Kentucky, the 11th of August, 1804, and received a good English education. He studied law, practiced his profession, and carried on farming at the same time. He was elected a Representative to the Legislature in 1831, and also in 1833. In 1846 he was elected to the State Senate. In 1849 he was elected a member of the convention which formed the last Constitution of Kentucky. In 1853 he was elected a Representative in Congress for the unexpired term of Presley Ewing, and was again elected in 1859 to the Thirty-sixth Congress, and served on the Committee of Agriculture. He died at his residence at Elkton, Todd County, Kentucky, June 10th, 1864.

PRESLEY EWING.

The Hon. Presley Ewing was a son of Judge Ewing, of Logan County, and a relation of his successor, the Hon. F. M. Bristow. He was born in Logan County, Kentucky, and represented that county one year in the Kentucky Legislature. He was afterward elected a member of the Thirty-third Congress, and was canvassing the district when he was taken sick from home, and died at the Mammoth Cave, September 27th, 1854. He was a great favorite of the renowned Henry Clay, and his constant companion in his last illness. Mr. Ewing was held in high regard in Congress, and considered one of the most promising young men of the State of Kentucky at the time of his death. The mother of Mr. Ewing was Jane McIntire, one of the most beautiful, intelligent, and accomplished ladies of her day. Her parents died when she was young, and she was raised and educated by her maternal uncle, Charles Helm, of Elizabethtown, the father-in-law of the writer, and father of Thomas J. Helm, Esq., who was so long the clerk of the House of Representatives of Kentucky.

HENRY C. BURNETT.

Henry C. Burnett was the son of Dr. Isaac Burnett, of Kentucky, but he was born in the county of Essex, in the State of Virginia, on the 5th of October, 1825. He studied law as a profession, and entered on its practice, but at the first election under the new Constitution of Kentucky was elected clerk of the Circuit Court of Trigg County, which office he held some two years. In 1853 he was elected a Representative in the Thirty-fourth Congress, and was also re-elected to the Thirty-fifth Congress. At the first session he was chairman of the Committee of Enquiry in regard to the sale of Fort Snelling and a member of the Committee on the District of Columbia. He was re-elected to the Thirty-sixth Congress, and also to the Thirty-seventh, but was expelled from the House in December, 1861, for treasonable conduct. Mr. Burnett was regarded as a young man of good talent and promising usefulness as a statesman. He died about the close of the late rebellion.

THOMAS J. HELM.

Thomas J. Helm was a native of Hardin County, Kentucky. He was born near Elizabethtown, in the year 1800, and was the son of Charles Helm, who, for thirteen years in succession, was a member of the Legislature from Hardin County, serving in both branches of that body with great acceptability to his constituents, and who was associated with Henry Clay in the House of Representatives in 1807, and voted for him for Speaker. A warm friendship ever existed between them whilst they lived. I have in my possession a letter written by Mr. Clay to Mr. Helm some forty years ago, couched in terms of profoundest respect and friendship. It was received by the family the very day on which Mr. Helm died, Mr. Clay being unapprised at the time of the illness of the latter.

Thomas J. Helm, the subject of this sketch, went to live with his maternal uncle, Henry Crutcher, Esq., of Glasgow, before he (Thomas) was yet grown. He there completed his education and studied law. Soon after this Mr. Logan, who had been clerk of the Barren County Court from its formation in 1798, died, and Mr. Helm was appointed his successor, in which office he continued until the adoption of the new Constitution. Mr. Helm was the successor of Robert S. Todd, Esq., in the office of clerk of the House of Representatives of Kentucky, which office he held by re-election for twenty-two consecutive years, and until the state of his health forbade his continuing longer. Mr. Helm was also secretary of the convention which formed the present Constitution of Kentucky. Mr. Helm, when a boy, wrote for some time in the clerk's office of the Court of Appeals under the instructions of Achilles Snead, Esq., then clerk of that court.

Mr. Helm was a man of good native sense, greatly improved by education and extensive reading. He had no superior as a clerk of a deliberative assembly. He could read indifferent handwriting with greater facility than any man I ever saw. He had a perfect recollection of names and dates, and was acquainted, personally, with more men in Kentucky than perhaps any other man in the State. Mr. Helm died at his residence, in Glasgow, some ten or twelve years ago.

JOSHUA F. BELL.

Mr. Bell's father was an Irishman, who was an early settler at Danville, and was extensively engaged in mercantile pursuits. He became wealthy. The son acquired a fine education, principally at the Danville schools, at which place he was born. He studied law, and soon obtained an extensive practice. He served in Congress from 1845 to 1847, and was a member of the Committee on Invalid Pensions. He declined a re-election to Congress, but afterward served as a member of the Kentucky Legislature. He was a member of the Peace Convention of 1861. He was distinguished as an able lawyer, and was one of the finest orators of Kentucky. Mr. Bell acted for a time as Secretary of State under the administration of Governor Morehead, and died some few years since.

GEORGE A. CALDWELL.

The Hon. George A. Caldwell was the son of Wm. Caldwell, who was clerk of the Circuit and County Courts of Adair County from the formation of that county to the time of his death, a period of nearly fifty years. George was the eldest son, and attended the best schools in that section of the country. Being apt to learn, he acquired a good education. He studied law, and commenced practice in Adair County. Being regarded as a talented young man, he succeeded well for one of his age and experience. At about twenty-four years of age he was elected the Representative of Adair to the Kentucky Legislature. He was a Representative in Congress from 1843 to 1845. After this he acted a conspicuous part as colonel of a regiment in the war with Mexico. Again, in 1849, he was elected from his district a Representative in Congress, and served the term ending in 1851. Upon his return from Congress he removed to Louisville, where he continued to reside until his death, devoting himself exclusively to the practice of his profession, which proved quite lucrative. At his death he had accumulated a very handsome estate, which was divided among his brothers and sisters, never having married, and his parents being dead. Mr. Caldwell had been in precarious health for several years previous to his death. He was discovered dead in his bed in attempting to awaken him for breakfast.

JOHN CALHOON.

The Hon. John Calhoon was born in Henry County, Kentucky, in the year 1797. He studied law, and settled in Breckinridge County, and was several times a Representative in the Legislature from that county. He was a Representative in Congress from 1835 to 1839. Mr. Calhoon was a man of marked ability, not only as a lawyer but as a statesman. He died some years since, the date unknown to the writer.

BEVERLEY L. CLARK.

The Hon. Beverley L. Clark was a man of decided ability. He commenced the practice of law at Franklin, Simpson County, Kentucky, and soon acquired an extensive and lucrative practice. He was several times a member in the Representative Branch of the Legislature of Kentucky, and served in Congress from 1847 to 1849, but was defeated in his election for a second term by the talented Presley Ewing, whose history we have already sketched. Mr. Clark was also defeated in a race he made for the gubernatorial chair; but was afterward appointed by the President to a foreign mission, and died while on this mission, in a foreign country. Mr. Clark claimed Virginia as his birth-place.

ALBERT G. HAWS.

The Hon. Albert G. Haws was born in Caroline County, Virginia, and was the younger brother of the distinguished Richard Haws, Jr., of Clark County. He settled in the county of Davis, Kentucky, and represented his district in Congress three terms, embracing the years from 1831 to 1837. He died at home, April 14th, 1849.

JAMES LOVE.

The Hon. James Love was born in Nelson County, Kentucky, in 1801, and was educated principally at Bardstown. He studied law, and settled in Barboursville, Knox County. He represented that county in the Legislature of Kentucky in 1829, and perhaps afterward. He was a Representative in Congress from his district from 1833 to 1835. Several years after this he removed to Galveston, Texas, where he died, the date not remembered.

RICHARD H. MENIFEE.

I have been unable to obtain any reliable information in regard to the life and public services of the Hon. Richard H. Menifee. I know that he was regarded as a young man of a high order of talents, and that he was greatly appreciated. I know also that he served one term in Congress, from 1837 to 1839, and occupied a high stand in that body. He died at Frankfort, February 21st, 1841.

STEPHEN ORMSBY.

The Hon. Stephen Ormsby, in his day, was one of the principal men of renown in Kentucky. He was a Representative in Congress from 1811 to 1817, lived to quite an advanced age, and died in Kentucky. He was a candidate for re-election to Congress in 1813, but was defeated by John Simpson, who was killed at the River Rasin before his service commenced. Mr. Ormsby, being again a candidate, was re-elected, and served, consequently, three consecutive terms.

WILLIAM WRIGHT SOUTHGATE.

Hon. William Southgate was a Kentuckian by birth, was respectably connected, and a young man of fine talents. He was several times a member of the House of Representatives of Kentucky, and was an active and efficient legislator. He represented his district in Congress from 1837 to 1839, and died some years since.

JAMES C. SPRIGG.

The Hon. James C. Sprigg was a young lawyer of great promise, and was elected to Congress from the Louisville district in 1841, serving his term of two years. He became somewhat intemperate, lost his popularity in some degree, and was not again returned to Congress. He died some years since, in the city of Louisville, the place of his residence.

GEN. LESLIE COMBS.

I cannot close my sketches of distinguished lawyers of Kentucky without a passing notice, at least, of that sterling patriot and statesman, Gen. Leslie Combs, of Lexington, Kentucky, though he yet lives, active in the busy scenes of life. Gen. Combs was born in Clarke County, Kentucky, about the year 1795, and is consequently at this time about seventy-six years of age; yet he retains in a great degree all the buoyancy and vivacity of a man of forty. During the War of 1812 he was a brave and gallant soldier under Gen. Harrison, and was then a youth only sixteen or seventeen years old, but was highly distinguished for his vigilance, bravery, and efficiency as an officer. He was with the force under General Green Clay, which went to the relief of Fort Meigs in the month of May, 1813. He was deputed to carry to Harrison the intelligence of Clay's approach. To accomplish this, he started at the head of five men, in a canoe, and had necessarily to encounter the annoyance of hostile savages, who occupied every beleaguered avenue to the fort. In this mission he lost nearly all his men, and narrowly escaped with his own life. He was an active participant in the disastrous attack made by the brave Colonel Dudley on the British batteries. In this attack he was severely wounded, and afterward taken prisoner.

Gen. Combs was often a member of the Kentucky Legislature. At the session of 1829–30 the writer had the honor of serving in that body with him, a session eminent for the talents of its members; and the writer, from his personal knowledge, can testify that there was no more efficient member in the House. At the session of the Legislature of 1846–7, Gen. Combs was chosen Speaker of the House, the duties of which he discharged with ability and becoming dignity. General Combs ran a race for Congress some time after this in the Lexington district, but was defeated by a small majority. In 1860 General Combs was elected clerk of the Court of Appeals for the balance of the term of Rankin R. Revill, who had died. This office he held for about six years, and declined the race for re-election. The writer had the honor of being his most formidable rival before the convention which nominated him as the candidate of the Union party, at that time greatly in the ascendant, and was beaten in that respectable body by a solitary vote. General Combs was every way worthy the distinction conferred, and discharged the duties pertaining to the office faithfully.

General Combs is a gentleman of high repute in his profession as a lawyer, and of ripe experience in public affairs; of courteous and graceful manners, and high mental accomplishments, rendering him worthy of association with the most illustrious of the land. He was the friend, associate, and confident of the great Henry Clay, whose esteem he enjoyed in no small degree, and without interruption, as long as the venerable statesman lived. As a neighbor, and as a polished gentleman in the relations of private and social life, General Combs may be regarded as a model. He is a man of great benevolence of heart and disposition. He feels for others woes, and stands ready to relieve distress, as far as in his power lies, in whatever form presented. These characteristics of the man were unmistakably manifested in him during the prevalence in Lexington of that dreadful scourge, the cholera, in 1833, which decimated the city. For weeks in succession his time was employed in constant attention to the sick and dying, and making provision for the needy and distressed. When such a man dies he will be greatly missed, "and mourners will go about the streets!"

WILLIAM J. GRAVES.

William Jourdon Graves was born in 1805, and was a lawyer of high reputation. He served as a member of the Legislature of Kentucky. He was in Congress for six consecutive years, from 1835 to 1841, and was an aspirant for the gubernatorial chair of Kentucky in 1848 at the convention which selected, by acclamation, J. J. Crittenden as the candidate. Mr. Graves died the 27th of September, 1848, in the city of Louisville, aged forty-three years. He was a highly esteemed and talented man.

ARCHIBALD DIXON.

The Hon. Archibald Dixon was born in Caswell County, North Carolina, April 2d, 1802, and was only three years old when his father came to Kentucky and settled in Henderson County. He received only a common English education, but he was studious, and read to great advantage. At twenty years of age he commenced the study of the law, obtained license at twenty-one, and soon acquired a high reputation as a lawyer as well as a lucrative practice. In 1830 he was elected a Representative to the Legislature of Kentucky, in 1836 to the State Senate, and in 1841 again to the Lower House. In 1843 he was elected Lieutenant Governor of Kentucky. In 1849 he was elected a member of the convention which formed the last Constitution of Kentucky, and was a member of the United States Senate from 1852 to 1855, being elected to fill the vacancy occasioned by the resignation of the Hon. Henry Clay. He is the present father-in-law of the distinguished John Y. Brown. Since his retirement from Congress, I think he has devoted himself exclusively to the practice of his profession.

THOMAS P. MOORE.

The Hon. Thomas P. Moore was not a lawyer, but he was a man of sound sense, a good speaker, and reasoned well. He was an efficient electioneerer, and decidedly popular. He ever discharged faithfully the duties of any trust confided to him, whether as a soldier or statesman. He was born in Charlotte County, Virginia, in 1795. He was an officer in the War of 1812 at seventeen or eighteen years of age, and as such was vigilant and brave. He was several times a member of the Legislature, and a member of Congress from 1823 to 1829. He was a lieutenant colonel in the regular army during the war with Mexico. His last public position was that of member of the convention for revising the Constitution of Kentucky. Previous to this, however, in 1829, he was Minister to the Republic of Columbia. He died at his residence, in Harrodsburg, Kentucky, the 21st of July, 1853.

RICHARD FRENCH.

The Hon. Richard French was a native of Kentucky, but I am not familiar with his general character. He was, I know, an amiable, sensible, and interesting man, and a lawyer of high repute in Kentucky. He was the nominee of the Democratic or Cass party for the office of Governor in 1840 in opposition to the renowned Robert P. Letcher, but was badly beaten, not on account of his lack of moral worth, but because of his opposition to what was called at that day the log cabin and hard cider candidate. Mr. French was several times a member of the Legislature of Kentucky, and a Representative in Congress from 1835 to 1837, from 1843 to 1845, and again from 1847 to 1849. He died some years afterward, but the date of his death is not known to the writer.

BENJAMIN TOBIN.

The writer was personally well acquainted with Benjamin Tobin, a distinguished lawyer of Elizabethtown, Kentucky, and the gentleman with whom Governor Helm studied law. He was a man of great eccentricity of character, forming but few attachments, yet manifesting no ill-feeling toward any one. He was, however, always particularly severe in his remarks when he spoke against the opponent of his client in a suit at law. He was a taciturn man, but always spoke sensibly. He was much given to the habit of making remarks concerning ladies passing along the streets, criticising their form, beauty, or homeliness. He was an own cousin of the distinguished Ben Hardin, studied law with him, and partook of many of his qualities and eccentricities. Mr. Tobin was thirty-five or forty years of age when he married. His first wife was a widow Llewllyn, formerly a Miss McIntire, who was a sister of the wife of Judge Ephraim M. Ewing, and cousin of the wife of the writer. She lived but a short time, when he married the very accomplished Miss Haynes. After her death he married the widow Poston, of Elizabethtown, a most estimable lady. He died a few years afterward. He was a lawyer of high reputation, but never aspired to office of any kind.

He was a native of Washington County, and perhaps over fifty years of age at the time of his death.

GENERAL SAMUEL HOPKINS.

General Samuel Hopkins was a man of no inconsiderable distinction in Kentucky, and is elsewhere mentioned in this history. He was a good man, of untarnished reputation, and of great popularity. He was born in Albemarle County, Virginia, and served with distinction in the Revolutionary War, having fought at Princeton, Trenton, Monmouth, Brandywine, and Germantown; and also as a lieutenant colonel of a Virginia regiment at the siege of Charleston. He removed to Kentucky in 1797, and served a number of years in the State Legislature. In the year 1812 he led, as has before been stated, two thousand troops against the Kickapoo Indians. He was a Representative in Congress from Kentucky from 1813 to 1815. He died October, 1819, at a very advanced age.

CAPTAIN WILLIAM HUBBELL.

There are but few names in the history of Kentucky more distinguished than that of Captain Wm. Hubble, not only as a soldier of the Revolution, but as a soldier of Kentucky in our early contests with the Indians. He was a native of Vermont, and served five years and a half in the war of the Revolution; first as a private, and afterward as a subordinate officer. He was engaged in many skirmishes during the war, and participated in the capture of St. John's and Montreal. Some years after the close of the Revolution he came to Kentucky and settled in Scott County, where he continued to reside until his death, which occurred many years ago, at a very advanced age. No man enjoyed in a higher degree while he lived the confidence and esteem of his fellow-citizens. In the year 1791 Captain Hubbell went to the east on business, and returning home on one of the tributary streams of the Monongahela, he procured a flat-bottomed boat, and embarked in company with Daniel Light, William Plascut, and others, destined for Limestone, now Maysville. Soon after passing Pittsburg they saw a boat aground on an island, which, doubtless, became a prey to the Indians, as it never arrived, and was never heard of afterward. Before Hubbell's company reached the mouth of the Great Kanawha they had, by several additions, increased their number to about twenty, consisting of men, women, and children. Constantly anticipating an attack, Captain Hubbell was appointed commander of the boat, and the poor arms of the men aboard put in the best condition possible for service. About sunset, on the 23d of March, 1791, his party overtook a fleet of six boats, but being unwilling to remain with them in consequence of the disposition manifested on their part to fiddle and frolic rather than be in readiness for battle, Hubbell and his party proceeded on their journey. Just at the dawn of day, on the succeeding morning, and before the mist had disappeared from the river, three Indian canoes were seen rapidly advancing towards them. About twenty-five Indians were in each canoe. Capt. Hubbell ordered his men not to fire until the savages approached so near as that the flash from the guns might singe their eyebrows. The savages commenced a general fire as soon as they approached within gunshot, and Tucker and Light were both badly wounded. The fire from the boat, however, small as was their effective force, soon checked in a considerable degree the confidence and fury of the Indians. The captain, after firing his own gun, took up that of one of the wounded men, and, when about to discharge it, a ball from the enemy took away the lock. Being ready for any emergency that might arise, he coolly took a brand of fire from the kettle, and, applying it to the pan, discharged the piece with effect. The captain, in the act of raising his gun a third time to shoot, received a ball through his right arm, which, for a moment, disabled him. The Indians now attempted to board the boat, and had actually seized hold of its sides with their hands; but, wounded as he was, he caught up a pair of horseman's pistols, and, rushing forward, discharged a pistol with effect at the foremost. The Indians fell back, and after firing the second pistol, being then without arms, he was compelled to retreat; not, however, until he had wounded one of them with a stick, taken from a pile of small wood which lay in the boat. The Indians now gave way, and directed their course to the boat of Captain Greathouse, which was then in sight and descending the river. This they entered without opposition, and rowed it to the shore, where they killed the captain and a lad fourteen years old. They then placed the women in the center of their canoes, with the hope, no doubt, of deriving protection from their presence, and again pursued Captain Hubbell. There were now but four men on Captain Hubbell's boat capable of defending it. The second attempt of the Indians, however, was resisted with incredible firmness and vigor. Notwithstanding the disparity of numbers, the Indians finally despaired of success, and retired to shore with their canoes. Captain Hubbell discharged his piece at an Indian in one of the canoes just as they were departing, and, as he believed, wounded him mortally. The sparcity of hands now on Hubbell's boat could not prevent it from drifting toward shore, which, being perceived by the Indians, four of five hundred of them rushed down to the bank of the river. Ray and Plascut, the only men remaining unhurt, plied the oars, and pushed forward with the utmost practicable rapidity. While in this condition, nine balls were shot into one oar, and ten into the other. During this dreadful exposure Mr. Kilpatrick received a ball through his mouth and the back part of his head, and another through his heart, killing him instantly. The boat, providentially, was carried out into the middle of the stream and taken by the current beyond the enemies' balls, when, afflicted as they were, yet unsubdued in spirit, with an appearance of triumph they gave three hearty cheers, calling to the Indians to come on again if they were fond of the sport.

Thus ended this awful conflict, in which, out of nine men, two only escaped unhurt, and reached Limestone by twelve o'clock that night. Hubbell, from pain and fatigue, was unable to walk, and was obliged to be carried to the tavern, where his wounds were dressed, and in a few days he had sufficient strength to proceed homeward. They found a considerable force at Limestone about to march against the same Indians from whose attacks they had suffered so severely, which force, on arriving near the scene of action, discovered several dead Indians on the shore, and the bodies of Captain Greathouse and the men, women, and children who had been on board of his boat. The boat which had been the scene of such heroism was literally filled with bullet holes. There were one hundred and twenty-two holes in the blankets which had been hung up as curtains in the stern of the boat to conceal them and the horses from the enemy. Four out of the five horses on board were killed.

GENERAL JEFFERSON DAVIS.

No two individuals, perhaps, ever lived in the United States of wider spread fame than Jefferson Davis and Abraham Lincoln, and nothing that I could say would add to or detract from either of them; but, both being natives of Kentucky, I deem it proper that I should give them at least a passing notice.

Gen. Jefferson Davis was born in Christian County, Kentucky, on the 3d day of June, 1808, but his father removed to Mississippi in his infancy. He commenced his education at the Transylvania University, Kentucky, but left it for the West Point Academy, where he graduated in 1828. He followed the fortunes of a soldier until 1835, when he became a planter. He was a cadet from 1824 to 1828; second lieutenant of infantry from 1828 to 1833; first lieutenant of dragoons from 1833 to 1835, serving in various campaigns against the Indians; was an adjutant of dragoons, and at different times served in the quartermaster's department. In 1844 he was a presidential elector; in 1845 he was elected a Representative in Congress from Mississippi for one term, but resigned in 1846 to become colonel of a volunteer regiment to serve in Mexico. In Mexico he received the appointment of Brigadier General. In 1847 he was appointed a Senator in Congress to fill a vacancy, and was elected for the term ending in 1851, but resigned in 1850; was re-elected for a term of six years, but again resigned. He was appointed Secretary of War by President Pierce, serving throughout his administration. In 1857 he again took his seat in the United States Senate for the term of six years, serving as chairman of the

Committee on Military Affairs, and a member of those on Public Buildings and Grounds, and on Printing. In February, 1861, he resigned his seat in the Senate, became identified with the Great Rebellion, and was elected President of the so-called "Southern Confederacy." He still survives, being now in the sixty-fourth year of his age.

ABRAHAM LINCOLN.

Abraham Lincoln, late President of the United States, was born in Hardin County (now Larue), Kentucky, February 12th, 1809 He removed with his father to Indiana in 1816. He spent two years at school in Stafford County, Virginia, and taught school and studied law for a time in Culpepper County of that State. Removing to Illinois in 1830, he turned his attention to agricultural pursuits. He served as a captain of volunteers in the Black Hawk War; and was at one time postmaster in a small village in Sangamon County. He served for four years in the Illinois Legislature, during which time he again turned his attention to the study of law, and settled at Springfield in the practice of his profession. He was a member of the National Convention which nominated Gen. Taylor for President in 1848, and was a Representative in Congress from Illinois from 1847 to 1849, serving on the committees on the Post Office, Post Roads, and Expenses in the War Department. In 1858 he acquired distinction by stumping the State of Illinois for the United States Senate against Stephen A. Douglass. In 1860 he was nominated by the Republican party as their candidate for President of the United States, and was duly elected to that position for the term of four years, commencing the 4th of March, 1861. By the Baltimore Convention, held in 1864, he was nominated for reelection to the Presidency, and, being again successful, commenced the duties of the office for a second term on the 4th of March, 1865. About six weeks afterward, on the 15th of April, 1865, he was wickedly assassinated in the theater at Washington City.

MR. WILLIAM MITCHELL.

One of the early pioneers of Kentucky, whose name has not heretofore been mentioned, was Mr. William Mitchell, brother of Thomas Mitchell, who lived for more than half a century within a few hundred yards of Camp Knox, in Green County, of which I have heretofore given a full account. Thomas Mitchell was the father of John A. Mitchell, who still lives at the same place, now in the seventy-fifth year of his age, and beloved and respected by all who know him for his intelligence, sociability, and eminent Christian character.

Mr. William Mitchell first settled at the station of James Davies, at Walnut Flat, Lincoln County, but soon after commenced a settlement himself at what was afterward called Paint Lick, in what is now Garrard County. This settlement was made at a time when Indian incursions were yet frequently made into that portion of Kentucky, to the great annoyance of the settlers. On one occasion Mr. Mitchell, his wife, and child, having left home to visit a neighbor, found, on their return, that their cabin had been visited by the Indians during their absence. Most of their household and kitchen furniture, or at least such portions of it as could be carried away, had disappeared, the Indians having ripped up the bedticks and used them as sacks for the purpose. Mr. Mitchell, as he approached his cabin, observed the Indians at a distance, who were fleeing with precipitation in the direction of the knobs in that neighborhood. Mitchell had left two horses in a sort of pen or pound near the house. These, too, the Indians tried to secure and carry away, but, being wild, they had escaped from the pound to the woods. The Indians made their escape unmolested, Mr. Mitchell having no means of pursuing them. A short time before, in the neighborhood of Gilman's Lick, Mitchell, with his comrades, had rescued a Mrs. Roberts and Mrs. Davies, and their children, from the Indians.

PHILIP SWIGERT.

Philip Swigert, worthy to be numbered among the most distinguished citizens of Kentucky, departed this life on the morning of Sunday, the 31st day of December, 1871, in the seventy-fourth year of his age, at his residence in the town of Frankfort. For the last fifty years he has lived and acted in that community as one of its most useful, enterprising, and distinguished citizens. He was of German descent, and was born of poor but respectable parents, in Fayette County, Kentucky, on the 27th day of May, 1798. When quite a young man he wrote as a deputy in the Woodford Circuit Court under John McKinney. He removed to Frankfort about the year 1822, where he continued to reside until his death. The first situation which he filled after his arrival there was that of commissioner or agent for the old Bank of Kentucky to collect its assets and settle up its affairs. This duty he performed in the most satisfactory manner, in the prosecution of which he visited nearly every county in the State. On the 22d of October, 1830, he received the appointment of Circuit Court Clerk for Franklin County, being the successor of Francis P. Blair, Sr., who, about that time, left for Washington City to edit the "Globe," the organ of General Jackson's administration. Mr. Swigert continued as Circuit Court Clerk by appointment, and then by election under the new Constitution, until 1862, a period of thirty-two years, when, wishing to embark in other pursuits, he declined being again a candidate. Mr. Swigert was a life-long Whig, and all the time devoted to the fortunes of Henry Clay, and was one of the leaders of what was called the American or Know-Nothing party. During the late war he was an ardent Union man, but opposed to the excesses of the war party, and as such was elected to the Senate of Kentucky from the counties of Franklin, Anderson, and Woodford in 1865, for the term of four years. He was remarkable for his financial ability, which was clearly manifested whenever opportunity was afforded him for action—especially as chairman of the State Board of Internal Improvement, and as president of the Farmers Bank of Kentucky. Mr. Swigert was a most distinguished member of the Masonic Fraternity, and was more extensively known in that respect than any other man in the State. He became a member of the order in 1819, at twenty-one years of age. In 1820 he represented Landmark Lodge No. 41 in the Grand Lodge of

Kentucky, which was the same year Henry Clay was elected and installed Grand Master. After serving, alternately, as Grand Junior and Grand Senior Deacon, he served some years as Grand Treasurer, and for twenty-one years afterward acted as Grand Secretary of the Grand Lodge. On his retirement from this office, as a testimonial of the high estimation in which he was held by his brethren, he was presented with an elegant Grand Secretary's jewel of gold. In 1858 he was elected Grand Pursuivant of the Grand Council, which office he held several terms. He was elected Grand Master of the Grand Lodge of Kentucky in 1857. He was elected Grand Secretary of the Grand Chapter of Royal Arch Masons in 1822, which office he held till his death, with only an interval of two years. For a period of forty-three years he was a constant and efficient member of Hiram Lodge No. 4, of Frankfort. He was a Knights Templar also, the members of which order, together with all other Masons in convenient distance, were present to bury him with the full honors and imposing ceremonies of that ancient and time-honored institution. Mr. Swigert was a man of great energy of purpose, untiring industry, and methodical habits. It mattered not how multifarious were his duties, whatever he undertook he accomplished with fidelity and ability; whether of minor or greater importance made no difference, he did his duty and did it well. He was nearly always one of the chief directing spirits in the public affairs pertaining to his county and town, and yet his fidelity to duty and rectitude of character were never called in question. No man enjoyed more fully while he lived the respect and confidence of the community of his neighborhood, and the thoughts of all who ever knew him were sorrowful and sad at his demise. Mr. Swigert was fond of home, and shone most eminent in the domestic circle. He was a lover of horticultural and agricultural pursuits, and was noted as a skillful cultivator of choice fruits, and as a breeder and importer of fine cattle. The writer, nearly every year, for a period of forty-seven years, was associated with Mr. Swigert in some capacity or other, but especially as a member of the Grand Lodge of Kentucky, and knew him well, and knew him but to love him. At his house his friends ever met a most cordial welcome. It has often been the pleasure of the writer to enjoy the hospitality and society of his family, where he felt as unrestrained as around his own fireside. He was eminently a self-made man. Possessing no advantages of fortune, and but few for education, in early life, by the force of native genius and indomitable perseverance he attained fortune and a high standing with the best informed men of the State.

COLONEL ACQUILLA WHITAKER.

Among the most intelligent and prominent pioneers of Kentucky, Colonel Acquilla Whitaker may justly be ranked. He was born in Baltimore County, Maryland, in the year 1755, and came to Kentucky in an exploring company in the year 1775. He was a man of medium size, of great nerve, strength, and energy, and fond of adventures. He was a bold and active leader, and took part in many dangerous and thrilling scenes, perilous incidents and trials, in the exploration and settlement of Kentucky. In 1779 he moved his family to Kentucky and settled near Sullivan's Station, near the Falls of Ohio. In 1788 he moved to the neighborhood of Shelbyville, where he lived for many years. At this place his brother, John Whitaker, was killed by the Indians, near the present town boundary, while clearing up the ground for cultivation. In the important military and aggressive movements made by Colonel George Rodgers Clark in and from Kentucky he was a lieutenant and captain, and ranked high as a brave, efficient, and intrepid officer, adding greatly by his ability as an officer and soldier to the achievement of the great success attending these movements. Prior to 1794 he was captain of the different parties from Boone's, Well's, and Whitaker's stations, and other stations (now Shelby and Jefferson), in pursuit of marauding bands of Indians, and many were the rencounters with them while engaged in their descent and forages on the settlements in that section of the State.

In March, 1781, the Indians entered Jefferson County, committing many crimes and depredations. They killed Colonel William Lynn, Captains Tipton and Chapman. They were traced and pursued by Captain Whitaker and fifteen others with great vigor to the foot of the Falls of the Ohio. Supposing that the Indians had crossed the river, they embarked in canoes to follow them. While pushing from the shore of the river, they were fired upon by the Indians, who were concealed on the bank, and nine of the party were killed or wounded. They immediately relanded, took cover, and, after a desperate and determined fight, defeated the Indians, killing over twenty of them. The survivors, five or six in number, escaped by flight in the undergrowth into the swamps below Louisville. A personal rencounter took place in the skirmish between Captain Whitaker and an Indian chief. Each one, from his sapling, eyed the other; both raised their rifles for work, and both fired simultaneously. The Indian's bullet cut the lock of hair off of Captain Whitaker's left temple, while his went crashing through the chief's mouth and head.

Mrs. Frances Young, wife of the late James L. Young, late of Trimble County, the eldest daughter of Capt. Whitaker, has described this engagement, as detailed to her by those engaged, as a most terrific and deadly struggle. The Indians outnumbered their opponents, and had greatly the advantage at the beginning; but a stubborn and unconquered will, and endurance, overcame and bore down the wily cunning and fierce daring of the Indians. A brief outline of this skirmish has been given both in Collin's and Marshall's History of Kentucky, but not so fully in detail as here given, especially as to numbers engaged and incidents.

The Indians having attacked Robert P. Barbee's house, on Bullskin, Captain Whitaker commanded the pursuing party, overtook them, killed two, and wounded several. John Owen got one of the scalps and Abraham Whitaker the other. An assault having been made on Well's Station, and a number of horses stolen, the men at the station sent Capt. Whitaker word to meet them at a given point, as they had reason to believe the Indians had gone that way. He could only get one man (James Scott) to go with him to the place of rendezvous, and on their way they fell in with the Indians, seven in number, with the stolen horses in their possession. Upon consultation between the two, it was agreed that Whitaker should make the first shot, as he was the best marksman. The Indians had stopped at a branch to let the horses drink, when Whitaker fired at the leader, as he supposed. The Indian tumbled over his horse's head into the branch, when the two men raised the shout, "Come on, boys," and rushed on the others, who became alarmed, scattered, and fled precipitately, leaving their dead companion and the horses.

There were many instances of daring deeds done by Capt. Whitaker and his comrades in the exploration and settlement of Kentucky from its native wilderness, an account of which were among his private papers, but they were years ago lost by fire. Captain Whitaker was a major in the division commanded in the Indian War by Major General Thomas Barbee, in 1794. Captain Bland Ballard commanded a company in his batallion, in which company two of Major Whitaker's brothers served as private soldiers, Abraham and Levi Whitaker. This company, composed of stern, uncompromising men, of sagacity, nerve, and endurance, waged terrible destruction with their deadly rifles on the bloody route of the Indians on the Miami or Maumee. He was the compeer of Colonel John Allen, Captain Bland Ballard, A. Owen, General Winlock, Colonel Ben Logan, Colonel Clark, and Colonel Floyd, and the brave men who wielded the rifle more than they did the pen in Indian hostility and border warfare.

Colonel Acquilla Whitaker was married twice. By his first wife there were born to him nine children, seven sons and two daughters; by his second wife there were born to him four daughters and five sons. The country becoming thickly populated, and being fond of adventure and the natural wilderness, he emigrated with the larger portion of his family to West Florida, where he died in the year 1824.

JAMES SULLIVAN WHITAKER.

The second son of Colonel Whitaker was James Sullivan Whitaker, born in October, 1782. By application and energy he obtained a good education, and, for several years, assisted

C. Columbus Graham
Ag. 85

James Craig, who was the first clerk of Shelby County. He then acted as sheriff of the county several years, studied law, and was admitted to the bar about the year 1816. In 1818 he was made clerk of the Shelby County Court, which office he held for over thirty years. He held other positions of honor and trust, discharging his duties honestly and faithfully. In the War of 1812 he was an active participant, raised a company of fine, vigorous, brave men, and was commissioned as their captain. He served with distinction as such until he was promoted to major. His military life was not of as long continuance as that of his father, but it was most honorably and usefully passed in service to his country. He died in Shelbyville, in the eighty-sixth year of his age. He was a serviceable, intelligent, and honored citizen.

RICHARD T. WHITAKER.

Lieutenant Colonel Richard T. Whitaker was the third son of Major James S. Whitaker, and was born in Shelbyville, Kentucky. He graduated with distinction at Bacon College, Harrodsburg, and was a merchant for several years in his native town. He volunteered as a soldier in the late civil war in the service of the United States. For military knowledge and efficiency he was promoted from the regiment in which he enlisted to the position of second lieutenant in the regiment commanded by his brother, Gen. Walter C. Whitaker. He was next promoted for courage and military acquirement to the position of major. After a hard and arduous service, for distinguished gallantry on the battle-field he was promoted to the rank of lieutenant colonel of that veteran regiment, the Sixth Kentucky U. S. Volunteer Infantry. He died at the age of thirty-eight years, respected for his truth, honor, and accomplishments, loved and esteemed by all who knew him.

CHRISTOPHER GRAHAM, M. D.

The life of Dr. Christopher Graham is so identified with Kentucky, that I would feel that I had not completed my work without a sketch of his most eventful career. A more remarkable man, in many respects, never lived in the State.

He is, moreover, the only link and witness that remains between the living and the dead—the present and the former inhabitants of Kentucky—having a perfect recollection of Boone, Clark, Harrod, Ray, and all the old heroes of those trying days and bloody struggles in Kentucky. And now, though they have all passed away, and sleep in their silent graves, the last remains to speak of acts he witnessed, and of things he heard from their own mouths. There have been but few men anywhere, acting in his sphere, of more wide-spread fame, or who have been more extensively known. Born with no other heritage than poverty, he has attained the high position he occupies in the community by the force of his own talents alone. His native genius, assisted by the ardor of his exertions, has carried him to the goal of highest perfection as a bold and fearless adventurer, as a successful financier, of indomitable courage and perseverance, of most unquestionable integrity and unbounded liberality. He was born the 10th day of October, 1787, at the station of his uncle, four miles southeast of Danville, in what is now Boyle County. His uncle was from Cork, Ireland, and in the conquest of the West was a captain under General George Rodgers Clark. His mother was Irish, his father one of the celebrated Long Hunters of Kentucky and a native of Virginia, and his grandfather hailed from the house of Montrose in Scotland. Dr. Graham was born at that period of time in the history of Kentucky most propitious to develop and render healthful the native energies of a man. At this early period, except around a few stations, Kentucky was almost a trackless wilderness. The fertility of the soil and the abundance of game had only attracted a few early adventurers, who suffered all the fatigues and inconveniences which the first settling of a new and uncultivated country could produce. These adventurers knew nothing of Lycurgus, or Greece; but as the same causes, under the same circumstances, produce the same effects, the Kentuckians of that day all became Spartans, and, war being their trade, muscle, manhood, and endurance were necessary in their numerous encounters with the wild beasts and savages. Shooting, swimming, running, hunting, climbing, wrestling, and fighting were their constant exercises, and contributed to make them soldierly, bold, and manly.

The subject of this sketch was five years old at the time Kentucky was first formed into a State, and was only eight years old when Indian incursions and hostilities ceased to afflict and disturb the tranquility of the State. His age, of course, forbade that he should have had much to do with the Indians, but he was often engaged, before he was ten years old, in the chase or hunt of panthers, bears, wolves, deer, and turkeys. On one occasion, when quite a boy, he drove a panther from a deer not quite dead, cutting the throat of the deer, and chasing the panther away. Running home to his father's cabin and procuring assistance, he saved the venison, which was exceedingly fat and fine. Upon another occasion, having killed a fawn and hung up as high as able, when he returned to take it home, he found that a panther had eaten the most of it and hid the remainder under the leaves; and now, determining to watch the thief, he, at the approach of night, hid himself behind a log. While awaiting the return of the panther, he saw a coon descending a tree, and when within six or eight feet of the ground, a panther leaped up the tree and caught it, the coon squalling terribly as the panther leaped off with it. Whether the panther or the Doctor got to this spot first, he could not tell, as the coon tree was some fifty paces from him, down in a dark ravine. The claw marks, said he, are yet upon the tree, as panther and bear scratches are seen upon many of the forest trees of Kentucky up to this day.

The extraordinary activity of the Doctor at his present extreme age, both of body and mind, is, doubtless, mainly attributable to his early habits of life; for even now, in the eighty-fifth year of his age, he can walk twenty miles a day as a pleasure exercise, and, without glasses, can beat, I doubt not, any man in the State at off-hand rifle shooting, which requires both muscle and vision. To show the influence of early habits in giving, even to boys, boldness and manly intrepidity, even to Roman endurance, I mention a single case of many related to me by the Doctor. His father was one of a party who pursued some Indians who had murdered several families and taken a lad prisoner; but, when they saw the whites in sight, they knocked the boy down and scalped him. When the boy's friends came up he had gotten upon his knees, and was soon upon his feet and foremost in the chase, exclaiming, with pointed finger: "That tarnal Indian has my scalp; catch him! catch him!" A nursed and effeminate boy of modern times would have felt that he was dead, and been without power to help himself.

The father of Dr. Graham, at an early day, moved to the Beach Fork, in what is now Nelson County, where game was more abundant, and better opportunities presented for fishing. Hunting and fishing were sources of enjoyment to his young mind beyond any other pursuit in which he could engage at that early day. He became so accustomed in that locality to the nightly howl of the wolf, the scream of the panther, and the whoop of the owl around their cabin, as to divest him of all fear. He became proficient in all the sports and exercises common to the youth of that day. His skill in swimming and diving was unsurpassed; even the great Mississippi was no terror to him. At a very early day he steered two flatboats out of Kentucky River to New Orleans; one of them long before there was a steamer on the Western waters; and he could swim across any part of that great stream. While at New Orleans, on the occasion alluded to, and on a wager, he swam across this sire of waters and back again without resting, a skiff following close after him for fear of accident. Since that period he has been to New Orleans some twenty different times, and on one of these occasions, while standing upon the wharf, he saw a man, to him an entire stranger, fall from the deck of a ship into the river. Though there were many persons present, none dared venture to help the poor fellow in his struggles for life, until young Graham, the soul of sympathy, and with that confidence which his early training inspired, plunged in and saved the drowning stranger from a watery grave.

Dr. Graham, in his younger days, learned to climb, too, as well as swim, and often followed the coon to the top limb of the tallest tree to shake him down. Once, upon such an occasion, the coon took to the water for escape, and, when about midway of the river, became engaged with the dog which usually accompanied his master. The coon seized the dog by the nose and struggled for the mastery, in which he seemed likely to prove successful, when young Graham swam into them, grabbed the victor by the back of the neck, and held him under the water with his left hand, while with his right he swam to shore.

The Doctor facetiously remarks, that he has twice died during his long life, once by water, and another time by a horse. When netting below a mill-dam, on one occasion, where the water was very swift, one of the men in company took him astride his neck and carried him to an island, leaving him with the fish they had caught while they passed further on Becoming chilled, and thinking he could swim out, he pitched off upon the tossing wave; but being alternately beaten down upon the rocks, and hoisted high on the waves, he soon lost his senses. Coming to himself, he was hanging to the bushes, having been drifted out into an eddy not knee deep. All this, however, was regarded as a small circumstance compared with the cruelties and death so common at that day, the result of savage warfare and other adventures. "Next," says he, "I was killed by a horse throwing me against a tree, from which I was picked up as lifeless." The common way of riding in those days was with what was called tugs, or leather bits, and tow reins, and a wild horse biting the leather in two could not be controlled, and the accident mentioned was the result.

Dr. Graham, after relating to me some of the numerous incidents of his eventful life, then remarked as follows: "The power of circumstances upon the human character is a principle of greatly more practical importance in the improvement of the human family than the history of his or any other man's life. More than two thousand years ago, in the days of Greece and Rome, men then and there lived with more muscle and mind than now exists, with all the advantages of time. Necessity and energy made those nations great, and luxury and indolence afterward destroyed them. Kentucky's necessities gave to her sons minds and bodies ample for great ends if properly directed, and that, too, with all the privations of education. Native energy produced a galaxy of men such as, it is to be feared, will never exist again in Kentucky— Clay, Rowan, Crittenden, Allen, Davis, Hardin, Robertson, Brents, Buckner, Letcher, Underwood, Menifee, Guthrie, Hays, and many others, nearly all of whom were self-made men, and sons of Kentucky." Said he, "I have often heard Judge Rowan say that he worked hard all the day, dressed in buckskin, and pursued his studies at night by a pine-knot fire. The productiveness of Kentucky's soil, with her commerce, wealth, luxury, and indolence, will as certainly lead to effeminacy and consequent decay, as it did to Greece, Rome, and Spain, notwithstanding their early energy, chivalry, and conquest. In my early days," he continued, "such things as dyspepsia, gout, rheumatism, consumption, hysteria, hypochondria, and suicide were unknown, while all had a relish for their food and for manly and social enjoyments. That our race in Kentucky is degenerating is as certain as that we have laws of our existence; and it cannot be otherwise with the present habits of our people. Our fashionables, dissatisfied with the taste of their Maker, have given to themselves fancy forms, both ludicrous and destructive. How," says he, "can a fashionable lady, with ribs crushed together and respiration (which gives vitality to the blood and heart) thus obstructed, expect to enjoy health, or give constitution to her offspring? An additional drag to their health is the great weight of skirts they hang to their hips, and the perching of themselves upon stilts, with their bodies thrown forward of the line of gravitation, causing a constant strain of the spine to preserve a balance, which has to be done upon an inch-wide heel. This is exceedingly trying to the constitution, disturbing all the vital functions, and must, in the nature of things, degenerate posterity. And now, what is not so injurious, but equally ludicrous, is the sticking of a peck of hair on the back of their heads (sweaty, and ponderous to be borne), and all this mounted mass to be crowned only with a droll, buffoonish-looking little thing, giving to the face a most unnatural and farcical appearance; and all this, though ridiculous, is not to be laughed at by the statesman and the philosopher, but to be treated with solemn gravity; for the mother who murders her child after birth, and she who murders it before birth, or brings it into the world without a constitution, to suffer a thousand deaths, should be held equally responsible."

The foregoing remarks may be regarded as a digression from the subject in hand, but they are worthy the appreciation of all, and too true to be omitted; and, besides, may in some degree, coming from such a source, act as a corrective of a very growing vice. It may be said, for the encouragement of the youth of our country, especially those in destitute condition, that Dr. Graham started in life an orphan, without education, friends, or money, and worked many a day in boyhood at twenty-five cents a day. His father being a philosopher after the order of Diogenes, desired nothing more than a cabin for shelter and a corn-patch for bread; for the river close by abounded with fish, and the forests around with all kinds of game. He thought his title good to a large body of land; but after the country was rid of all danger from the incursions of Indians, a gang of perfidious sharpers came in, and his father, sharing the fate of poor old Boone, lost his land by superior title.

Dr. Graham had two brothers, John and Robert, each occupying a high standing in the communities in which they respectively lived. Each, like the Doctor, was successful in the accumulation of wealth. John, at his death, was the judge of a court, an elder in the church, and worth one hundred and fifty thousand dollars. Robert died young, worth some thirty thousand dollars, whilst the Doctor, some years since, retired on a fortune of one hundred and thirty thousand dollars. These three brothers were all men of sterling integrity, and of sober, industrious habits; fit examples for the poor youth of the country to emulate. Dr. Graham's education was exceedingly deficient until after he became a man, and had returned from his service in the army in the War of 1812. In speaking upon that subject he says: "'Baker' was the desideratum and ultimatum of the day, over which but few passed. We all used thumb papers, and I have seen every leaf worn through to the back before reaching that point in Dillworth. Our pedagogue was, of course, a man of deep learning (compared with his pupils), of high temper, long nose, and a stern and wrinkled brow, with a voice of hoarse thunder; so much so, that when he, with conscious dignity and despotic power, filled the cabin door after a recess and belched forth 'Books! Books!' the wild forest echoed, and every urchin trembled. If, perchance, he was caught in error, and confronted by the book, the book was always wrong, and no one dared disputing such authority. A forked stick hung on a peg at the door, and when it was absent no one dared budge, but all eyes askant, there was generally a great uprising on its return; and though many might complain of the aches common with boys, but one was allowed to go out at a time. Boys and girls got their lessons openly and audibly, every one screaming at the top of his voice, 'ba, be, bi, bo,' &c.; and when the blessed hour of eve came for standing rank and file, to turn each other down in spelling, they became emulous and mirthful."

The account given of this school attended by the Doctor in his boyhood will answer well for nearly all the schools of Kentucky at that early day.

I will now relate an incident which occurred with the youthful Graham while attending the school alluded to. Although but ten years old, his father often allowed him to carry his gun to school with him, a distance of three miles, through a tangled and wild forest, where he generally killed something on the way. One evening, returning late, he saw four coons playing round the root of an old broken-top tree. At his approach they ran up it, when he shot them, one by one, bringing them to the ground. Swinging them on his back with papaw bark, hero-like, with fortune blessed, he started for home. He soon, however, sighted a deer, which stopped and stood within a short distance of him. He fired, and the deer fell with a broken back; but seeing it rise upon its forefeet, he mounted it, and with his small and dull old barlow strove to cut its throat. While thus engaged, alternately under and on top, the wounded deer desperately struggling for life, a pack of wolves, smelling the blood, came close upon him, with sharp and hideous barkings and howlings, such as he had never before heard. He was now no longer the hero, but made tracks for home, leaving gun and trophies all behind. This incident is given as illustrative of the times of his boyhood.

I have omitted as yet to mention the proficiency which the Doctor attained in the use of the rifle, especially as a marksman. Benjamin Mills, of Harrodsburg, Kentucky, was regarded by many as the best rifle-maker in the United States, and it was universally conceded that Dr. Graham was the best shot. He has had matches with all the most noted off-hand rifle-shooters in the United States, and never found a man who could equal him. This fact was well established and known to target-shooters, North, South, East, and West. Dr. Graham was at the head of the noted club formed at Harrodsburg, and of which Governor Magoffin was a member, known as the Boone Club of Kentucky, which was, perhaps, the best shooting club in the world. It consisted of twelve members, all men of the highest respectability, and in every way responsible. Such was the confidence of the shooting men of Kentucky in the skill of the Doctor, that they challenged the world on a ten thousand dollars wager, and no one dared to take it up; and this fact did much to establish Kentucky's skill with the rifle. He has been published in papers and magazines as the William Tell of Kentucky. Dr. Graham says, in speaking on the subject of rifles, that he had tried the rifles of Manton, of London, Wesson, of Massachusetts, and Morgan James, of New York, the most celebrated gunsmiths in the world, but gives it as his opinion that Mills's make is superior to them all. The challenge made was to shoot a Kentuckian, and a Kentucky rifle, against the world, which challenge was published in Europe as well as throughout the United States. Mr. Mills had kept and published a record of the Doctor's target-shooting for the space of some ten years, and it being so superior to any ever known, forced a conviction as to his marvelous skill, and is the reason the challenge was never accepted.

We pass over many events in the history of Dr. Graham, a

relation of which would be exceedingly interesting, but which we omit for want of space, and begin now with his services in the army of the United States in the War of 1812. Dr. Graham, then a young man, entered the army as a recruiting sergeant in Springfield, Washington County, Kentucky. The captain of the company, becoming dissipated, was called off and cashiered, but the Doctor enlisted thirty men with his own money, two dollars being then the bounty, and eight dollars per month the pay. At the time of his entering the army he was engaged in the silversmith business, and had opened a shop for himself; but the war cry being raised, he sold out the few effects he had accumulated, and used the money in recruiting as above related. It was his misfortune to have some hard cases in his company, particularly a desperado, who was at all times mutinous. On one occasion he became so outrageous in a drinking-house, that the Doctor, being the commander, was sent for to curb, if possible, his fury. The Doctor, arriving at the place, ordered him peremptorily to his quarters, upon which the man struck him, and for a time they had a rough and tumble fight; but the man, having grasped a poker, struck the Doctor with it, felling him to the floor. He soon recovered, however, and drawing his side weapon, at once laid the man out as dead. He ultimately recovered, and lived a sober life.

The recruits which Dr. Graham commanded were soon marched into active service, after which no act of insubordination occurred on the part of any of his men, but all did their duty. The successful training the Doctor gave his men, and the fine appearance they presented while under drill on the streets of Springfield, obtained for him, especially among the young ladies of the town, the sobriquet of the young Sir William Wallace. The Doctor was in many engagements during the three years' war, and wounded but once, and that was at the battle of Mackinaw, in his colonel's ill-planned, rash, and desperate effort to storm the fort, and where they were repulsed with great loss, considering their numbers. Major Holmes, one of the most promising and efficient officers of his rank in the army, fell in this battle, having received two balls through his breast. Dr. Graham was by his side at the time, was himself wounded by a musket-ball, and narrowly escaped death from a grape shot, which shaved his hair and burnt the side of his face, whirling him round, and throwing him to the ground. The night after this battle, when all thought themselves safe aboard, the vessel was suddenly struck with a dreadful tornado, which drove and tossed them throughout the darkness of as dark a night as ever came. The vessel was often furiously forced over shallows, in water much less than it drew, while every wave swept over deck, so that it was with difficulty the men could stand to throw their cannon overboard in an effort to lighten the vessel. They at last anchored in the Straits of St. Joseph; and having taken all the enemies' vessels on the upper lakes previous to their attack on the fort, they felt safe, and all hands turned in to sleep. Their fancied security was of short duration, for a British lieutenant and some Indians, in bark canoes, with muffled oars, came along side, boarded them, and shut them all under the hatches. Being soon afterward exchanged, the Doctor was at once reported for service.

When at Malden, and thinking of no danger from Indians, the Doctor, with several others, went out into a hazel thicket to gather nuts. Being farther advanced than the rest, he was surrounded by five Indians, and taken prisoner. His companions were fired at, but made their escape. This was at dusk, and the Doctor was hurried on till a storm of rain came up, and the darkness of the night stopped their further progress. A fire was then kindled, and a hasty supper broiled. The Indian, who seemed to claim the Doctor as his victim, touched him with his finger, and pointing to the fire, with a waive of his hand from east to west, intimated to him that next day he would be broiled. The Indian gave him to understand by signs, that a white man had killed his brother, and that his life had to pay the penalty. They now tied his hands with bark, and placed one of the party to watch him, with tomahawk in hand. The rain soon extinguished the fire, and all but his guard fell asleep. The frequent flashes of lightning, after a time, showed him that his guard had also fallen asleep, when he suddenly laid himself down on the earth, and, seemingly unconscious, rubbed his wrists together until the bark parted. His first thought was to sink the tomahawk into the head of the guard, then with the energy of desperation dispatch the others; but his second thought prompted him to leap into the dark, and thread the tangled forest as best he could. His progress was slow, depending in the main upon flashes of lightning to make his way. Coming to a stream they had before forded waist deep, he found it so swollen that he had to swim it, and, in so doing, felt the advantage of his early training to meet the emergencies of a rough and adventurous life. When approaching the fort, and feeling himself safe, he was fired on by the guard, and came near running upon his bayonet in the darkness which hid them from each other.

From Malden he was called to Fort Erie to reinforce Gen. Brown, who was beset by the English in force. After some desperate fighting, principally at the cost of the enemy, winter setting in, they crossed over to Buffalo, then a small village, every house but one having been burnt by the British. From this they marched to Erie, Pennsylvania, on the lake, and camped for the winter. The next spring (1815) the news of peace was received, and they returned home.

Dr. Graham, in passing through Lexington on his return from the army, was very politely addressed by a stranger, who said:

"Young man, I see you have been in the army," to which he answered in the affirmative.

"Have you," he continued, "ever studied a profession?"

"No, sir," he replied.

"How would you like that of medicine?"

"Very well," said he, "but I have neither money nor education to carry me through."

"That matters not," said the stranger; "go home and see your friends, and, if you like, return to Lexington and inquire for Dr. Dudley, who every body knows, and you shall neither want for education nor money."

The subject here dropped for a time. Home becoming too

monotonous for his restless spirit, he joined Captain Ben Sanders, of Lexington, Lieutenant William Baylor and Charles Mitchell, of Paris, and Colonel William Milam, of Frankfort, and others, all of whom joined Mina, at San Antonio, Texas, in the war for Mexican independence. Soon, however, becoming dissatisfied with the Spanish character, he returned to New Orleans, and, being in want of money, he walked up the Mississippi some eighty miles to Bayou Lafourche, and down it, in a French craft, through the Attakapas lakes, and up the Teche to its head, hunting a man who owed his father. He was disappointed in making any collection, but felt that he had been fully remunerated by the sport and adventures he enjoyed with numberless alligators. On returning to New Orleans without a dime in his pocket, he entered the school of Dr. Hull, an Episcopal clergyman, occupying the church on Canal Street (now the church of Dr. Lacock), and who had opened the first American female school of note in the city. The Doctor took charge of the urchin class, learning as they learned, and keeping a little ahead. Some of the first ladies of New Orleans (if yet living) were of that little class. Dr. Hull was a good-hearted old Irishman, of much learning, and who took his bottle of wine every Sabbath before going into the pulpit. The yellow fever, now entering the city, raged with fearful effect, and feeling its encroachments upon himself, he took a vessel for New York as his best way back to Kentucky, there being no steamers or railways at that time, and feeling too weak to walk. They had hardly gotten into the gulf before the fever broke out with such fearful intensity that several of their number, both passengers and seamen, were soon heaved overboard. The Doctor's attack came on so suddenly and severely as to strike him down like a shot. On his arrival at Staten Island, seven miles below the city, they were quarantined for thirty days, and ordered to approach no nearer; but to unload, whitewash, and ventilate. This did not suit the Doctor; so procuring a skiff, he got ashore, and took it afoot back to Kentucky by way of Virginia and Cumberland Gap.

Now it was that he gladly accepted the generous offer of

Dr. Dudley, who became his preceptor, and under whose instruction he graduated. Dr. Dudley's first step was to send the youth for whom he felt so special a regard to Transylvania University; and such was the assiduity and application of young Graham, that he quickly outstripped his fellow-students, and passed all his classes. Having completed the sciences in quick time, he entered on the study of his profession, and has the honor of being the first graduate of medicine west of the mountains.

Dead bodies for dissection were not articles of commerce in those days, as they now are; and young Graham strove to furnish the hall of Dr. Dudley with subjects for demonstration, which he disinterred himself, however disagreeable and arduous the task might prove; and, I might add, very hazardous also. On one occasion young Graham and two others, one of them a brother of Dr. Dudley, were taken prisoners, and suits instituted against them; but the distinguished John J. Crittenden, then a young lawyer, volunteered in their behalf, and acquitted them easily. On another occasion they had exhumed a subject in the neighborhood of Nicholasville, when a party came upon them as they started from the grave, the young doctor having the subject on his back, in a bag, carrying to the horses hitched outside of the fence. They were fired upon, the ball lodging in the body of the corpse. By fleetness on that occasion they were all enabled to make their escape. The disinterment of human bodies for dissection is in violation of the laws of the country, at the same time it is essential for the benefit of the living; for without the practice of dissection, no man can become an expert surgeon. Dr. Dudley, by this knowledge, which he attained in an eminent degree, was regarded one of the greatest surgeons the world has ever produced. In cataract and lithotomy, I suppose he never had an equal. He performed two hundred and fifty operations for stone in the bladder without ever having lost a case; in fact, never lost a case of any kind by the knife.

Passing many events of interest for which I have not space, I come to the year 1822, when he went to the city of Mexico with Stephen Austin to obtain a grant in Texas, and was there during the civil war that dethroned the Emperor Iturbide. General James Wilkinson, of Burr notoriety, was also in the city the same winter. Anticipating a change of government, he secretly wrote out, in Dr. Graham's room, a constitution for a new congressional government, and, ripping off the outer soles of some old brogan shoes, put the sheets between them, sewed them up, and gave them a good coating of mud. These shoes were carelessly thrown into the Doctor's baggage-cart; and thus he passed through warring parties undisturbed, and delivered the new constitution to Marquis Vianca, then at the city of Puebla. He also brought to New Orleans letters to several persons written in hieroglyphics, which could not endanger him from the fact that they could not be deciphered or understood without the alphabet. Many incidents of interest might here be related, especially Wilkinson's conversations in regard to the Burr conspiracy, if we had space; but, for want of it, is omitted.

During the Black Hawk War, Dr. Graham acquired a large lead interest about Galena; and at the close of it, to-wit, in the spring of 1833, being the owner of a boat then plying the Mississippi River, he took aboard Black Hawk, his two sons, the Prophet, and Keokuk, the great Indian orator; in other words, the whole royal family, and landed them at the mouth of the Des Moines River, there being at that time not a single white man in the now great State of Iowa. The city of Keokuk was named after this Indian, and Davenport was named after an Indian bearing that name. Davenport was a half-breed Indian, and an interpreter at Rock Island Fort, and piloted Dr. Graham's boat over Rock Island Rapids. The distinguished Jefferson Davis, rendered so conspicuous in the late civil war, was at that time a lieutenant in the Black Hawk War, and was at Galena, with Dr. Graham, during the winter of 1832. Across the river, at that time, the lead lay in great quantities all over the surface of the earth, and was so tempting that large numbers of miners went over from Galena, though the country yet belonged to the Indians, who complained to Government of the depredations of the miners. Lieutenant Davis had been ordered to expell them, but being greatly outnumbered by the miners he could do nothing. The miners soon started a village, and asked Dr. Graham, as a friend of Wm. T. Barry, then Postmaster General, to get them a post office. Dr. Graham, upon applying, received for answer, that nothing was known of the country or its necessities; therefore, the whole matter was left to his discretion. They at once obtained an office, though not within the United States, and appointed as postmaster one of his clerks, named Prentice, who remained in office until the Government purchased the country, and Dubuque became a city.

Leaving untold, for want of space, many interesting incidents, we arrive at the year 1852, being the year he sold his celebrated property at Harrodsburg to the United States Government for the sum of one hundred thousand dollars, as a site for a "Western Military Asylum." The Doctor, being then largely in funds, turned his attention to Texas for investments, making a visit to the State for the purpose. Whilst in Texas, he fell in with Colonel Gray, who was sent out, in part by Robert J. Walker & Co., and in part by the Government, to survey the route of the Southern Atlantic and Pacific Railroad under the line of thirty-two degrees. He joined the party as surgeon of the expedition, and continued with them until they arrived at El Passo, where the commandant calculated to remain some six weeks to recruit his men and mules. This arrangement not suiting him, he selected four men, his son Montrose being one of the number, and filed off to the left. Having read in Humbolt's Mexico of a vast mountain of pure iron (sufficient to supply the world) near the city of Durango, he resolved to prospect a road for himself, and such others as might join him, for the getting of this iron out. A Spanish train had just left for the city of Chihuahua, three hundred miles distant, and he soon joined them; but when some half way on the route, upwards of one hundred Appache Indians bravely charged upon and surrounded them. The Spanish merchants, who headed the train, had twenty-one wagons, loaded with goods, and about fifty men, badly armed. A council of war and a smoke of the pipe was demanded by the chief, or, in the event of a refusal, an immediate battle. It became obvious that the five Americans would have to do all the fighting, for the Mexicans turned pale, trembled, and crawled into the wagons. Sudelwizer, the merchant, and leader of the five Americans, seeing that he was in the power of the savages, determined upon any terms they might offer; and meeting the chiefs some two hundred yards distant, agreed upon terms, which were, that if they thought their scalps worth twenty dollars apiece, they might keep them; and, if not, they would take them. This, the owner of the train made known to Dr. Graham, who promptly replied, that he would pay no *black mail*, but would do his part of the fighting. But the owner of the goods, seeing it was his interest to do the paying, at once turned out a fifteen gallon keg of brandy, bags of tobacco, and quantities of beads and ribbons, and departed, leaving the Indians to the enjoyment of their trophies. Dr. Graham remarks, that he has seen nearly all the northwestern tribes of Indians, but never saw any equal to the Appaches for manly form and genteel appearance, all being well clad, and perfectly armed with lances and the best of guns. No cavalry in the United States, says he, ever had better horses, being the select of those which they would take from the Mexicans. One of them rode a dappled gray, and displayed him before them, going at full speed to and fro, turning his head with as much ease and grace as a fine waltzer upon a floor; now perfectly erect, with his hair streaming at right angles, and next disappearing on the opposite side of his horse. No circus rider, says the Doctor, was ever superior. This tribe, with the Southern Camanches, had penetrated some three hundred miles into Mexico, taking everything before them.

From Chihuahua the Doctor's little company traveled some six hundred miles to Durango, where they were confined for several days by the savages, some three hundred in number, who had surrounded the place, keeping in terror and alarm a population of perhaps twenty-two thousand. They daily displayed themselves on the plain, between the city and the Iron Mountain. One day, while there, they dashed into the city and took a quantity of goods, and tearing the calico into slips, attached them to their spears as banners, which sailed in the wind like kite tails.

From Durango, the Doctor's little company pursued their journey to Mazatlan, on the Pacific Ocean, a distance of three hundred miles, free from any attacks of either guerillas or savages, though they saw blazing fires on the mountain's side nearly every night. One night they cooked their supper on the coals of a burnt house, where seven persons had been shortly before murdered and burnt, their bones yet lying in the ashes. They often passed murdered bodies, both of Americans and Indians; and, on one occasion, they rode under a carcass suspended by the heels, the flesh dripping from the bones. A little beyond this they saw in the distance, across a necked space, something strange hanging on the bushes, which they took to be a new tropical fruit, but which, on approaching, proved to be human skulls; and beyond this, again, in the same day's travel, and at a great elevation, they saw a number of fresh mounds, with a cross erected upon them. Upon enquiry of their guide and muleteer, they were told that here a whole train, composed of fifty whites, were murdered by the Indians. Looking around they saw a board nailed to a pine tree, and on it this inscription, written in Spanish : "Here was the lovely daughter of Bishop Trespilas murdered by the cruel savages. Peace be to her soul." To show the condition of the country at this time, the Doctor related the following:

" On descending a very high mountain, between the cities of Chihuahua and Durango, we came to a beautiful little stream, where agate pebbles and shining silver were seen in the sand. Here I camped for the night. My son, wandering up the river for some distance, met with a man, who he addressed in English, and received an answer in the same language. Both were mutually surprised. The man asked

" 'Where are you from ?'

" 'Kentucky,' being the answer, he remarked—

" 'Do you know a Dr. Graham ?'

" 'I am his son,' was the response, ' and my father is now camped just below here.'

" 'Is it possible ? He saved my life.'

"Hurrying to the camp, he took me to his house, where two of his farm-hands were then dying, they having been shot that morning by the Indians. This man was Dr. Wilkerson, of the Galt House tragedy, who, having been a surgeon in the invasion of Mexico, had married a Spanish woman, with a considerable landed estate, but the Doctor had determined to abandon his possessions to the savages, and to return to Mississippi." Dr. Graham was the main witness in the Wilkerson tragedy, and through the influence of himself and Judge Rowan a change of venue from Louisville to Harrodsburg was obtained from the Kentucky Legislature.

"Upon another occasion," said the Doctor, "we had traveled hard all day, within sight of a smoking ranche, in order to reach a place of safety. On our arrival at the village, and while talking with the alcalde, his wife came in wringing her hands and crying aloud, 'the savages have burnt the village of Alecko and murdered all the people.' The alcalde most nobly, instead of detaining me to fight with and for them, advised me to travel all night, and furnished me with a guide. A hard travel it was, both upon self and mule. I felt badly," said he, "in leaving the village in such terror and confusion, but the safety of myself and party demanded such a course."

The most hazardous enterprise ever undertaken by any small company was that of Dr. Graham's. He ran the gauntlet for twelve hundred miles, through a border warfare, where nearly every man able to bear arms had been drafted, leaving old men, women, and children only, to the mercy of savages. It may be said with truth, that Dr. Graham's little company ran this distance with no hope of safety, except that they were well armed and were Americans; for it was a truth undoubted, that the Indians entertained greater fear and respect for Americans, by far, than they did for Spaniards. They seem to have slain the Spaniards on many occasions without remorse and with relentless vengeance—having a tradition of Cortez's cruelties to themselves.

On their travels they passed many mining furnaces which had been abandoned, and saw silver shining in the rocks everywhere. The Doctor looked upon the country as blessed by nature, but as cursed by man. The valley beneath the mountain range, even in mid-winter, abounded in tropical fruits. Birds of paradise, parrots, and black pheasants almost as large as turkeys, were to be seen in great numbers. The staple of the country is mahogany, rosewood, ebony, and logwood, which is packed upon the back to the seaboard, a distance of fifty miles. Chunks of silver were offered them in exchange for coin, two for one. In this village, though a paradise, many of the nations go as naked as when they were born, wearing not even a fig leaf. By some freak of superstition no hostile Indian has ever been seen in this valley, or even below the mountain range. The road to this valley is, perhaps, the roughest road in the world, and though millions upon millions of silver have been packed out of it, it remains unimproved. Much of the road passes through narrow and fearful passes, with a thousand feet perpendicular rock above you, and precipice as great and equally terrifying below you. In such places the solid rock is worn into pits, and unless your mule places his foot carefully in them, he is most sure to go overboard. Dr. Graham says his guide gave him this instruction in passing along: "Give your mule the bridle, shut your eyes, and hold fast to the horn of your saddle, which," says he, "I did, and, moreover, held my breath till I got through." Then it was that the Doctor gave up his railroad project, leaving the iron mountain, even as yet, to its undisturbed repose.

On arriving at Mazatlan, there being no steamers, they took passage for San Francisco in an old rotten whaler which had brought Walker and his fillibusters down to Wymers. It was soon seized by the Mexican authorities, and the captain thrust into prison. He purchased his liberty, however, yet found trouble in being ordered not to leave the port. Not regarding the order, he hoisted anchor at midnight, cleared the straits, and was on the wide ocean by daylight. When off Cape St. Lucas, they were struck by a tornado, which rent their rotten sails into ribbons, and left them with naked masts to the mercy of the foaming waves. In this condition they were tossed about for sixty-two days, laboring at the pumps both day and night. The hatches had to be kept shut tight, for the vessel was frequently under water, the waves rolling entirely over her. Provisions growing scarce, a demand was made by the sailors and steerage passengers for an equal division; and as life was equally dear to all it was granted, and, on open deck, each trembling hand grasped his last morsel with feelings not to be described. The trying hour had not come yet—to draw lots as to who should be eaten. But by-and-by the hour arrived, when it was secretly determined to butcher the captain, who weighed about two hundred and fifty pounds; and though the sailors were urgent and anxious for the feast, Dr. Graham's squad opposed it on the ground of there being no one on board who understood the quadrant and navigation, so that the death of the captain was the certain destruction of all; besides which, he promised them from day to day, that as he had been forty years whaling upon this part of the ocean, they would soon strike a counter wind, which would drift them into the Golden Gate; and, moreover, they had by that time mended and got up some little sail. In the meantime, the captain had found in the hold of the vessel some old, dried, mouldy beef—though riddled out by a hairy worm, called the moth-worm—which he had boiled up in black, stinking water, calling it soup. Their water had given out some days previous, but they accidentally found some old, half rotten casks, containing some water, but thick with wiggle-tails, which, when boiled up with the worms, furnished some little fuel to the spark of life remaining. On the sixty-third day from their embarkation they entered the harbor of San Francisco. Montrose, the Doctor's son, with others, were down with a nervous fever at the time, produced by the whetting of the stomach upon itself.

Relating nothing of the events connected with the Doctor in California, I speak next of his operations on Rockcastle River, in Kentucky, where, in the wilderness, he built up a place by legislative charter, called Sublimity, or Rockcastle Springs. At this place he spent some ten years labor and twenty thousand dollars, building a fine lumber and flouring mill, a hotel and cottages. Out of the bed of the river he blasted large rocks, cut out islands, felled leaning trees, to make the river navigable. He also opened roads to Somerset, Crab Orchard, London, and Barbourville, thus enhancing the value of property in that section to double its former worth. The mountain counties in that section of Kentucky owe him a debt of gratitude in this respect of which no doubt they are fully sensible. For Harrodsburg and Mercer County, nay, I might say for the whole State, he did even more than for the mountain counties. I have elsewhere spoken of the grand improvements and great expenditure of money at the Harrodsburg Springs, by his individual exertions, bringing to the State from other States more than three millions of dollars.

To recount the almost innumerable events and hairbreadth escapes in the most eventful career of Dr. Graham, would occupy a quarto volume of three hundred pages. Let it suffice to say, that in his travels he has checkered the continent, from the head of the Mississippi to the capes of Florida, and from Maine to California. He has hunted the moose in the Adirondacks (mountains) at the head of the Hudson, an account of which was published years ago, in the Home Journal of New York, written out by Mansfield Walworth, a son of Chancellor Walworth, who was with him at the time alluded to. He has had camp-hunts innumerable, especially with the Boone Club, in the Cumberland mountains, for forty years past, of which I have heretofore spoken. He has traveled much on horseback. Near fifty years ago he traveled through Tennessee and Alabama into Florida, and once barely escaped being murdered in the pine-flats of Florida, where cabins, then, were scarcely less than forty miles apart. His first adventures to the Galena lead mines were on horseback, and many a night he has slept on dirt floors, in Illinois cabins, where the grass was not yet worn off.

I have heretofore omitted to mention in this sketch that Dr. Graham was an author of no inconsiderable notoriety. The first production from his pen which I have seen noticed was a book entitled "*Man, from his Cradle to his Grave.*" The next, a book entitled, "*The True Science of Medicine.*" But the crowning work of his labors and eventful life which I have noticed is a book written and published by him at the age of about eighty-two years, entitled " *The Philosophy of the Mind.*" I never read a book upon the same subject that developed, illustrated, and, I may say, demonstrated the laws of the mind so fully to my satisfaction. To show the estimation in which Dr. Graham was held by that distinguished writer, Mr. Walworth, I make the following extract from the "Home Journal" above referred to. He says:

" Descriptions of the lower Hudson engross the attention of tourists, while these superb Adirondacks and woods, so much nearer and more accessible to Saratoga Springs and Lake George, have no chronicler. I conducted that famous traveler, scholar, author, and master of the rifle, Dr. Graham, of Harrodsburg Springs, Kentucky, to this locality on a moose deer hunt. He had explored all the grandeurs of nature throughout Mexico, from Maine to California, yet this unchronicled locality thrilled him, aroused his enthusiasm, inspired him. The view he had from a mountain, whose base was washed by the pellucid waters of the Hudson, drew from him the enthusiastic remark: 'This must be the mountain to which the devil took our Saviour, when he showed him *the whole world!*' Crane Mountain uprears its bald head about a cannon shot to the northwest of Dr. Graham's lofty lookout. I had often circled its base in pursuit of deer, with my rifle eagerly grasped, and my ears ringing with the wild music of the hounds on the trail. From the dense woods which cling to its sides and extend away up to its bald crown, I had many a day caught the cry of the dogs as they drove the antlered monarch of the glen around it in circles."

It was never the nature of Dr. Graham to indulge in idleness at any period of his protracted life. Whether in adverse or prosperous circumstances, he was continually moving, either for the advancement of his own interest, or for the benefit of others. I have before spoken of the expenditure and great amount of labor bestowed by Dr. Graham to the wilderness country in which the Rockcastle Springs are situated, and the beneficial results to the sparse population of that section, especially by increasing the value of their lands, and consequently increasing the revenue of the State; but he paid attention also to the moral culture of the youth of that neighborhood, especially in the establishment of a Sunday school at Sublimity, the name of a little town which he built up at that place, and for the establishment of which he procured a charter from the Legislature. This being the first Sabbath-school ever organized in that neighborhood, it attracted great attention, and some of the boys living a distance of ten miles from it were punctual in attendance, though they had frequently to go on foot. The Doctor remarked, that some of them were the brightest little fellows he ever saw, and made surprising progress, and ever manifested pride and pleasure when a book was given them.

Dr. Graham is noted for his munificence and acts of benevolence. No man in the community in which he has lived has contributed more willingly or more liberally to colleges, churches, and any and every object of charity which might be presented. He has given of his substance, during his life, more than ten thousand dollars for such objects; and in these things he has evinced nothing of sectarianism. He is quite tolerant in his religious views. He attached himself to the Methodist Church in his youth, during, he says, "the olden days, when that exercise called the '*jerks*' prevailed in Kentucky; when our good old preachers, with trumpet voice, beat the Bible with their fists and blistered their feet in the pulpit. This startled me," says he, "and when the shades of night fell thick, silent, and solemnly around me, I saw the 'old fellow,' hoof, horns, and all, seeking whom he might devour. So next morning I hurried to our little log church, gave in what was called a first-rate experience, and joined the Methodist Church, to which I yet belong. All my family are Presbyterians, but I have a liking for this church." He says, an upright, conscientious, Howard life, is his religion. "To do justice, love mercy, and walk humbly before God," is all He asks of His children.

I have stated before that Dr. Graham was surgeon to the expedition which made the first survey of the Southern Atlantic and Pacific Railroad, under the direction of Colonel Gray, but I omitted to relate an incident connected with his history, which I now give. When they arrived at the great Blue Spring, at the head of the Colorado River, they pitched tents early in the evening. The Doctor, perceiving a large flock of antelopes not far distant, sought to secure one, and had proceeded alone less than a mile from camp, when he was fired at by two Indians, who, missing him, rose up from behind a bluff and sent a shower of arrows after him. He rode into camp with one of the arrows sticking in the hip of his mule. Gray, having forbid any of the men to straggle away from camp, was angry with the Doctor, and pettishly remarked, " that he hoped the next time he ventured out he might return with a dozen arrows in his hinder parts."

There are two or three other incidents in the history of the Doctor which should be mentioned before I close this already protracted sketch. They will serve to exhibit, unmistakably, the iron nerve, fearlessness, and indomitable courage of the man. He owned, while he kept the Harrodsburg Springs, a band of colored musicians, who were doubtless one of the best bands to be found anywhere in Kentucky. During the watering season they played at the Springs, and during the winter at Louisville and Frankfort, but by the solicitation of the distinguished Judge Robertson (a musician himself), and his old preceptor, Dr. Ben. Dudley, he permitted them to locate in Lexington. From Lexington they ran off to Canada, and the fact having been announced, he followed them; but being anticipated by the blacks of Canada, through the perfidy of his agent whom he had sent ahead, a large and furious mob had assembled before his arrival, who at once set upon him with great violence, calling him by all manner of names, such as thief, kidnapper, slave-driver, etc. They spit upon him, grated their teeth at him, rubbed their fists in his face, and pinched him until he was black in many places. He said, he " felt as though the black jaws of perdition had belched forth their fiery fiends to torment him." Many of them were bare-headed, bare-footed, and half naked, red-eyed and taggy-headed, with their faces distorted with hideous grimaces. And now, at a moment when all felt that he was to be torn to pieces, he saw a man rush into the dense and suffocating crowd, and they disperse as fast as possible. This was General Ironsides, who, having at once dispersed the crowd, took the Doctor to a boarding-house, and ordered a guard to protect him against molestation or insult.

Ironsides was a General in the British Army, a half-brother of the celebrated Indian chief, Tecumseh, who fell at the battle of the Thames, October 5th, 1813. The question has ever been, Who killed Tecumseh? and now it is, Who killed Zollicoffer? General Ironsides gave to Dr. Graham a full account of his brother and of his death. He said that no white man had laid sight upon his brother, till he detected three Yankees taking him out of his grave to exhibit his skeleton, which, to them, would have been a fortune; but he took the body from them and buried it under the floor of his own house. He said his brother fell by a musket-shot, the ball passing through his heart, and he fell across the trunk of a fallen tree, near the roots. The top of this tree was very large, and pointed towards where the whites made the charge. Taking all the circumstances into consideration, he was of the opinion a random shot killed him. In answer to the Doctor, upon being asked if his brother had been mutilated by knives, and whether the rumor was true, that his back had been skinned for razor straps, he replied, that no white man in that battle could have touched him, for he was instantly picked up and borne off. He said, however, that there was an Indian chief killed, and literally skinned, who was so much like his brother that they were often taken for each other. The Doctor was not in that battle, but he had heard persons boast of having razor straps from the back of Tecumseh, which elicited from him the inquiries of Ironsides above mentioned.*

---

* The foregoing statement in regard to the killing of Tecumseh accords more fully with the views of the author than any other of the numerous accounts he has seen. Forty-two years ago, the author, being a member of the Legislature of Kentucky, and a boarder with Colonel James Davidson, then Treasurer of Kentucky, and who had commanded a company from Garrard county in the battle of the Thames, in the regiment of Colonel Richard Johnson, had frequent conversations with Colonel Davidson in regard to the

General Ironsides was as well known in Canada as was General Jackson in the United States; and no officer in the British service stood higher when Doctor Graham was there. This was just at the close of the Patriot War (so called) in Canada, at which time Ironsides had all his Indians, both of Upper and Lower Canada, in camp near Malden, the place where the Doctor was mobbed, and where he was invited out by Ironsides, and treated by him with all respect and kindness.

The servants of Dr. Graham did all in their power to assist him in recovering them, saying to the people that he had been

---

killing of Tecumseh, who made in substance the following statement: He said it was frequently claimed in after years by the friends of Colonel Johnson, that the renowned chief was killed by him (Johnson), but that Johnson himself knew that he did not kill him, and never claimed the honor. Colonel Davidson believed that a soldier in his company by the name of John King killed the Indian who, after the battle, was pointed out and recognized as Tecumseh. King, then a young man, about eighteen years of age, was a constant attendant of Colonel W. Whitley on his scouts. Whitley was then about sixty-five years of age, and being old, and having rendered essential services in the early settlement of Kentucky, was not restrained at all in his movements with the army, but was allowed pretty much to take his own course. He seemed to have a presentiment that he would be killed in the anticipated battle, and so expressed himself to one of his companions in arms. When the battle was over, Colonel Davidson went with King to the place Whitley had fallen, and pointed to a dead Indian not distinguished by his dress from the other Indians, but who was afterward recognized as Tecumseh. King said that the Indian had killed Colonel Whitley, and that he had shot the Indian. "Our guns," said he, "cracked together. I saw the Indian aiming at Whitley, and Whitley saw it also, and was about to shoot, but the Indian was too quick for him, and he fell without discharging his gun, the load remaining in it." The Indian was found to be shot in the left breast with two rifle balls, and Whitley's habit, as generally known, was to load his gun with two balls. This fact induced many to believe that Whitley had killed Tecumseh, or else that he was killed with his gun. King, being the constant associate of Whitley, had doubtless learned to load his gun with two bullets also, and the Indian killed, we are inclined to believe, was the Indian who bore so striking a resemblance to Tecumseh, and not Tecumseh himself. The foregoing statement corresponds with a statement lately made by A. K. M. McDowell, upon the authority of Mr. W. L. Floyd, a soldier of the War of 1812, still living, and who was a mess-mate with John King in Captain Davidson's company. John King was the son of a poor widow of Garrard county, who, after the war, removed with her son to Tennessee, of whom nothing was afterward known in Kentucky.

a father to them. They professed to be anxious to return, and said to him, secretly, that they would slip off and come home by and by. But they never did so. This incident occurred in the winter of 1840–41, just after General Harrison went on to Washington after his election to the Presidency of the United States. The band had been sent for to play at the reception of General Harrison in Kentucky; they took advantage of the occasion, and ran off to Canada.

A while after this, Dr. Graham instituted suit against Gorman & Strader, two very wealthy citizens of Cincinnati, who owned the line of mailboats from Louisville to that place, one of which boats carried off the slaves; and, from them, after long litigation, he succeeded in recovering about six thousand dollars. Guthrie, Pirtle, and Wolfe were the lawyers of the Doctor at Louisville; Harlan and Robertson, in the Court of Appeals; and Crittenden and Badger, before the Supreme Court at Washington City.

Another incident, marvelous in its result, occurred with the Doctor nearly fifty years ago, and which is not undeserving a place in history as an additional testimonial of the intrepid bravery and daring courage of the man. It was in the year 1822 that he determined on a trip to Mexico. At New Orleans, when about to start on a vessel bound for Tampico, he had the good luck to meet with a man who spoke Spanish well, and who desired to accompany him on his trip. His name was Alfonso Vacara. About the same time he was approached by a young Englishman by the name of Charles Chambers, who desired to go to that country also, but said he was without means, and proffered to accompany him as a servant. In response to his humiliating offer, the Doctor said: "Young man, I learned in early life to wait upon myself, but if you desire to go, I will take you along as my companion, and as an aid in any dangers we may encounter upon the road." The offer was gladly accepted, and the three were quickly off. To his gratification, the Doctor soon found that the young man was not only an accomplished gentleman, but spoke with fluency the French language. Fitted out with three mules, a guide and muleteer, they were soon on their way from Tampico to the City of Mexico, deterred not by the dangers which lay in their way, or mountain rising upon mountain to impede their progress. They gained the summit hights of some twelve thousand feet without molestation, and approached the celebrated silver mines of Real del Monta, which, though very rich, were then abandoned and in ruins, a result of the civil war in which the country had engaged. Here they were met and stopped by a wild looking beggar, when suddenly four armed men emerged from an adjoining chapparel, who darted upon them, firing as they came. Perceiving at once the danger which surrounded them, the firing became mutual and simultaneous. The man at whom the Doctor directed his aim soon tumbled from his saddle and expired. About the same time his own mule fell under him, dead, while the other two were wounded. The guerrillas, seeing that their foe was doubly armed, passed on, and were no more seen. The Doctor believed, from the character of the shooting, that it was not the intention of the guerrillas to kill, but simply to cower, and then rob, which they would doubtless have done had it not been for his lucky shot; for his companions were panic-stricken and attempted no defense. During the fight the affrighted horse of the man whom the Doctor had killed had run over the guide, disabling him to such an extent that he had to be carried on one of the mules, the others riding and walking by turns, as the guide had done before. In the progress of their travels they passed several dead bodies, but so plebeian in appearance as to indicate that they had not been murdered for their money. Such sights were not uncommon anywhere in Mexico.

Inquiring of the Doctor, why, in our previous conversations, he had not related to me before so important an event of his life, he replied : " I have been averse to giving any sketch of my life to any one for publication until I should attain a hundred years of age, for I now feel as though I shall cast my century behind me, and live in another age to meditate upon that past, demonstrate the fore-knowledge of God, or destiny of man (which are inseparable), and thus furnish something worthy of record; for then, time itself would head the list, and give importance to events otherwise uninteresting. In the little pittance of man's life I see nothing worthy of record, for I have ever looked upon him as an ephemeral and helpless being, whose life at best is but a flitting shadow, and whose acts are destined, by the laws of his organism, to be a fated link in the eternal chain of casualty. He is forced into existence, forced through his existence, and soon forced out of it, a mere bubble upon the rapid stream of time, which rises to view, sinks, and is gone forever. Ages past, and mouldering nations, tell the tale of our fated and rapid succession. I have in my own short life already outlived some three thousand millions of my race. There being a thousand millions of human beings on our planet, and thirty years being a full average of life, the startling and melancholy fact comes forcibly before me. With these views of God's eternal supremacy, and man's mortality and humble dependence, I claim no merit in life. I did not give it, nor can I prolong it beyond its destined end; and hence, though often asked by publishers of high repute for a sketch of my eventful life, I have hitherto refused, and even now yield a reluctant assent, influenced only by the desire manifested by my children."

Another incident in the life of the Doctor I will here relate: Becalmed in a trip between the capes of Florida and the island of Cuba, the sea rolling smoothly, he and another passenger aboard concluded to take a swim, but had not proceeded far, until they heard from the ship's deck the startling exclamation, "a shark! a shark!" A ladder was lowered, and he quickly ascended the ship; but his friend being behind, had one of his feet caught and severely torn by the shark. The shouts from the vessel, and the missiles showered upon the shark, caused him to let go his hold and sink; but soon rising again and making for the vessel, a sailor stuck a chunk of beef upon a tackle-hook and threw it to him, which he instantly swallowed, and by it was caught in the gills. They were thus enabled to draw his head above water, with his great mouth wide open, down which a crow-bar was pitched with such force as to protrude through his side; around the crow-bar a lasso was quickly thrown, with the other end made fast to the capstan, and he was soon hoisted on deck; but such were his frightful throes, that all took to the bulyards and the rigging, giving him a clear deck for action. When death had calmed him, and they approached the monster, a sailor remarked that he did not wonder that these "critters" were called heartless, when their hearts were not much larger than his thumb. This remark induced the Doctor to open the animal, upon doing which he found the declaration of the sailor to be true.

Lest I may have done injustice to the Doctor in remarks heretofore made in regard to his religious predilections, I subjoin remarks subsequently made by him on the same subject: "I have," said he, "always taken the ten commandments of the Bible and the life of Christ as my guide; and though I never subscribed to any man's dogma, I have ever been respectful and kind to the clergy. During the thirty-two years I kept the Harrodsburg Springs, it was a standing order to my clerks, never to charge a preacher; and, when traveling with them, my habit was to ask the privilege of paying their bills. It was a fact understood by all the different sects at Harrodsburg, that, at the State meetings of the clergy (so often held there), it was my custom to accommodate all sent to my house, however great the number, without charge. This I did, not because I thought they could do more for me than I could do for myself, but because they were honestly spending their lives in striving to prepare us for our destined end."

Dr. Graham, in the course of his life, has had many rencounters and combats, but in no instance can it be said, with truthfulness, that he was ever the aggressor; he never acted on such occasions, except on the defensive. The last incident of the kind which we will take time to record occurred at Crab Orchard during the late civil war, when the Doctor had attained the age of seventy-five or seventy-six years. It was understood that Kirby Smith had passed the mountain defiles and was approaching Richmond. Such was the excitement at that time, that many Southern-Rights men often received insult and maltreatment from the hands of the inconsiderate and unscrupulous among the Federals. While Judge Higgins and the Doctor were sitting quietly in a room at Crab Orchard, and some five thousand troops were hurrying through the streets, a soldier (some six feet two), with a number at his back, burst suddenly into the room, with the exclamation, "Here are two damned rebels, and I will give them hell." At this, Higgins wisely slipped out through the crowd, but the Doctor, not willing to retreat, stood his ground, when the assailant seized him by the throat, saying, "Now, damn you, I will blow your brains out," at the same time pointing a pistol at him and exploding a cap. Thus seeing his danger, the Doctor quickly grasped the pistol arm, while with his right he drew his bowie-knife, when two soldiers caught him and strove to disarm him. He held on to the arm of the soldier, and every time he turned the pistol toward him, he threw it up; and thus they went round and round the room, amid the noise of the scuffle, and the rattling of the chairs. The Doctor, in his efforts to extricate his knife arm, cut a soldier deeply and dangerously, which created tremendous excitement, not only in the room, but upon the streets. A rumor was circulated, that the Doctor had killed one soldier, and cut up several others. He now surrendered, and, with bayonets pointed at him, was ordered to march to the woods. Believing that they intended to shoot him, he refused to go, and stood firm upon the street, though pricked with bayonets on every side. Growing impatient, a soldier more desperate than the rest stepped back, with the exclamation, "Clear the way, I'll move the damn rebel, or send him to hell." "At this instant," says the Doctor, "I felt sure of death, but the soldier flinched in his charge, and only ran his bayonet into me about an inch." At this juncture, a citizen, whom he knew to be a friend, said to him, "Go, Doctor, go; they only want to take you to the army," which they did, with his consent. By this time it had become dark, and was snowing and sleeting. On his arrival he was put into a rail pen, knee deep in mud and snow, with several others they had taken into custody. He was in this disagreeable condition for a week, the officer of the guard allowing no friend to speak to him, and refusing all applications for his release by *habeas corpus*. The army having left to meet the Southern forces, except the guard commanded by a corporal, an officer stationed at Stanford was appealed to, to give him a trial, which being had, he was released. The only thing proved against him was his resistance, which was not only justifiable, but unavoidable.

Such is the indomitable perseverance of Doctor Graham that he is sure to succeed in whatever he undertakes; and I believe he is now engaged in an enterprise that will tend to identify his fame with Kentucky, and Kentucky history, as much, perhaps, if not more, than anything else in which he has ever engaged. I mean the effort he is now making to collect a Cabinet of Natural History for the State of Kentucky, of which he will be the sole distinguished author.

And now, it may be asked, why have we devoted so much space to the history of a man who is no politician, who has never been in public life, or even aspired to any public position? We answer, for the very reason, that by the force of his energy and native talents he has been enabled to render greater and more essential services to his country in the sphere in which he has acted than hundreds of our profoundest statesmen have been able to do in the capacities in which they have acted, and is, therefore, the more worthy of our emulation.

In 1819, Dr Graham went to Harrodsburg with twenty dollars in his pocket, borrowed money, which, with his scanty apparel, was all he possessed. From this time on his prosperity was uninterrupted, and he became one of the most enterprising men, if not a benefactor, of his native State. Instead of taxing the people for his support as a politician, he has, on the contrary, contributed largely to their support, asking no higher or greater reward than the peace of his own conscience and the approval of his fellow-citizens.

By a fair calculation, it is estimated that, in the thirty-two years he kept the Harrodsburg Springs, he brought to Kentucky some four millions of dollars, thus aiding the State, as well in its financial condition as in its character abroad for public enterprise. He created a good market for a whole country, and gave employment to thousands in his extensive improvements, greatly enhancing the value of property in his town and neighborhood, and in this respect contributed to the treasury of the State. He was among the first appointed on the part of the State to direct public improvements; and, for twenty years, devoted much of his time and money to that object, never asking or even desiring remuneration. He was regarded about Harrodsburg as the author and leader of all public improvements in that neighborhood, and was the originator of the turnpike road from Lexington, through Shakerstown, to Lebanon, etc. The very next day after his arrival at Harrodsburg, he gave the twenty dollars he had taken there with him to aid in rebuilding a church which had been blown down, and subscribed a hundred dollars more in aid of citizens who had sustained loss by a tornado. Shortly after this, he contributed five hundred dollars to the new Presbyterian Church, and an equal amount to Bacon College, which, by his subsequent aid and influence, was established at Harrodsburg.

The Presbyterian Female College and the Christian Baptist Female College, at Harrodsburg, owe their existence to Dr. Graham more than to any other man. To the first he gave the ground upon which it is situated, the rock necessary for its erection, bestowed upon it a cabinet of natural history, and planted every tree which now so beautifully shades its grounds. To the latter college he gave off of his Greenville tract twenty-four acres of land, with the buildings thereon. This college, while in the hands of Professor Mullin, was unfortunately consumed by fire; and while the flames were still raging, and sympathy at its highest pitch, the Doctor, taking advantage of the moment, raised upon the ground an amount of money amply sufficient to rebuild it. To this college he sent three of his relatives, paying their tuition fees, etc., until they graduated. To Professor Shannon, President of Bacon College, he gave the four acres of land upon which is erected his fine edifice. Through his intercession and influence the County Court of Mercer County was prevailed upon to enclose with a good fence the public square of the town, when the Doctor, without compensation or remuneration, graded the ground, sowed the grass seed, and planted the trees which now so beautifully adorn it.

The first street in Harrodsburg ever graded and paved was done by the Doctor at his own expense, whilst he contributed of his means to the making of all the others. In short, he was the foster-father, or *sine qua non*, of the town, and not until he left the place did the price of property begin to decline in Harrodsburg.

As an instance of the enterprise of Dr. Graham and his penchant for improvements, he took his own servants and tools to the Three Forks of Kentucky River, where there were no settlements near, cut timber, and built him a boat. This boat he ladened with mountain shrubbery to beautify the grounds of the Springs, and with his own hands assisted in rowing it to the landing at Shaker Ferry. He scoured with his wagons the cliffs of the Cumberland, across to the Kentucky River, with a similar view. With these collections, together with importations from almost every portion of the world, his possessions at Harrodsburg were rendered superlatively attractive; and when Generals Scott, Wool, and others, were deputed by Congress to purchase an asylum in the West for invalid soldiers, this spot was preferred above all others they had examined, and was purchased by the Government at the price of $100,000, as has heretofore been stated. The splendid edifice situated on these grounds was some years since laid in ashes by the devouring flames, but so beautiful a spot cannot long remain neglected; and I presage for the future some towering edifice upon its ruins, dedicated to literature and benevolence. And often will those who loiter in the ambrosial shades which surround it be carried back in contemplation of him who planted those trees with his own hands, and this, perhaps, long years after he shall have passed from the busy scenes of life.

I have to omit much of the history of this extraordinary man for want of space; but few if any have acquired more extended fame, or accomplished more good for his native State, either as a statesman or politician, nor has any man's life and character developed more fully that practical moral which his history fully presents. Raised from obscurity to affluence, and occupying the front rank of society, he has become a fit example for the poor youth of the country to emulate. We are by no means the first to herald the fame and merits of Dr. Graham. Years ago, when he occupied the Springs, he was published in the journals of the day as the prince of landlords. Poets sung of him, and prose-writers eulogized him for his excellence, nay superiority, as an off-hand rifle shooter, as a man of unbounded benevolence and unswerving morality, great industry, and indomitable perseverance and courage. Particularly lavish in his praise was the renowned N. P. Willis, the poet and journalist, who selected our subject as his friend and second in his affair of honor with Forest, the celebrated tragedian. So, too, was Frederick Peel, eldest son of Sir Robert Peel, Prime Minister of England, who, on visiting the Springs, brought with him a letter of introduction from the Hon. Henry Clay, a sure passport to the best society in any part of the world. Mr. Peel, on his return to Europe, recorded the facts in his tour, of having " met in the far West with a man of great intelligence and public enterprise, by whom he was kindly entertained, and from whom he acquired valuable information in regard to his travels to the Mammoth Cave, and thence to the Falls of St. Anthony on the Upper Mississippi," etc. In fine, it may be said that Dr. Graham was truly a remarkable man, and has obtained for himself a name and a fame which the fewest can ever attain.

The plan of this work forbids any further account of the adventures of Dr. Graham. Other incidents, equal in importance to many we have mentioned, we are compelled to omit, upon which the future historian will dwell and enlarge. The cruelties he has suffered, his narrow escapes from death, his alternate good and bad fortune, his dangerous adventures and successful escapes, his hardships and privations, etc., in many instances appear more like the inventions of a novelist than a narrative of the incidents of real life; yet romantic as they may appear, they are nevertheless true; and hence, as we have before said, he may be regarded as one of the most remarkable men of the age, and too many monuments of his history remain for us to cease to remember him through generations even yet remote.

JOHN P. MORTON.

I feel it my duty, as a faithful chronicler of men and events connected with the history of Kentucky, to mention conspicuously another self-made man, still living, and now in the sixty-fourth year of his age. I allude to Mr. John P. Morton, of Louisville, Kentucky. Like Dr. Graham, he never aspired to any public station or political preferment; and yet he has been more essentially serviceable, and conferred greater benefits on the community at large, than thousands of our wisest statesmen and most astute politicians. He was the first man in Kentucky to commence the publication of books, and the manufacture of blank books, and as a publisher and printer has established for himself a business and reputation of the very highest character. He began business in Louisville in 1825, without capital; but the course he pursued, and the rules he adopted, secured to him the confidence of all who had any transactions with him or his firm. One of his rules was to avoid incurring debt, which he never departed from; consequently, the financial storms which repeatedly swept over the country ever passed harmlessly over him. Another rule was to observe strictly and to the letter all his engagements, whether written or verbal. In short, in truth it may be said of him, that he is spotless in character, of a highly cultivated mind, a polite, agreeable, high-toned, and genial gentleman, always interesting and instructive in conversation, and success in his business has attended his career through life to the present time. Mr. Morton was born on the 4th day of March, 1807, in Lexington, Kentucky. He was a student in Transylvania University until he arrived at the age of sixteen, by which time he had gone through the Sophomore class, but his circumstances would not allow of his going to school longer, and the failure of his father in business, who had a large family to provide for, demanded of him that he should provide for himself. His school-fellows of that day, who subsequently became men of high distinction, were Jefferson Davis, General Albert Sidney Johnson, Governor Morehead, and Senator Hannegan. He became a tutor for a short time; but finally became a clerk in a bookstore in Lexington. In 1825 he went to Louisville, where he at first acted as the agent of Mr. W. W. Worseley, and took the entire charge of the publishing business of that gentleman. In 1826 Mr. Worseley started a paper called the Focus, in which Mr. Morton became a partner; at the same time they had a bookstore. Subsequent to this, the firm of Morton & Co. was established, which continued until 1829. Morton and Smith bought out Mr. Worseley, whose business was prosperous and continued to increase. In 1839, another change took place in the firm; and still later, some young men in the counting-room were admitted as partners, when the firm took the name which it now bears, that of John P. Morton & Co., and their establishment is now, perhaps, the largest publishing house south of the Ohio River. It is the only house in the South engaged in the publication of school books of all kinds. Mr. Morton's commencement of this business was in a small way. In the first place his means were limited; and in the second place, having no experience, he was venturing on an untried experiment in Kentucky. Their first effort was directly in the interest of the community, for their first publications were an elementary speller and primer, and an almanac. The business was profitable, and he was soon enabled to enlarge his sphere, until his establishment now ranks among the foremost in the West.

GENERAL HUMPHREY MARSHALL.

General Humphrey Marshall was born at Frankfort, Kentucky, January 13th, 1812. He graduated at the West Point Academy, but resigned his military commission and studied law, which he practiced with success. For some years previous to the Mexican War, he took an active part in the military affairs of the State, as a captain, major, and lieutenant colonel. He was a colonel of cavalry in the Mexican War, and led the charge of the Kentucky volunteers at Buena Vista. In 1847, after declining several important nominations, he retired to a farm. In 1849 he was elected to Congress as a representative, and re-elected in 1851. He was appointed by President Fillmore Commissioner to China. On his return he was elected a representative in the Thirty-fourth Congress. In 1856 he was a member of the American National Council held in New York, where he caused to be thrown off all secresy in the politics of his party; and in 1857 he was re-elected to Congress, serving as a member of the Committee on Military Affairs. He took part in the Rebellion of 1861, and was a general in the Confederate Army. He was a member of the Confederate Congress at Richmond, and distinguished himself in that body as a debater and orator, equaling similar honors achieved by him previously in the Congress of the United States at Washington City. General Marshall was a man of considerable corpulency, and died suddenly in Louisville, March, 1872, in the sixty-first year of his age. He belonged to a family which has added luster to our State and country—in the senate, upon the bench, at the bar, and before popular assemblies. He was the son of John J. Marshall, and grandson of Humphrey Marshall, the latter a distinguished politician of Kentucky in his day, and author of the History of Kentucky, sketches of whose lives I have given.

CHAPTER XI.

History of Kentucky more particularly relating to Green County—When Established—Its present Area—First Representative, Richard Thurman—Sketch of General James Allen, first Lawyer of Greensburg—Sketch of his Life and Family—Incidents in the Life of himself and Brothers, John, Robert, and David—David Kills an Indian—Early Military Services—Clerk of both the Courts in the County—Military Service in the War of 1812—In the Legislature of Kentucky—Governor Shelby's Confidence in him—General Adair's Opinion of him—His Death, &c.—John Emerson, Sketch of—Alexander McGinty—Isham Talbot—James Nourse—Ninian Edwards—John Rowan—Felix Grundy—Judge Allen M. Wakefield—Robert Coleman—Samuel Work—George Semple—Samuel Brents—Ezekiel Allen—Robert Wickliffe, Sketch of—Judge John Bridges—Judge Henry P. Broadnax—Francis Emerson—Benjamin Hutcheson—W. W. Irvine—General John E. King—Richard A. Buckner—Nathan Haggard—David Walker—Wm. Owens—John A. Coke—Thomas M. Emerson—Wm. J. Adair—Wm. T. Willis—Wm. B. Booker—Benjamin G. Burks—Thomas Waller Lisle—Christopher Tompkins—Jesse Craddock—George Washington Towles—James T. Goalder—John Pope—Benjamin Hardin—General Samuel A. Spencer.

Although much of the History of Kentucky will be embraced in this chapter, yet it will relate more particularly to Green County than to any other portion of the State. We will speak of its earliest settlers, so far as information can be obtained; of the earliest lawyers of the Greensburg bar, who have passed away; of the doctors, merchants, mechanics, etc., and also of the leading farmers of the county as far as anything can be learned of their history, together with such matters as will be most interesting to their descendants who still survive. I would gladly embrace in this history a particular account of each county in the State, but I cannot as readily obtain the desired information in regard to them: besides, the relation would occupy more space than the design of this work would justify, and would make it so voluminous as to put it out of the power of persons in ordinary circumstances to procure a copy. With the history of Green County the writer is more familiar than, perhaps, any other man now living. His father and uncles were among the earliest settlers of the county, and have related to him in his youth numerous incidents of early history, which he has cherished in his memory and never forgotten; many of them worthy in importance to be transmitted to posterity, and well calculated to afford a pleasant repast to the rising generation.

Green County was established by the first Legislature which met after the formation of the first Constitution of Kentucky, in 1792, and was the thirteenth county in the State. From this county eight counties and parts of counties have been formed, which reduces her area at this date to less than almost any other county in the State. The last county formed from Green was Taylor County, and under the last apportionment Green and Taylor together are only entitled to one representative in the Legislature. The first representative of Green in the Legislature of Kentucky was Richard Thurman, of whose history I know but little. He emigrated from Virginia at a very early period, and settled about two miles from Glover's Station, where Greensburg was afterward located. He was an honest man, of good native sense, of a popular turn of character, but very illiterate. I have heard persons who were acquainted with him say that he could not even write his name. Many men who rendered essential service to the country in its first settlement were illiterate, but they were honest men, of good judgment and sound discretion. Of this character were such men as Boone, Kenton, Harrod, Whitley, and many others.

I shall commence this part of my history with a sketch of the lives of the attorneys who practiced at the Greensburg bar. To perform this labor faithfully will involve some delicacy, but my ultimate aim and wish is, that I may be impartial. The history commences ten years before I was born; of course, I must draw to some extent on tradition, and such other sources as may furnish the desired information. I shall speak particularly only of those whose names and actions have made a history for themselves.

The first lawyer, so far as we know to the contrary, that ever located in Greensburg was James Allen, an uncle of the writer. He was born in April, 1770, in Albemarle County, Virginia, four miles from Charlottesville, and about the same distance from the residence of the sage of Monticello. His grand-parents were from the county of Armah, in Ireland: both Allens, and remotely related. His father was a blacksmith, and manufacturer of cutlery by trade, and a captain in the War of the Revolution, having risen from a private soldier to the command of an independent corps, and was in many skirmishes and a number of battles. When the war was over he turned his eyes to Kentucky as his future residence. He sold his lands in Virginia, and received in payment for it Continental money, and starting on his way, arrived in what was then Augusta, afterward Rockbridge County, where he was taken sick and died, leaving a widow, (who now lies buried at Greensburg), and six children, who remained there some four years or more before they proceeded to Kentucky. Having purchased a small farm near New Providence Academy, then under the care of the Rev. John Brown, father of John, James, Samuel, and Preston Brown, all of whom afterward became distinguished in Kentucky, James Allen, being designed for the bar, was placed at the school above mentioned, and was a class-mate of Samuel, and fellow-student of James Brown. He studied Latin and Greek in this school, and became proficient, and often in his advanced years read his Testament in the original Greek. After some three or four years in this Academy, he went to an institution near Staunton, under the presidency of a learned Scotchman by the name of James Scott, where he studied the sciences and reviewed the classics. In 1787, the family, then consisting of the mother, four sons, and a daughter, viz: John, Robert, James, David, and Mary, and a few slaves, removed to Kentucky, and settled near what is now Hustonville, in Lincoln County. All the boys understood well the use of the rifle, and at once united themselves with the gallant defenders of the exposed frontiers, and became distinguished for great activity and dauntless courage.

An incident occurred in connection with David Allen, the father of the writer, then a boy fourteen or fifteen years old, and the youngest of the four brothers, worthy of record in this place. The first twelve months of the residence of the young Allens in Kentucky was occupied in guarding the defenseless families of the surrounding country, pursuing parties of hostile savages, and often encountering them in perilous conflicts, recovering horses and other property of which the inhabitants had been robbed. The incident alluded to is this: A party, consisting of about twenty Indians, had come into the settlement secretly, and stolen several horses. When morning came, the horses were missing, and signs clearly indicated who the depredators were. Accordingly, on short notice, a band of about seventeen dauntless and brave fellows were prepared for pursuit. David and two of the older brothers were among the number. About ten o'clock in the morning they started from Carpenter's Station, in Lincoln County, and late in the evening, having journeyed about fifteen miles, near the stream called the Rolling Fork they overtook the marauders, between whom and the whites a conflict was commenced. The Indians were soon dispersed, flying in different directions. David, by some means, had become separated from the rest of his companions, and looking round to discover how or in what manner he could most safely direct his footsteps, he beheld with amazement a large Indian, about thirty paces distant, endeavoring to creep silently upon him. As instantaneous as thought David wheeled, and ran at the top of his speed in an opposite direction. The Indian pursued, evidently with the design of taking him captive; for, having his gun in hand, he might have shot at any instant. David had not proceeded very far, when suddenly, and unexpectedly, he came to a deep ravine or gully. It was very wide, insomuch that he felt persuaded that he would not have leaped its bounds under any ordinary circumstances. His situation was perilous; the Indian was close behind him; the gully before him; he knew he must submit to be the captive of a savage and unrelenting foe, or save his own life by leaping the gully; so with a desperate effort, and determination of purpose, he sprang as for his life, and barely reached the opposite bank, near which was a large tree, to which he instantly sprang for protection. Having then time to turn round, he raised his gun to shoot his pursuer, who at this instant had reached the gully also, but terrified at the prospect of death from the youthful Allen's rifle then leveled at him, or else lacking confidence in his ability to leap the gully, he suddenly wheeled and ran in an opposite direction. Young Allen fired upon him, and was soon convinced that the ball had taken effect, as he saw the Indian stagger and place his hand to his side. Young Allen was then in turn the pursuer, and could trace him by the blood from the wound he had inflicted by the shot, and finally came upon him, lying dead upon the ground, some two or three miles from the place at which he was shot. He found, upon examination, that he had shot him in the side, a little above the hip, the bullet-hole being plugged with bark chewed by the Indian. Night had now overtaken young Allen, and he had proceeded but a short distance in the direction homeward, when he thought it most prudent to provide for himself such repose as was possible under the circumstances. Being much wearied with the fatigues of the day, he soon found rest in a bed of leaves which he had scraped together against a large log. Having slept soundly during the night, he felt by morning greatly refreshed, although he had eaten nothing since the previous morning. He reached the station about three o'clock that evening, where he found all his companions, the others having returned in safety a few hours previously, greatly apprehending that David had been killed.

After safety in some measure had been obtained on our borders, James Allen commenced the study of law. He read about two years with Judges Sebastian and Ormsby, and in 1790 obtained license to practice from the Judges of the Superior Court for the District of Kentucky, and came to the bar before he was twenty-one years old. He practiced some two years in the counties of Lincoln, Washington, and Madison, in successful competition with Greenup, Todd, McDowell, Ormsby, Overton, McClung, and other able counselors. When the State of Kentucky was formed, and the county of Green

HISTORY OF KENTUCKY. 343

was established, he was appointed clerk of both the County and Quarter Sessions courts, and thereupon settled himself permanently in Green. The Indians being occasionally troublesome in this section of the State south of Green River, soon after his arrival in Green he raised a company of mounted riflemen, to be in constant readiness to repel savage aggressions. This organization continued until the enemy were entirely expelled from our borders. When the Quarter Session Courts were abolished, and the Circuit Court system established, Mr. Allen was appointed clerk of the latter court. On receiving the appointment as clerk, he withdrew from the practice of the law, and devoted himself to the duties of his offices and other affairs in which he was engaged at that time.

Mr. Allen early imbibed a taste for military science. In 1802 he was commander of the Sixteenth Regiment Kentucky Militia, and in a few years attained the rank of brigadier general. In 1811, the war with Great Britain was loudly threatened, and General Allen was appointed to the command of the Tenth Brigade. He ordered brigade drills, and attended and instructed in person the officers until he advanced them to a perfection seldom witnessed in the militia. Encamping for days together in the open fields, they were also instructed in the duties of the camp, and every other branch of actual service. On war being declared, General Allen answered the first summons of his country. Immediately on the proclamation of Governor Shelby, General Allen raised a company of mounted riflemen for a campaign against the western Indians, and in a few days was at Vincennes, the place of rendezvous. His younger brother, David, was lieutenant of the company. General Hopkins had been appointed to the command of the army, and upon their arrival at Vincennes he ordered them to be formed into battalions and regiments, and that the soldiers should proceed to the election of their colonels and majors. General Allen was elected colonel of his regiment by unanimous voice, and David Allen captain of the company from which James had been promoted. General Allen was stationed with his command in the van of the army, and was subject only to the orders of the Commander-in-chief. He marched on the campaign in front, and on two occasions acted, by general concurrence, as General-in-chief. There was scarcely a soldier in the whole army who would not have preferred General Allen as the Commander-in-chief, and steps were being taken by some of the officers to bring about that result; but General Allen, upon being informed of the movement, repelled it at once, and suppressed and put at rest every attempt which seemed likely to produce insubordination of any kind in the army. General Hopkins was a worthy and meritorious officer and citizen, but was "not born to command." But little, if any good, was effected by that campaign.

Shortly after his return from that campaign, General Allen laid before Governor Shelby a plan, devised by himself—a corps of Kentucky volunteers, to be armed, equipped, and provided in a manner admirably suited to the frontier service —for an expedition against the Illinois Indians, and the protection of that suffering border. It was so highly approved of by the Governor, that he urged its adoption, and the appointment of General Allen to the command. The design was superseded, however, by the plan of invading Upper Canada, to cut off the communication of the British, and to stop the supply of arms and ammunition to the latter. The General Assembly of Kentucky, after the disaster to the Northwestern Army and the massacre of Kentuckians at Raisin, requested Governor Shelby to take the field himself, to which he consented, and at once appealed to General Allen to join with him, and exhorted him to exert his influence to bring as many volunteers into the field as he could to support him in the enterprise. Governor Shelby's letter to General Allen, of the 31st of July, 1813, we omit on account of its length. He concludes by saying: "I will write you again by express soon, or by next mail, and write this hasty scrawl to apprise you of my wishes and expectations." This letter was enough for General Allen; he did not wait for either "the express or next mail." He at once responded to the Governor that he would meet him at the rendezvous on the day to be appointed, and raised the flag, and commenced beating up for volunteers. In a short time two full companies were raised in the county of Green, commanded by Captains Warner Elmore and Thomas S. T. Moss. With these he met Governor Shelby at Newport, on the 31st of August, 1813, according to appointment, and was greeted with joy by the old Governor, who immediately handed him a commission of brigadier general. The brigade of General Allen was constituted of two regiments, formed of the companies from the counties of Lincoln, Garrard, Mercer, Madison, and Shelby. In this arrangement, as well as throughout the service, Governor Shelby manifested for General Allen the most unbounded confidence. The army under the command of the Governor arrived at Lake Erie just as Commodore Perry was in the act of landing the British prisoners he had taken in the great victory achieved on the lake, an account of which I have elsewhere given; also an account of the leading incidents of the battle of the Thames, which occurred the 5th of October, 1813, in which General Allen bore a conspicuous part. The result of the battle was glorious from the fact that it gave security to the North for the remainder of the war.

No officer in the army enjoyed in a higher degree the confidence of his superior officers than General Allen. General Adair, who never spoke flattery of any man, has frequently said, "he had no superior of his rank in the army." The officers and men under his command were sincerely attached to him, and not more so than he was to them, which he manifested by his willingness on all occasions to share with them every privation and his last morsel.

The war having ended in the victory of New Orleans, General Allen resigned all public office, determined to spend the remainder of his days in retirement and domestic and social enjoyment. Thus retired, he was induced to accept the presidency of the Independent Bank at Greensburg, one of the forty chartered by the Legislature; but finding it could not be made useful and safe to the public, he hastened to wind up its concerns, which was soon effected without the loss of a dollar by its bills, whilst a loss of thousands was sustained in many other of similar institutions chartered at the same time. Soon after this he was called by the suffrages of the people to a seat in the Senate of Kentucky, where he discharged his duties with such satisfaction to his constituents, that, at the end of four years, he was re-elected for a second term by a greatly increased majority, and would have been elected for a third term had he not positively refused. He consented, however, to serve them one year in the representative branch, was accordingly elected, and this ended his career in the political arena. At the close of his last term in the Senate, his political friends warmly urged him to consent to his nomination for Governor of the State; but, with that modesty so characteristic of him, he persistently refused to permit his friends to urge his claims for that high and responsible station.

There were few men in Kentucky better qualified for public office than General Allen. Endowed by nature with a strong mind, possessing the advantages of an early education, and the experience of seeing, as it were, the foundations of the government laid, and having witnessed the growth of our wilderness into a flourishing and great State, and been engaged extensively in her commerce, and exercised various public offices and employments, he had embodied a stock of information and experience which falls to the lot of but few men. The latter years of his life were devoted to farming, in which occupation he was both industrious and skillful. He was just, generous, and a peace-maker among others, and was deservedly esteemed by his neighbors. He had the advantage of an excellent person, being six feet, two inches high—erect, lean, and well-formed; strong features, steady eyes, high forehead, of commanding appearance, good constitution, and cheerfulness of temper. Free and social in his intercourse with society, he exhibited an openness of manner which evinced an honesty of purpose and a kindness of heart.

On the 24th of November, 1836, General Allen went to Lebanon on some business, and returning home the next day by a by-path to his residence near town, when within half a mile of home he fell from his horse and was killed, in the sixty-seventh year of his age. He was soon afterward found, lying upon his side, with knees drawn up, his whip clenched in his right hand, hat barely removed from his head, and a slight scratch on his face. He was lying under a beach tree, the limbs of which hung low over the path. It was supposed that he had become unsettled in his saddle while passing under the limbs of the tree, and that the fall had killed him instantly, for there were no apparent indications of his having moved or struggled after the fall. He was the last survivor of the four brothers who came to Green County shortly after its formation—John, the eldest, having died in 1808; Robert in 1809; and David, the youngest, and father of the writer, on the 14th of November, 1817, all having died at the age of about forty-three years, except General Allen.

John Emerson was admitted to the bar at the August Court, 1794. He must have been about forty years old at that time. He was one of the earliest settlers of the town, being there the year before Greensburg was laid off and established as the county-seat. He was raised to some mechanical art, but never followed it in Kentucky. He studied law after he came to Greensburg. He emigrated from Pennsylvania in company with his brother-in-law, John Johnson, who was one of the first justices of the peace for Green County. Mr. Emerson was a man of good natural sense, and possessed of considerable wit. His education was quite limited, writing a poor hand, and reading badly. He was voluble, however, as a speaker, and spoke with intense animation and rapidity—never appeared at a loss for words to express his ideas. When he became greatly enlisted in a cause, or rather under the excitement of his feelings while speaking, his face would redden and his mouth froth, and his gesticulations become vehement. He was an advocate rather than a special pleader; for the latter he, for the most part, relied upon those who were engaged on the same side of the cause with him. He was a man of great goodness of heart and benevolence of feeling. He was a great friend of the poor, and would do anything in his power to alleviate their distress or to calm their afflictions. He abominated misers, usurers, hard masters, and cruelty in any form. As a lawyer, he never prosecuted in any case. When employed, it was always for the defense. If the criminal was too poor to give a fee, he was certain to volunteer in his behalf. He had a great desire for office, especially a seat in the Legislature. He was a standing candidate for the Legislature for a period of nearly thirty years, except on one occasion when a candidate for Governor. In that period he was elected to the House of Representatives five or six times; but never two years in succession. One year he would get but few votes; another year his majority would be overwhelming. For the office of Governor he obtained very few votes. He was one of the earliest justices of the county, and held the place until by seniority he became entitled to the sheriffalty of the county under the Constitution, but for some reason was not permitted to qualify. In 1795 Mr. Emerson was dismissed from the bar of the Quarter-Session Court, and the year following from the bar of the County Court, but for what cause cannot be ascertained from the record. At the May Court, 1801, however, the records show that he was readmitted, and that he continued to practice until his removal from Greensburg. About the year 1826, being quite old, he removed to Burksville, Cumberland County, where nearly all his children then resided. At this place, a few years afterward, he died of cancer.

He served several years in the Army of the Revolution, and was a true patriot and good soldier, having rose to the rank of lieutenant in the company to which he belonged. In the War of 1812 he joined the company of Captain David Allen, though then between fifty and sixty years of age, and was a subordinate officer in that company in the army of General Hopkins; but he returned home before the campaign was ended on account of failure of health by exposure.

Alexander McGinty was admitted and sworn as an attorney of the Greensburg bar at the August Court, 1794, but that is all that I can say of him. The records of the Green Quarter Session Court show nothing else in respect to him, and no man living in the county at this day ever knew or heard of him.

Isham Talbot was also admitted to the Greensburg bar at the August Court, 1794, being then just twenty-one years of age. He was born in the county of Bedford, State of Virginia, in 1773. His father emigrated to Kentucky while Isham was quite a youth, and settled near Harrodsburg, Kentucky, in Mercer County. Young Talbot became a good scholar, having been sent to the best schools in Harrodsburg; but, beside this, he acquired, without the aid of teachers, a respectable knowledge of the ancient and some of the modern languages. On arriving at manhood he studied law with the distinguished Colonel George Nicholas, and commenced the practice of his profession in the town of Versailles, Woodford County. Soon afterward he removed to Frankfort, and entered the list with the most distinguished lawyers of Kentucky who adorned the bar at that day, and was generally regarded as one of the brightest in the galaxy of illustrious names. In 1812 Mr. Talbot was elected to the Senate of Kentucky from Franklin County, and continued in that office until his election to the United States Senate, in 1815, to fill the vacancy occasioned by the resignation of Hon. Jesse Bledsoe. In 1820 he was re-elected to the Senate, and served in that body until the 4th of March, 1825. Mr. Talbot was a true patriot, and one of the most eloquent of statesmen. He died at his residence (Melrose), near Frankfort, on the 27th of September, 1837.

James Nourse was also admitted a member of the Greensburg bar at the August Court, 1794. He is spoken of by those who knew him as a good lawyer, an excellent surveyor, and highly esteemed by a large circle of acquaintances. He resided in Bardstown, and died by his own hand, deeply regretted by all who knew him, leaving a family of the highest respectability and numerous friends to mourn his loss.

Ninian Edwards was admitted to the bar of Greensburg at the March Court, 1795. He was born in Montgomery County, Maryland, March, 1775. He graduated at Dickinson College, and was the intimate friend of William Wirt. He studied both medicine and law, but devoted himself to the practice of law exclusively, and with eminent success. After his removal to Kentucky he was twice elected to the Legislature, was afterward appointed a circuit clerk, then Judge of the General Court of Kentucky, then of the Circuit Court, then of the Court of Appeals, and finally Chief Justice of the State, and all before reaching the thirty-second year of his age.

In 1809 President Madison appointed him Governor of Illinois Territory, to which office he was re-appointed three times. Before Congress had adopted any measures on the subject of volunteer rangers, he organized companies, supplied them with arms, built stockade forts, and established a line of posts from the mouth of the Missouri to the Wabash River, and, during the Indian wars on the frontiers, was most devoted to his country's service. In 1816 he was appointed a Commissioner to treat with the Indian tribes. When Illinois became a State he was elected a Senator in Congress, serving from 1818 to 1824, when he was appointed Minister to Mexico, but declined the office. In 1826 he was elected Governor of the State of Illinois, which office he filled until **1831**. He died of cholera, July 20th, **1833**.

John Rowan was admitted an attorney of the Green Quarter Session Court at the May term, 1795. He was an able jurist and statesman, and one of the most distinguished men in the Western country. He was born in Pennsylvania, in 1773. His father, William Rowan, removed to Kentucky in 1783, and settled in Louisville, then a small village. In 1784 he, with five other families, made a settlement at the Long Falls of Green River, then about one hundred miles from any white settlement. At the age of seventeen John entered a classical school at Bardstown, conducted by the distinguished teacher, Dr. James Priestley. In this school was educated, about the same time, many of those men who figured so conspicuously in the history of Kentucky as jurists, politicians, and divines. Among them were Grundy, Davies, Pope, Allen, Cameron, etc. Thirty years afterward the writer was a fellow-student with two of John Rowan's sons and a son of Felix Grundy, under the same teacher. The school was on the Cumberland River, between the Hermitage and Nashville, four miles from the former, and eight from the latter. Upon leaving this school Mr. Rowan went to Lexington, where he commenced the study of law, and was admitted to the bar in 1795. He soon attained a high rank in his profession. Of those eminent for talent, learning, and eloquence, he was generally regarded as among the foremost, especially as an advocate in criminal cases. He was a member of the Convention which formed the Constitution of Kentucky of 1799. He was Secretary of State in 1804, a member of Congress from 1807 to 1809, and, was for many years, at intervals, a member of the Legislature of Kentucky. He was Judge of the Court of Appeals in 1819, and was a Senator in Congress from 1825 to 1831. In 1823 he was appointed in connection with Henry Clay a Commissioner to defend what were called the occupying claimant laws of the State before the Supreme Court of the United States. The petition drawn by him is regarded as the ablest vindication of those laws ever published. Several speeches of great celebrity, delivered by Judge Rowan both in Congress and the State Legislature, have been published. The writer, when a boy, often heard him at the bar with extreme delight. His last public position was that of Commissioner for carrying out a treaty with Mexico. He died in Louisville, Kentucky, July 13th, at the age of seventy.

Felix Grundy was admitted an attorney of the Green Quarter Session Court at the August term, 1795. He was not less distinguished as a jurist and statesman than John Rowan, and was some three years his senior. He was born in Berkeley County, Va., September 11th, 1770 (one account says 1777, which may be correct). If so, he commenced his career as a public man at the age of twenty-two, and as a member of the Convention for revising the Constitution of Kentucky in 1799. He was afterward, for six or seven years, a member of the Legislature of Kentucky. In 1806 he was appointed one of the judges of the Supreme Court of Kentucky; and was Chief Justice soon afterward. When the Circuit Court system went into operation in Kentucky, Mr. Grundy was appointed the first Commonwealth Attorney for the district of which Green formed a part. In 1807 or 1808 he removed to Nashville, Tennessee, and became very eminent as a lawyer. From 1811 to 1814 he was a representative in Congress from Tennessee, and for several years after was a member of the Legislature of that State. From 1829 to 1838 he was United States Senator, and in the latter year was appointed by President Van Buren Attorney-General of the United States. In 1840 he resigned this position, and was again elected Senator. He died at Nashville, Tenn., December 19th, 1840. Mr. Grundy was married in Green County, Kentucky, while he resided at Springfield, Washington County, to a Miss Rodgers. He received his education at Bardstown Academy, principally under the instruction of Dr. James Priestley. A year or so previous to his death, Mr. Grundy, on his way to Washington, spent a day in Greensburg, in the course of which he related many scenes of early times which occurred at this place, with the relation of which I was greatly delighted as well as highly edified.

Allen M. Wakefield was admitted to the bar at Greensburg, November 10th, 1795. Mr. Wakefield was the first county attorney appointed for the county of Green, which office he held for several years at a salary of £18 ($90) per annum. When the Circuit Court system was instituted and organized instead of the Quarter Session Courts, Mr. Wakefield was appointed the first judge of the circuit of which Green County formed a part. He held this office until his death, which occurred in 1808 or 1809, and he lies buried in the cemetery at Greensburg, without a stone or any other mark to distinguish his grave. He was a thorough business man, and regarded as a profound lawyer for the times. There were more students of law under his instructions than perhaps any other lawyer in this region of the country. His wife was a Miss Thurman, of that part of Green County which in 1798 was cut off into Cumberland, and of wealthy and influential family. I suppose he was sometimes given to profanity. I come to this conclusion from the fact, that at August Court, 1800, he was indicted for profane swearing. No man stood higher in the community at that day than Allen M. Wakefield. He was about thirty-five years of age when he died.

Robert Coleman was admitted an attorney at the Greensburg bar at the May Court, 1797; Samuel Work, at October Court, 1798; and George Semple, at August Court, 1799. I have no other information in regard to these names, and this I obtain from the records of the court.

Samuel Brents was sworn and admitted an attorney of the bar at Greensburg at the November Court, 1798. He was born in North Carolina, about the year 1778, and was but a youth when his father emigrated to Kentucky and settled in Green County. He had two brothers older than himself, Peter and Solomon, and one younger, whose name was Joshua. He had several sisters, some older and others younger than himself. His father and mother both lived to a remarkable age, and died at his house, aged, respectively, near one hundred years. Joshua died about ten years since, aged about eighty-four years.

Mr. Brents was one of the profoundest lawyers of his day. He was especially proficient as a land lawyer, and accumulated a great amount of property by his profession, especially of lands situated in different parts of the State. His practice of the profession was extensive and lucrative ; and besides being an adept in special pleading, prepared his cases better than any lawyer I ever knew. He was also a good surveyor, and in early life did a considerable business in that way. He was indefatigable in his professional labors, and equally so as a statesman. He was elected to the House of Representatives of Kentucky the first time in 1803, and frequently at intervals afterward. Before he came to the bar he was a deputy clerk in the offices of General Allen, who was clerk of both courts, and for a year or two a deputy sheriff. He was a justice of the peace nearly all his public life, and was of great advantage to the county in that respect, as also to the other justices who were less informed. He was good at figures, wrote a beautiful hand, and though he wrote with great rapidity, yet his writing was well-punctuated and easily read. He was for many years a trustee of the town, a trustee of the Academy of Greensburg, and generally acted as the clerk of those boards. He was addicted to no habits of dissipation, and of a happy and social disposition. He was possessed of great benevolence of feeling, was liberal in every public enterprise, and had a heart to feel for the woes of others.

He had great equanimity of temper, not easily aroused by passion, but would resent an insult quickly. I never heard of his having but one fight in his life, and that was with one between whom and himself the most kindly relations had ever existed. It occurred with Judge Buckner, another able jurist and statesman. Court was in session at Greensburg, Judge Tompkins presiding. The evidence had been heard in the case, and Mr. Brents was addressing the jury, when some remarks he made gave offense to Buckner. Words of crimination and recrimination were banded, when the Judge remarked that such conduct would not be permitted in the presence of the court, and that they must go out of doors to settle their difficulties. Brents, in the midst of his speech, left the court-house, and Buckner as quickly followed, when a real fisti-cuff fight took place in the court-yard, which continued until they were separated by mutual friends. Brents was made somewhat bloody by the bleeding of his nose; but, having washed, he returned to the bar and resumed his speech with as much coolness and deliberation as if nothing had happened, addressing the jury with "Gentlemen of the jury, as I was about to remark," etc. At this point the whole house were convulsed with laughter, in which even the combatants joined as heartily as others. The parties were as friendly ever afterward as they had been before.

Mr. Brents was always interesting, jovial, and witty in conversation with his intimate friends or in the social circle; besides, he was something of a soliloquist. On a certain occasion the Hon. Thomas W. Lisle and myself were traveling to the country with him, when he, being a few paces in advance of us, commenced talking audibly to himself. Mr. Lisle enquired:

"Mr. Brents, why do you talk to yourself so much?"
"Oh," said he, "because I like to talk to a man of sense."

Although Mr. Brents was a man of considerable property, yet he often felt the need of ready money. He was so liberal and accommodating in his disposition, that he never refused when asked to go security for a friend; and the consequence was, that he often had large security debts to pay, and was unable frequently to meet his own pressing demands. On one occasion, when traveling to the Cumberland Court, he stopped on the way at the house of an old friend, to whom he had owed one or two hundred dollars for a long time. Before he left, his friend dunned him for the debt, but Brents did not have the means with him to pay, and so stated.

"Well," says the old man, "Mr. Brents, you have owed me this debt a good while; but if you will pay me the interest now, I can afford to trust you longer for the principal."

"Ah," says Brents, "Mr. Freeman, it is not my principle to pay the interest, nor is it my interest to pay the principal; but if you will take cash notes on safe men, I will pay you all now."

"Well," says Freeman, "I will do it."

Brents accordingly paid over the cash notes to an amount even more than was due, and started on to Cumberland. Having realized some cash fees at court, on his return he called on Mr. Freeman again, but had scarcely alighted from his horse when Mr. Freeman, addressing him, said:

"Mr. Brents, every one of those notes you let me have are on men in the penitentiary."

"I know that," said Brents; "you said you would take notes on safe men, and if men in the penitentiary are not safe, I don't know who are."

Having amused himself sufficiently at the old man's expense, he paid him the debt, and took back the notes, to the old man's great delight.

Mr. Brents, as I have before stated, was frequently elected a member of the Legislature; in fact, never was defeated in his election for that office when a candidate. Old Squire Skaggs, of Brush Creek, was always his friend when a candidate, and could control more votes at an election than any other man in the county. On one occasion, when Brents was a candidate, the old man entertained great fears of his success on account of some vote Brents was said to have given in the Legislature at a previous session, which was offensive to a good many of the voters of his neighborhood, and the old man was very anxious that Brents should clear up the report, or in some way dispel the prejudice which had been engendered in the neighborhood. On the Sunday before the election the Baptists had appointed a great meeting, to be held at the house of old man Skaggs, on which occasion the whole neighborhood turned out. Brents was also in attendance. After the sermon was over, the male portion of the congregation, and some of the women too, collected around Brents in the yard, and he commenced talking to them, at first in rather a conversational way, but gradually raising his voice so as to be heard by all the crowd, speaking generally in regard to his action on those subjects most likely to be pleasing to the people whom he addressed, but never once alluding to the subject of which the old man and his neighbors complained. When about to retire, the old man remarked:

"Mr. Brents, there is one report concerning you about which you have said nothing, and which we would like to have you explain." Brents, feeling his guilt, and conscious of his inability to clear it up satisfactorily, at once gave it a turn which satisfied the people, and to which the old man made no further objection:

"Oh yes," says Mr. Brents, "I had like to have forgotten it. It is reported that I am too great a friend to the poor people; that I show my partialities for them in preference to the rich and well-born. I acknowledge my guilt, fellow-citizens; if I am to be beaten in this race upon this ground, why be it so; I will not give up my predilections on this subject to be elected. It is true that I have ever been the friend of the poor man. When they have been charged with crimes of which I believed them not guilty, I have ever volunteered in their behalf. I voted for the occupying claimant law, and all laws which enabled the poor man to pay for his land in the easiest way, and I have no reflections on myself for doing so. I know I have many times committed unintentional errors, but in this I do not think I have erred; if you think otherwise, gentlemen, forgive me; for if it be an error, it is of my head, and not of my heart." So saying, he retired, and was elected by an increased majority over any former vote.

To relate all the anecdotes or occurrences of this nature in regard to Mr. Brents with which I am familiar would occupy more space than the design of this work will allow or I would gladly do so. He was my preceptor in the law, my friend and social companion. I was devoted to him as a man, and ever enjoyed myself in his society. Mr. Brents made no pretensions to religion, but he respected it highly, and was a moral man. His wife was a most devoted and exemplary Christian, and a member of the Methodist Church. His house was the home of the preacher of any denomination, and the temple for worship before the erection of churches in Greensburg. Mr. Brents died of cholera on the 14th of June, 1833, in nine hours from his attack.

Ezekiel Allen was admitted to the bar at Greensburg, October 11th, 1796; Samuel Work at the October Court, 1798, and George Semple at the August Court, 1799. We have no other account of either of the three named above except what this record shows. Semple, we believe, was a son of Dr. James Semple, of Virginia, who resided near Greensburg for a few years, but afterward moved to Cumberland County, near where the town of Albany, Clinton County, now stands, where he continued to reside until his death. His widow afterward became the wife of Duff Green, Sr., who was the father of General Duff Green. Dr. Semple was the brother of the distinguished Robert Semple of Virginia, a Baptist preacher and a cotemporary of Richard Broadus and Alexander Campbell.

Robert Wickliffe settled in Greensburg, Green County, in 1799, and was admitted a member of the bar at that place the 16th of April, 1799. He continued to reside at this place for some four or five years, but finally settled at Lexington, where he lived the remainder of his life. He erected a good log building in the town, in which he lived and kept house. His sisters were occasionally with him to superintend his house affairs, for he was not then married. He was the owner at that time of but little property, but became exceedingly wealthy in after years, and at his death he was perhaps the wealthiest man in the State. Mr. Wickliffe acted as one of the trustees of the town during most of the time he resided at Greensburg, and for a year or two was the County Attorney for Green. After he removed to Lexington he attained great distinction, not only as a lawyer, but as a statesman also. He was regarded as one of the ablest land lawyers of the State, was frequently a member of the Legislature, and for almost half a century bore an active and conspicuous part in all the leading questions which agitated the State in his day—especially during the pendency of the *Relief* and *Anti-relief*, *Old* and *New Court* questions. He discharged creditably and honorably other important public trusts besides legislation. He died at Lexington some years since, at about the age of eighty-four years. The father of Mr. Wickliffe removed from Virginia to Kentucky in 1784, at a time when our forests were still exposed to the horrors of savage warfare. His mother was a sister of Col. John Hardin, so celebrated in Kentucky for his heroism and tragical fate. Robert was the oldest of his sons. At the age of twenty-one he commenced the study of the law under the celebrated George Nicholas, and by his talents and industry made himself one of the most eminent of his profession.

John Bridges was sworn and admitted an attorney at the bar of Greensburg at the March Court, 1798. I have learned but little of his history worthy of record. He was somewhat unsteady in his younger days, but became thoroughly reformed. He was a gentleman of high refinement, though somewhat eccentric—a profound lawyer, and an able judge. He was a judge of the Circuit Court longer, perhaps, than any other man in the State. His wife was the daughter of Governor Adair, a most estimable lady. He raised a large and highly respected family, and died a few years since, at a good old age, deeply regretted by all who knew him.

Henry P. Broadnax was also admitted to the Greensburg bar at the March Court, 1798. He was judge of a circuit court for a great number of years in the southwestern portion of Kentucky, and attained great celebrity as such. He died at a good old age, and was never married. He was over eighty years old when he died.

Francis Emerson was admitted to the bar at Greensburg, May 22d, 1801. He was the eldest of seven sons. Of his father, John Emerson, we have already spoken. Francis Emerson was a promising young man, and of fair talents. When about twenty-one years of age he married a Miss Thurman, and was the brother-in-law of Judge Allen M. Wakefield. He settled in Burksville, Cumberland County, but died three or four years afterward, leaving two children, and a good estate for their inheritance. His widow afterward married his brother, Thomas M. Emerson, a lawyer also, but some six or eight years his junior.

Benjamin Hutcheson was admitted to the Greensburg bar the 22d of June, 1802, when about twenty-one or twenty-two years of age. He had studied law under Judge Wakefield, and by close application to books had impaired his health. He was a good scholar for his opportunities. He taught school a year or two, and was highly appreciated as a teacher by his patrons; but his health finally gave way, and he died February, 1807.

William W. Irvin was admitted to the Greensburg bar the 15th of March, 1802; Stephen Chenault and George C. C. Harbison, on the 23d of May, 1803. I know nothing concerning the history of these gentlemen, nor have I ever seen their names outside of this record.

John E. King was admitted to the bar of Greensburg at the August Court, 1803. He settled in Greensburg about the year 1796 or 1797, and kept a tavern. In 1798 the county of Cumberland was formed from Green, and Burksville established as the county-seat, when Mr. King removed to near that place, and upon the organization of the county received the appointment of clerk of both the county and circuit courts. I do not think he made any pretentions to the law until after this period. He was a Virginian by birth, and emigrated to Kentucky at an early period. He was a military genius, and an excellent tactician. He rose to be a brigadier-general in the militia; and when the War of 1812 broke out, General King, though considerably advanced in years at that time, assisted greatly in raising the flag for his country. He was a brigadier-general in the army of Shelby, and did his duty at the battle of the Thames, the 5th of October, 1813. In that battle he bore a conspicuous part, and, with the other officers engaged in the battle, received from Governor Shelby his share of the praise At the ninth presidential election (1821), General King was elected one of the electors for Kentucky, and cast his vote, as did the other electors, for James Monroe as President and Daniel D. Tompkins as Vice President. General King was a sensible man and true patriot, a polite gentleman, a good neighbor, a devoted friend, and of great benevolence of heart. He died a good many years since, at a good old age, greatly lamented by all who knew him.

Richard A. Buckner was admitted to the Greensburg bar at the August Court, 1804, at twenty-one years of age. He was born in Fauquier County, Virginia, and received there a liberal education, being an excellent Latin and scientific scholar. He came with his father from Virginia about the year 1803, and settled in Green County. I think he studied law in Virginia; but he did not obtain his license to practice until after his arrival in Kentucky. He was a timid, retiring young man, and for several years after his arrival neither sought or obtained an extensive practice. About 1810 or 1811 he taught school for a year at Greensburg, and about that time removed from the country to town. His school being ended, he turned his attention with greater assiduity to the law, and soon obtained an extensive and lucrative practice. He was Commonwealth's attorney for some years, and county attorney at the same time for Green County. He was prosecuting attorney in the trial of Alexander Hamilton, at Glasgow, for the murder of Dr. Sanderson, in 1818, and succeeded in convicting him upon circumstantial testimony alone. The distinguished John Rowan appeared for the defence, and it was the opinion of many who witnessed the trial, that Buckner on that occasion greatly eclipsed his noble and valiant adversary in the argument. There was more intense desire and excitement manifested in that trial than any other similar case I ever heard of. From that date the fame of Mr. Buckner began to grow and spread with unparalleled rapidity, and his powers as a prosecuting attorney were ever afterward dreaded by the friends of the accused. Finding that his services for the defence in all criminal cases would be in demand, and would yield greater profit in his profession, he resigned his office as Commonwealth's attorney, and refused ever afterward to take a fee upon the side of the prosecution. In 1822 Mr. Buckner was elected to a seat in Congress, and was re-elected in 1824, and again in 1826, serving in that body six years. He was one of those from Kentucky who voted for Adams in the House in preference to Jackson. A great storm was raised against him in his district on this account, and every effort was brought into requisition to defeat him at the succeeding election, but he was triumphant over all opposition. Having served this term, he retired from Congress; but was soon called to the bench of the Court of Appeals. After serving a short time in this position he resigned, and was several times elected a member of the House of Representatives of Kentucky. After this, he received the appointment of Judge of the Circuit Court, which office he filled with great ability for several years, and until his death. Judge Buckner was born in 1783, and died at his residence in Greensburg, December 8th, 1847.

Aylett Buckner, eldest son of Judge Buckner, was admitted to the bar of Greensburg about the year 1828, and twice elected to the Legislature of Kentucky, and served in Congress one term, from 1847 to 1849. He was beaten in the race for the succeeding term, on account of his free-soil proclivities, by the Hon. George Alfred Caldwell. Soon after this he went to St. Louis to live, where he remained until about the year 1864; but being in bad health returned to Kentucky and practiced law as his health might permit. He died at his brother's, Judge R. A. Buckner, Jr., in the city of Lexington, Kentucky, at about the age of sixty-three years. He was never married.

Nathan Haggard studied law with Judge Wakefield in 1804, and was admitted to the Greensburg bar, December, 1805. He soon after located in Tennessee. I corresponded with him in 1825, at which time he was doing a successful and profitable business. I have heard nothing of him since. It is presumable that he has long since died. He boarded at my father's while engaged in the study of the law, and was regarded by the family as a very worthy and excellent man.

David Walker was admitted to the bar of Greensburg, November, 1806. He was a small man, of fair abilities, and was for a long time a clerk of one of the county courts of the State. He has been dead some years.

William Owens was admitted to the bar of Greensburg at the June Court, 1809. He was born in Fauquier County, Va., on the 4th day of May, 1773. At ten years of age (1783) he came to Kentucky with his maternal uncle, the justly renowned Simon Kenton. Colonel Owens was captain of a company in Wayne's campaign, was a good soldier, and an efficient officer. Colonel Owen was poor and of humble pretensions, but had an indomitable will, and was a man of great perseverance. His early advantages of education were poor. He was emphatically a self-made man—of towering native intellect. Soon after his return from the army he formed the acquaintance of the Hon. Judge Bridges, through whose influence he was induced to engage in the study of the law. After six months close application he was enabled to obtain a license, and at once commenced the practice of his profession. He settled in Danville, and practiced in Mercer and the adjoining counties several years. In 1805 he married Miss Mary McClain, of Newcastle, Henry County, a most estimable lady. In 1807 he removed from Danville to Columbia, where he continued to reside until his death, which occurred on the 7th of November, 1847.

Colonel Owen was for many years a senator, representing Green, Adair, etc., in that department of the Legislature. He was the opponent of Judge Buckner in 1826 in one of the most exciting and strongly contested races for Congress I have ever known. He was defeated by a very small majority. For many years he acted as Commonwealth's attorney for the district in which he resided. He was a devoted Mason, took great pleasure in the order, and was what is called bright in the degrees of the Lodge and Chapter. He was a man of great benevolence of heart, and of unbounded liberality. He was ever the friend of the widow and the orphan, and the minister of Christ, of whatever name or persuasion. The poor, distressed, and friendless were never turned away empty from his door.

John A. Coke was admitted to the Greensburg bar in 1804,

and Thomas M. Emerson, another son of John Emerson, in January, 1814. Cake's name I never saw or heard of, other than in this record. In 1809 Emerson taught a small school in Greensburg, being the first school I ever attended. I was then six years old. He taught me the alphabet, to spell, and to read. Shortly after this he went to Burksville to live, and there married his brother's widow. He carried on the business of merchandise for some time; occasionally practiced law, but never to any great extent. He was a kind-hearted and clever man, fond of fun, and a great joker. He devoted a great portion of his life and expended much money in his attempts to make discoveries or new inventions, but never succeeded in perfecting any. Among the discoveries he was trying to make was that of "perpetual motion." He removed to the western part of Kentucky, where he died a few years afterward, at about seventy years of age.

William J. Adair was admitted to the bar of Greensburg the 25th of November, 1805, at which time he settled in Greensburg. Two or three years afterward he was elected to the Legislature from Green. He was a gentleman of high standing and intelligence, and of good family. Governor Adair was his paternal uncle. When the War of 1812 came up, he joined the regular army, was appointed to the rank of major, and was first engaged a considerable time as a recruiting officer. After the war he settled in Alabama, became a general of the militia, and had a high reputation as a jurist, being a judge of one of the higher courts for many years. He visited Greensburg in 1835, spending a week or two with his old friends and former acquaintances. He died at home, in Alabama, some time during the year 1836.

William T. Willis was admitted to the Greensburg bar about the year 1819 or 1820. He was born about the year 1796. His father was an early emigrant from Virginia, and settled in Adair County. Mr. Willis, at about the age of seventeen went to school to the Rev. John Howe, at Greensburg, and devoted himself principally to the study of the classics. At about twenty years of age he married the daughter of his preceptor, Miss Hetty Howe, and, quitting school, engaged in mercantile pursuits, settling himself in the little town of Summerville, in Green County. In the course of three or four years his reverses were such as to occasion his failure in business, when he removed to Greensburg and commenced the study of the law. In the course of a year he obtained license, and became a successful practitioner. In 1824 Mr. Willis was elected to the Legislature as the colleague of Samuel Brents, Esq., and both of them voted in that body against the act which afterward became so odious and obnoxious, called the Re-organizing Act. This act was the beginning of troubles in Kentucky, which continued some five or six years before finally settled.

About 1832 Mr. Willis changed his politics. After being the greatest political enemy and most embittered opponent of General Jackson he ever had, he suddenly became one of his greatest admirers and most devoted friends. After this change he was elected to the Senate of Kentucky; first, for a part of a term, and then for a full term, as a Jackson man. In 1839 Mr. Willis was a candidate for Congress in opposition to Willis Green, Esq., a staunch Whig, but Mr. Green was elected by a considerable majority over him. Soon after this Mr. Willis removed to Harrodsburg, where he thought to obtain a more lucrative practice of his profession. His wife died within a year or two after his removal, and some time afterward he married a lady of Jessamine County, of wealth and high standing; but unhappy family difficulties arising, and the war with Mexico about to commence, he raised a company of volunteers, to which he was elected captain, and immediately proceeded with the army to Mexico. He was a brave man and a good officer, and valiantly fell in the battle of Buena Vista. His remains were afterward brought to Frankfort, and lie buried in the cemetery at that place. Captain Willis was a good lawyer and an able advocate, and but few excelled him as a speaker.

Wm. B. Booker, a younger brother of the distinguished jurist, Paul J. Booker, came to the bar at Greensburg about the time that Paul was appointed to the bench of the Circuit Court in the district of which Washington County formed a part. Mr. Booker was a gentleman of fair talents, and became a good lawyer. He was several times elected a member of the Legislature from Washington, and was afterward appointed clerk of the Washington County Court, which office he held many years, and was the incumbent at the time of his death, which occurred some years ago. His brother, the Judge, still survives, and is eighty odd years of age.

Benjamin G. Burks was admitted to the Greensburg bar about the year 1823. He was born in Green County. His father was Silas Burks, who came with his father to Green County at a very early period. He was educated at the school of the Rev. John Howe, in New Athens Seminary, Greensburg. His education was a fair one, he having acquired some knowledge of the Latin and Greek languages. After quitting school he wrote in the clerk's office for a time under John Barret, Esq., who was clerk of both the County and Circuit Court. Reading law during that period, he was licensed and admitted, as before stated. He married Miss Winn in 1824, who was a niece of Governor Clark. His manner of address obtained for him a good practice in the circuit, though he had a far greater reputation as a speaker than for his profundity in legal lore. He was one of the counsel of John U. Waring, at Frankfort, on his trial for the murder of Thomas Q. Richardson. Waring having dispensed with the further services of Mr. Crittenden in his cause, employed, as a substitute, Mr. Burks. The trial of the case excited great interest and feeling in Kentucky, and the effort of Mr. Burks on that occasion exceeded that of any other effort of his life, and gave him considerable notoriety in that part of Kentucky as an advocate. He had been elected to the Legislature from Green the preceding year. About this time he changed his residence and located in Lexington, where he practiced law for a few years. Separating from his family, he went to Texas. A short time afterward, being out on his circuit, he retired to bed one night, to all appearance in usual health though slightly inebriated, and was found dead in the morning.

Thomas Waller Lisle was admitted to the bar of Greensburg in 1826. His father, Daniel Lisle, was a carpenter by trade, and came to Greensburg in the year 1802 to assist in building the substantial stone court-house which still stands on the public square of Greensburg, impregnable to storm or time.. Waller Bullock, of Lexington, was the undertaker of the work, through the influence of Mr. Robert Wickliffe, who was then a citizen of the place and one of the commissioners appointed by the court to superintend and receive the work when done. The work was completed and the building received the next year (1803). During the progress of that work Mr. Daniel Lisle was married to Miss Dolly Miller, of Green County, a highly esteemed and most exemplary lady, and the subject of this sketch was her first-born. Mr. Thomas W. Lisle was a good English scholar, and for several years prior to his maturity was engaged as a school-teacher himself, having by that means accumulated several hundred dollars. He wrote for a time in the clerk's office of John Barret, Esq., who was clerk of both courts. During his stay in the office he studied law, and also speculated on his money to great advantage, insomuch that when he commenced the practice of law he was possessed of about one thousand dollars in cash. With his speculations, and the practice of his profession combined, he continued to increase in property, and soon became what is called in this quarter of the State, wealthy. In 1833 two of our citizens of greatest property died, Elijah Creel, an extensive trader and merchant, and Samuel Brents, Esq., a lawyer of affluence. They both had an immense amount of unsettled business to wind up and control, and Mr. Lisle had been selected by each as executor. In winding up the affairs of these estates a great deal of business was necessarily thrown into his hands, which he turned to profit. Mr. Lisle was elected the member from Green to the convention which formed the present Constitution of Kentucky. He was twice married, and raised a large family; and a more worthy family, including himself, never lived. He was a man of great benevolence, a public-spirited and high-toned gentleman. He was, in the true sense of the word, an honest man. He died at the age of about fifty-two years.

Christopher Tompkins was appointed to the bench of the Circuit Court in 1809 to supply the vacancy occasioned by the death of the Hon. Allen M. Wakefield, and continued in that office until 1824, when he resigned, and was a candidate for Governor of the State in opposition to General Joseph Desha. He was defeated in the race by a considerable majority. He then resumed the practice of the law. In 1831 he was elected to Congress from the Glasgow district, and was re-elected in 1833. After this, he served one term in the Legislature, and was again appointed to the bench of the Circuit Court. He died in 1845, full of honors and full of years. He was over seventy-five years of age. No one stood higher in public estimation as a man and a jurist than Judge Tompkins. He was without reproach, and one of the noblest works of God. Scarcely any man's death was ever more regretted.

Jesse Craddock came to the bar of Greensburg about 1836. He had practiced but little out of his own county (Hart) previous to that time. He was married and had one child (the Hon. George W. Craddock, of Frankfort) before he learned to read. His wife was his teacher. As soon as he got to be a moderate reader he commenced the study of the law, and a year or two afterward he obtained license and commenced practice at the Munfordville bar. Business increased with him every year, and he soon began to extend the circuit of his practice, attending the courts of Green, Barren, Edmonson, Grayson, and Hardin counties, and doing a respectable business in each of those counties. He became a good lawyer, and was one of the most forcible and impressive speakers at the bar. On some occasions he was truly eloquent. His native abilities were unsurpassed, and if he had had the polish of early education but few men in Kentucky could have excelled him. He was several years a member of the Legislature, and served one term in the Senate, while his son, from the same county, was a member of the House of Representatives. He paid great attention to the education of his children, having felt severely the want of it himself. Several of his sons became lawyers, and inherited much of that native talent which their father possessed. Mr. Craddock was very sociable in conversation, full of anecdote, and could tell one with great zest. He was a very large man, weighing perhaps three hundred pounds or more, and was about five feet ten or eleven inches in hight. He died at home, in Munfordville, between fifty and sixty years of age.

George Washington Towles was admitted to the Greensburg bar about the year 1840, when he had attained the age of about fifty years. His business of life had been that of a farmer, but he lived in a neighborhood of Green County where there was a great deal of litigation, and which had become notorious for outbreaks of different kinds, and violations of law generally. Parties litigant, or those who had been arrested, charged with the commission of crime, were very frequently unable to procure the assistance of lawyers from Greensburg or elsewhere; and Mr. Towles, living convenient, and known to be a man of respectable education, of good native sense, a man of wit and influence, and, withal, a good speaker, was frequently called upon to act the lawyer on those occasions, which at first he did without fee or reward, and was usually successful in his efforts. These calls were so frequently made upon him that they finally became irksome, and determined him to study law and obtain license. This he was enabled to do in a very short time, when he commenced regular practice in the courts, making the law his principal occupation. Mr. Towles now moved to Summerville, a small town of Green County, six miles from Greensburg, and attended the courts regularly of Green and Hart.

About this time Governor Stewart, of Missouri, while in full practice as a lawyer at St. Joseph, I believe, took occasion to visit his uncle, a Mr. Wyatt, of Hart County, and during his stay a case of considerable importance came up before a magistrate of the neighborhood. One of the parties to the cause engaged the services of Mr. Stewart; the other employed Mr. Towles. The evidence being heard, Mr. Stewart commenced the argument, not at all dreading his opponent or the final result. Mr. Towles, in ordinary conversation, was given a great deal to stammering; but, in making a speech, he was sufficiently free from the impediment to render his speech more interesting than otherwise. In this respect Stewart was greatly disappointed upon first acquaintance. Towles, in reply, was particularly fluent, quite cutting in his remarks, and not a little demagogical, in which last he was not at all deficient when occasion required it. He was triumphantly successful, to the great delight of his client, who was looking only for defeat, being opposed by a lawyer so distinguished for talent. The writer, some years afterward, met with Stewart at Jefferson City, whilst Governor of Missouri, who enquired kindly after Mr. Towles, related the circumstance, remarking, to use his own language, "I tell you, Mr. Allen, that man Towles is no slouch."

Major Towles was twice elected to the Legislature from the county of Green; was always a great partisan in politics, and took an active part in every election. He emigrated from Virginia, where he had married, about the year 1816 or 1817. He was an own cousin of the distinguished William T. Willis, of whom we have spoken, and his wife was a cousin of the Hon. John T. Mason, representative in the Thirty-fifth Congress from Kentucky. The only survivor of the large family of Major Towles is his son, David T. Towles, clerk of the Green County Court, and a lawyer of prominence. Major Towles died at sixty-six years of age.

James T. Goalder was admitted to the bar of Greensburg in the year 1845. He was married, and had several children, before he commenced the study of law, and was twenty-eight or thirty years old at the time. Judge Buckner had a law-class of about twenty students in the winter of 1842-'43, and Mr. Goalder commenced the study at that school. Misfortunes had made him poor, and he determined upon the profession of law as a means of support. He applied himself closely, and was soon enabled to obtain license, and acquired at once a good business in several of the counties of the district. He was a kind-hearted, liberal man; very social and agreeable in his intercourse, loved his friends, and gave them frequent social entertainments, where wine sparkled on the board and the richest viands spread the table. He was a devoted Union man, and came to the belief that there were some of the Confederate party who would kill him, or do him some great injury, if they could capture him. With this belief he left his home, and went to Springfield, Kentucky, to remain awhile with his brother-in-law, Mr. J. W. Reinhart. While there he contracted the disease of small-pox, of which he died, at the age of about forty-eight or fifty.

Benjamin Hardin was justly regarded as one of the ablest men of the State. He was admitted to the bar at Greensburg about the year 1813, and continued his practice at the bar for many years. He was an antagonist always to be feared. His style was pungent, sarcastic, pointed, and energetic. John Randolph, of Roanoke, in allusion to Hardin's style of oratory, used to call him " the kitchen knife, rough and homely, but keen and trenchant." As an advocate at the bar he had but few if any superiors in the State. He has frequently been a member both of the Senate and House of Representatives of Kentucky, and several times elector of President and Vice President of the United States. He was a member of Congress from 1815 to 1817, from 1819 to 1823, and from 1833 to 1837. Few occupied higher rank as a debater whilst he was in Congress. In 1844 he was appointed by Governor Owsley Secretary of State, but in consequence of some differences or difficulties between him and the Governor he resigned in February, 1847. He was tall in person, had a keen, penetrating eye, and his countenance exhibited the strongest indications of decided talent. He was born in Westmoreland County, Pennsylvania, and died at Bardstown, where he lived, September 24th, 1852. In his last sickness he made a profession of religion and joined the Methodist Episcopal Church.

Hon. John Pope, who, though not a regular practitioner of the Greensburg bar, was occasionally there in special cases. At the August Court, 1820, he appeared for the defense in the case of the Commonwealth against Joseph Alerdice, for the murder of David Allen Forbes. It was regarded at first as one of the most unprovoked cases of murder that had ever occurred in the country, and the excitement against the accused was very great. The case had been twice continued by the defendant, but finally came up for trial at the time mentioned above. Alerdice was a native of Philadelphia, and respectably connected in that city, his mother being a devotedly pious woman of the Presbyterian Church. An uncle and a cousin of his, of high standing, good appearance, and intelligence, came from Philadelphia to be present at the trial. They were here some days previous to the trial, made quite a favorable impression upon the community, and the excitement which had prevailed died away to some considerable extent. Alerdice, at the time he committed the act complained of, was a stranger in the county, had been here but a few days, was known personally to but few persons, and was slightly intoxicated. The effort of Mr. Pope, on that occasion, was equal, perhaps, to any he had ever made before on like occasions. Alerdice was acquitted.

Mr. Pope was a distinguished politician and statesman as well as lawyer. He was born in the year 1870, in Prince William County, Virginia, but emigrated to Kentucky while quite a boy. In early life he had the misfortune to lose his right arm from a severe wound received while attending a cornstalk mill. By this accident he was induced to turn his attention to the profession of the law, in which he soon attained eminence. He first settled in Shelby County, but afterward removed to Lexington. He was frequently a member of the Legislature. In this body he was conspicuous and influential. In 1807 he was elected to the Senate of the United States, and was for many years a distinguished member of the House of Representatives. He was appointed by Governor Slaughter Secretary of State in 1816. At that time Mr. Pope was unpopular in Kentucky on account, while Senator, of his opposition to the war with England. It was supposed by many that the fierce agitation of the new election question, after the demise of Governor George Madison, was attributable more to the unexpected appointment of Pope than to any other cause, and Mr. Pope, regarding himself in this light, resigned his office. In 1829 he was appointed Governor of the Territory of Arkansas, which office he held for six years. He died at his residence, in Washington County, on the 12th of July, 1845. In early life Mr. Pope belonged to what was then known as the Federal party, but in after years attached himself to the party which has assumed to itself the name of Democratic.

General Samuel A. Spencer was admitted to the bar of Greensburg about the year 1827 or 1828. His occupations were somewhat varied, though he never at any time relinquished the practice of law, from his first embarkation therein. Many of his characteristics furnished a model which challenged our admiration and commanded our highest regard, they being every way worthy of imitation and deserving our emulation. He had a pure heart and a correct judgment, was a man of strict integrity and disinterested benevolence, of industrious habits, and one who faithfully discharged whatever duty devolved upon him in any sphere he was called to act. For many of his good qualities he was doubtless indebted to the early training of his widowed and pious mother, who emigrated to Kentucky from Virginia in the fall of 1817, and settled near Greensburg. Inspired by the sentiment of the great Dr. Franklin, that "He that hath a trade hath an estate," she placed Samuel, at the age of about fifteen years, as an apprentice to learn the trade of saddler and harness-maker, in the town of Greensburg, under the instruction of the very capable and worthy firm of White & Nolley. He resided in Greensburg till his death, a period of over fifty-three years. Having completed his trade he set up business for himself. Though denied the advantages of early education, he had contracted during his apprenticeship a great fondness for books; and while other boys of the town, in the same condition of life, were spending their time in frivolity and idleness, he was poring over books and storing his mind with useful knowledge, which told well for him in his future life, and which he never regretted.

Soon after commencing business for himself as a saddler, his attention was attracted to the study of the law, with a view to its practice as a profession. Having provided himself with a copy of the Commentaries of Sir William Blackstone, he devoured its contents with avidity, and soon attained that proficiency which enabled him to answer readily any question pertaining to it. It was not long until he obtained license to practice, when he devoted himself exclusively to the profession. He had become an excellent lawyer, especially in land cases, and his earnest manner and peculiar style of speaking attracted and interested, not only his brethren of the bar, but the judge and jury also; and his speeches were never without effect.

General Spencer was for many years surveyor of Green County, in which branch of mathematics he was an adept; but it yielding little profit he relinquished it. For the last twenty-five or thirty years he connected with his profession the business of "pension agent," in which he attained great proficiency, and obtained a run of business unequaled, perhaps, by any man in the State. For some years his office was the daily resort of soldiers, widows and orphans, both white and colored; and, while in health, he was ever to be found at his place of business from early dawn till late at night. Such has been his press of business in that line as almost to exclude him from society, and even the enjoyment of his own happy family circle, except on the Sabbath day, which was ever remembered by him with that reverence and respect most becoming every Christian gentleman.

General Spencer filled many offices of high trust and responsibility in his county. He was a justice of the peace for many years; afterward county judge for the term of four years. Previous to that time he served for four years in the Senate of Kentucky, and was often the incumbent of minor offices under the corporation laws of Greensburg, such as trustee of the town, of the academy, of the common schools, etc. For several years he held the office, by appointment, of Commissioner of the United States Court for the county of Green. Until sickness prevented his attendance, he was superintendent of a Union Sunday-school of Greensburg, but resigned shortly before his death on account of ill-health.

General Spencer was a good man in every relation of life, and his loss was deeply felt by all. As a husband he was kind, and provided well for his household; as a father he was affectionate; as a friend he was devoted; as a gentleman he was courteous; as a Christian he was pious. In him the widow and the fatherless ever found a true friend; the suffering and the distressed had his sympathies, and they were never turned empty away. Early in life he became a member of the Masonic fraternity, and was greatly devoted to the institution in the light of its benevolence, and as being the handmaid of religion. In later years he became a member of the Baptist Church, and died one of its honored members, in the triumphs of faith, and in prospect of a glorious immortality beyond the grave. He was born in Charlotte County, Virginia, February, 1803, and died Sunday morning, the 12th day of March, 1871, in the sixty-ninth year of his age.

But few States in this Union can boast of a greater amount of legal talent than the bar of Kentucky, and but few counties in the State a greater amount than the bar at Greensburg, even from the first organization of the county through the lapse of a great number of years. Of all those admitted to the bar previous to the year 1800, not one survives; and many, even of those who attained a good old age long before their demise, took up their residence in larger towns and cities, or emigrated to newer States, where there was greater prospect of gain and acquisition of fame.

I have, in the preceding chapter, given sketches of the lives of those jurists and lawyers of the State of Kentucky at large who have passed away from the transitory scenes of earth, and who were most distinguished in the profession—that is, so far as I have been enabled to obtain reliable information concerning them, believing that such history will add greatly to the interest of a work like this; and I have added a few names of those most distinguished who still survive, but have grown old in the profession, and are still in the public service of their country.

CHAPTER XII.

First Settlers of Green, where from—Of High Character and Good Property—Names given of the Early Settlers—Names of Early Ministers of the Gospel—Rev. Manoah Lasley, Sketch of—Rev. Thomas Lasley, Sketch of—Rev. John White, Baptist Minister—John Chandler and James Larimore, Baptist Ministers—Isaac Hodgen, Baptist Minister, Sketch of his Life—First Judges of Green Quarter Session Court, Sketch of them—General Barbee, the Founder of Deaf and Dumb Asylum—An Account of it—Colonel Wm. Casey, Sketch of his Life—John Tucker, Sketch of—A Number of Names of Emigrants to Green in 1795 and 1796—Nathaniel Owens, Sketch of—Joseph Logston, Sketch of—William Skaggs—His Trial for Murder—The Last Judges of Quarter Session Court, Jonathan Cowherd, John Chandler, and John C. Allen, Sketch of them—John Y. Taylor and David Willock, first Assistant Judges of Green Circuit Court, Sketch of—First Circuit Court, its Officers—First Order of Record—First Constable—First Licensed Tavern-keeper—First Overseer of Road—First Pauper—First Mill—First Reviewers of a Road—First Administrator of an Estate—First Deputy Sheriffs—First Coroner, and first Commissioners to take Depositions—First Lawyer Sworn to Practice—First Keeper of Standard Measures—First Ferry on Green River—First Jailer—First Inspectors of Tobacco—First Keeper of Stray Pen—First Merchant, Daniel Brown, Sketch of—John Barret, Sketch of—Names of his Deputies who acquired Distinction—Robert Barret, Sketch of—First Silversmith—First Hatter—First Tanner—First Saddler—Captain William Hobson, Sketch of—Alexander Irvin, first Physician, Sketch of—Most noted Tavern, an account of it—Incidents there Occurring—David Allen, Incidents related of him—Silas Burks, Sketch of—Jenkins Asten—Fight with Burks—First Tailor Shop—First Dancing School—First Classical School—First Tobacco Warehouse Established—Wm. H. King, Sketch of—First Tobacco Manufactory—Distinguished Arbitrators—First Singing School Taught—First Resident Carpenters—Robert Ball—Thos. Parsons, Sketch of—Revolutionary Pensioners—Wm. Finn, Centenarian—List of Earliest Justices of the Peace, Constables, and Assessors—Creed Haskins, Sketch of—First Baptist Church Organized—List of Early Coroners—First Undertakers of Public Buildings—First Man Tried for Vagrancy—First Will Admitted to Record—Gabriel and Benjamin Chisham—Jonathan Hobson, Sketch of—Bank at Greensburg, its Officers—Uncommon Names who were Early Settlers of Green—Life and Villainies of Carrington Simpson, the Murderer, in Detail.

The first settlers of Green County were principally from the State of Virginia; a portion from North and South Carolina, and a few from Pennsylvania and Maryland. Except from the States mentioned, there was scarcely to be found an emigrant from any other State. The first emigrants to Green were generally farmers, men of intelligence, good property, and high standing in the old States from which they came; especially so the settlers from Virginia, who, in point of numbers, exceeded all the rest put together. A better state of society did not exist anywhere west of the mountains than the early population of Green County. They were proverbial for all those characteristics which have ever been ascribed to the old Virginia gentleman and lady—frank, free, open, generous, hospitable, and sociable; fond of pleasure and good living; and enjoyed themselves greatly in those innocent sports common in the country at that day, such as the chase, the dance, &c. Among those to whom these remarks apply I would mention the names of William Barret, Thomas Miller, Daniel White, David Allen, William Buckner, William Winlock, Jesse Mills, Pouncy Anderson, David Anderson, Jonathan Cowherd, James Cowherd, Creed Haskins, Thomas Marshall, Thomas Higgason, Thomas Merriwether, John C. Allen, Allen M. Wakefield, Robert Allen, James Allen, William Barnet, William Casey, Nicholas Burks, Richard Yates, James Mitchell, John Thurman, James Spillman, John P. Con, Adam Mitchell, John Mitchell, Samuel Burks, Benjamin Cook, Henry Embry, Charles Patteson, Elias Barbee, Benjamin Chisham, Christopher Brooks, John W. Semple, John Baldwin, John E. King, Thomas Eastland, John Barret, Edward J. Bullock, William Hobson, Jonathan Hobson, Alexander Irvin, William H. King, Daniel Brown, Simeon Bohannon, Luke Ford, Jas. Munford, F. C. Dickinson, William Sympson, Robert Barret, Anthony Thornton, Thomas Pettus, Joseph Akin, David Willock, James Harris, Liberty Green, James Murray, Daniel Lisle, John Walker, Thomas Johnson, Stephen Biggs, Samuel Combs, Elijah Adams, Adam Campbell, Robert Jarboe, Andrew and David Campbell, George Speers, Thomas Mitchell, Daniel Williams, Andrew Chaudoin, James Durham, James Scott, Mark Lively, Wm. Mann, William and James Lisle, John Sandridge, Robert and Abraham Woodward, Thomas

Robinson, Dr. Joseph Winlock, Nimrod H. Arnold, William Gray, John Durrett, Horace Buckner, Chapman Lobb, James Dobson, Daniel Turner, John McKinney, William and John Brownlee, James Sharp, William Vance, Charles Gum, William Rhea, Joseph Hutcherson, Ignatius and Richard Hazell, Thomas Wisdom, George Sexton, Hugh Paxton, Jacob Bale, John Hawthorn, William Adams, Moses Mann, Drury Despain, Jesse Roberts, James Calhoon, Thomas Bass, Edward Lewis, Joshua Lee, David Hutty, B. and Matthew Hutcherson, Hugh Wilson, William Penick, James Murry, William Elmore, Bartholomew and William Curry, Joseph Akin, John Brents, Joseph Burton, John McBrayer, William Phillips.

Nearly every person above named were men of good sense, judgment, and discretion, and at an early day filled the highest positions in the community, such as judges, clerks of courts, justices of the peace, sheriffs, surveyors, coroners, legislators, foremen of grand and petit juries, &c. A few of them were men highly educated.

To the foregoing list of early settlers of Green County I would add the names of ministers of the Gospel of that day who are remembered, viz:

David Rice, John Howe, and Jeremiah Abell, whose history has been given under the head of Sketches of the Presbyterian Church of Kentucky. Manoah Lasley, of the Methodist Church, was authorized by the Green County Court to solemnize the rites of matrimony, February, 1797. He was a pious and useful man in the community, lived to a very advanced age, having married a second time at the age of seventy-five years. His son, Thomas Lasley, was also a Methodist minister of some note as early as 1809, and was authorized to solemnize matrimony in 1810. The renowned Peter Cartright, who yet survives at nearly ninety years of age, rode his first circuit in Kentucky, in what was called Stockton's Valley Circuit, under the charge of the Rev. Thos. Lasley.

John White, a Baptist minister, was authorized by the County Court of Green to solemnize matrimony in 1798. Of his history I have no information.

John Chandler was one of the earliest Baptist ministers of Green, and was authorized to solemnize matrimony in 1806. Mr. Chandler was the last appointed judge of Green County under the Quarter Session Court system.

James Larimore and Isaac Hodgen were among the early Baptist ministers of Green County. Larimore moved to Missouri about the year 1820, where he lived many years and died.

Isaac Hodgen was a leading minister of the Baptist denomination, and became pastor of the Mt. Gilead Church about 1801-2. He was born in Frederick County, Virginia, the 8th of August, 1779. In the fall of 1784 his father came to Kentucky, and lived for a short time at Philip's Fort, near Nolin Creek. The next year he settled on a farm where Hodgenville, the county-seat of Larue County, now stands. About the year 1800 or 1801, Isaac, being of age, left his father's residence, and commenced business for himself as a deputy sheriff of Hardin County. It was about that time he made a profession of religion and attached himself to the Baptist Church. He received baptism by immersion at the hands of Joshua Morris, in Nolin Creek. He soon began to exercise himself publicly in prayer and exhortation, and in a short time was licensed to preach, and went to the neighborhood of Mt. Gilead Church, Green County, to live. The 27th of December, 1804, he was married to Miss Phebe Trabue, daughter of William Trabue, deceased, who resided on an eminence near Skinhouse Branch, and within a few hundred yards of where Mt. Gilead Church now stands. After Isaac's marriage he resided with his mother-in-law until her death, and afterward becoming himself the owner of the place, he continued to reside there until his death, which occurred on the 22d of March, 1826, when in the forty-seventh year of his age. The pastor of Mt. Gilead Church at the time Mr. Hodgen was married was a Baptist preacher by the name of Elijah Summers; his predecessor a minister by the name of John Mulky, who many years afterward joined in the reformation begun and carried on by B. W. Stone, Alexander Campbell, and others.

The Rev. Isaac Hodgen was a man of exemplary piety, and a man of God, as was admitted by all who knew him; in consequence of which, revivals always followed his preaching wherever he went. He generally had the care of four churches at the same time, and traveled a great deal besides. At the time of his death he was pastor of the churches at Greensburg, Friendship, Union, and I believe of Mt. Gilead also, but of the latter I am not certain. He was so constantly engaged in preaching that he was at home but little, but traveled in almost every direction in the mission to which God had ordered him. He was popular with all denominations of orthodox Christians; his sermons were never sectarian or partisan; he persecuted none, and labored with all. The chief theme of his discourses was "Christ, and him crucified;" "Repent, or you will all likewise perish;" "Repent, for the kingdom of heaven is at hand;" "God has commanded all men everywhere to repent." These, and such like texts, were always favorites with him. Whilst his congregation were being assembled, he was to be seen in the pulpit, with his head bowed, and resting upon his hands, as if engaged in silent prayer; and when he arose to begin the service, he was often seen wiping the tear from his eyes. His delivery was clear, distinct, and forcible; his manner persuasive and inviting. His greatest fort was in exhortation. In the close of his discourses, he became animated, and exhorted with irresistible power and effect. He was fervent in prayer, and sung with the spirit and understanding. But few preachers could wield a greater influence with a congregation. When about to lead in prayer he would say, "Let us all now bow before the great, the eternal God, for unto him every knee shall bow, and every tongue confess," and the whole congregation would at once fall upon their knees, sinners as well as saints, and, when they arose, saints were found rejoicing and sinners weeping. In the year 1818, he, in company with another good man (William Warder), was sent by the association to Philadelphia on some missionary errand, passing through Virginia on their return home. At a point not now recollected, they held a meeting, protracted for a few days, at which more than one hundred persons were hopefully converted and added to the church. A short time previous to his death there was a revival in his immediate neighborhood, at which his two eldest children made a profession of religion, to-wit: Robert and Elizabeth, to both of whom he administered the ordinance of baptism. Robert afterward became a member of what is denominated the Christian Church, and Elizabeth became a member of that church also, having intermarried with Mr. Robert Caldwell, who was a minister of the Christian Church. Mr. Caldwell having died, Elizabeth became the wife of Mr. John Scott, of Greensburg, who still survives, now in the eighty-eighth year of his age, retaining his intellect in an extraordinary degree for one of his age, an eminent Christian patron of piety, and a member of the Baptist Church for seventy-one years past. Two more worthy and exemplary old people live not in any community.

The Rev. Isaac Hodgen was in person good looking, about five feet, eight or nine inches in hight, square shouldered, weighing near two hundred pounds, with a form indicative of great strength; his countenance bland, hair sandy, and eyes blue. In conversation he was always interesting, especially when animated. No minister was ever more universally beloved by all who knew him, of whatever persuasion or denomination. He lies entombed on the farm where he died, and these simple words mark the headstone of his grave, "Prepare to meet thy God."

The first judges of the Green County Quarter Session Court were William Buckner, Elias Barbee, and William Casey. They were all farmers of respectable education and strong natural endowments, and very well suited to the office they filled. They all attained the age of eighty years and over, having filled many important offices and positions of distinction. They all, at some period of their lives, were members of the Legislature — General Barbee more frequently than the other two.

To General Barbee is ascribed the honor of being the starter and founder of the Deaf and Dumb Asylum of Kentucky, situated at Danville, which went into operation in the spring of 1823, and up to the present time has proven to be a success. The officers of the institution, besides the instructors, who are in constant attendance upon the pupils, are a physician, and a superintendent and matron, in whose family all the pupils reside. Those whose circumstances will admit of it are required to pay for board and instruction; and for the indigent the law makes ample provision.

Mr. Buckner was surveyor of Green County for many years, and acquired considerable wealth, especially in lands and negroes. At his death he was the owner of about one hundred slaves, and had distributed among his children, as they married, quite a number. Mr. Buckner was one of the largest stock raisers of the county, and in his earlier days had produced some of the best and swiftest racers to be found anywhere.

Colonel William Casey was a native of Frederick County, Virginia, and removed to Kentucky in the early part of the winter of 1779-80; and, during the intensely cold weather of that memorable winter, lived in a camp on the Hanging Fork of Dix River. He was one of the company who, with the Logans, Montgomeries, McClures, and Whitleys, established Logan's Station at Buffalo Springs, near the present town of Stanford. From this point Colonel Casey formed a company of some thirty hardy and well tried men, with the view of establishing stations south of Green River. In the spring of 1791, Casey, with his party, composed of the Butlers, Tuckers, Montgomeries, Dudleys, Fields, Lawsons, Harveys, Fletchers, and others, started down Green River, crossing at the mouth of what was afterward called Casey's Creek. At a large spring of most excellent water, now on a farm owned and occupied by Mr. James Callison, they erected a block-house and fort, which, in honor of their captain, they called Casey's Station. Here, at a distance of fifty miles from any white settlement, he, with the families who had pushed their fortunes with him, though feeble in numbers, maintained themselves gallantly and victoriously against many attacks from the Indians. His station was subsequently reinforced by several families, whose presence was instrumental in preventing any further assault on the part of the Indians. It was in one of the incursions of a small band of savages that Mr. John Tucker, a Methodist preacher, together with his wife and some others, were cruelly murdered at Tucker Station, which had been established about a mile from Casey's Station. Many of the inmates of this station were enabled to make their escape in safety to Casey's Station, where information was given of the attack, the marauders suddenly pursued, and overtaken just as they were in the act of crossing the Cumberland River on a raft. The Indians were fired upon by Casey's company and several killed, and some horses recaptured which the Indians had taken from Tucker's Station.

The Casey farm was the first farm opened south of Russell's Creek. The Fletcher and Hunt farms, all in what is now Adair County, were opened to some extent, and houses built, several years before their owners dared to occupy them.

Colonel Casey was a man of strong natural mind, of great benevolence and goodness of heart. No man was ever more beloved by his acquaintances, or deservedly more popular. When the election came up for delegates to the convention of 1799 to remodel the Constitution of Kentucky, he was elected by a large majority over all opposition. In this capacity Colonel Casey served the people ably, and with entire satisfaction. After the county of Adair was stricken from Green, Colonel Casey's residence then being in that county, he was by them often honored with high and responsible trusts, and lived to the age of more than four-score years, leaving an only son (Green Casey) and several daughters, all of whom inherited, in a good degree, the good sense and moral worth of their father, and occupied a high stand in the community in which they lived. Colonel Casey, in person, was large and corpulent, and of prepossessing appearance. His forehead was prominent, his eyes black, keen, and piercing, and voice stentorian. He made no pretensions to oratory, yet he spoke with power, and never failed to interest his auditory and to carry his point, though this result, perhaps, was more from the unbounded confidence of the people in him as a sincere and honest man than from any other cause.

In the years 1795 and 1796 a set of very wealthy and worthy farmers removed from what is called the blue-grass regions of Kentucky to Green County, and settled for the most part on Caney Fork, Skinhouse Branch, and Big Creek. They were the Trabues, the Haskins, the Creels, the Dahoneys, the Hunts, the Whites, the Conovers, the Gilmers, Denisons, Paxtons, Votaws, Weases, &c. The Stapps, Burbridges, Bowmers, Kelsoes, Briants, and Youngs settled on Glenn's Fork of Russell. John Stapp settled in that part of Green which is now Adair County; also William Lair, Edmund Greer, Thomas Carter, Gabriel Hays, and the Joneses, Holts, Holmes, Silveys, Oldacres, McClures, Moores, Kens, Dunbars, Frenchs, Chamberlains, &c. All the persons named were regarded as worthy and highly respected citizens. It is a remarkable fact, that of the whole number of persons who accompanied Colonel Casey to the country south of Green River, not one of them was addicted to habits of intemperance, and many of them were honored with high positions in the community in which they lived.

The first high sheriff of Green County was Nathaniel Owens. He was a farmer of good education for the times, and of a high order of native intellect He was a man of untiring perseverance and industry, and acquired considerable wealth. He bestowed great attention to the education of his children, sent them from home to the best schools, and occasionally employed in his family a private teacher for their instruction. He was among the earliest pioneers to Green County, and participated largely in the hardships which the first settlers had necessarily to encounter. He was thought by many to be selfish in his disposition, and like the old woman, who, after keeping house many years, bought her a tea-kettle, and determined from that period that she would neither borrow or lend. He was a close, economical, money-making man, but punctiliously honest in all his dealings. He dispensed but little, if any, of his property to his children in his life-time, but they and their descendants received it all after his death. Mr. Owens acted for a time as justice of the peace, and also as a judge of the Green County Quarter Session Court previous to 1801, when the Circuit Court system was established. Mr. Owens lived to be eighty odd years of age, and died about the year 1846, at his residence, on Little Brush Creek, where he lies buried.

Joseph Logston was the first person ever tried in Green County for a high crime. The court before which he was tried thought him guilty, and sent him to the Court of Oyer and Terminer, which was held at Lexington, for final trial. I think on final trial he was acquitted, and immediately left for the territory north of the Ohio River. Joe Logston came to Green County at a very early period, from near the source of the north branch of the Potomac River, and resided for some years in the family of Andrew Barnett, another individual of great notoriety at that day. It was said of Logston, that he could out-run, out-hop, out-jump, throw down, drag out, and whip any man in the country. Collins, in his History of Kentucky, gives the particulars of a fight, said to have occurred in Green County at a very early period, between Big Joe Logston and an Indian. The rencontre related was one of the most desperate ever seen or read of, and possibly did occur on the frontiers of Illinois. I have the best authority for saying that the fight alluded to did not occur in Green County, and that Logston never returned to the county of Green after he had been taken to Lexington for final trial.

In 1798, William Skaggs, heretofore in this history prominently mentioned, was sent from Green County to the District Court held at Bardstown for further trial, charged with the murder of one Martin Frazer, who kept a ferry on Green River, two miles below Greensburg. Wonderful excitement existed in the neighborhood for a long time on account of this murder. No one at all acquainted with the facts hesitated for a moment to state as his belief that Skaggs was the slayer of Frazer, and that he did it with an augur he had purchased in town on the day of the murder. Skaggs, however, after the continuance of the case for several courts was finally acquitted. The lawyer in his defense was John Rowan, whose effort on that occasion, young as he was, was masterly indeed, and obtained for him a reputation, which followed him through life, as one of the ablest lawyers at the bar of Kentucky, especially in a criminal case. It is stated as a fact, that at the instant the verdict of the jury was delivered, the court-house was struck by lightning, accompanied by a terrible peal of thunder, and Rowan and several of the jurymen knocked prostrate to the floor..

The last judges on the bench of the Green Quarter Session Court, under that system, were Jonathan Cowherd, John Chandler, and John C. Allen. They were all men of good sense, sound judgment and discretion, and every way worthy the position which they held. Cowherd and Chandler lived to an advanced age, each being over eighty years of age at his death. Allen died at the age of about forty-three years. Chandler was a Baptist minister for a great number of years before his death. Cowherd's mind became impaired in the latter years of his life, from which he never recovered.

John Y. Taylor and David Willock were the first and only assistant judges for Green County under the Circuit Court system, Allen M. Wakefield, presiding judge, whose history I have heretofore given. Judge Taylor was born in Virginia on the 11th of January, 1765. He removed to Green County in 1803, and died at the residence of his son, Dr. R. A. Taylor, in Greensburg, October 6, 1845, in the eighty-first year of his age. He was a man of extensive reading, possessed of a fund of information, and well-posted on religious as well as political subjects. He was tall, slim, and a little stoop-shouldered; in form, weight, hight, and general appearance, always reminding me of General Jackson. He was a man of exemplary morality, and in religious sentiment, Unitarian. He was sociable, and always interesting in fireside conversation.

Judge Willock was from Virginia also, a worthy, sensible, and exemplary man, with whose history I am not familiar. He was for many years a justice of the peace for the county, and high sheriff. He died some thirty or more years ago.

The first Circuit Court ever held in Greensburg under that system was begun the 28th of February, 1803, A. M. Wakefield the first judge, and James Allen the first clerk.

The first order of record in the Green County Court was

for the building of a court-house, and the first licensed tavern-keeper was Samuel Burks.

The first constable was Frederick Skaggs.

The first appointed overseer of a road was John Chisham.

The first allowance made by the court for the support of a pauper was for the wife of Jacob Niece.

The first grant of privilege to build a mill was to Joseph Anderson, in February, 1795.

John C. Allen was the first overseer of a road proceeding from the court-house.

The first reviewers of a road appointed were Moses Kirkpatrick, Alexander McFarland, Joseph Black, and William Pepper.

The first administration of an estate in Green County was by Wm. Casey, of the estate of John Reynolds.

The first deputy sheriffs of the county were Archibald Kenedy and Isham Burks.

The first surveyor appointed was Thomas Hall.

The first coroner was Joshua Armstrong.

The first commissioners to take depositions in regard to land titles, by improvement, were William Buckner, Elias Barbee, and John Rogers.

Allen M. Wakefield was the first lawyer sworn to practice law in the county court. He was also the first county attorney.

William McMurtry built the first mill in Green County of which we have any record, and David Pierce a fulling-mill.

Robert Erwin was appointed first keeper of standard measures, and Jesse Gray the first overseer of a road in Green, south of Green River.

The first ferry was established at the mouth of Mill Creek, on Green River, by Robert Todd and John Thurman.

John C. Allen was the first jailer of Green County, and Stephen Biggs the first keeper of stray-pen.

Bartlett Hilliard and John Moss were the first inspectors of tobacco at Greensburg warehouse.

Daniel Brown was the first merchant of Greensburg. He was born in Pennsylvania about the year 1763, came to Greensburg with a stock of goods about the year 1792-93, and continued to reside here until his death, which occurred in October, 1845, at the age of eighty-two years. He was one of the early justices of the peace, but held the office only for a short time, when he resigned. He attended closely to his business as a merchant, and was very successful for many years; but, finally, engaging in tobacco speculations, and buying horses for the southern trade, he became considerably embarrassed. He was enabled, however, to pay all his debts, with a sufficiency left to support him in his declining years. He and his brother, Alexander Brown, and brother-in-law, Samuel Findley, became the proprietors of the town of Greensburg, having purchased from Walter Beall, the original proprietor. They sold many of the lots at a considerable advance upon the price given. Mr. Brown was a man of most exemplary piety, and a ruling elder of the Presbyterian Church for nearly fifty years. He was the father of the Rev. John H. Brown, a distinguished minister of the Presbyterian Church, now of Chicago, Illinois; for many years pastor of the church at Richmond, Kentucky; afterward at Lexington; and for twelve years past, and until lately, ministered to the church at Springfield, Illinois.

John Barret was born in Virginia in 1785, and was a boy some eight or ten years old when his father came to Kentucky. At the age of about fifteen years he became the deputy of General James Allen in both the circuit and county court. He continued as deputy, doing the entire business of the offices, until some time during the War of 1812. General Allen being an active participant in that war resigned his position in both courts, and John Barret was appointed in his stead, and continued to hold said offices until the coming in of the new Constitution of Kentucky in 1851, a period of nearly forty years, and as deputy and clerk together, a period of more than fifty years.

Mr. Barret had but few superiors as a clerk in the State of Kentucky. He was decidedly a business man, and never left anything undone that ought to be done. He was so careful in the order and arrangement of the papers of the offices, that he was never at a loss to find a paper though called for immediately; and he always exacted of his deputies the same particularity. With very few exceptions, every deputy he ever raised in his office became distinguished, either as a lawyer, or as a clerk of some of the courts. To instance some of them, well-known in Kentucky, I would mention the following: Augustus M. Barret, a brother, for many years clerk of the courts of Edmonson County, Kentucky, and who afterward removed to Missouri and was the acting clerk of Pettus County at the time of his death, which occurred some twelve or fourteen years since; the Hon. George T. Wood, of Munfordville, Kentucky, who was clerk of the county and circuit courts of Hart County from its formation until a few years since; Hiram S. Emerson, a lawyer of distinction, and at the time and at the present time the clerk of a court in Tennessee; Robert H. Buckner, who removed to the State of Mississippi, where he became eminent as a lawyer and a judge; Rutherford H. Rountree, of Lebanon, Kentucky, a lawyer of high standing, and for many years clerk of the Marion County Court; Thomas W. Lisle, for many years a prominent lawyer of the Greensburg bar, an extended sketch of whom has heretofore been given; Wm. F. Barret, at the present time one of the leading lawyers of the city of Louisville; John G. Barret, the present cashier of a bank in Louisville, but who practiced law with considerable success in that city previous to his appointment as cashier; John Richard Barret, an eminent lawyer of St. Louis, Missouri, and twice elected to the Congress of the United States from that city; John Barret, Jr., a lawyer of prominence, and Commonwealth's attorney in the Henderson district at the time of his death, which occurred a few years since; James D. Allen, of Kansas (brother of the writer), who served as a clerk in the Kansas Legislature, and police judge of the city of Shawnee; Andrew Monroe, a lawyer of eminence, and judge of the county court of Jefferson County for several years; William H. Otter, a lawyer of considerable prominence, now of the city of Kansas, in the State of Missouri; Samuel T. Wilson, now of Louisville, the successor of Mr. Barret in the circuit court office, serving seventeen consecutive years by re-election, when he resigned and became the principal agent in the Kentucky Southern Life Insurance Company. Nearly every one of the persons named were men of industry and perseverance, and occupied a high standing in the communities in which they lived. All prospered greatly, and most of them attained the distinction of being called wealthy; and all of them, with scarcely an exception, acquired his habits, and imbibed his notions in regard to business, which they have retained through life.

Mr. Barret was punctiliously prompt in all his transactions, and equally exacting from those with whom he had to do. He scorned a mean action, and never hesitated to remind either friend or foe of his faults, whether he offended or not. He was quick to resent an insult, and free to forgive. He amassed largely of this world's goods, but contributed liberally to the poor and to the church of which he was a member. He was, in all respects, a useful member of the community in which he lived. He was jovial and sociable in his disposition, fond of anecdote, enjoyed much the company of ladies and young persons, to whom he gave frequent and sumptuous entertainments, and was himself the life and soul of the company. His house was the resort and stopping-place of high preachers of all denominations; and strangers of high character, visiting the town, were always invited to, and made welcome guests at his house. Mr. Barret's prudence, discretion, good sense, and qualifications for business, placed him in many important as well as subordinate positions, in town and county. He was a director of the Independent Bank of Greensburg, established by an act of the Legislature of 1818. He was a director also, and for a time president of the Bank of the Commonwealth, established at Greensburg by the act of the Legislature of 1820. He was a director all the time, and nearly all the time president, of the Greensburg Branch of the Bank of Kentucky during its continuance at that point, a period of twenty-five years, and under his management it yielded a greater profit, considering the amount of capital invested, than perhaps any branch of that institution in the State, or even the mother bank itself. Mr. Barret acted as a trustee of the town of

Greensburg for a great number of years, and was usually the president of the board. He acted as executor or administrator of more estates in Green County than any other man; and such was the unbounded confidence in him by those, who, by last will, appointed him to the executorship, that it was in the fewest instances required of him that he should give security on his bond for the faithful discharge of his duty. When the act passed by Congress allowing pensions to soldiers of the Revolution took effect, Mr. Barret was the man to whom they applied to make out their papers in proper form for the obtention of their pensions, which business he continued to perform successfully so long as any of them remained to be recipients of the honor.

Mr. Barret never held any military position, except that of paymaster to the Sixteenth Regiment of Kentucky Militia. The duties of this office he fulfilled for a great number of years. At a very early period he was the postmaster at Greensburg. He was a ruling elder in the Presbyterian Church for more than thirty years, and several times a member of the General Assembly of that church at Philadelphia.

Mr. Barret died at his residence, adjoining the town of Greensburg, on the 6th of April, 1860, in the seventy-sixth year of his age. His venerable widow still survives, at the age of about seventy-five years, respected for her virtues by all who ever knew her. Mr. Barret had seven children living at the time of his death, four boys and three girls, all of whom still survive, are in prosperous circumstances, and occupying the highest standing in the communities in which they live. Most of the family reside now in the city of Louisville. Wm. F. Barret, his eldest son, whose name has heretofore been mentioned, is a lawyer of fame, and for a number of years a resident of that city.

Robert Barret, an elder brother of John, was also a prominent citizen of Green. He was born in Virginia about the year 1784, came to Kentucky when a boy, and learned the art of a silversmith and jeweler. He was for many years a justice of the peace. He was elected from the county of Green a member of the Legislature of Kentucky for three successive years, during the administration of Lieutenant and acting Governor Slaughter, viz: 1816, 1817, and 1818. He was a major in the militia, and participated in the War of 1812 as a subordinate officer. He was first lieutenant in the company of Captain David Allen, in General Hopkin's campaign. He was a man of fine native sense, of great physical strength, robust form, good looking, and of prepossessing manners; he sympathized deeply with distress wherever encountered, and was ever ready, to the extent of his ability, to alleviate its necessities. After his last term in the Legislature, his health became impaired, and he died in 1821, in the thirty-sixth year of his age. He was the first silversmith that ever established a shop in Greensburg, and was a perfect master of his trade.

The first hatter's establishment in Greensburg was carried on by James Lasley, son of Manoah Lasley, who was the first Methodist preacher of Greensburg. James Lasley was for many years a justice of the peace for Green County, and highly esteemed for his many good qualities.

John Parks established the first tanyard in Greensburg, with whom William Workman, a man of celebrity in that line of business (in after years), learned his trade.

Thomas K. Slaughter was the first saddler of Greensburg, and was the brother of the wife of General Elias Barbee, of whom we have spoken.

Captain William Hobson, father of General E. H. Hobson, learned his trade with Slaughter, and afterward set up in business for himself, following his trade until his death, which occurred the 6th of April, 1853. William Hobson was a true man, to be relied upon in all respects. He was just, generous, and honest, and a faithful soldier in the War of 1812. He killed an Indian at the battle of the Thames, of which fact no doubt existed. He was engaged in mercantile pursuits for several years, in connection with the saddler's business. He was for some years a justice of the peace, trustee of the corporation of Greensburg, and for many years president of the Board. Captain Hobson was a model of industry, applied himself closely to his business, and acquired considerable property. He sustained great loss in the commencement of his career by suretyship. He was never known to refuse a friend, of however doubtful circumstances he might be. No more worthy citizen ever lived in any community. In his death the community around him sustained irreparable loss.

Alexander Irvine was the first physician of Greensburg. He was born, raised, educated, and studied medicine in Ireland. He was regarded as a most excellent physician, and obtained a most extensive practice, though very laborious. He often visited patients a distance of forty-five miles from his residence, there being no physician nearer. In 1814 he was elected a member of the Legislature from the county of Green, a colleague of Colonel Liberty Green. After his service in the Legislature, he became somewhat intemperate, and obtaining but little practice at that time he removed to the country, where he married at the age of more than fifty years. He afterward removed to the southern part of the State, where he died. He had no relations in America.

The first tavern in Greensburg of special note was kept by Benjamin Graves, or rather by his wife Polly, who was principal manager. The log house, now weather-boarded, in which the tavern was kept is still standing, and in good repair. It was customary at that day, on the night of every court day, to have what is called a frolic, or dance, at this tavern. On such occasions the house was always crowded, especially by those who participated in the dance. Ordinarily, the men appeared in their hunting-shirts, and the ladies in their calico, or nice cotton dresses. On one of the occasions alluded to, Robert Allen attended in more costly attire than was customary, wearing a nice broadcloth coat. This so excited the envy of a fellow present, that he stealthily slipped behind Allen, caught hold of the skirts, and tore them asunder. David Allen, the father of the writer, and brother of Robert, being present and witnessing the outrageous and unprovoked act, struck the fellow a violent blow with his fist, which felled him near the door, through which he was quickly ejected by the application of Allen's foot to his person. The fellow dared not enter the house again. Scenes like this were not unfrequent at that early day and time. David Allen, at twenty-one or two years of age, weighed about one hundred and seventy-five pounds, was raw-boned, square-shouldered, and nearly six feet, two inches high. He was regarded as one of the strongest and most active men in the country at that day. Though a remarkably peaceable man, he was fearless, yet cool and deliberate, and never exhibited any extraordinary excitement from passion. Besides the incident I have related, of knocking a fellow down for tearing his brother's coat, I do not remember to have heard of his having but one fight in the course of his life, and that was with a man who, up to the time of the occurrence, he had never known, and with whom no animosity had ever existed. The circumstances, as related to me by a gentleman who was present, are about these: William Twyman, a very stout man, living in the new county of Barren, came to Greensburg one county court day, and stated that he had come for the express purpose of having a fight with David Allen, whom he had heard was the stoutest man in Green County, and he desired the honor of whipping that man. David Allen was immediately hunted up, and introduced to Mr. Twyman. A fight was agreed upon, seconds chosen to see that all was done fairly, coats thrown aside, a ring formed, over which no man was to intrude; the combatants with their seconds entered the ring, and the fight commenced. In a short space of time the cry was heard from Twyman, "Take him off! take him off!" Allen desisted. They then repaired to Graves' tavern, where they washed the blood from their faces, took a social glass, shook hands, and parted. Twyman, mounting his horse, started for home, apparently in as good humor as when he came. By an examination of the order-book of the Quarter Session Court, I find that at the August Court, 1799, Allen was sued by Twyman for an assault and battery, but at the August Court, 1800, said suit was dismissed upon payment of costs by Allen.

Benjamin Graves had several portly, fine-looking daughters, with two of whom the writer was well acquainted. One of them married Mr. William Price, a highly respected farmer, who lived in the neighborhood of Greensburg, and died some fifteen or sixteen years since, at an advanced age; the other (Betsy) married Mr. Silas Burks, the father of Benjamin Graves Burks, whose history I have heretofore given.

Mr. Silas Burks was quite a noted man in the early history of Green County. He was more famed as a pugilist than for any other quality he possessed, having had more fights than perhaps any other man in the county, and often with the stoutest men. He whipped, on one occasion, Jenkens Asten, a great fighter, and much his superior in point of size. Burks took, it is said, a foul start upon him, which soon made him cry "enough." Burks weighed, in his best days, about one hundred and seventy-five pounds, and was one of the best made men for strength and activity I ever saw. He was a perfect stranger to fear. He was apt to get the start of any one with whom he fought, and was generally the champion even with those of superior size. He was once badly whipped by Reuben Vaughn, the father of Fielding Vaughn, Esq., a worthy and respectable citizen of this county, who yet survives, at the age of about seventy years. The last fight Burks had was about the year 1814 or 1815, with Robert Barret, a maternal uncle of the writer. Barret, by an unfortunate blow, in the beginning of the fight, knocked out the eye of Burks, or, rather, so injured it as to destroy the sight. Burks was the aggressor in the affair, and the result seemed to have humbled his pride and ambition in matters of the sort. Mr. Burks, though a farmer, paid but little attention to that sort of business. He was much given to the sports very common at that day, horse-racing and gambling, and was a good judge of horses and a successful jockey trader. He died from home, some thirty years ago, at the age of about seventy-five years.

John O'Hara carried on the first tailor's shop ever established in Greensburg. He was a man very much deformed in his legs, yet walked about without crutches or cane.

Christopher Brooks was the first dancing-master in this section of country, and gave lessons in dancing in Greensburg at a very early period. One of his legs was an inch shorter than the other, but the imperfection was not discoverable when dancing. An improper intimacy having sprung up between himself and a lady of the neighborhood, he was compelled by her relations to marry her, when they left the country. In 1843 the writer met with him at Nashville, Tennessee. He was then an acting constable of that city, doing a profitable business, and was highly respected by the community. His age at that time was about seventy years.

The first classical school ever taught in Greensburg was by General James Allen, whose history I have given in detail. He taught a select class of young men in his clerk's office, instructing them only in the higher branches of literature. Of this class were the Rev. Thomas Cleland, Hon. Samuel Brents, James McElroy, and Francis Emerson, sketches of whom I have given, except as to McElroy.

The first tobacco warehouse ever established in Greensburg was by a merchant from Prussia, whose name was William H. King. He was a man well-educated in the country from which he came. He spoke plainly and fluently the English language, was sociable and interesting in promiscuous companies, and enjoyed himself in the society of Greensburg at that day. His associates among the young men of that time were John, Robert, and Captain Jack Barret, Wm. J. Adair, Dr. Alexander Irvine, Barret Cook, Judge Wakefield, and others whose names have been heretofore mentioned. In statue he was small, but good looking, and of very gentlemanly demeanor. He committed suicide by drowning, in a deep hole of Green River, in the latter part of the summer of 1811. The hole is near Greensburg, and is known and called by the name of King's Hole to this day. The act was attributed to disappointment in a love affair with a beautiful and accomplished young lady of the town.

The first factory for the manufacture of tobacco in Greensburg was established by James Harris, of Richmond, Virginia, and conducted by his brother, Thomas Harris, and Gabriel M. Buckner, who were interested in the establishment.

A suit instituted in the Green Circuit Court by James Simpson against Boston Damewood, in the year 1802, was referred to the arbitration and award of Governor Isaac Shelby, Wm.

Logan, and Samuel Brents, whose award was made a judgment of the court. Three more distinguished men were scarcely to be found in the State of Kentucky.

Samuel Harding, an elder brother of the Hon. Aaron Harding, taught the first singing-school remembered to have been taught in Greensburg. Mr. Harding afterward became a Baptist preacher, and removed to Indiana at an early day, where he died. His brother, John Harding, a Baptist preacher also, of high reputation for good sense and strict piety, died some fifteen years ago in the town of Greensburg.

The first resident carpenters and house-joiners of Greensburg remembered, were Edward J. Bullock, whose wife was a sister of Governor James Clark, and Daniel Lisle, the father of the Hon. Thomas W. Lisle. They came to the town as workmen on the court-house, built in 1803, of which Waller Bullock, of Lexington, was the undertaker. The building is of stone. The foreman in the masonry was Robert Ball, who died some two or three years since, in Green County, at the advanced age of about ninety-five years.

Thomas Parsons attained the greatest age of any man who has died in Green County. He died at his residence, three miles from Greensburg, a few years since, in the one hundred and sixth year of his age. He was less a dotard than most men at eighty years of age. He rode horseback to within a week of his death. He was a Democrat in politics, and never failed to exercise his privilege of voting. He was a soldier of the Revolution, and a pensioner of the Government to his death. A great many soldiers of the Revolution, residing in Green County, lived to a very advanced age. Joshua Phipps was in the hundreth year of his age when he died. James H. Sherrill lived to see his ninety-ninth year. Major James Cowherd, Jonathan Cowherd, Sherrod Griffin, John Thurman, Andrew Barnett, Wm. Barnett, Thomas Gaines, John Emerson, James Spilman, John Defevers, Elias Barbee, Gentleman John Smith, Thomas Smith, Benjamin Cook, and John Chaudoin, all died between eighty and ninety years of age. A Mrs. Speak, of Robinson's Creek, Green County, died some years since at the advanced age of one hundred and thirteen years. Wm. Finn, now living in Green County, is over one hundred years of age, and delights yet occasionally in the sport of fishing. All the persons above named were among the early settlers of Green County.

The following are the names of the earliest appointed justices of the peace for Green County, to-wit: Moses Skaggs, Samuel Burks, John Hall, John Johnson, Samuel Watts, George Clark, John Rodgers, James Blain, Robert Hill, Daniel White, David Willock, John Emerson, Robert Allen, Wm. Simpson, and John Trotter—all commissioned as justices of the peace previous to the year 1801.

The earliest appointed constables of Green County were Frederick Skaggs, Johnson Graham, Jesse Handy, and William Trible.

The first county assessors, or commissioners of tax, were John Chandler and Creed Haskins. The first named was a Baptist preacher; the second, a prominent young man just entering on business. Mr. Haskins was born in Frederick County, Virginia, December 2, 1773, and came to Kentucky with his father, Robert Haskins, when a small boy. Creed grew up, married well, became a respectable and wealthy farmer of the county, and died in the neighborhood of his first settlement on the 21st of April, 1851, at the age of seventy-seven years, four months, and nineteen days. He was a man of exemplary life and conduct, and no aspirant for office. Daniel Trabue, Henry Hatcher, and three others of the Trabues, all brothers, married his sisters. The family, with their connections, were all Baptists, and constituted the first church organized at Mt. Gilead, on Skinhouse Branch of Caney Fork Creek. Edward Haskins, brother of Creed, died the 12th of April, 1837, in the seventy-second year of his age. Colonel Daniel Trabue died the 10th of September, 1840, between eighty and ninety years of age. Henry Hatcher died the 19th of July, 1836, over eighty years of age.

The coroners of Green County previous to 1800 were first, Joshua Armstrong; second, David Allen. David Allen was also the first captain of an organized militia company of

Green County, and was deputy sheriff for a short time in the year 1800.

James Scott, when the county of Warren was formed, was appointed to run the line between that county and Green.

Henry Embry was the undertaker for the building of the first jail. Robert Ball, a stone-mason, performed the work.

The first man tried for vagrancy in Green County was Benjamin Hopkins; the second, was Wm. Pringle.

The first will proven and admitted to record in the county of Green was that of Richard Chisham, the father of Gabriel, Benjamin, and John Chisham, all of whom were men of note in the county afterward. Gabriel was a man of fine sense, but was distinguished most as a very successful and accomplished professional gambler. Benjamin was a good farmer and surveyor, and was once (1820) the representative of the county in the Legislature. John followed farming and school-teaching. In his latter years Gabriel became intemperate, lost his fortune, and died on a trip from home, at St. Louis, about the year 1826 or 1827.

Jonathan Hobson, an elder brother of Captaim William Hobson, was born in Virginia about the year 1788. His parents died when he was very young, and he came to Kentucky, when a small boy, with his maternal uncle, Jonathan Patteson. At about sixteen years of age he commenced writing in the clerk's office of William Caldwell, of Adair County, soon after its formation, where he continued until the formation of Butler County, when he was appointed the first clerk of the courts of that county. A short time afterward, a vacancy occurring in the courts of Warren County, he became, by appointment, clerk of the courts of that county, in which situation he continued near thirty years, when he resigned, and his deputy and nephew, Atwood G. Hobson, was appointed in his stead, and served as such for many years. Mr. Hobson, after this, was elected a member of the Legislature from Warren County, of which body he was an efficient and influential member. Mr. Hobson acquired considerable property during his life, and was liberal in dispensing it to his relations and to the poor. He contributed liberally also to churches and ministers, and to anything tending to the promotion of the public good. No more exemplary man ever lived in any community, and no man was ever more universally beloved than he. In his latter years he lived on his farm near Bowlinggreen, making an annual visit to his relations in Green and elsewhere. On one of those visits, in the fall of 1863, he was taken sick at the house of his widowed sister, Mrs. Thomas W. Edwards, in Green County, where he died, at about the age of seventy-six years. Many years ago he proposed to his negroes, of whom he had a good many, that he would manumit such of them as would go to Liberia. Eleven of them, I think, embraced the offer, and went; the rest remained with him during his life. He provided liberally for those who went; and was the kindest of masters to those who remained and preferred slavery with him to freedom in a foreign land.

The first bank ever established in Greensburg was one of the independent banks, chartered by a Legislative act of 1818, which I have heretofore mentioned under another head. Its first president was General James Allen; its cashier, William D. Barret; and its clerk, James C. Sympson. Its duration was only for a year, or such a matter. The next chartered bank of Greensburg was called the Commonwealth's Bank, of which I have heretofore spoken also. One of these banks was established in each judicial district of Kentucky. General James Allen was the first president of this bank also; William D. Barret, its cashier, and Anthony Waggener clerk. The last bank established at Greensburg was a branch of the Kentucky Bank, chartered by the Legislature at the session of 1834-5. Its first president was John M. S. McCorkle, now of the city of Louisville; William D. Barret, its cashier, and the writer was its clerk, notary public, and attorney. A year or two after its establishment, John Barret was appointed its president, who was succeeded some years afterward by Josiah Brummal, who was succeeded by the appointment of John Barret once more, who remained in office until his death; after which, Brummal was again president whilst the institution remained. Three years after the appointment of Wm. D. Barret as cashier, he resigned and removed to St. Louis, Missouri, and the writer was appointed in his stead, and acted in this capacity nearly twenty years, when he resigned and was succeeded by the Hon. Henry C. Wood, who, after a year's service or more, was elected to a judgeship in the Court of Appeals of Kentucky. His successor in the bank as cashier was William B. Fairman, who had previously been the clerk of the institution from 1839 to 1860.

I have omitted the mention of many names connected with the early settlement of Green County equally noted and meritorious as many who are mentioned, but the limits of the work contemplated forbid any further extension under this head. A complete history of Green County would constitute a large volume of itself; and so would the history of each one of many other counties of the State.

I subjoin, more for curiosity than any other purpose, a list of uncommon names which appear on the record books of the Green County Court during the first eight years after the organization of the county. But very few of the persons who bore them are remembered by any one living at this day. The names are as follows, to-wit: John Rock, Abijah Stone, Bailey Corder, J. W. Crank, George Spear, Wm. Syckle, Jno. Steele, Thomas Stubbs, Stephen Biggs, Wm. Bigger, Thomas Slaughter, Job Little, James Killing, John Killpatrick, Absalom Birch, Wm. Oaks, Samuel Rountree, Isaac Crabtree, Wm. Bush, Julius Bunch, Henry Grove, John Park, John Wood, Boston Damewood, Joe Logsdon, Sylvanus Pipes, Daniel Pepper, Stephen Scales, George Wolfscale, Joshua Matlock, Thomas Highsmith, Frederick Slinker, Wm. Peace, George Fought, Alexander Whip, Albert Dunce, Job Carlock, Joshua Matlock, John Votan, Stephen Vittatoe, Marcus Followay, James Tay, Peter Demas, Wm. Hoorcrous, John Huggurt, Jacob Yoder, Joe. Swing, Enoch Schoolfield, Jacob Cork, Hugh Carigan, John Willing, Isham Ready, John Stahl, Thos. Hall, Elijah Stillwell, Wm. Meadows, John Fields, William Summers, Elisha Winter, Philip Wells, Joseph Akin, Adam Payne, Duquid Ford, Wm. Rivers, Wm. H. King, Solomon

Priest, Moses Meeker, Philip Weas, Isaac Plummer, William Razor, Elijah Fishback, John Fisher, Titus Hunter, James Harpur, Levi Blunt, Wm. Hoehammer, Jesse Shoemaker, Caleb Handy, Wm. Tandy, John Stringer, Jose Philpot, Isaac Skinner, John Bridgewater, John Take, Wm. Tribble, Norris Bass, Jarrot Brickey, John Silcock, Joseph Winlock, Jacob Wilcox, Abraham Babcock, Wm. Hancock, Wm. Nance, Jacob Niece, John Sally, John Mouser, John Long, Horatio Short, Daniel Brown, Jeremiah Black, Liberty Green, Jesse Gray, John White, Adam Lamm, Eli Bull, John Crowe, Enos Bird, Christopher Wren, Ediah Owing, Wm. Wright, Michael Archdeacon, Jacob Yokum, James Goin, John Goodnight, John Trice, Abraham Lets, Abijah Links, Wm. Cake, Henry Neitz, Wm. Hoocouse, Allen Gundell, Jos. Carter, and Thos. Waggener. Besides these, were the Williamsons, the Johnsons, the Jacksons, the Robertsons, the Petersons, the Stephensons, the Jemmiesons, the Richardsons, the Wilsons, and the Clarksons.

CARRINGTON SIMPSON.

The trite saying, that "murder will out," was fully verified in the case of Carrington Simpson, of Green County, who was a *particeps criminis* in one of the most diabolical deeds of murder that was ever perpetrated in this, or, perhaps, any other country. A history of the affair, and of the man who was the principal actor in that tragic scene, will now be given, as far as my memory serves me, being greatly assisted by extensive notes taken at the time by General Samuel A. Spencer, who was one of the attorneys for the defense on the trial of the case in the Green Circuit Court.

In the month of July, 1838, Lucinda White, a widow lady of about forty-five years of age, and her two sons, Lewis Charner and John Quincy, and her daughter-in-law, Mrs. Matilda White, some twenty-two years of age, and her infant son, William Franklin, about two years of age, were all foully murdered, and their bodies deposited in an old potatoe-hole in a dilapidated cabin, situated in an unenclosed waste old field on the farm of Carrington Simpson, on the south side of Green River, about seven miles from Greensburg, and about one mile from the place the murdered persons lived. The bodies were slightly covered, principally with rotten tobacco stalks, the house having been used some years previously as a tobacco barn.

When the bodies were exhumed, they were found in the hole, or grave, in the following order, viz: The son, Lewis Charner, on top; next to him, Lucinda, the mother; next, the son, John Quincy, and the infant, William Franklin; and at the bottom, Matilda, the daughter-in-law. Although in a high state of putrefaction, the bodies were all identified and recognized by those who had known them well; one by the comb in her head and the ring upon her finger; another by her teeth and the color of her hair; another by the peculiarity of his teeth, &c. It seems that all of them were stript of their clothing before interment, except Matilda, the daughter-in-law—her clothing appeared to have been pulled up and tied over her head; she had also a rope about her body and arms, as though she had been tied. The skull of each one was broken, apparently, and, in the opinion of the physician present at the exhumation, with the same instrument, except that the head of the child was mashed and severed from the body. The coroner having held his inquest and made out his report, old Daniel Kesler, the father of young Mrs. White, collected the remains of his daughter (Matilda) and her child and placed them in one coffin, and those of Lucinda and her two sons, which he placed in another coffin, and deposited both coffins in the same grave on his farm, not far distant from the scene of the direful atrocity.

Carrington Simpson was an intemperate man in the use of liquor, petulant and fearless, especially when under its influence, had a great many quarrels and fights, and, in short, a general wrong-doer, and a terror to the neighborhood in which he lived. Some eighteen months had elapsed from the time of the murder to the discovery of the bodies spoken of, and during that whole period there was not even a suspicion that a murder had been committed; but the universal belief in the neighborhood was, that this family had moved clandestinely to the State of Alabama. The facts which influenced this general belief were, that Lucinda White had a brother and other relations living in that State, who were anxious for the removal of her family thither; she was anxious to go, and often spoke of going; her eldest son, the husband of Matilda, had gone there some months previously, with the view of securing a home for the family by the time they might arrive; the husband of Matilda, who had gone, was by no means in good odor with his father-in-law, old Daniel Kesler, but on the other hand was regarded by him as a very sorry chance, and who consequently opposed vehemently the going of his daughter to Alabama; but she was determined to accompany her mother-in-law, Lucinda, whenever she went, at all hazards, and it was agreed among the family that Matilda should go to her father's (old Daniel Kesler's) to spend the day, and while there collect some articles of clothing belonging to her, and bring them away; in the meantime give her father's family to understand that she had abandoned all idea of going to Alabama. The arrangement was further made, however, with Carrington Simpson, who was present at the time, that he was to remove them five days' journey with his ox team, and that they were to start at a late hour that night. Lewis Charner, the eldest of the murdered sons, had been started off a day or two previous to the contemplated movement of the rest of the family, on an old worn-out gray horse, which they feared would not be able to hold out, and that he possibly might have to return before he had traveled very far, which the sequel will show was the case.

The night appointed for the removal was the first Saturday in July, 1838. Jason Bell, who lived about six miles from Greensburg, and three or four miles from Simpson's, on the same side of the river, had a still-house of very low character, where rowdies frequently met to carouse. Carrington Simpson was one of the most frequent attendants. On the Thursday before the murder, Simpson went to this still-house. Pleasant Sadler was there also, who was the step-son of Bell. Simpson's account of that meeting, as related in his testimony on the trial of Bell and Sadler, was that after talking awhile on other matters he remarked to them that Lucinda White wanted some one to remove her to Alabama. Sadler remarked that she had a purse of money as long as his arm. Bell then said, that would be a pretty good haul. Sadler then proposed to him and Bell, that they should kill old Lucinda and all the family, throw them into the river, and get her long purse of money. Bell agreed to the killing, but objected to throwing them into the river, as it might lead to their discovery, and inquired of Simpson if he did not know of some deep hole in which they could throw the bodies. Simpson mentioned as a very suitable place, near by, an old potatoe-hole, in a falling-in waste-house, in an old field of his. It was then agreed that Simpson should go to Lucinda's on Friday, and tell her that Bell and Sadler would move her five days' journey for ten dollars; that she must be ready to start by Saturday night; that they would all be there with a cart and ox team by dark, prepared to start on the trip.

They were at the place by the time appointed, with the cart and ox team, but had previously murdered Matilda and the child in the old field in which the waste-house was situated. They had met her on her return from her father's. Lucinda and her son John Quincy were murdered at her house after their arrival there with the cart, and their bodies taken to the old waste-house and thrown into the same hole with Matilda and her child. The cart was then loaded up with Lucinda's plunder, which was carried off to Simpson's house, where the division of spoils took place.

The next day, Lewis Charner, who had started off beforehand on the old gray horse, returned, alleging that the horse was about to give out, that he was satisfied it could never perform the trip, and that he had concluded to leave the old horse and travel with the rest of the family. Arriving at Lucinda's house he found it vacated, and supposing they had started on their trip and that he had missed them on the way, he hunted up Sadler, who prevailed upon him to conceal himself (under some pretext, not now remembered) in an old barn until night, when he was inveigled into the old field, murdered, and deposited in the same hole with the rest, there to remain until time and circumstances should reveal to public observation the whole affair.

I should have mentioned that the poor old gray horse was also taken to the old field and killed near the waste-house, so that any disagreeable effluvia which might arise from the decomposing human bodies would be attributed to the carcase of the dead horse.

After the night of Saturday, the 7th of July, 1838, the whole of this family were known to be missing; yet nearly eighteen months had elapsed before even the faintest suspicion had been aroused in the neighborhood that they had been foully dealt with, because it was generally understood in the neighborhood that they intended to move to Alabama. Many months afterward, however, the anxiety of old Mr. Kesler in regard to his daughter Matilda induced him to write to Alabama to ascertain where they had settled, how they were doing, &c. After waiting a long time and receiving no reply, he wrote again, and again, with no better success. About this time various articles of clothing, such as ladies' dresses, children's clothes, bed clothing, &c., were seen worn and used by Simpson's family, which were recognized by the neighbors as having been worn and used by Lucinda and Matilda; but still their suspicions were slight, from the fact that Simpson had repeatedly stated openly that he had received his pay for moving them in such articles, they having no money to spare for that purpose. About this time the suspicions of the neighbors began to gather strength, daily, from new discoveries of articles worn by the Simpsons, articles which it was unreasonable to suppose those persons would have parted with, such as under-dresses, flannels, shirts, shoes, children's clothing, and new calico dresses which these people were seen making a few days before they started. These suspicions and circumstances led to the arrest of Simpson, in March, 1840, under a warrant obtained by Daniel Kesler, the father of Matilda, and he was brought before Justices J. D. Mottley and Isaac Gibbons, who, after hearing the evidence and duly deliberating thereon, committed him to jail, to be held for trial at the ensuing circuit court for the murder of the five persons before mentioned.

Some few days after his commitment, a number of persons of the neighborhood in which the murder was supposed to have been committed assembled, divided themselves into different parties or companies, intending to search the neighborhood thoroughly, in every direction, for the bodies supposed to be murdered. One of the companies having with them a grubbing-hoe, proceeded immediately to the old field and waste-house of which I have spoken, which they all entered; and, after casting their eyes about a little, the man with the grubbing-hoe, without the expectation of making any discoveries, made two licks with his hoe, in quick succession, into the loose looking tobacco stalks which covered the hole. The second lick brought up the rib of a human body. The rubbish being cleared away, several human forms were discoverable, but they were not disturbed until the arrival of the coroner. An inquest being held, the remains were disposed of as heretofore stated. Before his arrest, Simpson's statements in regard to what had become of this family were very contradictory. In regard to their manner of leaving he was generally consistent. At one time he said he did not know where they had gone, at another, that he did know, but would not tell; and at another, that he could go to them in three hours, and that but one person besides himself knew anything about them. He said that some of them left on Saturday night, and the rest on Sunday night; that the reason they left separately and in the night was that old man Kesler, the father of Matilda, intended to stop her from going, and this plan had been adopted to escape him. These evasive answers went far to strengthen the suspicions already afloat.

On the evening of the day on which the dead bodies were found, Simpson was visited at the jail by several persons, who communicated to him the fact of their discovery, and all the circumstances which conduced to prove him, beyond all reasonable doubt, a guilty participant at least. He, however, denied, as he had uniformly done before, any participation in the affair. One of the visitors, upon leaving the jail, addressing himself to Simpson said, "As regards you, Simpson, your guilt is conclusive, and your doom is fixed, but I have no doubt there were others connected with you in the affair, for no one man could have accomplished so tragic an act unaided and alone, and you had as well come out fully and tell all about it." To these remarks Simpson made no reply. Early next morning, however, he gave information that Jason Bell and Pleasant Sadler were his accomplices in the affair, and that Sadler, a stout young man, had done the killing in each instance.

Some months previous to this time Bell and Sadler had removed from the neighborhood in which they had lived to the head waters of Brush Creek, in Green County, some twelve or fifteen miles distant; but a warrant was forthwith obtained, and an officer immediately dispatched for their arrest. They were soon brought to town, delivered over to the justices, an investigation had, mainly upon the testimony of Simpson, who made a full confession of his own guilt and of their participation, which resulted in their commitment also for further trial, without bail. At a subsequent circuit court, they were all tried, condemned, and sentenced to be capitally executed.

Soon after the sentence Bell became sick, and in a few days afterward was found dead in the cell. His illness was not thought to be dangerous, and he and Sadler being confined in a room together, separate from Simpson, it was generally believed that Sadler, his step-son, had smothered him to death. A short time after this, Sadler made a rope out of his bed-clothing and hung himself, fastening one end of the rope around his neck and the other to the grating of a small window in the dungeon some seven or eight feet high from the floor. Simpson abided his time, and was hung in the suburbs of Greensburg on the 21st of September, 1841. Bell and Sadler were to have been hung on the 27th of the same month. The throng of people who attended the hanging of Simpson was tremendous. I would say there were present on that occasion ten thousand persons at least.

After the trial, conviction, and sentence of Simpson, and when he had no hope of executive clemency, he detailed to General S. A. Spencer the following history of his life, viz:

"I was born in the county of Chesterfield, State of Virginia, on the 10th day of August, 1782, about twelve miles from Manchester, near the coal pits, where I lived until about the year 1818, when I removed to the county of Rockingham, in the State of North Carolina. I remained at this place about ten years, when I removed to Green County, Kentucky, in the year 1828, and settled some seven or eight miles southwest of Greensburg, where I have resided ever since. My mother's name was Jenny Simpson. She was never married. I had three brothers, Langhorn, Robert, and Jack, and four sisters, Betsy, Rhody, Polly, and Lear, all raised in Chesterfield County, Virginia. My father was said to be Judge C., of Virginia, from whom I took my given name. I was married about the year 1809 to Dicy Powell, daughter of James Powell, of Chesterfield.

"In 1814 I was drafted a soldier, and marched in a company commanded by Captain Berfoot for a term of six months, and was stationed at Camp Holley, near Richmond. During the service I was discharged, and I returned home. While in the service I was not idle in supplying myself with any and everything needful which fell in my way. The hen-roosts of the neighborhood, the stores of the commissary and of my brother soldiers, suffered no little from me in a small way.

"From ten years of age to the time I went into the service, I was engaged in the grocery business, first as an assistant to my brother Jack, and afterward as partner in the profits, and finally became individually interested and sole proprietor. After this, I connected with my business that of butchering, in which I continued until I left Chesterfield.

"The stand, or situation I occupied for business, I rented from a man by the name of Roberts, and I occupied it for the space of fifteen years, at $50 per year. I was not slow in forming the acquaintance of all such persons as seemed disposed to become my instruments or aiders in stealing, and such like. I formed an alliance with one Archibald Casey, the overseer of Colonel Thomas Harris, who supplied me regularly and abundantly with corn, oats, and wheat, taken from Harris and others. I was supplied in this way for several years with almost everything I needed. Colonel Harris had a wealthy sister by the name of Nancy, who owned a negro man named Peter, who was an efficient striker for me, and supplied me continually with sheep, hogs, cattle, turkeys, &c. I formed a partnership in the butchering business with a man by the name of Chelsey Wooldridge, who lived near the line of Powhattan County, and who was every whit as bad a man as myself. To carry on the business, each put in the sum of $40 capital. Although doing pretty well, we concluded we were not making money fast enough, and prevailed on the negro man Peter to leave his mistress and come into our service, to which he consented, and we kept him concealed for about eighteen months, during which period he brought to us a number of beef cattle, sheep, shoats, &c., taken from his mistress and others in the neighborhood. After getting what service we could out of him in this way, we concluded to turn him into money. It was agreed that Wooldridge should take him off to Kentucky and sell him, and return and divide the price that might be obtained; but that was the last I ever heard of Wooldridge or the negro.

"The last difficulty which occurred with me in Virginia was concerning some sheep. A man by the name of Kidd, and a free negro by the name of David Landrum, procured for me by stealth some twelve or fifteen sheep from a man by the name of Reuben Winfrey, and I took them to Richmond and sold them for a good price. On the way from Winfrey's to my house, one of the sheep got away, and ran into the field of Erasmus Reams and got with his sheep, and David, in trying to get this sheep afterward, was found out, and told that I had sold the other sheep at Richmond. Upon this charge I was tried before the justices and acquitted, but the grand jury, which met soon afterward, found a true bill against me, and process was issued for my arrest, to avoid which I removed to North Carolina as before stated.

"I bought land in North Carolina of a man by the name of Pirtle, and lived upon it until I moved to Kentucky; but I had never paid for it, and Pirtle took it back. Whilst living in North Carolina, I visited my friends stealthily in Virginia five or six times, but was never overtaken by the officers of the law. Kidd and Landrum, from time to time, had supplied me with a great deal of stolen goods. Erasmus Reams, whose name I mentioned, was the overseer of Judge Fleming, of Virginia

"Previous to this last incident mentioned, I had several times been arrested and tried before an enquiring court for petty offences, of some of which I was guilty, but always managed to escape punishment. My character was generally bad in the neighborhood in which I lived, and on one occasion, upon a charge of robbery, though innocent, I would have been found guilty had it not been that I was able to prove an *alibi* by a minister of high character, by the name of Benjamin Watkins, who stated that on the night of the alleged robbery I was at a meeting at Anderson Johhson's, where the said Watkins preached, and sat under the pulpit all the time. I was tried on that occasion by Esquires Locket and Mosely.

"Whilst in North Carolina I perpetrated a good many petty offences without detection, and was once arrested for horse-stealing. I went on one occasion to a barbecue in company with one Wm. Wortley. We remained on the ground until after dark, when each of us stole a horse. The horse taken by me belonged to a man by the name of Wm. Bethel. On our way we overtook the owner of the horse I had stolen, who immediately recognized not only the horse, but myself also. Bethel caught hold of the bridle of the horse and stopped him, when I dismounted and made off at once. Bethel afterward obtained a warrant and had me arrested, but no one appearing at the trial to prosecute I was discharged.

"In Green County I was generally regarded as a suspicious character, and believed to be guilty of many offences in the neighborhood, of which sufficient proof could not be obtained to sustain the charges; consequently, I was suffered to escape."

The fall before his arrest for murder he was arrested for stealing the hogs of an old preacher in the neighborhood by the name of Joseph O. Gentry. Upon examination before the justices, he was committed for trial at the next circuit court in default of bail; but was afterward released from prison by executing a bond for his appearance, with his son as surety.

To show the mischievousness and cruelty of his disposition, I will relate an incident which occurred a while before his arrest for murder of the White family. Being at the still-house of Bell and Sadler, on a certain occasion, at night, with some others, he proposed to a young man who was there (G. B.), a somewhat verdant youth, but of respectable family, to initiate him into the secrets of Masonry. The confiding young man agreed to the proposal, suffered himself to be denuded of his clothes, then tied, and soaped all over with soft soap. He was then taken to a deep water trough, where they dipped and washed him till he was thoroughly cleansed, after which the final ceremony was performed by branding him with a hot iron. This operation was carried on nearly the whole night; but a while before day he was released and permitted to go home, satisfied with his own concupiscence, and desiring no further light in Masonry. Bell was present on the occasion, but had no participation in the operation.

Bell and Sadler were willing strikers for Simpson, who was shrewder than they, and under his plans and directions rendered him essential service in diabolical deeds of his planning, such as slaughtering neighbor's cattle and hogs, curing the meat at home, and always making a liberal division with Simpson. A rehearsal of all the deeds of infamy charged against these men would occupy more space than we are willing to allow; let it suffice that three worse men than Simpson, Bell, and Sadler never lived, perhaps, in any country; but they have passed from earth, and must appear at the bar of God, to be judged according to their deeds.

THE HARPES—THEIR TRAGICAL HISTORY.

About seventy years ago two men, who stated in answer to inquiries made by Colonel James Davidson and others of Lincoln County, Kentucky that their names were Harpe, and that they were emigrants from North Carolina, made their appearance in Kentucky. Accompanying them were three women. The first that was known of them was that they had encamped about a mile from the present town of Stanford, in Lincoln County, near what was called the Wilderness Road.

The appearance of the individuals composing the company, as related by Colonel Davidson, was wild and rude in the extreme. One of the men was a large man, in stature above the ordinary size; the other was smaller than the ordinary size of men. The females were coarse, sun-burnt, and wretchedly attired. The clothing of all of them was shabby, weather-beaten, and dirty, indicating continual exposure to the elements, as though they had dwelt far away from the habitations of men. The frame of the large Harpe, who seemed to be the leader of the band, was bony and muscular, with gigantic limbs and broad shoulders. His countenance was bold and ferocious, and, from his strongly marked expression of villainy, appeared exceedingly repulsive. He exhibited the appearance of one of ungovernable passion, in whose breast was extinguished every noble feeling of the heart. His eyes glared upon the beholder with brilliancy, and yet with unpleasant fixedness. He wore no hat, but had very thick, coarse hair, of fiery redness, being uncombed and matted. His arms were a rifle, knife, and tomahawk; the two latter in a broad leathern belt, drawn closely around his waist. The smaller Harpe was similarly armed, and had the same suspicious exterior of his brother, with countenance equally sinister, bold, and fierce.

The party remained at their encampment the greater part of two days and a night, spending the time in rioting, drunkenness, and debauchery. When they left their camp, they took the road leading to Green River. On the Wilderness Road, which runs through Rockcastle Hills, a young man of wealth from Virginia was, on the day succeeding their departure, robbed and murdered. His name was Lankford. The Harpes were at once suspected as the perpetrators of the foul deed; and Captain Ballenger, at the head of a few bold and resolute men, started in pursuit, and after encountering some difficulties finally came upon them while encamped in a bottom of Green River, near the place where the town of Liberty, Casey County, now stands. At first they made a show of resistance; but being threatened that, if they did not immediately surrender, they would be shot down, they yielded themselves prisoners.

They were brought back to Stanford, where they were examined, and among their effects were found fine linen shirts, marked with the initials of Lankford. One had been pierced with a bullet, and was stained with blood. A considerable amount of gold was also found, and it was ascertained afterward that this was the kind of money that Lankford had with him. The evidence against them being regarded as conclusive, they were confined at first in the Stanford jail, but were afterward sent for trial to Danville, where the district court was in session. Here they broke jail, and succeeded in making their escape.

They were soon heard of again in Adair County, near Columbia, where they met a small boy, the son of Colonel Trabue, with a pillow case of flour, whom they doubtless murdered. Many years afterward, human bones, answering to the size of the boy at the time of his disappearance, were found in a sink-hole near the place he was said to have been murdered. Their path, at intervals, all along in the direction to the mouth of Green River, was marked with murders and robberies of the most brutal character. They seemed inspired with hatred against the whole human race, as is evidenced by their often killing where there was no temptation to rob. One of their victims was a little girl, whose helpless and tender age afforded no protection against fiends so merciless. A man by the name of Dooley was murdered by them not far from the place where Edmonton, now Metcalfe County, is situated; they also murdered a man named Stump, on Big Barren River, below Bowlinggreen.

The last dreadful act of barbarity, which led to their punishment and expulsion from the country, exceeded all others in atrocity. This was the murder of Mrs. Stagall, her child, and a man named Love, who was staying at Stagall's that night. Assuming the guise of Methodist preachers, they obtained lodging at Stagall's, in his absence from home. They conversed freely, and made inquiries about the Harpes, who were said to be prowling through the country. In the dead hour of night they crept stealthily down stairs, and with an axe they had procured before retiring, assassinated all the above named persons while asleep. They then set fire to the house, and made their escape.

Stagall had gone to the Robinson Lick, north of the river, for salt. Two men, one by the name of Hudgens, and the other Gilmore, who had been to the lick also, and who were on their return, had camped for the night not far from Stagall's, of which fact the Harpes were informed. About daylight the Harpes went to the camp of these men and arrested them, under the pretense that they had committed murder, robbery, and arson at the house of Stagall. Soon after the arrest they shot Gilmore, who died on the spot; Hudgens broke and run, but was overtaken and put to death also. This was stated by the women after Big Harpe's death.

When Stagall returned and discovered what had been done, almost distracted with grief and rage he turned from the smouldering ruins and repaired to the house of Captain John Leeper. Leeper was a powerful as well as a fearless man; and collecting four or five men, well-armed, they started in pursuit of vengeance. It was agreed that Leeper should attack Big Harpe, leaving Little Harpe to be disposed of by Stagall; the others were to assist as circumstances might require.

When they arrived at the camp of the Harpes, they found only the women, the men having gone aside into the woods to shoot a traveler by the name of Smith who had fallen into their hands, and whom the women did not wish to see killed before their eyes. It was this halt that enabled the pursuers to overtake them. The women immediately gave the alarm, and the Harpes, mounting their horses, which were large and fleet, fled in separate directions. Leeper singled out the Big Harpe, and, being better mounted than the others, soon left them far behind. Little Harpe succeeded in escaping.

After a chase of about nine miles, Leeper came within gunshot of Big Harpe and fired upon him; the ball striking his thigh and passing through it, entered the horse he was riding and both fell. Harpe's gun escaped from his hand. Leeper, re-loading his rifle, ran up to where Harpe lay weltering in his blood, and found him with one thigh broken and the other crushed beneath his horse. Rolling the horse away, he sat the outlaw in an easier position. Harpe begged that he might not be killed. Leeper told him that he need not fear him, but that Stagall was coming up, and probably could not be restrained. Harpe appeared frightened at this, and implored Leeper to protect him. In a few moments Stagall appeared, and, without uttering a word, raised his rifle and shot Harpe through the head. They then severed the head from the body, and stuck it upon a pole where the road crosses the creek, ever since which time the place has been called "*Harpe's Head.*"

Thus the country was rid of one of the boldest and most noted freebooters that ever lived, perhaps, in any country. This account is given principally on the authority of Colonel James Davidson, who lived in Lincoln County at the time the occurrence took place, and who was a man of high standing, and for many years Treasurer of the State of Kentucky.

The Little Harpe, when next heard from, was on the road which runs through the Choctaw grant to Tennessee, and had joined the band of outlaws led by the celebrated Mason. Mason and Harpe committed many depredations upon the road mentioned, and upon the Mississippi River. This course was continued by them for a long time, and until they grew wealthy. Finally, Mason and his band became so notorious for their villainy, that the Governor of Mississippi Territory offered a reward of five hundred dollars for his head. Harpe immediately determined to secure the reward for himself. It is said, that finding Mason one day in a thick canebrake counting his money, he shot him, cut off his head, and carried it to the village of Washington, then the capital of the territory. Here a man, who had before that time been robbed by Mason's band, recognized Harpe, and upon his evidence he was arrested, tried, condemned, and executed. Thus perished also the Little Harpe.

I have lately seen in the newspapers of the day a long account of the tragedies, capture, &c., of the Harpes, from the pen of the Hon. Joseph R. Underwood, upon the authority of a Mr. Ruby, who was long a neighbor of Mr. Leeper, who was the captor of Big Harpe, and who had often heard him speak of the affair. This account is varied in many respects from the account here given, though I regard the variance as unimportant, the facts stated being pretty much the same.

Judge Underwood's account, in some respects, is more in detail. He gives the christian names of the Harpes, which we had not before seen. The name of Big Harpe was Micajah, and that of Little Harpe was Wiley. Two of the women with them were the wives of Big Harpe. The third was the wife of Little Harpe. Judge Underwood states on the authority of Major Steward, who was sheriff of Logan County in 1799, that after Big Harpe was killed, and the Little Harpe had fled from the State, their wives and children (for each of the women had a child) were brought to Russellville, where the women were tried as accomplices of their husbands, and acquitted. Stagall, and a party of his associates, intended to murder the women after their acquittal, and sought opportunities to do so. The accomplishment of this design was prevented by the wise conduct of Judge Ormsby and Sheriff Stewart. The judge, seeing that the women would be murdered by a mob, ordered the sheriff to put them in jail, as though it never would do to turn them loose upon society; but secretly told the sheriff he would intrust the safety of the women to him, and he might remove them after night to a place of safety. The sheriff accordingly put them in jail; but fearing they might not be safe there, as soon as he could do it undiscovered, he removed them after dark from the jail, and hid them in a sink. The next night he removed them five miles from Russellville to a cave, where he kept them hid and supplied with food until Stagall and his party had left, and they could safely make their escape.

Judge Underwood's account speaks of Big Harpe's wives as coarse women, but Little Harpe's wife as a beautiful young woman that had been well raised; and that after Little Harpe was hung in Mississippi, she had married a highly respectable man, and raised by him a large family of children, all of whom were much esteemed for their honesty, sobriety, and industry. His informant, however, would not tell the name of the person she had married, because a silly world might take occasion to reflect upon her children in consequence of her connection with Harpe.

Mr. Stewart, the sheriff, told Judge Underwood that the women seemed to be grateful to him for the manner in which he provided for them, and related to him with apparent candor the history of their lives and connection with the Harpes. Among other things they told him that their husbands had once been put in jail at Knoxville, on suspicion of being guilty of crime when they were innocent; and when they got out, they declared war against all mankind, and determined to murder and rob until they were killed.

The company selected to pursue the Harpes after the Stagall murder were all pioneers of the wilderness, whose names were as follows, viz: John Leeper, James Tompkins, Silas Magby, Nevil Lindsey, Matthew Cristy, Robert Roberson, and the infuriated Moses Stagall. The last mentioned name is spelled by Mr. Underwood, in his account, *Stigall;* all other accounts that I have seen spell it as I have done. The character of Stagall, according to Ruby's account given to Underwood, was very bad, and states that he was afterward killed for aiding Joshua Fleehart in running off with Miss Maddox. The place called Harpe's Head is about twenty miles from the town of Henderson, just within the line of Hopkins County (now Webster) where the roads from Henderson, Morganfield, and Hopkinsville intersect, which is a very wild and lonely spot. The bloody legend connected with it has been made the foundation of a thrilling border romance by Judge Hall, of Cincinnati, much famed as a pleasing and interesting writer.

27

APPENDIX.

THE ALIEN AND SEDITION LAWS.

Six years after the admission of Kentucky into the Union as a sovereign State, an agitation of the public mind took place which has scarcely ever been equaled on any questions which have arisen since that day. This agitation was produced by the passage of two acts of Congress, known as the "Alien and Sedition Laws." These laws met with almost the unanimous condemnation of Kentucky.

The Alien Law authorized the President of the United States "to order all such aliens, as he shall judge dangerous to the peace and safety of the United States, or shall have reasonable grounds to suspect are concerned in treasonable or secret machinations against the government thereof, to depart out of the territory of the United States." By another section, the President was authorized to "grant license to any alien to remain within the United States for such time as he shall judge proper, and at such place as he may designate." It was likewise enacted, "that should any alien return, who had been ordered out of the United States by the President, unless by his permission, he shall be imprisoned so long as in the opinion of the President the public safety may require."

The passage of the Sedition Law by Congress was clearly an attempt to protect the official conduct of the government officers of the United States from a free and unrestrained discussion; and the act held any person answerable "by fine and imprisonment, who should print, utter, or publish any false, scandalous, and malicious writing against the government of the United States, the President of the United States, or either House of Congress, with intent to defame, either of them, or excite against either of them the hatred of the good people of the United States."

Subjecting to condign punishment malicious falsities is by no means objectionable; but the great objection to this law was the subjection of men's opinions, however honestly expressed, to the punishment of fine and imprisonment. Opinions can only be successfully combated by argument. Mental freedom should be open to the excursions of all minds, and never be trammeled by any fears of prosecution, or apprehensions of legal penalties. This idea is well supported by the Constitution of the United States, which declares in its very first amendment that "Congress shall make no law respecting an establishment of religion, or prohibiting the free exercise thereof; or abridging the freedom of speech, or the press." The spirit of the Constitution clearly prohibits all legislation on subjects so vitally sacred as tending to encourage factions, and endanger the liberty and prosperity of the people.

The sense of Kentucky in regard to these laws was fully expressed in resolutions adopted by the Legislature of Kentucky at the session of 1798. The same resolutions had been previously adopted by the Legislature of Virginia, and Mr. Jefferson regarded as the acknowledged author of them; and being communicated by him to Mr. Breckinridge, the leading spirit and statesman of Kentucky, were by him introduced into the House of Representatives of Kentucky on the 8th day of November, 1798, and passed both branches of that body by a vote nearly unanimous. These resolutions, independent of their protestations against the "Alien and Sedition Laws," convey the doctrine that the several States composing the United States of America are "united by a compact, under the style and title of a Constitution of the United States; that to this compact each State acceded, as a State, and is an integral party, its co-States forming to itself the other party; that the government created by this compact was not made the exclusive or *final* judge of the extent of the powers delegated to itself; but that in all other cases of compact among parties having no common judge, each party has an equal right to judge for itself, as well as of infractions as to mode and manner of redress."

Mr. Wm. Murray, the representative from the county of Franklin, opposed vehemently these resolutions, casting his vote against each and every one them, nine in all. Against the first, Mr. Murray's was the only vote cast; against the second, Brook and Murray; against the third, Murray and Poage; against the fourth, fifth, sixth, seventh, and eighth, Murray alone; against the ninth, Brook, Murray, and Poage. Mr. Murray, in some remarks he is reported to have made on that occasion, said: "We were not sent here to fabricate theories of government, and pronounce void the acts of Congress. The Constitution was not merely a *covenant* between integral States, but a compact between several *individuals* composing these States. Accordingly, the Constitution commences with this form of expression: 'We, the people of the United States,' not 'we, the thirteen States of America.'" In another place he remarked, that "the authority to determine that a law is void is lodged with the judiciary."

His remarks on this occasion corresponded with those of the distinguished Daniel Webster on a subsequent occasion, when he so triumphantly vindicated the supremacy of the Constitution of the United States over all State laws. He said on that occasion, in answer to Mr. Hayne: "The gentleman has not shown, it cannot be shown, that the Constitution is a compact between the State governments. The Constitution itself, in its very front, refuses that proposition; it declares that it is ordained and established by the people of the United States."

On the adoption of the resolutions of 1798, moved by Mr. Breckinridge, he in their support, and in reply to Mr. Murray, said: "I consider the co-States to be alone parties to the federal compact, and solely authorized to judge in the last resort of the power exercised under the compact, Congress being not a party, but merely the creature of the compact, and subject, as to its assumption of power, to the final judgment of those by whom, and for whose use, itself and its powers were all created." He said, also: "If, upon the representation of the States from whom they derive their powers, they should nevertheless attempt to enforce them, I hesitate not to declare it as my opinion, that it is then the right and duty of the several States to *nullify those acts and protect their citizens* from their operation."

It is asserted that all the States passed counter resolutions to those of Kentucky of 1798, except the State of Virginia. The effect of the resolutions of 1798, proceeding primarily as they did from so high authority as that of Mr. Jefferson, was to influence in no small degree the administration of the General Government; and had, besides, a very fatal importance in the misconstruction of the Constitution given by leading men of South Carolina and other leading men of the United States. The false, dangerous, and unconstitutional doctrines of these resolutions have long since been disclaimed and disavowed by the constituted authorities of Kentucky; especially in resolutions approved by Governor Breathitt, which were adopted by the Legislature on the 2d of February, 1833. The following is the substance of the resolutions of disavowal by Kentucky:

"That so long as the present Constitution remains unaltered, the legislative enactments of the constituted authorities of the United States can only be repealed by the authorities that made them; and if not repealed, can in no wise be finally and authoritatively abrogated or annulled, than by the sentence of the Federal Judiciary declaring their unconstitutionality; that those enactments, subject only to be so repealed or declared null, and treaties made by the United States, are supreme laws of the land; and no State of this Union has any constitutional right or power to nullify any such enactment or treaty, or to contravene them, or obstruct their execution; that it is the duty of the President of the United States, a bounden, solemn duty, to take care that these enactments and treaties be faithfully executed, observed, and fulfilled; and we receive with unfeigned and cordial approbation the pledge which the President has given to the nation in his late proclamation, that he will perform this high and solemn duty."

THE LATE GREAT REBELLION.

Although a history of the late disastrous Rebellion belongs properly to a history of the United States, yet it seems to me that a passing notice, at least, would not be improper. I propose, therefore, to give a synopsis of the cause which produced it, and its results. Many large books have already been written on the subject, to which the reader is referred for a fuller account.

Slavery has existed, at some period, in almost every portion of the civilized globe. The introduction of slavery into the country was during the reign of Queen Elizabeth of England, in the year 1620, when twenty were landed by a Dutch man-of-war in Virginia. This was the beginning of a traffic which continued for more than two hundred years. The utility of negro slavery in the warm regions of the South was found of great advantage in the cultivation of cotton, sugar, and rice. In the Northern and Western States there were very few slaves, the climate not being so well suited to their nature, nor the agricultural products such as to better enable them to render more essential or better service; hence the Northern and Northwest States were called Free States, and the Southern were called Slave States.

The people of the free States were, in general, opposed to slavery, and thought it wrong to hold a portion of the human family in bondage; and although they had no right under our Constitution to interfere in that matter, yet they would talk, write, and speak against it, seeking to show that the South, by the toleration of slavery, were acting injuriously even to their own interests. The South regarded slavery not only as a blessing, but as having the sanction of Holy Writ. The subject of slavery finally became greatly agitated. Southerners claimed the right to take with them their slaves to the territories lately acquired by the United States, with the view of extending our slave territory. The Northerners denied the right, and parties arose entertaining these opposite opinions; and in 1857, James Buchanan, a Northern man with Southern principles, was elected President of the United States by the pro-slavery party. Slavery agitation continued with increased rancor. The Southerners believed that the next election would result in the election of an anti-slavery man, and that slavery in the territories would finally be prohibited; in that event secession was threatened by the South, who believed that the North were threatening the liberties and honor of the South. The South regarded secession as a right granted by the Constitution, and many having long cherished the idea with great fondness, determined now to carry it out.

As anticipated by the South, at the November election, 1860, Mr. Lincoln, opposed to the extension of slavery into the territories, was duly elected President of the United States; and although the South had the majority in the United States Senate, and it was yet four months before Lincoln would obtain power, they immediately seized the forts, arsenals, mints, custom-houses, and other property of the United States in their limits. To this Mr. Buchanan, still in office, offered no resistance. He admitted that the Constitution gave no right to the States to secede, but at the same time contended that the Government had no right to "coerce," or use force, to prevent secession. The South therefore proceeded in their career unmolested, and every fort in South Carolina was seized, except Fort Sumter, and Fort Pickens in Florida, and batteries erected in order to drive out their small garrisons of United States troops; and by the 4th day of March, 1861, when Lincoln came into power, seven of the Southern States had seceded, and four others making ready to follow them. A Southern government for these States had been established in Alabama, with Jefferson Davis at the head of it. Most of the ships of our navy had been sent to distant seas, and most of the small garrisons of United States troops had either been captured, or else had joined the Southern party. Sumter and Pickens were the only two forts in all the South where the "Star Spangled Banner still waved." Upon the flag at Sumter the first shot was afterward fired. This fort was garrisoned by only seventy men, under the command of Major Anderson, and was in an exhausted and helpless condition. General Beauregard, commanding the forces then in Charleston, numbering about seven thousand, supposing an attempt would be made to throw supplies and reinforcements into Sumter, on the 11th of April, 1861, summoned Anderson to surrender, to do which he refused, and at 4 o'clock, on the morning of the 12th, the first shot was fired from Fort Moultrie, and the fight began, continuing until the afternoon of the 13th, when the garrison capitulated and marched out with the honors of war, no one being killed on either side.

Thus commenced a war of four years' duration, disastrous in the extreme to the whole country, but especially to the South, and such a one as is to be hoped may never again occur in this "land of the free and home of the brave." Troops were immediately called for by the President; and throughout the loyal States raising soldiers, building ships and gunboats, forging cannons, and manufacturing muskets and small arms, and such like, were the topics of all conversations.

Among the first measures of the Government was the blockade of the Southern ports. At the entrance of every harbor men-of-war were stationed, to prevent ships from going in or coming out. By July, an army of fifty thousand men had been collected in the neighborhood of Washington, and commenced their march on Richmond, which had become the Southern capital. The battle of Bull Run ensued, in which the Union troops were defeated, and retreated upon Washington. This unlooked for event aroused the North to more energetic action. Volunteers sprang to arms in great numbers, and the army of the Potomac soon amounted to two hundred thousand men.

Battles were now fought all over the country, with varying results, the particulars of which the limits of our work will not allow to be given. In 1862 General Grant was sent with forty thousand men to the Tennessee and Cumberland rivers, then closed by the enemy's forts. The 6th of February Fort Henry was captured, and on the 15th Fort Donelson; and the rivers cleared for hundreds of miles, and the Mississippi opened as far as Island No. 10, the enemy falling back to the South.

In April of the same year occurred a six days' bombardment of the forts defending New Orleans by the fleet under

Farragut. The same month, it was confidently expected that McClellan, with his magnificent army of the Potomac, would capture Richmond, the enemy's capital, and at once end the war, but it was a signal failure. In less than three months his army was so reduced by disease and battle, that the enemy no longer feared them, and prepared to march on Washington. General Pope, opposing them, was compelled to retreat, and before McClellan could afford any aid, Pope was a second time defeated at Bull Run.

The enemy continued their march upon Washington, but were met by McClellan on a stream in Maryland called Antietam, where, after a bloody battle, victory perched upon his standard. No pursuit being made, the enemy crossed the river on the 18th of September unmolested.

General Burnside succeeded McClellan in command of the army of the Potomac, and in December of the same year fought the enemy at Fredericksburg, and was defeated with a loss of twelve thousand men.

In April, 1863, the same army, under General Hooker, attacked the enemy, but were defeated, losing eighteen thousand men. General Lee, of the Confederate Army, crossed the fords of the Potomac in June, of 1863, and met the Union Army at Gettysburg, Pennsylvania, commanded by General Meade, who, after a three days' battle, signally defeated the enemy, with a loss on their part of not less than thirty thousand men.

Rosecrans, in the mean time, had gained the signal victory of Stone River. The Mississippi River had been opened its entire length, except between Port Hudson and Vicksburg. The 4th of July, 1863, Vicksburg surrendered to General Grant; and on the 9th of the same month Port Hudson surrendered to General Banks, which opened the Mississippi from its source to its mouth. In the series of battles mentioned, the loss of the enemy was forty thousand men and seven hundred guns. On the 9th of September of this year, General Rosecrans having marched from Murfreesboro, entered Chattanooga. The battle of Chickamauga was, of course, a check to his progress; but General Grant succeeding him, before the close of the year forced the enemy into the fastnesses of Georgia.

General Grant was made Lieutenant General in March, 1864, and thus became Commander-in-Chief. Sherman commanded the army at Chattanooga, and Grant, with the army of the Potomac, on the Rappahannock, whose eyes were still on Richmond. From the 5th of May to the 18th of June, Grant's forces were in constant collision with the enemy, sixty thousand men losing their lives in six weeks, when Petersburg, the key to Richmond, was besieged and held. Sherman's army, too, was in constant contact with the enemy, and in three days killed twenty thousand men, and entered Atlanta early in September. Before Christmas, Sherman's army reached and captured Savannah, on the Atlantic coast. He cut loose from the base of supply of the enemy a railroad which connected them with the north. A more wonderful march than that accomplished by Sherman is scarcely, if anywhere, to be found on record. Sherman's army, after resting and re-equipping, turned to the north to assist General Grant in destroying the army defending Richmond, and made their way through the marshes, floods, and high lands of North Carolina. All the cities in their march surrendered on their approach. When they were near the Virginia line, Grant fell upon Richmond remorselessly for a week, and received their surrender on the 6th of April, and here ended the rebellion.

In the very midst of the rejoicing of the country at the result, Abraham Lincoln, President elect of the United States for a second term, and who had but a few weeks previously entered upon the discharge of his duties, was basely assassinated. This occurred the 14th day of April, 1865, at the theater in Washington. He lived until the morning of the 15th, when he expired.

Andrew Johnson, who had been elected Vice President, succeeded him, and the Government went on as though nothing had happened; thus proving unmistakably the strength of a government capable of withstanding the greatest possible trials.

GOVERNMENT OF KENTUCKY.

The first Constitution of Kentucky was formed and went into effect the first of June, 1792. The experience of seven years exhibited clearly many defects in that instrument; accordingly, in 1799, the second Constitution of Kentucky was formed and went into operation. The distribution of the powers of the government were the same in both instruments; yet, as a whole, many important changes were made. In order to any future amendment, the Constitution of 1799 provided that the vote of the people at two annual elections be taken as to whether it be expedient to call a convention for this purpose; and if, at both elections, a majority of all the votes in the State be found in favor of the proposed call, a poll is to be opened for the election of delegates to a convention, with full power to modify, amend, totally abolish, or establish any system whatever, provided it be Republican.

After a lapse of nearly fifty years, the Reform question had become considerably agitated in Kentucky by the politicians of the day; and the Legislature of 1846-7 having authorized the submission of the question to the people, at the August election, 1847, the first vote upon the expediency of calling a convention was taken, which resulted overwhelmingly in favor of the call of a convention. In August, 1848, the second vote on the proposed call was taken, and the result was an expression of public feeling in favor of a call far more decided than the previous vote had indicated. In pursuance of a legislative enactment, delegates were elected at the August election of 1849 to compose a convention, who assembled at Frankfort in October of the same year, and, after a session of three months, produced the present form of government, or Constitution of Kentucky. It was not proclaimed as the Constitution, however, until it was once more referred to the people for their final approval or ratification. The action of the people was coolly and deliberately had, after a full discussion by the ablest men in the State, whose arguments on both sides were evincive of learning as well as research, and a thorough acquaintance with the science of government; and though the positions of each were stoutly maintained, the result was by no means changed, but was fully approved of at the polls in May, 1850, and the convention, which re-assembled the succeeding month, proclaimed and published the present Constitution to be the fundamental and inviolate law of the land.

As to the general principles of government contained in this instrument, it might not be regarded as objectionable; but its minuteness gives it more the appearance of a code than of a constitution. It is destitute of that simplicity of plan, style, and arrangement which characterizes the Constitution of the United States, or even theConstitution of 1799 of Kentucky. Some of the brightest intellects of the nation adorned the Convention of 1799, men who could not be swayed by interest or self-promotion; but whose grand aim and object was public good and universal happiness. It emanated from the heads and hearts of such men as Breckinridge, Logan, Allen, Adair, Rowan, Grundy, McDowell, Marshall, Wallace, Ewing, Taylor, Bledsoe, and others. It had been tested by time, and met fully all public expectation.

The writer was one of those who opposed a change of that Constitution at the time it was made. Changes of fundamental law, except from great necessity, he regarded as pernicious to the people, alienating their affections in consequence of a lack of fixedness of principles, and rendering us insecure in the enjoyment of life, liberty, and property. The writer believed that the change proposed at that time was principally instigated to suit the whims and caprices of noisy demagogues and political aspirants, who, as we know, are only satisfied when themselves are the recipients of the loaves and fishes, regardless of the general prosperity and happiness of the people.

The writer was ever opposed to an elective judiciary; and more so since the test which has been made under our present Constitution than before. Opinions expressed by him twenty years ago have been fully verified. He then believed, and still believes, that impartial justice will not at all times be administered by those who depend for their stations upon the sycophancy which they breathe toward the wealthy, the influential, and the powerful; and who, instead of reading their books and qualifying themselves for the station, are electioneering and swaggering in grog-shops and groceries. The judiciary, as one of the three great departments of the government, deserves as much, if not more, to be preserved than either of the other two. Unlike the legislative or executive departments, it possesses neither power nor patronage; neither sword nor purse. Of all the departments it is the feeblest by far, for it neither makes laws nor does it execute them. Its powers are merely to decide and declare what the law is when proper cases are brought before them by others; and yet feeble as their power is, it is one of the most important stations in our government; and to ensure justice, all must admit, should be the most independent. Their independence is the strongest support to our liberty and the safest guard to our happiness; nay, it is the best armor and ablest tower of protection to any government. The independence of the judiciary alone preserved the liberty of England amidst divers changes; it has preserved our country; and will ever do so whilst its independence is maintained. My observation and experience within the last twenty years have satisfied my mind, that the election of judges by the popular vote is not the surest protection to the poor or to the fallen in fortune—a leaning is often discoverable on the side of wealth and influence. Under the former constitution, though salaries were far lower than at present, the wisest and best men of the legal profession occupied seats upon the bench, especially of the Court of Appeals. It is not always the case now; nay, but seldom the case; and it is to be feared that no better condition can exist in Kentucky as long as the present system continues; and, finally, the decisions of our courts of highest jurisdiction will be no more regarded than the *dictums* of a county court. These were the views of the writer expressed more than twenty years ago, which time and observation have only tended to confirm.

Of all the people in the State of Kentucky, how few there are who ever read or even know anything about her Constitution, the very thing that every man ought to read and understand before he attempts to vote. There is some excuse, however, from the fact that the Constitution is scarcely to be found anywhere else than in the Revised Statutes of Kentucky, which, for the most part, are accessible only to lawyers, clerks, and magistrates, while the great mass of the people are deprived of the privilege of perusing it, except at the expense of the purchase of those books. To remedy this inconvenience, I have thought it advisable to present here a synopsis of the Constitution of Kentucky, which, as I conceive, will add greatly, not only to the interest, but to the value of the work.

The powers of the government of the State of Kentucky are divided into three distinct departments, each confided to a separate body of magistrates, to-wit: Those which are Legislative to one; those which are Executive to another; and those which are Judiciary to another. No person being of one of these departments can exercise any power properly belonging to either of the others, except in such instances as are directly expressed or permitted by the Constitution.

EXECUTIVE DEPARTMENT.
GOVERNOR.

The supreme Executive power of the Commonwealth is vested in a Chief Magistrate, who is styled the Governor of the Commonwealth of Kentucky. He is elected by the qualified voters of the State for a term of four years. In case of a tie, the election is to be determined by lot, in such manner as the General Assembly may direct. The Governor is ineligible for the succeeding four years after the expiration of the term for which he shall have been elected. He shall be at least thirty-five years of age, a citizen of the United States, and an inhabitant of the State at least six years next preceding his election. He commences the execution of his office on the 5th Tuesday succeeding the day of the general election on which he shall have been chosen, and shall continue in the execution thereof until his successor shall have taken the oaths prescribed by the Constitution.

No member of Congress, or person holding any office under the United States, or minister of any religious society, shall be eligible to the office of Governor. The pay of the Governor for his services can neither be increased or diminished during the term for which he was elected.

He shall be Commander-in-Chief of the army and navy of the Commonwealth, and of the militia thereof, except when they are called into the service of the United States. But he shall not command personally in the field unless so advised by a resolution of the General Assembly.

He has power to fill vacancies that may occur, by granting commissions, which shall expire when such vacancies shall have been filled according to the provisions of the Constitution.

He has power to remit fines and forfeitures, grant reprieves and pardons, except in cases of impeachment. In cases of treason he can only grant reprieves until the end of the next session of the General Assembly, in which the power of pardoning shall be vested. He can not remit the fees of the clerk, sheriff, or Commonwealth's attorney in penal or criminal cases.

He shall, from time to time, give the General Assembly information of the state of the Commonwealth, and recommend to their consideration such as he may deem expedient.

He may, on extraordinary occasions, convene the General Assembly at the seat of government, or at a different place if that should become dangerous from an enemy or from contagious disorders; and, when the two houses can not agree as to the time of adjournment, he may adjourn them to such time as he shall think proper, not exceeding four months.

He shall take care that the laws be faithfully executed.

LIEUTENANT GOVERNOR.

The Lieutenant Governor is chosen at the same time of the election of Governor, to continue in office for the same time, and to possess the same qualifications. By virtue of his office he is Speaker of the Senate, and when in committee of the whole has a right to debate and vote on all subjects; and when the Senate is equally divided, he is entitled to give the casting vote.

Should the Governor be impeached, removed from office, die, refuse to qualify, resign, or be absent from the State, the Lieutenant Governor shall exercise all the power and authority which belongs to the office of Governor until another be duly elected and qualified, or the Governor, absent or impeached, shall return or be acquitted.

The Lieutenant Governor, as Speaker of the Senate, receives the same pay which is allowed the Speaker of the House of Representatives. During the time he may administer the government he receives the same compensation the Governor would have received.

SECRETARY OF STATE.

The Secretary of State is appointed by the Governor, with the advice and consent of the Senate, who is commissioned during the term for which the Governor had been elected. He keeps a fair register, and attests all the official acts of the Governor; and, when required, lays the same before either House, or both, of the General Assembly, and peforms all other duties required of him by law.

TREASURER AND OTHER OFFICERS.

The Treasurer is elected for the term of two years, and the Auditor of Public Accounts, Register of the Land Office, and Attorney General, for the term of four years. The duties of these officers are prescribed by law.

LEGISLATIVE DEPARTMENT.

The Legislative power shall be vested in a House of Representatives and Senate, which, together, shall be styled the General Assembly of the Commonwealth of Kentucky.

Members of the General Assembly receive from the public treasury compensation for their services, not however to be increased or diminished, to take effect during the session at which the alteration is made. And a session can not continue more than sixty days, except by a vote of two-thirds of all the members of both Houses. The present pay of members is $5 per day, and twelve and a half cents per mile for necessary travel going and returning.

The sessions of the General Assembly are held at the seat of government. At every apportionment of representation, the State is laid off into thirty-eight senatorial districts. No person can be a Senator who at the time of his election is not a citizen of the United States, has not attained thirty years of age, and has not resided in the State six years next preceding his election, and the last year thereof in the district for which he may be chosen. One-half of the Senators go out of office biennially. Senators are chosen for the term of four years, and the officers of the Senate are chosen biennially.

HOUSE OF REPRESENTATIVES.

Representatives are chosen on the first Monday in August every second year. The qualifications of each at the time of his election are to be a citizen of the United States, twenty-four years of age, and a residence in the State two years next preceding his election, and the last year thereof in the county, town, or city from which he may be chosen. Their term of service is two years from the day of the general election. They choose their speaker and other officers. The number of Representatives shall be one hundred.

JUDICIAL DEPARTMENT.

The Judicial power of the Commonwealth, both as to matters of law and equity, are vested in one Supreme Court, (styled the Court of Appeals), the courts established by this Constitution, and such courts inferior to the Supreme Court as the General Assembly may from time to time erect and establish.

COURT OF APPEALS.

The Court of Appeals shall consist of four judges, any three of whom may constitute a court for the transaction of business. The State is divided by counties into four districts, in each of which is elected a judge of the Court of Appeals. When a vacancy shall occur for any cause, the General Assembly has power to reduce the number of judges and districts; but in no event can there be less than three judges. Eligibility to the office of judge is to be a citizen of the United States, a resident of the district for which he may be a candidate two years preceding the election, thirty years of age, and a practicing lawyer of eight years. Judges of the Court of Appeals hold their offices for eight years, but are removable by the Governor on the address of two-thirds of each House of the General Assembly. They are, at stated times, to receive for their services an adequate compensation, to be fixed by law, which shall not be diminished during the time for which they shall have been elected. After the first election it was determined by lot the length of time each should serve; and at the expiration of the service of each, an election in the proper district shall take place to fill the vacancy. The judge having the shortest time to serve shall be styled the Chief Justice of Kentucky. The Court of Appeals has appellate jurisdiction only coextensive with the State, under such restrictions and regulations as may be prescribed by law, not repugnant to the Constitution. It is to hold its sessions at the seat of government, unless otherwise directed by law. The General Assembly has power to direct that the court should hold sessions in any one or more of the said districts.

A clerk of the Court of Appeals is elected for a term of eight years, and should the General Assembly branch the court, a clerk of each district is to be elected. To be eligible to the office of clerk, it is required that he be a citizen of the United States, a resident of the State two years, twenty-one years of age, and have a certificate from a judge of the Court of Appeals, or a judge of a circuit court, that he has been examined under his supervision, and that he is qualified for the office for which he is a candidate.

A reporter to the Court of Appeals is indefinitely appointed by the judges.

CIRCUIT COURTS.

Circuit Courts are established in each county now existing, or which may hereafter be erected. The General Assembly is to divide the State into districts, and a judge is to be elected in each district. Their term of office is six years. He must be a citizen of the United States, a resident of the district two years preceding his election, thirty years of age, a practicing lawyer for eight years. They are to be commissioned by the Governor, and continue in office until their successors are qualified; but may be removed from office in the same manner as the judges of the Court of Appeals. The removal of a judge from his district vacates his office. When a vacancy occurs in the office, the Governor shall issue a writ of election to fill the vacancy, unless the unexpired term be less than one year. In that event the Governor appoints a judge to fill the vacancy. The General Assembly has power to change or alter the jurisdiction of the court. The right to appeal, or sue out a writ of error to the Court of Appeals, remains as it now exists until altered by law, which power the General Assembly has.

A Commonwealth's attorney is elected for each district at the same time, and for the same term, with the circuit judges. To be eligible to the office, he must be twenty-four years of age, a citizen of the United States, resident two years preceding his election in the State, and one year in the county or district for which he is a candidate, and shall have been a licensed practicing attorney for two years.

DEPARTMENT OF COUNTY MATTERS.

A County Court, consisting of a presiding judge, is established in every county of the State. The presiding judge is elected for a term of four years, and continues in office until his successor is duly qualified. His eligibility consists in his being a citizen of the United States, over twenty-one years of age, a resident of the county one year next preceding his election. The County Court, composed of the presiding judge, has the same power and jurisdiction possessed by the courts lately abolished, except as restricted by the exclusive jurisdiction conferred upon the October terms. At this court the presiding judge shall make all settlements with executors, administrators, and guardians within his county. The clerk of this court, the sheriff, and other officers, perform the same duties, and bear the same relation to this court, as formerly to the old courts.

The presiding judge shall also hold quarterly terms at the seat of justice of his county for the trial of all causes brought before him. He has jurisdiction concurrent with the justices of the peace, both in law and equity, and with circuit courts in all sums over fifty and not exceeding one hundred dollars, and in all actions of trespass on the case, and writs of replevin, where the damages complained of do not exceed one hundred dollars, except where the title or boundaries of land come in dispute, under the same rules and regulations prescribed by law conferring concurrent jurisdiction on justices of the peace and circuit courts. He shall have power to grant writs of injunctions, attachment in chancery, and *ne-exeat* in all cases; and when the amount does not exceed one hundred dollars, to hear and determine the same. He shall have power to grant, hear, and determine writs of habeas corpus; and concurrent jurisdiction with the circuit courts in granting writs in relation to idiots and lunatics. He shall have the same fees allowed to justices and circuit court clerks for similar services.

The October terms of the court are composed of the presiding judge and all the justices of the peace as associate judges. At this court the claims by and against the county are audited and settled; provision is made for the poor; necessary appropriations for repairing roads, building bridges, public buildings, &c., are made; the county levy is laid and directed to be collected; and, in short, the whole financial business of the county is transacted.

A circuit court clerk is elected in each county for the same term with the circuit judges; and a county court clerk is elected for the same term with the county judges. They must be citizens of the United States, have resided in the State two years, and one year in the county in which he is a candidate, and has procured from a judge of the Court of Appeals or circuit court judge a certificate that he has been examined by the clerk of his court, under his supervision, and that he is qualified for the office for which he is a candidate.

A sheriff is in like manner elected for a term of two years. He must be a citizen of the United States, twenty-one years of age, a resident of the State two years, and of the county one year, next preceding his election.

The county attorney is elected for the term of four years. Besides possessing the qualifications required of sheriffs, he must have been a practicing lawyer two years next preceding his election.

A coroner, jailer, assessor, and surveyor are also elected for the same term as the county judge, and possessing the same qualifications with the sheriff, except that they must each be twenty-four years of age. The counties are all laid off in convenient districts; in each of which two magistrates and a constable are elected for a term of four years. The same qualifications are required for these offices as of sheriff. Not less than two nor more than four examiners shall be appointed in each county to take depositions. Not more than three offices can be kept in one county, and one of them must be at the county seat.

I am clearly of opinion that the election of fiscal officers, such as sheriffs, constables, &c., is incompatible with the pecuniary responsibilities involved in the office. As was said by Mr. Butler, in his History of Kentucky, written nearly forty years ago: "Such elections are almost sure to make the sheriff and his securities the victims of indulgence, inconsistent with private safety and the punctual collection of taxes."

Under the first Constitution of Kentucky sheriffs were elective; but the second Constitution (1799) had become convinced by the experience of seven years that the plan did not work well. Under that plan it was found, in numerous instances, that the public revenue was continually squandered, and thousands of dollars annually lost to the State, that remain unpaid to this day; and I have heard it said by the men of those days, that there were a greater number of defaulters among sheriffs during that period than there was under the second

Constitution of Kentucky during the whole period of its existence. I believe with Mr. Butler, when he says, "that the incessant courting of the people for their favor, for every public employment, eventuates in corruption." There are hundreds in Kentucky at this day who can bear testimony to the fact under the operations of the Constitution of Kentucky of 1850. Mr. Butler says, and I agree with him, that "an intelligent and high-spirited people ought to feel above the low flattery, the servile compliance, and often the infamous misrepresentations that are often too inevitably incident to the practice of electioneering. It has grown with the growth of Kentucky at a most fearful rate, and tends greatly to supercede the popular superintendence of its own affairs, by tacitly surrendering them to professed candidates. Let discussion take its widest range within the limits of decorum; but let the parties whose qualifications and merits may be the subject be kept out of the interested, and, consequently, intemperate participation. The only effectual influence which can radically ameliorate society is the diffusion of moral and intellectual cultivation, with the protection of honest industry in the enjoyment of its fruits. No free government, and, therefore, generally no good one, can protect the people against their own will, however corrupt and indirect it may be; all, then, which the machinery of government can effect is to check the hasty and rash impulses of the popular sentiment for some short time, till it has the opportunity to correct itself. Popular power, when so administered as to forget or to violate the rights of others, becomes as rank tyranny, and as gross oppression, as at the hands of kings and princes. Right and justice are founded in distinctions as eternal as the Almighty Mind which created them; and no power, whether clothed in imperial purple, or the more unpretending though not the less significant insignia of a republic, can consecrate oppression, or lesson the wickedness of injustice."

STATES AND TERRITORIES OF THE UNION.

The first and original States that formed and confirmed the Union by the adoption of the Constitution are as follows:

NEW HAMPSHIRE.

This name was given to the territory conveyed by the Plymouth Company to Captain John Mason by patent, November 2, 1629, in reference to the patentee, who was Governor in Portsmouth, in Hampshire, England. It was first settled at Dover and Portsmouth, by the Puritans, in 1623, was embraced under the charters of Massachusetts, and continued under the same jurisdiction until September 18, 1679, when a separate charter and government was granted. A constitution was formed January 5, 1776, which was altered in 1784, and again amended February 13, 1792. This State ratified the Constitution of the United States June 21, 1788. The area of square miles of this State is 9,280. Its population in 1870 was 318,300, of whom 580 were colored, and 23 were Indians.

MASSACHUSETTS.

So called from Massachusetts Bay, and that from the Massachusetts tribe of Indians in the neighborhood of Boston. This State was first settled at Plymouth, by English Puritans from Holland, who landed December 22, 1630. It was chartered March 4, 1629; also chartered January 13, 1650; an explanatory charter granted August 20, 1726, and more completely chartered October 7, 1731. Formed a constitution March 2, 1780, which was amended November 3, 1820, and on several occasions since that time. The State ratified the Constitution of the United States February 6, 1788. Area of square miles, 7,800. Population in 1870, 1,457,854; of these, 13,947 were colored, 151 Indians, and 97 Chinese.

RHODE ISLAND.

So called in 1664, after Island of Rhodes, in the Mediterranean. It was first settled at Providence by Roger Williams, in 1636; was embraced under the charters of Massachusetts, and continued under her jurisdiction until a separate charter was granted July 8, 1662, which continued in force until a constitution was formed, September, 1842. She ratified the Constitution of the United States May 29, 1790. Area of square miles, 1,306; population in 1870, 217,353; of these, 4,980 were colored, and 154 Indians.

CONNECTICUT.

So called from the Indian name of its principal river, which signifies "long river." It was first settled at Windsor, 1635, by the Puritans, was embraced under the charters of Massachusetts, and continued under her jurisdiction until April 23, 1662, when a separate charter was granted, which continued in force until a constitution was formed, September 15, 1818. She ratified the Constitution of the United States January 9, 1788. Area, of square miles, 4,674; population in 1870, 2,530,561; of these, 9,668 were colored, 235 Indians, and 22 Chinese.

NEW YORK.

So called in 1664, in reference to the Duke of York, to whom this territory was granted by the King of England. It was first settled on Manhattan Island in 1614; granted to Duke of York March 20, 1664, April 26, 1664, and June 24, 1664. Newly patented January 9, 1674; formed a constitution April 20, 1777, which was amended October 27, 1801, and again on November 10, 1821. A new constitution was formed in 1846. New York ratified the Constitution of the United States July 26, 1788. Area, 46,000 square miles; population in 1870, 4,392,759; of these 52,081 were colored, 439 Indians, and 29 Chinese.

NEW JERSEY.

So called in 1664, from the Island of Jersey, on the coast of France, the residence of the family of Sir George Carteret, to whom the territory was granted. It was first settled at Bergen, in 1620, by the Dutch, and held under same grants as New York; separated into East and West Jersey March 3, 1677. The government surrendered to the crown in 1702.

and so continued until the formation of the constitution, July 2, 1776. She ratified the Constitution of the United States December 18, 1787. Area in square miles, 8,320; population in 1870, 906,096, of which 30,658 were colored, 16 Indians, and 15 Chinese.

PENNSYLVANIA.

Was so called in 1681, after William Penn. Was first settled on the Delaware River, in 1682, by him; chartered February 28, 1681; formed a constitution September 28, 1776. Ratified the Constitution of the United States December 12, 1787. Area, 46,000 square miles; population in 1870, 3,456,449; of which 65,294 are colored, 34 Indians, and 14 Chinese.

DELAWARE.

So called in 1703, from Delaware Bay, on which it lies, and which received its name from Lord de la War, who died in this bay. First settled at Cape Henlopen, in 1627, by Swedes and Finns; embraced in the charter and continued under the government of Pennsylvania until the formation of a constitution, September 20, 1776. A new constitution formed June 12, 1792, and amended in 1831. She ratified the Constitution of the United States December 7, 1787. Area, 2,120 square miles; population in 1870, 125,015, of which 22,794 are colored.

MARYLAND.

So called in honor of Henrietta Maria, Queen of Charles the First, in his patent to Lord Baltimore, June 30, 1632. First settled at St. Mary, in 1634, by Roman Catholics. Chartered June 20, 1632. Formed a constitution August 14, 1776, which was amended in 1795 and in 1799, and again in 1812 and 1851. Ratified the Constitution of the United States April 28, 1788. Area, 11,124 square miles; population in 1870, 780,894, of which 175,381 were colored, 4 Indians, and 2 Chinese.

VIRGINIA.

Was so called in 1584, after Elizabeth, the virgin Queen of England. First settled at Jamestown, in 1607, by the English. Chartered April 10, 1606, May 23, 1609, and March 12, 1612.

Formed a constitution July 5, 1776; amended January 15, 1830. Ratified the Constitution of the United States June 26, 1788. Area, 38,352 square miles; population in 1870, 1,225,-165, of which 512,811 were colored, 229 Indians, and 4 Chinese.

NORTH CAROLINA.

Was so called by the French in 1564, in honor of King Charles the Ninth, of France. Was first settled at Albemarle, in 1650, by the English. Chartered March 20, 1663, and June 30, 1665. Formed a constitution December 18, 1776, which was amended in 1835. Ratified the Constitution of the United States November 21, 1789. Area, 50,704 square miles; population in 1870, 1,071,361, of which 391,650 were colored, and 1,241 Indians.

SOUTH CAROLINA.

First settled at Port Royal, in 1670, by the Huguenots. Embraced in the charters of Carolina, or North Carolina, from which it was separated in 1729. Formed a constitution March 26, 1776; amended March 19, 1778, and June 3, 1790. Ratified the Constitution of the United States May 23, 1788. Area, 29,585 square miles; population in 1870, 705,606, of which 415,814 were colored, 124 Indians, and 1 Chinese.

GEORGIA.

Was so called in 1732, in honor of King George the Second. First settled at Savannah, in 1733, by Oglethorpe. Chartered June 9, 1732. Formed a constitution February 5, 1777; a second in 1785; a third May 30, 1798; and amended in 1839. Ratified the Constitution of the United States January 2, 1788. Area, 58,000 square miles; population in 1870, 1,184,109, of which 545,142 were colored, and 40 Indians.

STATES ADMITTED.

The following States were admitted into the Union after the adoption of the Federal Constitution:

VERMONT.

First settled at Fort Dummer, in 1764. Formed from the territory of New York. Admitted March 4, 1791. A constitution adopted July 9, 1793. The State called Vermont by the inhabitants in their declaration of independence, January 16, 1777, from the French "*verd monte*," the Green Mountains. Area, 9,056½ square miles; population in 1870, 330,359, of which 924 were colored and 24 Indians.

KENTUCKY.

Was so called in 1792, from its principal river, which is an Indian name for "dark and bloody ground." First settled near Lexington, 1775. Formed from territory of Virginia; admitted June 1, 1792. The constitution laid before Congress November 7, 1792. A new constitution adopted August 17, 1799, and again in 1850. Area, 37,680 square miles; population in 1870, 1,132,011, of which 222,210 were colored, 108 Indians, and 1 Chinese.

TENNESSEE.

Was so called in 1796, from its principal river. It is an Indian name, and is said to signify "*a curved spoon.*" It was formed from the territory of North Carolina in 1790. Adopted a constitution February 6, 1796; amended in 1835. It was admitted June 1, 1796. Area, 45,000 square miles; population in 1870, 1,258,523, of which 322,331 were colored, and 70 Indians.

OHIO.

Was so called in 1802, from the river of that name, which is its southern boundary. Ohio is an Indian name, and is said to signify *beautiful river*. It was first settled at Marietta, in 1788; formed from Northwestern territory, and adopted a constitution November 1, 1802, and amended in 1851. Admitted November 29, 1802. Area, 39,964 square miles; population in 1870, 2,665,200, of which 63,213 were colored, and 100 Indians.

LOUISIANA.

Was so called in honor of Louis the Fourteenth of France. First settled at Iberville, in 1699; formed from French territory. Adopted a constitution January 22, 1812; amended in 1845 and 1852. Admitted April 8, 1812. Area, 41,255 square

APPENDIX. 445

miles; population in 1870, 726,915, of which 364,210 were colored, 569 Indians, and 71 Chinese.

INDIANA.

Was so called in 1809, from the American Indians. Was first settled at Vincennes, 1730; formed from Northwest territory. Adopted a constitution June 29, 1816, which was amended in 1851. Admitted December 11, 1816. Area, 33,809 square miles; population in 1870, 1,600,637, of which 24,560 were colored, and 240 Indians.

MISSISSIPPI.

Was so called in 1800, from its western boundary. Mississippi is an Indian name, which denotes the whole river, or a river formed by the union of many. It was first settled at Natches, in 1716. Formed from the territory of South Carolina and Georgia. Adopted a constitution March 1, 1817, which was amended in 1832. Admitted December 10, 1817. Area, 47,156 square miles; population in 1870, 827,422, of which 444,201 were colored, 809 Indians, and 16 Chinese.

ILLINOIS.

Was so called in 1809, from its principal river, and is an Indian word said to signify "*the river of men.*" It was first settled at Kaskaskia, in 1720. Formed from Northwest territory. Adopted a constitution August 26, 1818. Area, 55,409 square miles; population in 1870, 2,539,891, of which 28,662 were colored, 32 Indians, and 1 Chinese.

ALABAMA.

Was so called in 1814, from its principal river. It is an Indian name, said to signify "*here we rest.*" It was formed from the territory of South Carolina and Georgia, and for two years bore the name of Mississippi Territory. Adopted a constitution August 2, 1819. Admitted December 14th, 1819. Area, 50,722 square miles; population in 1870, 996,992, of which 475,510 were colored, and 98 Indians.

MAINE.

Was so called in 1623, from Maine in France, of which Henrietta Maria, Queen of England, was at that time proprietor. It was first settled at Bristol, in 1624. Formed from territory of Massachusetts; and adopted a constitution October 29, 1819. Admitted March 15, 1820. Area, 31,766 square miles; population in 1870, 626,915, of which 1,606 were colored, 499 Indians, and 1 Chinese.

MISSOURI.

Was so called in 1821, from its principal river, and is an Indian name. Was first settled at St. Louis, in 1764. Formed from French territory. Adopted a constitution July 19, 1820. Admitted August 10, 1821. Area, 67,380 square miles; population in 1870, 1,721,295, of which 118,071 were colored, 75 Indians, and 3 Chinese.

ARKANSAS.

Was so called in 1821, from its principal river, and is an Indian name. It was formed from French territory, the Louisiana purchase. Presented a constitution March 1, 1836. Admitted June 15, 1836. Area, 52,198 square miles; population in 1870, 484,471, of which 122,169 were colored, 89 Indians, and 98 Chinese.

MICHIGAN.

Was so called in 1805, from the lake on its border. It is an Indian name. It was first settled on the Detroit River, in 1650. Formed from territory originally belonging to Virginia. Presented a memorial for admission January 25, 1833, with a constitution, which was revised in 1850. Admitted January 26, 1837. Area, 56,243 square miles; population in 1870, 1,184,050, of which 11,849 were colored, 4,926 Indians, and 2 Chinese.

FLORIDA.

Was so called by Juan Ponce de Leon, in 1572, because it was discovered on Easter Sunday; in Spanish "*Pascua Florida.*" It was discovered in 1497, and first explored by Ponce de Leon in 1512. Formed from Spanish territory. Presented a constitution February 20, 1839. Admitted March 3, 1845. Area, 59,268 square miles; population in 1870, 187,747, of which 91,689 were colored and 2 Indians.

TEXAS.

A Spanish word applied to the Republic. First settled in 1792. Was an Independent Republic. Admitted December 29, 1845. Area, 324,018 square miles; population in 1870, 818,879, of which 253,475 were colored, 379 Indians, and 25 Chinese.

WISCONSIN.

Was so called from its principal river, an Indian name. First settled at Green Bay, in 1670. Formed from Indian territory. Adopted a constitution January 21, 1847. Admitted May 29, 1848. Area, 53,924 square miles; population in 1870, 1,054,670, of which 2,113 were colored and 1,206 Indians.

IOWA.

So called from its principal river, an Indian name. First settled at Galena and Dubuque. Formed from Indian territory. Presented a constitution December 9, 1844. Admitted December 28, 1846. Area, 55,045 square miles; population in 1870, 1,191,792, of which 5,762 were colored and 48 Indians.

CALIFORNIA.

A Spanish word, and named from an arm of the Pacific Ocean. First settled on the Pacific slope. Formed from Mexican territory. Adopted a constitution November 13, 1849. Admitted September 9, 1850. Area, 188,982 square miles; population in 1870, 560,247, of which 4,272 were colored, 7,241 Indians, and 49,310 Chinese.

MINNESOTA.

The name of the above State is also an Indian name. First settled on the St. Peters River, in 1805. Formed from Indian territory. Admitted May 11, 1858. Area, 83,531 square miles; population in 1870, 439,706, of which 759 were colored and 690 Indians.

OREGON.

So called from its principal river, an Indian name. First settled by the Spaniards. Formed from Indian territory. Adopted a constitution in November, 1857. Admitted February 12, 1859. Area, 102,606 square miles; population in 1870, 90,923, of which 346 were colored, 318 Indians, and 3,330 Chinese.

KANSAS.

Kansas is an Indian name. Formed from Indian territory. Admitted December 6, 1859. Area, 114,798 square miles; population in 1870, 364,399, of which 17,108 were colored and 914 Indians.

WEST VIRGINIA.

Formed from the State of Virginia, and admitted December 31, 1862. Area, 23,000 square miles; population in 1870, 442,014, of which 17,980 were colored and 1 Chinese.

NEBRASKA.

Organized May 30, 1854, as a territory; afterward admitted as a State. Area, 122,007 square miles; population in 1870, 122,000, of which 789 were colored and 87 Indians.

ORGANIZED TERRITORIES OF THE UNITED STATES.

UTAH.

Organized September 9, 1850. Area, 109,600 square miles; population in 1870, 86,786, of which 113 were colored, 179 Indians, and 445 Chinese.

NEW MEXICO.

Organized September 9, 1850. Area, 124,450 square miles; population in 1870, 91,874, of which 172 were colored and 1,309 Indians.

WASHINGTON.

Organized November 2, 1853. Area, 71,300 square miles; population in 1870, 23,955, of which 207 were colored, 1,319 Indians, and 234 Chinese.

APPENDIX. 449

COLORADO.

Organized in 1861. Area, 106,475 square miles; population in 1870, 39,864, of which 456 were colored, 180 Indians, and 7 Chinese.

DAKOTA.

Organized in 1861. Area, 152,500 square miles; population in 1870, 14,181, of which 94 were colored and 1,200 Indians.

NEVADA.

Organized in 1861. Area, 83,500 square miles; population in 1870, 42,491, of which 359 were colored, 23 Indians, and 3,152 Chinese.

ARIZONA.

Organized in 1863. Area, 130,800 square miles; population in 1870, 9,658, of which 26 were colored, 31 Indians, and 20 Chinese.

IDAHO

Organized in 1863. Area, 310,000 square miles; population in 1870, 11,000, of which 60 were colored, 47 Indians, and 4,214 Chinese.

DISTRICT OF COLUMBIA.

This District was established under the First Article of the Constitution of the United States for the seat of the National Government, Maryland in 1788, and Virginia in 1789, having ceded lands belonging to their States respectively for that purpose. These cessions were accepted by Congress, and by an act passed and approved July 16, 1790, and amended March 3, 1791, the District, ten miles square, was located, and its lines and boundaries established by a proclamation of George Washington, President of the United States, March 30, 1791. And by an act approved the 27th of February, 1801, Congress assumed complete jurisdiction over the District, as contemplated by the framers of the Constitution. The area of the District is 100 square miles; population in 1870, 131,700, of which 43,404 were colored, 15 Indians, and 3 Chinese.

29

www.ingramcontent.com/pod-product-compliance
Lightning Source LLC
Chambersburg PA
CBHW022136300426
44115CB00006B/210